LEFT OF KARL MARX

THE

POLITICAL

LIFE OF

BLACK

COMMUNIST

CLAUDIA

JONES

LEFT OF KARL MARX

Carole Boyce Davies

Duke University Press   Durham and London   2007

© 2008 Duke University Press
All rights reserved

Designed by Heather Hensley
Typeset in Adobe Janson by Keystone Typesetting, Inc.
Library of Congress Cataloging-in-Publication Data
appear on the last printed page of this book.

CONTENTS

Acknowledgments   vii

Preface   xiii

Chronology   xxiii

Introduction. Recovering the Radical Black Female Subject:
Anti-Imperialism, Feminism, and Activism   1

1. Women's Rights/Workers' Rights/Anti-Imperialism:
Challenging the Superexploitation of Black Working-Class Women 29

2. From "Half the World" to the Whole World: Journalism
as Black Transnational Political Practice   69

3. Prison Blues: Literary Activism and a Poetry of Resistance   99

4. Deportation: The Other Politics of Diaspora, or "What is
an ocean between us? We know how to build bridges."   131

5. Carnival and Diaspora: Caribbean Community, Happiness,
and Activism   167

6. Piece Work/Peace Work: Self-Construction versus State
Repression   191

Notes   239

Bibliography   275

Index   295

ACKNOWLEDGMENTS

This project owes everything to the spiritual guidance of Claudia Jones herself with signs too many to identify. At every step of the way, she made her presence felt in ways so remarkable that only conversations with friends who understand the blurring that exists between the worlds which we inhabit could appreciate. The many anecdotes that surround this narrative are best left to that realm of Caribbean realism that we share over good food and drinks, wakes, and assorted rituals.

Diane Langford, the erstwhile guardian of the Claudia Jones papers, is owed a special debt of gratitude for her trust in me and her confidence that I was the person she was waiting for and that Claudia's papers would be safe with me. Diane has become a wonderful friend, supportive reader, and source of encouragement from across the Atlantic, providing at times surprising photos, letters, and other bits of information. Ricky Cambridge, a trusted comrade and Claudia's last assistant, came into my life at a particular time in this project, as though he were sent by Claudia herself to help guide me to her papers in Hampstead, to reassure Diane that all of this was going to be in good hands, to escort me through some of her ideas, to cross-check information and be good "keeping company" through numerous pleasurable hours of sharing. Janice Shinebourne has been an important link in all of the London processes. Also, in London, thanks are also due to several former friends and colleagues of Claudia Jones with whom I had interviews and conversations at various times. These include Ranjana Ash, Pansy Jeffries, the now deceased Billy Strachan, and John La Rose of New Beacon Books, Jessica and Eric Huntley of Bogle L'Ouverture Publishing, and Donald Hinds. Buzz Johnson is acknowledged for initially pointing me in the direction of this project.

Numerous libraries and librarians deserve acknowledgment: In London, the library at Race and Class and the Brixton Public Library; in New York, the Schomburg Research Library and Cultural Center, especially Diane Lachatanere and Howard Dodson; the Librarians at the University of the West Indies, St. Augustine, especially Margaret Rouse-Jones; the OWTU Library in San Fernando, Trinidad, the librarians at the Herskovits Library at Northwestern University; and the professional and competent support of Steve Switzer at Florida International University.

At Northwestern University, Dean Eric Sundquist and the African American Studies Department under the leadership of Sandra Richards and the African Studies Program under the leadership of Jane Guyer are gratefully acknowledged for the Herskovits Professorship 2000–2001, during which time I was able to advance this project considerably. Students in my graduate class there were always interested in the advancement of this project, and some provided assistance in the photocopying of documents. The Herskovits Library at Northwestern University provided old copies of the *Daily Worker* which provided invaluable documents on and by Claudia Jones and which I devoured. My research assistant at Northwestern, Laura, did an amazing job of photocopying and scanning materials from the Claudia Jones collection. Paul Lane of Photo/digital Imaging, Evanston, did a very professional job of reproducing some images used in this book. Reesom Haile, poet laureate of Eritrea, now chanting poetry in another realm, passed through my world like a flash of lightning but communicated his love of words and people from which I learned immensely.

At the Centre for Gender and Development Studies, University of the West Indies, St. Augustine, thanks are due to Rhoda Reddock for providing me with the space and congeniality in which to work. Her support staff helped with the assembling of the Guide to the Claudia Jones papers. Dr. Bridget Bereton has also been very supportive of this project. Thanks are also due to the Fulbright Foundation for a research fellowship from March to July 2002, which allowed me to complete the Trinidad portion of the research, the archival work in searching for Claudia Jones's birth certificate and her birthplace home in Belmont, Trinidad. Special thanks to John Donaldson Jr., for a useful lead that made this happen more efficiently. The chapter "Prison Blues" was completed in Trinidad during my period at the Centre and presented at the Caribbean Studies Association that year (Claudia May in the audience provided helpful affirmation). My brother Joseph A. Boyce and his wife, Marie, my cousins Margaret George and Isaac Thomas, my old Howard flatmate and friend, Ken Forde, and Yvonne Corbin of my Nigeria and Brasilia days, are acknowledged for helpful comments and questions at the seminar at the Centre for Gender and Development Studies at which I presented some of this work.

In Binghamton, Kelvin Santiago-Valles and Gladys Jiménez-Muñoz provided material on the Puerto Rican independence movement as well as their consistent friendship and support of this project. Chapters from this project were presented to a variety of audiences of wonderfully engaged students and faculty at the following universities: Spelman College (at the invitation of Beverly Guy-Sheftall); Michigan State University; SUNY Buffalo (at the invitation of Misani [Alexis] De Veaux, Monica Jardine and Women's Studies); the Coloniality Reading Group at Binghamton University; Syracuse University; Caribbean Feminisms Workshop at UWI, Cave Hill; SUNY Stonybrook; Vassar College; Oberlin College (at the invitation of Meredith Gadsby); the African Diaspora Conference in Ottawa Canada (at the invitation of Leslie Sanders and Rinaldo Walcott); the Caribbean Transnationalism Conference at the University of South Bank, London (at the invitation of Harry Goulbourne); Cornell University (at the invitation of Elizabeth De Loughrey); the University of Wisconsin, Madison (at the invitation of Stanlie James for the Black Feminism Graduate Seminars); the African Literature Association Annual Conference at the new Alexandria Library in Egypt; and the 2004 African Diaspora Research Conference at the Sorbonne in Paris. At these presentations, many members of the audience suggested leads, many of which I could never follow but for which I thank them. If I have neglected to identify anybody, it is not intentional.

At Florida International University, Associate Dean Joyce Peterson provided very early references about Elizabeth Gurley Flynn from a book she was reading by Rosalyn Fraad Baxandall. Rosalyn Fraad Baxandall herself has been very supportive of this project. The African-New World Studies Program at FIU which I directed from 1997–2000 and 2001 to 2006 and a variety of graduate and work-study students provided the institutional framework for this work to advance. Program coordinators Lillie McPhee and Rosa Henriquez have been wonderful people to have on one's team and helpful in various ways in this project.

A variety of other friends and colleagues have provided quick leads and directions that advanced this project substantially. These include Lydia Lindsey, Gerald Horne, Donna Weir-Soley, Buzz Johnson, Cecil Gutzmore, Winston James, Sharon Harley, Robert Hill, Rosemari Mealy, Sam Anderson, Geri Allen, Ulla Taylor, Tony Bogues, Michael Hanchard, Winston James, Brian Meeks, John McClendon, Rupert Lewis, Greg Thomas, and Linda Carty. Colin Palmer organized a Symposium at the Schomburg which provided one of the earliest fora on Claudia Jones and presented a range of figures who knew her such as Howard "Stretch" Johnson, Jan Carew, and George Lamming.

A number of colleagues who read the manuscript at its various stages and offered detailed suggestions are specially thanked, particularly Monica Jardine, Gerald Horne, Ricky Cambridge, Greg Thomas, John McClendon, Babacar M'bow, Rhoda Reddock, and George Lamming. Readers at Duke University Press and my editor Reynolds Smith are also acknowledged for their responses to this work and understanding the significance of this project.

The Sister Scholars — Women of Color Research Group from the University of Maryland — are acknowledged for providing the context in which to do this kind of work, particularly from the example of other colleagues like Elsa Barkley Brown doing her own work on Maggie Lena Walker, and Francille Rusann Wilson doing work on Sadie T. M. Alexander. Sharon Harley in particular is identified for friendship and leadership and amazing collegiality.

John McClendon, my colleague from graduate school at Howard University's African Studies and Research Program, has been a steady traveling companion and supporter of this project throughout its history and is recognized here for his allied work on CLR James and on other left activist scholars. Greg Thomas, former student and now dear friend, provided amazing bibliographic leads from his own reading and his quick brilliance cut through a mass of research tedium. Monica Jardine and Janis Mayes have been trusted phone buddies on this and a variety of issues. Leo Wilton another former student, now a professor in his own right, as always, consistently provided the pacing and questioning for the completion of this project and a desire to use some of this work in his teaching.

In Salvador-Bahia, my friends Rita and Lino de Almeida (whose painfully premature departure — June 17, 2006 — still hurts those left behind), provided supportive hospitality in their home as I re-edited the final version of this manuscript.

And finally family: My daughters, Jonelle and Dalia, from the start, have been the sister-friends I always wanted as a girl. I love them dearly and thank them for their unquestioning support through all our moves, turns and twists, and my various research ventures. Most importantly, Babacar M'bow, my dear and trusted best friend and companion knows how to love and support and advance intellectual work, how to be a woman's best friend and working companion more than anybody I have ever met. I thank him always for coming into my life at an important time, clarifying so many things for me, supporting everything from my mother's presence in ways that he and I alone know: my early morning hours research, providing the space, at times, the necessary cup of tea or glass of wine, or friendly shoulder, the technical help to input images to get the work out and above all love and context for this work to be brought to resolution. His energy pulled me back towards Florida and his example of unfailing understanding of the practice and politics of diaspora made all of this have practical life. As always, my mother, Mary Boyce Joseph is acknowledged for giving me the space to be brilliant!

Jonelle Davies, the artist, my daughter and friend is acknowledged for her technical assistance on this project, particularly with preparing the photographs for submission. So much has happened since this work started: I made two professional moves, one of them to help care for my mother who has since passed. I have grown in inestimable ways since I began this project which has taken much longer to complete than I thought. Friends and well-wishers have come into my life and good friends like Lino de Almeida have been "lost along the way." I thank all those here and no longer with us in this world, who have contributed in their own encouraging ways, with friendship, bibliographic references, suggestions, kind words, understanding, love, and, above all, a shared excitement about this project.

One love! (What about the one love?!)

One heart! (What about the one heart?!)

> She made of her life a fury against poverty, bigotry, ignorance, prejudice,
> war, oppression—for all our sakes.
> —RUBY DEE, *WEST INDIAN GAZETTE*, FEBRUARY 1965

Claudia Jones was a black woman and a communist, clear about her ideological orientation, as she was about her identity as a black woman writing and doing political work simultaneously. She saw her "activism through writing" as always linked to struggles for social change and for the creation of equitable societies. She also saw the implementation of Marxism-Leninism as a practical possibility, in the realization of a world in which resources were evenly distributed. But Claudia Jones also belonged to other traditions and communities, and she was willing to deploy all her positions in them. For her, the true creative fusion of these allied positions would be her major contribution to a distinctive anti-imperialist politics that positions her "left of Karl Marx."

This book is not a biography but a study of someone who, in my estimation, is one of the most important black radical thinkers, activists, and organizers in African diaspora history. The need to reintroduce Claudia Jones and account for her in all relevant discourses essentially drives this project. I read Claudia Jones as a black feminist critic of Afro-Caribbean origin. As someone whose primary fields are literature and culture with an emphasis on black women's writing, approaching the political life and intellectual corpus of Claudia Jones, I find a series of meanings immediately evident. Primary among them is that Jones was a black communist woman very conscious of her location in history and of her contributions to advancing her particular understandings of anti-imperialism. But her Trinidadian origin, identity, and Caribbean diaspora belonging are also always ever present, as is her African diaspora experience, all gained through a series of migrations and lived experiences.

My relationship to Claudia Jones's life and work has been intensely personal yet, at the same time, deeply professional and political. First, I met by chance, in Birmingham (England),[1] Buzz Johnson, who had just published *"I Think of My Mother": Notes on the Life and Times of Claudia Jones*. He urged those of us beginning work on black women to find room for Claudia Jones in our teaching and studies. Still, a subsequent reading of his book did not provide as full a sense of the importance, the personality, and the politics of Claudia Jones as I have today, though her presence lingered somewhere in my consciousness and I used excerpts of her work in my teaching from time to time. I had other fleeting encounters with Jones's presence in sources such as Angela Davis's chapter on communist women in *Women Race and Class* (149–171) and Bryan, Dadzie, and Scafe's *The Heart of the Race: Black Women's Lives in Britain*, which had a few pages of material on Jones (136–140).

A few years later in 1992, I decided to visit Jones's gravesite in Highgate Cemetery one grey London day and joined a group tour through the older part of the cemetery. I soon discovered that Karl Marx's grave, my landmark to finding Claudia's, was in fact on the newer side of Highgate Cemetery. A quick escape from that tour and an individual pilgrimage to Karl Marx's gravesite found me in the presence of Claudia Jones's tombstone, a flat stone in the ground, to the left of Karl Marx's as one stands in front of the huge Marx bust. The significance of her position in death as it relates to the spatial/historical dimensions of both figures is overwhelming. The towering Marx bust, emblazoned with the words "Workers of the World Unite" is frequently visited and always strewn with flowers. Next to it is a simple flat stone, minus all the power and might of Marx, and easily overlooked by all visitors not knowing that there is a black woman "left of Marx." A black woman's history is again, literally, overlooked by many, even as she remains, forever, and definitively, "the black woman buried left of Karl Marx."[2]

So, gradually, Claudia Jones's presence has consistently enlarged itself in my life and work, as it has in the larger communities of knowledge. Clearly Jones is determined to be seen and heard again. Writing a paper entitled

"Black Feminist Thought: Dancing at the Borders" for the Black Feminist Seminar of the University of Wisconsin, Madison (1996), in which I critiqued the U.S.-centeredness of popular black feminist formulations, I decided, deliberately, to go to the work of Ella Baker and Claudia Jones as illustrations of black feminist politics that crossed the logic of U.S. borders. I soon realized that I had little material with which to work. I began in earnest then to engage in research on Claudia Jones. In the Schomburg Library and Cultural Center at the New York Public Library, and elsewhere, there was almost a total void. The Schomburg file on Claudia Jones contained only a few clippings from the *Daily Worker* and two encyclopedia entries, by Robin Kelley and John Mc-Clendon.[3] In all honesty, not much material was available on Ella Baker either, beyond the film *Fundi*; not much existed on Marvel Cooke and most of the other left women, who were, like Claudia, radical black female subjects.[4] This absence also confirmed a tendency that I began to recognize as the deporting of the radical black female subject to an elsewhere, outside the terms of "normal" African American intellectual discourse in the United States. So I was excited about the ongoing research on Ella Baker by Barbara Ransby,[5] as I was by that of Joy James on political prisoners and black female revolutionaries. What began as a brief interest has since developed into a much larger project, as the paucity of material itself created a huge space that needed to be filled.

The identification of a number of people still living, who had been comrades of Claudia Jones, many now aging and living in London, New York, and Chicago, opened up a major resource. I decided to work my way back, beginning with those who knew her last in London. In 1997, in between my responsibilities for the London semester abroad program of Binghamton University, I made significant advances in the London phase of my research. There was nothing in the British Museum and its public library, but the library in Brixton produced old microfilms of the *West Indian Gazette*, albeit with poor-quality machines for reading and printing them. Also in Brixton I walked through the streets and looked at the buildings near where the *West Indian Gazette and Afro-Asian Caribbean News* (as it was later called) was housed. In London, the library of the Institute of Race Relations, which publishes the journal *Race and Class*, was a rich find, in that it had several original copies of the *West Indian Gazette*, which I could look through and photocopy. Buzz Johnson promised to share what is apparently an extensive collection of material, but he proved elusive, and his collection from all accounts is in storage at some unidentified place.[6]

Ultimately, the most fruitful source in developing a body of working material was the interviews[7] I conducted with people who knew Claudia Jones personally. Many showed me or handed me their own copies of newspapers, photographs, clippings, cards, letters, newsletters, and other archival material; they shared experiences and their own reminiscences, often provided missing pieces of information. Many were excited to meet me and learn that I had an interest in Claudia Jones; many were emotional, some still dealing with her loss. All were hospitable and offered repeated invitations to tea or lunch. Some, like Billy Strachan, who has since passed away and who was among the group of comrades who met her upon her arrival in London, wanted the interview to focus mostly on themselves, but even in these cases, the interviews provided quite a bit of contextual or relational material. Interviews and conversations with Pansy Jeffries and others who knew Jones personally produced details that fleshed out her human dimensions. (It was Barbara Castle, a member of Parliament in the Labour Party, who introduced Pansy Jeffries to Jones.) I learned that Jones was a helpful, sensitive person who could cook potatoes in five minutes. She liked having a nice coat, having her hair done, and looking good. She moved with a black, New York City style and tempo in the more formal London. Taking a taxi to get somewhere quickly was automatic for her, while other black Londoners tended to wait for the bus or tube. She was serious, intuitive, and nice without arrogance. She liked a good time. She was a human being who wanted to do what she could for black people, but she was not antiwhite. She developed the London Carnival, held in town halls before it moved to the streets. She saw beauty and talent contests and cultural programming as a way of bringing the black community out for carnival. She worked at all levels: with sympathetic whites, community workers, politicians, diplomatic representatives, musicians, entertainers, and writers and in schools and universities.[8]

A series of intellectual projects have begun to produce a body of scholarship on Claudia Jones. The proceedings of a symposium held in 1996 at the Institute of Commonwealth Studies (ICS) in London, which brought together a number of her friends and colleagues, has been edited and introduced by Marika Sherwood with Colin Prescod and Donald Hinds (*Claudia Jones: A Life in Exile*). Another symposium on Claudia Jones was organized by Colin Palmer in 1999, at the Schomburg Library, and was videotaped. Speakers on the panel included the now deceased Stretch Johnson, who was an intimate friend of Claudia, as well as George Lamming, Gerald Horne, Jan Carew, Lydia Lindsey, and this writer.

Significant encouragement and advancement of my research came from Lydia Lindsey, a historian at North Carolina Central University, who has been pursuing the intellectual history of Claudia Jones and working on a Jones biography for a number of years. Lydia was one of the first people to contact me about this project and to share information; she suggested we meet in Miami at the Association for the Study of African American Life and History (ASALH) Conference. When we did meet (on a day when I had also talked with John Hope Franklin about his impending visit to Florida International University in Miami to give the Eric Williams Inaugural Lecture), we talked like old friends about someone we knew. Lindsey handed me a portion of her copy of the FBI files on Claudia Jones, and a few copies of Jones's "Half the World" columns from *The Daily Worker*, wondering if I had seen them.

A new body of literature on Claudia Jones is also emerging from a new generation of scholars. A copy of a dissertation by Claudia May at Berkeley,[9] which I was aware of, came to me through a colleague who knew I was working on Claudia Jones. It includes several interviews with comrades of Jones in New York. A master's thesis on Claudia Jones was written by Yumeris Morel in the History Department at Binghamton University. Additionally, Claudia Jones is one of four women studied in Erik McDuffie's two-volume Ph.D. dissertation for New York University. So a growing number of younger scholars interested in black intellectual traditions is reversing that erasure which her deportation meant to achieve, incorporating Claudia Jones in their dissertations and theses.[10]

This attention is beginning the process of recovering the radical black subject that was Claudia Jones from the oblivion that was intended by the United States government, and brings her back into our conscious knowledge. While she is relatively forgotten in the United States, in London there are organizations named after her and a proposal to have a statue in her honor in Notting Hill. The Camden Black Sisters have done an exhibition in her honor and produced a booklet in her name. The Claudia Jones Organisation in London maintains a series of activities and projects in her honor, including a Claudia Jones supplementary school.

All the evidence points to an energy, a spirit, a dynamism that always would have resisted containment, erasure, or silencing. Through a number of encounters that could only be fortuitous, and exist in the very sphere of Caribbean "magic" realism, Claudia Jones is making it known that she wants to be heard. I have heard of other scholars pursuing a particular figure and feeling almost possessed by the subject of their study.[11] This has been my experience also, and I am a willing subject in this process. For one thing, Jones and I share a birthplace — Trinidad. We have made some of the same migratory journeys — to the United States and to London, though at different historical periods and with different results. In several interviews with people who knew and worked with Jones in London, there is always a moment when the interviewer, in describing her, stops and says, "She looked like . . . well, . . . very much like you do . . . about your height [some accounts put her at five foot, nine inches]. You share some of her bearing, behavior, Trinidadian style, mannerisms." I am flattered, of course, because for me Claudia Jones was the kind of beautiful and insightful woman that I can only approximate. Still, all of my attempts to develop enough work for a study on her have moved with amazing fluidity.

Once, in Café Jam in Brixton, soon after my arrival in London in 1997, I sat with a group of friends[12] following a presentation at Goldsmith's College. A tall, freckled man came in and sat in a corner of the café. After overhearing our conversation, he introduced himself to us. One of our group excitedly indicated that he was Ricky (Alrick) Cambridge, the founder of *The Black Liberator*[13] and someone absolutely essential to an understanding of black struggles in the United Kingdom.[14] I told him about my project and my inability to find material. To my absolute delight, he announced that he had been Claudia Jones's last assistant up to her death and pointed me to a series of sources, indicating all the time that her papers must be somewhere in Hampstead, in the borough of Camden in northwest London. This was the most fortuitous of meetings, and I immediately scheduled an interview. We have since developed a friendship and worked on assembling a volume of Jones's writings, tentatively titled *Claudia Jones beyond Containment*.[15]

Without a doubt, the most important of these experiences came after I had spent about six months in London, conducting interviews and tracking Claudia's papers, all to no avail. During a last, brief, one-week visit to London after the *Presence Africaine* fiftieth anniversary conference in Paris (December 1997), at which I had presented a paper titled "Trans-cultural Black Intellectual Presences,"[16] in which I had made a small mention of Claudia Jones, I received word from a London writer-friend[17] of a source who had her papers. I quickly pursued this lead and, two days later, with Ricky Cambridge facilitating the encounter, found myself in the living room of Diane Langford, in Hampstead. Diane Langford had been married to Claudia's partner, Abhimanyu Manchanda, after Claudia's passing. When Manchanda died, Langford and her daughter Claudia Manchanda (named in honor of Claudia Jones) inherited his estate, including his papers. Among the Manchanda papers, as Langford began to catalog them, was quite a bit of Claudia Jones material, that is, by all accounts, what remained after the Communist Party had come in and taken the first pick. Langford recounted that, throughout their marriage, Manchanda had retained, almost religiously, items such as clothing from Claudia Jones, which he would air out from time to time.

The room we entered in a house in Hampstead was dominated by a box and, deliberately arranged as though they were spilling out of it, were the papers, photographs, newspapers, poems, and letters that their curator, Diane Langford, had guarded with a passion. It is this first encounter with the box and its metaphors of containment and the spilling over of the contents of a life unwilling to be contained by limiting spaces that produced the title for the collection of Jones's writings that Ricky Cambridge and I are editing.[18] Cambridge lamented the small amount of available material, when, in his memory, Claudia Jones had amassed a substantial collection of papers, books, and other items, the majority of which seemed to have disappeared.

That collection now resides in the Schomburg Library and is called the Claudia Jones Memorial Collection. This writer is pleased to have been the person who, with Alrick Cambridge, convinced Diane Langford that depositing the papers in the Schomburg, of all other options available, would make sure that Claudia came "home to Harlem." I feel pleased that I was entrusted with bringing the collection to the United States and delivering it to the Schomburg.

But there are other intellectual homes to which Claudia Jones belongs: the black radical tradition; the Caribbean radical intellectual tradition, particularly the identification of Trinidadian scholars and activists who have contributed to world history in general; African American history and politics in the United States; African diaspora history; pan-Africanist politics; and feminist politics. All of these developing knowledges — that of black communists in particular, which is still being written — are other homes to which Claudia Jones belongs. So I do not see her as "a woman alone"[19] but as an important member of a group of black women communists internationally; as a member of a cadre of African American communists in the United States; and as a respected member of and participant in the London Caribbean community.

Left of Karl Marx is a study organized around six chapters and an introduction. The introduction, "Recovering the Radical Black Female Subject: Anti-Imperialism, Feminism, and Activism" gives a general overview of the subject. Chapter 1, "Women's Rights/Workers' Rights/Anti-Imperialism: Challenging the Superexploitation of Black Working Women," tries to account for the way Jones saw black working-class women as the representative subject for a range of allied political and economic positions. Chapter 2 is titled "From 'Half the World' to the World: Journalism as Black Transnational Political Practice" and concentrates on the range of Jones's journalistic praxes. Chapter 3, "Prison Blues: Literary Activism and a Poetry of Resistance," analyzes a group of fifteen poems found in the Jones collection. Chapter 4, "Deportation: The Other Politics of Diaspora, or 'What is an ocean between us? We know how to build bridges,'" details Jones's deportation and the criminalizing of communism that targeted Claudia Jones as a foreign national but which she transformed into another site of work. Chapter 5 is titled "Carnival and Diaspora: Caribbean Community, Happiness, and Activism" and details Jones's work in the London Caribbean community. By way of a tentative closure, Chapter 6, "Piece Work/ Peace Work: Self-articulation versus State Repression," studies the politics of life writing as it applies to political activism. In that chapter, I examine Claudia Jones's own self-construction in relation to the state's narrative. It identifies Jones's FBI file as the final framing mechanism of the state when it made its case for criminalizing her for being a thinking, writing, speaking black woman.

Claudia Jones, as I have already noted, is interred to the left of Karl Marx in Highgate Cemetery, London. In the general area of the Marx tomb are graves of several other communists, in what seems to be a decisively communism/ arts/journalism corner of the cemetery. Across from Claudia Jones is Carmen England, a sister Caribbean friend and cultural worker. Caribbean journalists and world communist activists are identified on several tombstones close by.

As I left Highgate Cemetery after my December 2004 visit there with my daughter Jonelle, who was photographing the grave site, the realization that Claudia Jones was in the company she would have wanted came over me and provided an amazing lift.

As I come to the end of this stage of my work on Claudia Jones, I see many other possible beginnings. There is so much more to be said, but for now, there must be a reluctant and temporary closure. The photograph of Claudia Jones that you will find toward the end of this book (figure 31), shows her, I am sure, as she would want to be remembered. It portrays her happily attending as a guest the Caribbean-style wedding of Fitz Gore and Patricia Reid in September 1959. Her beautiful smile and joyful expression are mature echoes of another stunning and beautiful photograph, which graces the cover of the *Young Communist Review* (figure 3). This is the energy of Claudia that transcended all the pain she endured throughout her life and endeared her to many.

CLAUDIA VERA CUMBERBATCH JONES

Chronology

This chronology uses dates from Claudia Jones's "Autobiographical History" and other sources that provide details about her public and private life. Exact dates of arrests, incarceration, and related matters are taken from official government documents available in the FBI's files under the heading: Claudia Jones/File number: 100-72390 Volume 1 and Volume 2. The ideological underpinnings of discrepancies between official and personal memory are the subject of the final chapter of this book.

1915   Born February 21, Belmont, Port-of-Spain, Trinidad, to Charles Bertrand Cumberbatch and Sybil (Minnie Magdalene) Cumberbatch, née Logan.

1924   Arrives February 9 on S.S. *Voltaire* in New York City with sisters Lindsay, Irene, Sylvia and aunt Alice Glasgow.

1930–1935   Attends Wadleigh High School. Active in Junior NAACP. Studies drama at Urban League; performs in Harlem and Brooklyn.

1933   Mother dies of spinal meningitis at age thirty-seven, two years before Jones graduates from high school.

1934   Committed to Sea View Sanatorium for almost a year after having been diagnosed with tuberculosis.

1935   Graduates from high school. Works in laundry, factory, millinery, and sales.

1935–1936   Involved in Scottsboro Boys organizing. Writes "Claudia's Com-
             ments" for a black newspaper; becomes editor of a youth paper,
             organ of Federated Youth Clubs of Harlem. Attends Harlem rallies.

1936   Joins Communist Party and Young Communist League; assigned to
        Youth Movement.

1937   Becomes Associate Editor of *Weekly Review* and Secretary of the
        Executive Committee of Young Communist League in Harlem.
        Employed in the business department of the *Daily Worker.* Attends
        six-month training school of the Communist Party.

1938   Becomes New York State Chair and National Council member of
        Young Communist League. Attends National Council of Negro
        Youth, Southern Negro Congress, National Negro Congress. Visits
        American Congress. Files preliminary papers for U.S. citizenship.

1940   Marries Abraham Scholnick.

1941   Becomes Educational Director of Young Communist League.

1942   Aggressive surveillance by FBI begins.

1943–1945   Becomes editor of *Spotlight*, American Youth for Democracy.

1943   Becomes Editor-in-Chief of *Weekly Review*.

1945–1946   Becomes Editor, Negro Affairs, *Daily Worker*. Elected full member
             of the National Committee of Communist Party USA at its annual
             convention.

1947–1952   Active in national women's movements and United Front move-
             ments, such as Congress of American Women and National Council
             of Negro Women.

1947   Divorced in Mexico (February 27). Becomes Secretary, Women's
        Commission, Communist Party USA.

1948   Arrested for first time (January 19); imprisoned on Ellis Island under
        1918 Immigration Act. Released on $1000 bail (January 20). Threat-
        ened with deportation to Trinidad (January 26). Speaks at May Day
        Rally in Los Angeles. Assigned by Party to work with working-class
        and black party women for peace and equality. Tours forty-three U.S.
        states, including the west coast, reorganizing state-level women's
        commissions, recruiting new party members, and organizing mass

rallies. Deportation hearing begins but is postponed because people will not testify against her.

1950   Deportation hearing resumes (February 16). Appointed alternate member of the National Committee, Communist Party USA. Gives speech in March ("International Women's Day and the Struggle for Peace"), which is later cited as "overt act" in her subsequent arrest. Arrested for second time (October 23) and held at Ellis Island under McCarran Act. Detained at New York City Women's Prison (November 17). Released on bail (December 21). Deportation order served.

1951   Speaks in Harlem while on bail. Arrested for third time (June 29) under Smith Act, along with sixteen other communists (including Elizabeth Gurley Flynn). Released on $20,000 bail (July 23, 1951). Deportation hearing continues.

1952–1953   Serves on National Peace Commission at end of Korean War.

1953   Convicted under Smith Act (January 21). Sentenced to one year and a day and $200 fine. Suffers heart failure and is hospitalized for twenty-one days at the end of her trial. December, hospitalized again. Diagnosed with hypertensive cardiovascular disease.

1954   Becomes Editor of *Negro Affairs Quarterly*.

1955   Imprisoned in Women's Penitentiary, Alderson, West Virginia (January 11). Released October 23 after numerous petitions for health reasons. Sentence commuted for "good behavior." Stays with her father. Hospitalized at Mt. Sinai Hospital, following heart attack identified as exacerbated by conditions of imprisonment. Deportation ordered (December 5). Leaves for London on the *Queen Elizabeth* (December 9). December 22, Arrives in London, welcomed by friends and Communist Party members, including earlier communist deportees from the United States.

1956–1957   Becomes affiliated with Caribbean members of Communist Party of Great Britain (CPGB); joins West Indian Forum and Committee on Racism and International Affairs. Works in various organizations in London, including the Caribbean Labour Congress (London Branch); reportedly helps with the editing of final issue of the Labour Congress's organ, *Caribbean News*.

1956   Hospitalized in London for three months.

1957   Co-founds West Indian Workers and Students Association. Becomes active in variety of ways against racism, immigration restrictions, and oppression of Caribbean community in London, and apartheid South Africa.

1958   Founds *West Indian Gazette* (later, *West Indian Gazette and Afro-Asian Caribbean News*) in London.

1958–1964   Edits *West Indian Gazette and Afro-Asian Caribbean News*; active in political organizing of Caribbean, pan-African, and third world communities in London.

1959   First London Caribbean Carnival, St. Pancras Hall, London (January 30).

1961   Afro-Asian Caribbean Conference, organized in part by *West Indian Gazette*, leads to formation of Committee of Afro-Asian and Caribbean Organizations.

1962   Visits Soviet Union as guest of editors of *Soviet Women*. Visits school and studies developments in health care. Is hospitalized while in Soviet Union. Tours Leningrad, Moscow, and Sevastopol. Returns to London (November 21).

1963   Visits Soviet Union again as representative of Trinidad and Tobago to attend World Congress of Women. August, organizes with Committee of Afro-Asian and Caribbean Organizations a "Parallel March" on Washington to U.S. Embassy.

1964   Works with African National Congress to organize hunger strike against apartheid, to boycott South Africa, and for freedom of political prisoners such as Nelson Mandela. Participates in protests outside South African embassy in London. Speaks at rally with novelist George Lamming and others (April 12). Meets Martin Luther King Jr. in London on his way to Oslo to collect Nobel Peace Prize. Writes editorial about King's visit in *West Indian Gazette and Afro-Asian Caribbean News* (it is her last editorial and is published posthumously). Gives speech in Japan as a delegate to 10th World Conference against Hydrogen and Atom Bombs. Serves as Vice Chair of the Conference Drafting Committee; proposes resolution in support of liberation struggles in the third world. Travels to China as guest of China Peace Committee. Meets Chairman Mao, along with a Latin American delegation. Interviews Soong Ching Ling, wife of Sun Yat-Sen. Dies of heart failure in London.

1965   Funeral draws recognitions from governments around the world, diplomatic representations, and media coverage. January 9, Cremated at Golders Green Crematorium, London. Memorial meeting held in Peking by Committee of British and American Friends of Claudia Jones (February 21). Interment of Jones's ashes in plot to left of grave of Karl Marx, Highgate Cemetery, London (February 27).

1984   Headstone erected; inscription reads: "Claudia Vera Jones, Born Trinidad 1915, Died London 25.12.64, Valiant Fighter against racism and imperialism who dedicated her life to the progress of socialism and the liberation of her own black people."

RECOVERING THE RADICAL
BLACK FEMALE SUBJECT

Anti-Imperialism, Feminism, and Activism

Your Honor, there are a few things I wish to say! . . .
I say these things not with any idea that what I say will influence your
sentence of me. For even with all the power your Honor holds, how can
you decide to mete out justice for the only act [to] which I proudly plead
guilty, and one, moreover, which by your own rulings constitutes no
crime—that of holding Communist ideas; of being a member and officer
of the Communist Party of the United States?
—CLAUDIA JONES, FROM "SPEECH TO THE COURT, FEBRUARY 2, 1953"

The only black woman among communists tried in the United
States, sentenced for crimes against the state, incarcerated,
and then deported, Claudia Jones seems to have simply disappeared from major consideration in a range of histories. The
motivating questions for my study have arisen principally from
this situation. How could someone who had lived in the United
States from the age of eight, who had been so central to black and
communist political organizing throughout the 1930s and 1940s,
up to the mid-1950s, simply disappear? How could such a popular public figure, an active journalist and public speaker, a close
friend of Paul and Eslanda Goode Robeson, a housemate of
Lorraine Hansberry, mentored by W. E. B. Du Bois, remain
outside of major consideration? How could someone who was so
central to Caribbean diaspora community organizing abroad, the

founder of the London Carnival and of one of the first black newspapers in London, the *West Indian Gazette and Afro-Asian-Caribbean News*, a close friend of Amy Ashwood Garvey, a female political and intellectual equivalent of C. L. R. James, remain outside the pool of knowledge of Caribbean intellectual history? The need to find answers to these questions, and thereby correct these omissions, provides the impetus for this book.

Tall, elegant, brilliant, and Trinidadian, Claudia Jones was deported from the United States in December 1955 after serving over nine months of a one-year-and-one-day sentence in the Federal Prison for Women in Alderson, West Virginia.[1] In my view, the deportation of Claudia Jones in a sense effected the deporting of the radical black female subject from U.S. political consciousness. By "radical black female subject," I mean both this black radical individual herself and the basic subject or topic of black female radicalism within a range of political positions and academic histories. Claudia Jones's politics were radical because she was seemingly fearless in her ability to link decolonization struggles internally and externally, and to challenge U.S. racism, gender subordination, class exploitation, and imperialist aggression simultaneously.

The fact that Claudia Jones is *buried* to the left of Marx in Highgate Cemetery, London, provides an apt metaphor for my assertions in this study. Her location in death continues to represent her ideological position while living: this black woman, articulating political positions that combine the theoretics of Marxism-Leninism and decolonization with a critique of class oppression, imperialist aggression, and gender subordination, is thus "left" of Karl Marx.[2]

Claudia Jones's position on the "superexploitation of the black woman," Marxist-Leninist in its formation, offered, for its time, the clearest analysis of the location of black women — not in essentialized, romantic, or homogenizing terms but practically, as located in U.S. and world economic hierarchies. It thereby advanced Marxist-Leninist positions beyond their apparent limitations. To develop her argument, Jones contended that if all workers are exploited because of the usurping of the surplus value of their labor, then black women — bereft of any kind of institutional mechanism to conquer this exploitation, and often assumed to have to work uncountable hours without recompense — live a life of superexploitation beyond what Marx had identified as the workers' lot.

1. Claudia Jones, on left on second row, with other defendants in front of Court House, Foley Square, New York. Pettis Perry is on the far right in the second row. Elizabeth Gurley Flynn is to Claudia Jones's left. From the *West-Indian Gazette and Afro-Asian-Caribbean News*, 1965.

Jones's argument regarding the superexploitation of the black woman is clearly a position left of Karl Marx, since Marx himself did not account for race and gender and/or the position of the black woman. Though her position may be identified as a logical extension of Marx's theory of surplus value, Marx had not, in his time, either the imagination or the historical context to argue for the gendered black subject. Lenin had taken a position on what was then called "the woman question," asserting from the outset that "we must create a powerful international women's movement, on a clear theoretical basis."[3] But Lenin spoke only of the enslavement of women within the social and economic structures that restrict them to domestic labor. Clearly this general position did not account for the specificities of any group of women, as it spoke of women generally and did not figure in the fact that black women at that time were already located in a superexploitative condition within the given productive labor sectors. This is the analytical space in which Claudia Jones began to provide intellectual leadership and to which subsequent scholars of black women's social and political history and condition in various societies would contribute.

This line of argument on the economics of black women's experience was to be made subsequently by Francis Beale in a 1970s black feminist articulation, "Double Jeopardy: To Be Black and Female," but it somehow disappeared from Beale's larger conceptual framework, which in the end she reduced to the "double jeopardy" of race and gender. Angela Davis took the formulation further than double jeopardy, as she identified instead, in *Women, Race and Class*, a "triple jeopardy" that was consistent with Marxist/feminist politics. Davis obviously had been aware of Claudia Jones's existence and ideas (167–171). But in my view, largely because her information was sketchy at best, Davis was not able to give Claudia Jones the full conceptual emplacement in an international "women, race, and class" formulation that she deserved.[4] It is important to recognize nevertheless that Angela Davis herself, having been imprisoned, like Jones, for her communist political views and activism, also occupied—and continues to occupy—the pole of the radical black female subject in black feminist conceptualizing. Claudia Jones thus functioned for Davis as an earlier example of a communist woman's struggle against state repression, as well as an earlier recipient of the state's reprisals.

It remained standard practice, during the 1980s and 1990s, for U.S. African American feminist scholars to deliberately reduce much of their analysis to either a race and gender approach (later including sexuality) or a straight U.S. linear narrative.[5] While a domestic U.S. approach is appropriate for fleshing out the specifics of African American feminist political history in the United States, such a position remains bordered within the U.S. narrative of conquest and domination and thus accompanies the "deportation of the radical black female subject" to an elsewhere, outside the terms of the given U.S. discourse. For this reason as well, there tended to be a consistent deportation of class analysis also to this elsewhere, though there would be fairly frequent mention of class in a variety of formulations.

For Claudia Jones, deportation was not the end of her life. Instead, "elsewhere" became creative space and another geographical location for activism. As will be explored in subsequent chapters, after deportation, Claudia Jones's life was full of political organizing in London: the founding, writing for, and editing of a newspaper; the organizing of cultural activities such as the first Caribbean carnivals in London; and travel to China, Russia, and Japan. Her untimely death in December 1964, nine years after she had left the United States, brought an abrupt halt to a vibrant life, full of activity and energy.

Some writers, such as Buzz Johnson,[6] have argued that her incarceration and the harsh treatment she experienced in prison in the United States—the denial at times of appropriate medical care and diet—weakened her to the point that it is possible to contend that the U.S. government technically killed her. While this is an important and credible assertion, others who knew her well[7] say that Jones never rested, even with a heart condition, and constantly minimized how serious her health issues were, so much so that many of her London colleagues never knew that she was as close to death as she was.

An African diaspora framework, internationalist in orientation, embraces this radical black female subject and begins a process of relational work, combating the imposed erasure and silencing of Claudia Jones that was the final goal U.S. officials intended by her deportation. *Left of Karl Marx* has the explicit aim, then, of recovering the radical black subject that was Claudia Jones for a variety of relevant discourses; this recovery of Claudia Jones, the individual subject, reinstates a radical black female intellectual-activist position into a range of African diaspora, left history, and black feminist debates.

Combating the Erasure and Silencing of Claudia Jones

The life of Claude Vera Cumberbatch (as she is identified in her birth certificate) was one that consistently resisted containment within the limitations of space, of time, and place.[8] Her declared political identification as a communist of Marxist-Leninist orientation functioned for her as a large enough ideological positioning within which to address the many other subject locations she carried: black, woman, Caribbean-born, pan-Africanist, antiracist, anti-imperialist, feminist. However, it also simultaneously marked her—if we are to use Joy James's distinctions—as minimally a black radical subject and maximally as revolutionary.[9] In my view, a "radical black subject" is one that constitutes itself as resisting the particular dominating disciplines, systems, and logics of a given context. The radical black subject, male or female, challenges the normalizing of state oppression, constructs an alternative discourse, and articulates these both theoretically and in practice. This is a resisting black subject . . . resisting dominating systems organized and enforced by states, organizations, and institutions in order to produce a complicit passive people and to maintain exploitative systems. The revolutionary subject works in a movement geared toward dismantling that oppressive status.

In the end, these distinctions, while useful, may still not mark a person for

the entire trajectory of her life, particularly since, for the revolutionary position to be effective, the individual act must be operational within some sort
of revolutionary movement for social change. James herself concludes that
"no metanarrative can map radical or 'revolutionary' black feminism, although the analyses of activist-intellectuals such as Ella Baker serve as outlines" (*Shadowboxing*, 79).

Another such outline would be the activist-intellectual work of Claudia
Jones herself. Along with her organizing and intellectual work, her own resistance to the variety of organized attempts to silence her are worth recognizing. Her speech to the court, excerpted in the epigraph to this chapter,
which begins "Your Honor, there are a few things that I wish to say," challenges linguistically, politically, and legally the state's illegal attempts to silence her. Indeed, she has her say, and this itself becomes a tangible document
within the corpus of material on state censorship and the creation of political
prisoners in the United States. Within the speech, she makes it clear that even
the judge was hamstrung by the legal prescriptions against communism and
confined by U.S. capitalist prescriptions about ideas. Jones became a political
prisoner, imprisoned — as she herself says explicitly — for her independent
ideas. Paramount in this imprisonment and subsequent deportation was the
fact that she dared to adopt a political philosophy that was anathema in the
McCarthy period of the 1940s and 1950s: Marxism-Leninism with an anti-
racist, antisexist, problack community orientation.

Claudia Jones also has to be seen as a writer articulating her ideas in a
variety of media (poetry, essays, articles, editorials, reviews, booklets). While
her dominant genre was the political essay, the creative was clearly also part
of her formation. Thus another form of resistance to silencing is her composition of a number of poems during periods of imprisonment, which also
thereby demonstrated her resolve and willingness to speak in the face of
perhaps the most concentrated and directed attack on her freedom and the
notion of freedom more generally. Her subsequent founding of the *West
Indian Gazette*, which opened up a wide space for free expression, also fur-
thered this process and provided some continuity with her essays in *Political
Affairs* and journalism in the *Daily Worker*. This conscious and deliberate
definition of herself as a black woman writer is another major means by which
she combated erasure and silencing, as it has been for numerous other dis-
carded writers now being brought back into full consideration.

Another related project in recovering Claudia Jones is a more developed understanding of the transnational/African diaspora subject, whose movement outside of circumscribing national space renders her nationless. Jones's emigration from Trinidad to the United States of America as a child of eight led to a full immersion in urban African American culture but also to being subjected to its racism. The implications of this location within U.S. racism and her understanding of the denial of citizenship rights for African Americans also produced her preliminary understanding of the need for black liberation and therefore ushered in her life of activism. Her secondary migration, to England, led to a participation in a broader Caribbean/African diaspora, as well as an international community of Asians and Eastern Europeans and other groups. But at the same time it also meant another location, within the contours of British racism and its explicit resentment of all black immigrants at the same time that Britain maintained colonial domination in the homes of those same immigrants. The internationalizing of this understanding of racism provided Jones with the means to operationalize her pan-Africanist politics in resistance to these various versions of racism in a way that was more obvious there than it was in the United States.

Thus, to understand Claudia Jones as an African diaspora subject is also to recognize her own placement outside of narrow nationalist identifications. Her alliances with other racial and political communities in a truly cross-cultural mode of community organizing similarly articulate that personal and political movement. The range of personal and political affiliations and subject locations that she consistently deployed — "Negro, Woman, Communist, of West Indian descent . . . born of working-class poverty" (Johnson, 130), and so on (much like Audre Lorde would subsequently do) — makes this point as well.

In the end, then, combating the erasure and silencing of Claudia Jones means simultaneously relocating her in the multiple discourses that she articulated and to which she belonged. For example, Marika Sherwood concludes a section on Jones's political activism with the strong assertion that "Claudia, despite her plethora of political activities, appears in no histories of the British Left. She, like so many other Black activists, has been written out of history."[10] Given these and a variety of other projects of deliberate scholarly recovery, however, the black woman buried left of Karl Marx can no longer remain willfully unaccounted for in the history of the Left.

My context for understanding the radical black female subject is a particular formulation of the black radical tradition that combines intellectual and activist work in the service of one's oppressed communities. I see this as represented well by Claudia Jones's own practice. Intellectual work in this understanding is not a "neutral process," nor one of distant academic reflection, but one of contending ideas — as Stuart Hall maintains — and struggles for social change and human justice. My assertion therefore is that Claudia Jones, though never located in the academy, engaged directly in intellectual-activist work that locates her solidly within Caribbean, African American, and black international radical intellectual traditions.

The role of the intellectual within the academy has been subjected already to some internal scrutiny. Several other attempts have been made over the years to identify the nature of intellectual work in and for black communities. Du Bois's formulation of the "talented tenth," despite its limitations, has been embraced by some scholars in the contemporary period, although Du Bois himself had repudiated it, finding in the end that he had not accounted sufficiently for the selfishness of that talented tenth. Still, one must read Du Bois's formulation along with Zora Neale Hurston's "pet negro system" and her subsequent articulations; in her recently published letters, for example, she describes the mutual benefit that accrued to the dominant white society and to the coopted black intellectual or creative figure.[11]

The Gramscian binary of the traditional intellectual and the organic intellectual is expanded by three descriptors: "the co-opted liberal intellectual" posture, which never sees knowledge as moving into transforming action; "the accommodationist-reformist" intellectual, who aligns her/ himself with popular struggles but cannot communicate with people the ideas of the academy; and the "guerilla intellectual" in the tradition of Walter Rodney, whose scholarship, life, and activism were all organized for transformative intent.[12]

Our contemporary U.S.-based realities reveal that two other categories are perhaps appropriate. I would add (1) the commoditized intellectual, whose entire exercise of academic production is hyper-market-driven and in the benefit of the state; and (2) the radically transformative intellectual,[13] whose entire praxis is organized around the production of knowledge directed at transforming the social contexts in which we live and operate in and out of the academy. This latter position comes out of not seeing the Walter Rodney position in idealistic terms, because, at its most extreme, it requires a certain martyrdom in order to be activated.

Still, I find most helpful Edward Said's analysis "The Limits of the Artistic Imagination and the Secular Intellectual," which offers six axes of activity and thought for the secular intellectual, not in terms of authority but "as an everlasting effort, an unendingly vigilant, prompt, energetic and reflective activity, an unstoppable energy." The axes, which Said sees as "orienting intellectual activity" and not prescribing it, comprise (1) providing counterinformation in an age where the media have the resources to manage and manipulate reality; (2) a reinterpretive function at the level of communicating ideas; (3) demystification by articulating the basic issues of justice and human good or evil surrounding these issues; (4) interfering and intervening across lines of specialization that attempt to privatize knowledge; (5) an insurgent and resistant position when consensus is arrived on the basis of domination; and (6), the task of "exercis[ing] a moral function of deploying the irreconcilable and irreducible oppositions between ideas, peoples, societies, histories, and claims" at the level of performance (32). Many of these qualities seem to mark the activist orientation of Claudia Jones. In the final analysis, then, Said's definitions may not be directly operational by the academy-bound intellectual, who is subject to a variety of institutional mandates, and may indeed work better for the activist-intellectual outside of the academy.[14]

I am suggesting then that one cannot talk about intellectual work and practice among black and women scholars without raising some questions on the role of its practitioners who occupy the "status identity" of the professoriat. Additionally, our contemporary (twenty-first-century) political realities make it clear that one cannot assume that, by virtue of any generic subject location, one's contribution is automatically radical just because it comes from a member of a subordinated group. The nature of the construction of power elites who function as spokespeople for subordinated communities in myriad locations testify to this.

Thus, one cannot locate all intellectual activity within the academy only, particularly when there exists (and existed) a Marxist tradition of the development of working-class intellectuals for whom the study of political theory and its praxis were critical. This is one of the traditions out of which Claudia Jones came. Thus, I am extending this critique of intellectual work to say equally that popular versions of black feminist thought, in many ways, simply retraced the basic academic terms of black studies and women's studies positions, as these have themselves retraced the larger academic structures. In that context then, it is important to give similar recognition to the kind of intellectual work produced organically outside of the academy and accord that work the same weight and space one gives to academic production. In the final analysis, in order to speak fully about the intellectual work that was Claudia Jones's contribution, as it was for several of her counterparts, one has to undo the narrow equivalence of intellectual work with the academy.

This introduction engages some of the questions surrounding black feminist work and its relation to work in black studies and feminist studies, to the academy as a whole, and to the larger public sphere in which it sometimes operates, in order to understand why someone like Claudia Jones remained outside the pale of black and feminist intellectual production. The entire project therefore locates itself within a certain form of radically transformative intellectual work, engaging some of the ideas advanced by Said, for example, on the role of the intellectual as identified above. It also relocates the issue of activism in black intellectual production at the level of praxis.

It is in this context that we account for the activist-intellectual who was Claudia Jones, as someone who was solidly located outside of any academic context but whose entire production of ideas rivaled many of those produced in the universities at the same time. This intellectual contribution is particularly important since black communities did not have the kind of access to academic institutions that they do following the civil rights era. As chapter 2, "From 'Half the World' to the Whole World: Journalism as Black Transnational Political Practice," will demonstrate, a great deal of this praxis came through the medium of journalism. But there are also theoretical contributions outlined in a range of political essays and journal articles. *Left of Karl Marx* represents the radical, political intellectual ideas of Claudia Jones, recovering them from erasure, and relocating them solidly within black, feminist, Caribbean, and allied intellectual traditions.

Relocating Claudia Jones in U.S. Black Feminist Thought

The advances in black feminist thought have been substantial in articulating a theoretics that has historically put together race, gender, class, and sexuality as intricately linked, and thus provided a model for the kind of contemporary theoretical work that builds on a logic of intersectionality. Black feminist analyses have allowed a series of articulations that have accounted for the missing black woman in a variety of discourses. Still, the absence of a geopolitical approach to black identity often replayed itself in seventies and eighties U.S. black feminist thought, in much the same way that mainstream feminist thought accounted only for white women. The tendency has been toward the articulation of a historically linear narrative that looks back in U.S. history to black women, either symbolic or actual, for verification and therefore stays within U.S. borders. The specifics of location raised by black women across various cultures became, by the end of the twentieth century, significant for reassessing various subject positions and redefinitions of black feminism.

It is important to say at the outset that in the second wave of black feminist activity (during the 1980s and beyond), the intent and spirit of the Boston-based group of black lesbian/feminist activists, the Combahee River Collective, was often overlooked. The "Combahee River Collective Statement," republished in Hull, Scott, and Smith's collection *All the Women Are White, All the Blacks Are Men, But Some of Us Are Brave*, began to formulate a discourse of black feminism with an activist and intellectual orientation (praxis model) in mind, as did the initial work of the Chicago-based National Black Feminist Organization. Much of this was unfortunately transformed to a singularly intellectual agenda in the post-1980s entry of black women into academic positions. To their credit, the formulators of the Combahee River Collective Statement addressed the relational, that is, the issues that relate African American women living in the United States to third world women in their assertion that "black, other Third World, and working women have been involved in feminist movement from its start" (14).

> The inclusiveness of our politics makes us concerned with any situation that impinges upon lives of women and those of Third World and working people in general. We are of course particularly committed to working on those struggles in which race, sex, and class are simultaneous factors in oppression. We might, for example, become involved in workplace organizing at a factory that employs Third World women or picket a hospital that is cutting back on already inadequate health care to a Third World community, or set up a rape crisis center in a black neighborhood. (21)

That this position is listed under "black feminist issues and practice" is significant because here were women working toward a "nonhierarchical distribution of power" within their own group and in a transformed society.

In the introduction to her 1990s reprint of *Black Macho and the Myth of the Superwoman*[15] titled "How I Saw it Then; How I See it Now," Wallace references postcolonial criticism and the problematizing of home but offers her critique as well: "I don't think they begin to exhaust what we can possibly say about our relationship to 'other worlds' beyond the hegemony of the West. Afro-Americans are not immigrants although we have always wanted recent arrivals from the Caribbean and Africa among us. As a group, we have been in the Americas longer than anyone apart from the Indians" (xxvi).

For Wallace, the particular black identity that is evoked is consistently only viable within U.S. African American formulations about race and history. Thus is sometimes enshrined a separation between those who do African diaspora (international) work and those who do U.S. African American (domestic) research in the United States without any attempt to conceptually account for what lies outside U.S. borders, as though the U.S. African American community was somehow not part of the African diaspora. Thus it was gratifying to see Wallace refer to the Jamaican side of her family, who were always there, even though this does not continuously inform her articulation of African diaspora women's experience from locations outside of the United States. Her visit to Jamaica that is narrated at the start of *Dark Designs and Visual Culture* is seen through the prism of U.S. citizenship privilege. Her statement "Suddenly, I understood how and why my own family, and all the other West Indians who lived in Brooklyn and Queens and Harlem, had fled this island" (3) makes it seem that the apparent poverty and unfinishedness that she witnesses in the Caribbean are not also found in poor black communities in the United States. For indeed, the amenities of good living (such as universities and bookstores and libraries) are available in certain classed communities everywhere and unavailable in others.

But it is precisely in that space between the domestic and the international that someone like Claudia Jones, though she had spent the bulk of her life in African American communities in the United States, continuously disappears.

It is for this reason that I want to foreground the logic of praxis, as opposed to the split between theory and practice. I also want to assert the spirit of contestation and production involved in work, not asserting that "thought" is not "work" but that "work" foregrounds labor-intensive aspects that must constitute any set of productive gestures. In fact, if we use the example of the same African American foremothers that are invoked — Sojourner Truth,

Harriet Tubman, Maria Stewart, and Ida B. Wells, for instance — we are talking of women who were actively involved in a variety of movements against oppression both inside and outside the U.S. government's legitimating mechanisms: women who often deliberately moved in search of an elsewhere that was not confining.

Defined as a leading black feminist scholar for her work on developing black feminist thought, bell hooks clearly also had a blind spot regarding third world feminisms, which disappear from her formulations, except, perhaps, in "Third World Diva Girls: Politics of Feminist Solidarity."[16] While the essay claimed to work toward "feminist solidarity between black women/women of color" (94), it homogenized all "third world women" into some generic "third world woman." In this formulation, clearly no room exists for black feminist discourse in some sort of transnational context.

Again, speaking of its limits, and not devaluing its contributions, it is helpful to examine the underlying principles of the work of Patricia Hill Collins. In her *Black Feminist Thought* one is even more struck by the way in which the definitions of black feminism are circumscribed by U.S. nation-state, patriotic Americanism; the ways in which racial discourse in the United States consistently effaces "transnational Afro-diasporism."[17] Thus she dismisses the analyses of internal colonialism that would link African American populations in the United States more solidly to the discourses of African diaspora. Her essay "Learning from the Outsider Within: The Social Significance of Black Feminist Thought" is perhaps most instructive. It is based entirely on a position grounded in U.S. parochialism and by its very construction marks the limits of "outsider within" positionality. Beginning with the case of the domestic worker who knows the house better than the mistress allows her to construct black feminist intellectuals within a similar relationship to white feminists. The subject of the address is white women, with a U.S. definition of naturalized, essentialized race as marker, which thus allows her to develop what she calls "standpoint epistemology," that is, that U.S. black women as a group all see the world from a particular angle. It is only logical that the discourse will turn in onto itself in her formulation of Afrocentric feminism.

Collins, like many other scholars, privileges her own subject position, that of the U.S. intellectual as the producer of "facts and theories about the black female experience that will clarify a black woman's standpoint for black women" ("Learning From," 516). But even more surprising is her inability to locate a black feminist position of non-U.S. origin operating within or outside of the United States. Her response in *Fighting Words* to the ways in which black feminist thought has been internationalized is telling.

The issue of imperializing gestures that crop up in a variety of articulations — even ones claiming to be resistant — has been raised in various quarters. Valerie Amos and Pratibha Parmar in England, in their essay "Challenging Imperialist Feminism," began the process of talking about imperialist feminisms in the context of women from dominant social positions who set the agendas for the entire group. Some examples of such discussion is found in the work of African women looking at the bases of U.S. feminisms.[18] Still, it was with surprise that I learned recently that the same Valerie Amos had recently been made a baroness and that Caribbean feminists from the former English Commonwealth had to address her by that title when she visited the Caribbean, with all the protocols in place.[19] Some critiques of imperialism from U.S. (African American) feminism similarly come from women who, in their home contexts, have equivalent class privilege to that of Baroness Amos.[20] The point is less that women operating in a certain class background cannot make significant contributions, or that they commit class suicide, but that those class locations have to be consciously interrogated in general race-based critiques and women's equality arguments.

In general, the idea prevalent in the United States that its people are the only "Americans" carries with it some specific imperialist baggage, as Michael Hanchard shows in his essay "Identity, Meaning and the African-American." The extent to which U.S. African American intellectuals buy this formulation uncritically is the extent to which they participate in the management of the crumbling house of U.S. imperialism. The Afro-Canadian Caribbean writer Marlene Nourbese Philip takes up the argument, made in the May 1996 *New Yorker* special issue "Black in America," that the existence of a successful and prominent black middle class of intellectuals, entertainers, and athletes is a counterpoint to the economic hopelessness of the larger population. Philip's view is that the existence of this class helps to "manage a situation that may already be unmanageable" (18). She notes: "As often happens with empire, specificities are erased and absorbed into a larger whole — the way, for instance, in which all black people in Canada are absorbed into the larger identity of Jamaican immigrant. And so, we could argue, the black in America stands in for being black in Canada, eh. In the Caribbean. In Africa. Everywhere" (15).

The articulation of the role of the intellectual with which I began provides space for a reading of the black and female intellectual as a manager of reality. I see a range of work—black feminist work included, if it remains uncritical of the boundaries that are being deployed—as fulfilling a similar role. The extent to which Claudia Jones remains unaccounted for (not even mentioned)[21] in most U.S. black feminist conceptualizing and remains unknown by the major black women historians is a clear index of that absence of relational work and of paradigms that are not exclusively gender- and race-based, even as the word "class" is mentioned.[22]

Thus the importance of Ella Baker's work and her essay "The Bronx Slave Market" (written with Marvell Cooke). Even as Baker and Cooke deal with domestic labor in New York, because of its identification with the contexts of the exploitation of this labor, they are able to produce a historical document with international import into which or against which contemporary analyses of the exploitation of Caribbean women as domestics in New York may be measured. This issue, we know, reappears in Paule Marshall's novel *Brown Girl, Brownstones*, which gives substantial narrative descriptions of Caribbean domestic labor in New York.

The accounts of Baker, Cooke, and Marshall are valuable, and for the same reasons I value Joy James's black feminist assessments, as I do her work on political prisoners. They come together in her work on the Angela Davis corpus and her critique of "talented tenth" formulations. James expresses a desire to restart black feminist articulations from a different theoretical place, one that accounts more deliberately for a tradition of radicalism that we know existed in the activism of people like Ida B. Wells. James's is a framework of black feminism in which radical black left female subjects like Claudia Jones can have tangible existence.[23] For James, "black feminist writings often pay insufficient attention to state repression and the conflictual ideologies and divergent practices (from liberal to revolutionary) found within black feminisms" (*Shadowboxing*, 78).

The gains of black feminist thought can be summarized as follows: it has put together a range of hitherto disparate identities and theories (race, gender, and sexuality, for example); it has opened intellectual scenarios where black women must be accounted for; and it has inaugurated a proliferation of studies in the social sciences, humanities, legal studies, and even current discussions of black masculinities and black queer studies. It has therefore transformed the subjects of a great deal of intellectual inquiry and the ways that it is conducted, post-1980s and at the turn of the century.

Yet the reasons why important figures in U.S. African American history like Claudia Jones are again deported to another location conceptually and literally, outside the borders of U.S. thought, scholarship, and understandings have to be understood. The "insider within" approach has as its limit a certain set of insular assumptions about the local. Learning from the "outsider outside" is another approach that can be used along with it, as Lorde does with her formulation of "sister outsider" — the woman who is outside of a range of discourses, privileges, opportunities, and access. Hers is the kind of work that sees the global and local imbrications. It allows a certain domestic agenda and activism even as it recognizes how interrelated these are with the international. But much of this work is only just beginning to take place, and my study of Jones contributes to that process. By these and other means, many of the gaps in black feminist thought internationally are gradually being filled. This opens the space for a position as radical as that of Claudia Jones to be re-inserted. A more recent collection of black feminist criticism, *The Black Feminist Reader*, includes Sylvia Wynter's important "Beyond Miranda's Meanings: Unsilencing the Demonic Ground of Caliban's Woman."

The work done by some black feminist historians in the United States has been extremely useful in this regard, even as it has built itself into its own particular domestic borders, as I describe above. Works like *Black Women in America*, edited by Darlene Clark Hine, Elsa Barkley Brown, and Rosalyn Terborg-Penn, are indispensable tools, providing extensive histories of black women's contributions to the world; their book includes an entry on Claudia Jones. And the timely collection of essays by black women *Words of Fire: An Anthology of African-American Feminist Thought*, edited by Beverly Guy-Sheftall, provides an easy way to work through the various positions coming out of U.S. black feminist articulations. To its credit, the collection includes the classic article by Jones "An End to the Neglect of the Problems of Black Women," almost always overlooked, despite what it calls for.

Black Communist Women

The study of black communist women remains one of the most neglected among contemporary examinations of black women for at least one of the reasons that Joy James identifies: "The revolutionary remains on the margin, more so than any other form of (black) feminism" (92). *Left of Karl Marx* contributes to the necessary unfolding of this area of research, but there are a few texts already available. Gerald Horne's *Race Woman: The Lives of Shirley Graham Du Bois*, which, although titled *Race Woman*, shows that one of Du Bois's important "lives" was her strong affiliation with the Left and details, in particular, her travel to China and experience there. Horne reports, especially in the chapter "Black, to the Left," her relationship to the American Left as being cemented when her husband, W. E. B. Du Bois, joined the Communist Party of America (CPUSA), putting the couple ideologically in the company of Esther Cooper Jackson and James Jackson, who published the journal *Freedomways*. But, not unusually, these relationships with the Communist Party were never smooth, always complicated by issues of American black nationalism and the responses to racism that invariably produce a "race first" narrative.

Some new work is beginning to be available that makes the appearance of Angela Davis not an aberration or the result of some exceptionalism but something located within a history of black communist women. Erik McDuffie's 2003 dissertation, "Long Journeys: Four Black Women and the Communist Party, USA, 1930–1956," studies the early and developing lives of black communist women, using oral histories, FBI files, and other available records. The women include Louise Thompson Patterson, Claudia Jones, Audley Moore, and Esther Jackson. One chapter in particular ("Black Women Communists and the United Front in Harlem, 1933–1935") focuses on Patterson and Moore but also provides considerable information on the activities of other women. We learn, for example, that in the period following the Harlem Riot of 1935 "Louise Thompson had become the most visible African American female personality within the Party" (195), becoming "a high-profile CPUSA spokesperson" (197) and therefore an important member of the cadre of black leadership that developed in Harlem. Audley "Queen Mother" Moore would have a different trajectory, moving from activism in the Garvey movement to the Communist Party and back out again into a more explicit African nationalism at the end of her years. My own study of Claudia Jones, one of the important members of this group, adds to the growing knowledge of the history of black women communists. And hopefully additional studies will flesh out the full dimensions of their story.

But even before Jones, as Mark Solomon reports, there was Maude White, who had studied in Russia, was one of a class of students that included Ho Chi Minh and Jomo Kenyatta, and returned to the United States as an activist in Harlem and subsequently in Pittsburgh. Solomon, whose dissertation is now published as *The Cry Was Unity: Communists and African Americans, 1917–1936*, had earlier written a short piece titled "Rediscovering a Lost Legacy: Black Women Radicals Maude White and Louise Thompson,"[24] which focused exclusively on black communist women, providing substantial discussion of Maude White, who was active in the Communist Party in the early 1930s. Thus, when Claudia Jones entered the Communist Party there were already examples of very active black communist or leftist women who had visible identities that she could emulate and positions she could advance. In this context, Claudia Jones was not a lone, singular figure, or unusual. What marks her instead is that she became both an *organizer* and a leading *theoretician*.

Additionally, as Solomon also reports, the Caribbean community was well represented in the early days of the Communist Party in the person of Richard Moore. Otto Huiswood, Cyril Briggs, and Grace Campbell, would be founding members of the radical African Blood Brotherhood. Grace Campbell, in particular (who is identified as of Jamaican descent and who has so far been also only marginally recognized), was among a group that according to Solomon, "found their way to the Communist Party when the Socialists continued to be unresponsive to the problems of African Americans" (4).

Kate Weigand, in *Red Feminism*, also reports that in Communist Party schools, courses on black women would become part of the curriculum with "teachers such as Lorraine Hansberry, Claudia Jones, Charlotta Bass, Eleanor Flexner, Yvonne Gregory and Doxey Wilkerson [who] offered lectures and courses that explored topics such as 'Negro Women in the Struggle for Peace and Democracy' and 'Negro Women in Political Life' " (110). While it was clearly a Communist Party project, this initiative was spearheaded by black party women like Claudia Jones and accompanied by ongoing activities to recruit black women members, as significant elements of black communist women's organizing and educating strategies.

It is in this context that the group known as Sojourners for Truth and Justice would exist. Dealing specifically with the conditions of black women, the links to the larger issues we have identified are among the fundamental markers of this manifestation of black feminist politics. Although not all its members were Communist Party members, and although there would be some conflicts between members such as Claudia Jones and Beah Richards on this issue, the project of the Sojourners would be identified by the state as a left, Communist Party–inspired project and guarantee their surveillance by the FBI. And even when they were not Communist Party members, black women like Charlotta Bass took positions that would be defined as radical in the challenge to racism and sexism and state oppression. For example, Bass later defended other women who, like Claudia Jones, were being hounded by the U.S. government. Bass had also traveled to the Soviet Union, shared the same optimistic view of that country as Thompson Patterson, and wrote about her experience. In *Forty Years*, a collection of her writings in *The California Eagle*, she says there was "no color question in the USSR" and expresses the favorable view that Russians, "held together in a common bond of brotherhood for the good of all, . . . were enthusiastic in the belief that there was no room for hatred, bitterness and strife. There was no problem of discrimination or segregation" (167). Bass describes stumbling upon the John Golden story, of a black U.S. family living under segregation in Mississippi who decided to move to the Soviet Union in 1931 (166). Bass also points out the important fact that Los Angeles was founded primarily by black people and includes a piece that recognizes black women from other locations, capturing the words of Adora Lily Ulasi from Nigeria, then a student and later a writer (155).

Some specific connections are yet to be made between the activism of left women in the 1940s and 1950s and the genesis of Angela Davis in the following decades. From some reports, one of those links might be Esther Jackson, who was president of the Southern Negro Youth Conference and who would also work on the Scottsboro Boys case. The Angelo Herndon case would provide another link, as it became, for its time, the legal struggle that would launch the careers of subsequent communists like Benjamin Davis. The point is that throughout our histories there have been black activists — many of them women — who would be defined as radical or revolutionary because they challenged oppressive state practices. In our own contemporary period, Assata Shakur stands as an example of a woman who refused to be cowered by an oppressive prosecutorial system. In her day, Harriet Tubman, though now celebrated, would have gone down as a radical woman, confronting the system of slavery at that time and moving in and out of it at will. Claudia Jones would be but one of a line of those radical women. As we shall see, comparable figures also appear in the Caribbean and in Africa.

Transnational black feminist work recognizes that our current geographical locations are products of multiple historical processes, many of which we had no control over, which have produced us, as subjects, in various "nation-states" of the world, having to interact with other similarly or differently produced individuals. These displacements are the end product of some very hateful processes: wars of domination, colonialisms, enslavements, holocausts, encampments, dispossession, and genocide. Thus, preliminarily, transnational or cross-cultural feminist work has to take into account how we were produced as subjects in the wake of European Enlightenment and modernism, colonialism, and their various enterprises. More recent structural adjustments, economic and corporate globalization, and the transnational movement of capital in its search for cheap labor sources worldwide are reproduced under various nationalist or regional and global imperatives.

A number of texts begin to engage feminism in the United States from a variety of other ethnic locations other than black feminist positions. Transnational feminism would arise preliminarily from one larger assumption: that working cross-culturally is an essential feature of our contemporary world, and our own specific locations and identities must be part of the bases of our analyses. With this in mind then, any contemporary cultural and political work that wants to move out of fixity and specific imperialistic interpellations has to account for its particular location, articulate its own specificity, and move toward the recognition of the existence of other cultures and political realities in some cross-cultural or translocational way.

In much the same way, gender, or the social categorization of "woman" as identified and understood by Western feminists, has already been significantly challenged and redefined by a variety of non-Western feminist scholars and lesbian philosophers.[25] The result is that gender now has to be spoken for and understood within very specific cultural contexts and also relationally. Similarly, the tendency for the category "black woman" or "black feminism" to be deployed in a limited way is still being challenged and thereby redefined, based on the experiences of a number of black women internationally.

"Migratory subjectivity," an earlier formulation of mine, attempted to account for the ways our identities are formed in movement.[26] In some ways, migratory subjectivity may be considered here, as it is through migration that one gets to the transnational. Perhaps most critical in doing transnational feminist work is the understanding that the nation-states in which we live as subjects have been produced out of specific political imperatives and histories and that they therefore seek to contain, arbitrarily, a variety of peoples subject to the whims of these same nation-state enterprises. If those nation-states attain dominance, as has happened in the case of the United States, then even those identities subordinated domestically in those states are unwittingly attached. Thus African Americans in the United States end up carrying some of the weight of U.S. imperialism and its manifestations in war efforts and capitalist expansion. Among the people in contemporary times who are unable to live with the domination instituted in order to maintain these nation-states are "gypsies," "nomads," "migrants," "migrant workers," "exiles," "refugees," the "imprisoned," "the deported," and "the homeless." Persons displaced by global economic processes, who must constantly reconcile themselves to existing emotionally and physically in different spaces, may enter what is popularly referred to now as a diaspora, a space that resists centering even as it identifies longing, homelands, and a myth of origin. Still, there are those who remain outside a diaspora or who live in intersecting or overlapping diasporas.

"Migrating subjects," I have argued, already consistently negotiate borders in assertive ways, challenging the entrenched meanings of those in intact locations, crossing and recrossing them, making them sites of transformation. But there are those who remain confined by state dictates as they deal with the realities of living in twentieth-century imprisonments: a variety of prisons across the United States and refugee camp and concentration camp situations such as Chrome in Miami or Guantánamo Bay in Cuba. A lingering question then has to be, "What are all the in/visible identities that remain hidden as a dominant discourse is constituted?" First of all, the critique of a variety of levels of exclusion is critical, as is the recognition of the many local, activist movements of the women themselves, and clearly the appearance of a variety of these women in the various metropoles. Amrita Basu, in *The Challenge of Local Feminisms*, speaking of participants at a 1985 Nairobi conference, says that "better communications between these groups of women . . . occurred once they abandoned the myth of global sisterhood and acknowledged profound differences in women's lives and the meaning of feminism cross-nationally" (3).

A growing body of scholarship, produced by black women and women of color, is systematically addressing the specificities of women's lives in myriad locations, identifying what the particularities of gender, sex, sexuality, race, class, and so on mean when looked at through different lenses or at least when removed from the fixed location of "under western eyes." See, for example, the recent work of Jacqui Alexander and Chandra Talpade Mohanty, including *Feminism without Borders: Decolonizing Theory, Practicing Solidarity*.[27]

Beverly Guy-Sheftall's overview "Speaking for Ourselves: Feminisms in the African Diaspora" offers a range of black feminist contributors and positions internationally across the African diaspora, beginning with Anna Julia Cooper and ranging through the Casely-Hayfords and Funmilayo Anikulapo Ransome-Kuti to contemporary contributors. Transnational black feminist work, which accounts for some of these movements and migratory journeys as they also attempt to make connections, makes meaning based on a variety of experiences and is reflected as well in the kind of gender work that Claudia Jones did, from a variety of political positions and geographical locations. There is sufficient evidence, as Guy-Sheftall reveals, that these women often worked collaboratively across continents. Amy Ashwood Garvey, Eslanda Goode Robeson, and Claudia Jones, for example, maintained an international friendship and communication. And Claudia Jones is identified as attending the same meeting as Mrs. Ransome Kuti, at the World Congress of Women in the USSR in 1963.[28]

With the various histories accounted for, it is not difficult to begin a process of recognition of the various positionalities we occupy and have occupied historically. This is the process that, for me, offers the possibilities for the transformation of the unequal bases of our arrangements. The context in which I want to locate this particular work on Claudia Jones is one that recognizes the transnational as it interacts with the local. For Jones herself was able to link the specific struggles of women from a variety of locations to those of women in world hegemonic powers like the United States.

As cultural critic, Stuart Hall appropriately asserted — well before the popular discourses of globalization — that the global has now become the local; indeed, the global and local are imbricated, one on the other. Separating them masks the ways in which capital traffics in global ways.[29] What some would call the postcolonial, the transnational, or the cross-cultural is a reality of our contemporary existences. Media, markets, and communications of various

lived and organized at the intersection of a variety of positionalities (anti-imperialism and decolonization struggles, activism for workers' rights, the critique of appropriation of black women's labor, the challenge to domestic and international racisms and their links to colonialism) and was therefore able to articulate them earlier than many of her contemporaries. In this regard, her ideas, as this book argues, have significant implications for contemporary articulations of transnational African diaspora/feminist politics.

Recovering Claudia Jones for the Caribbean

Claudia Jones was in effect a "sister outsider," as Audre Lorde[37] described herself in a variety of discourses, and she definitely remains a sister outside the Caribbean intellectual-radical tradition. The fact is that she is not well known in the Caribbean, just as she is also not remembered in the United States. This, we can say, is the result of emigrating from Trinidad to the United States as a child, and then being deported as an adult from the United States to the United Kingdom. But this lack of recognition is also related to the fact that women are not generally assigned importance as intellectual subjects, for she was sufficiently known in London, as was her compatriot C. L. R. James and many other writers who would be subsequently hailed as contributors from the United Kingdom to Caribbean politics and culture. One of the purposes of this book is to challenge the status quo in which Claudia Jones escapes a certain belonging in Caribbean feminist history and the larger Caribbean intellectual and political genealogy as well. The tendency has until recently been to identify only the men in this tradition, beginning with the early pan-Africanists and continuing up to our contemporaries.[38]

The particular process of recovery, for Claudia Jones, has meant beginning at the end: in London, the place where she spent the last ten years of her life and, paradoxically, the place where she is still best known. This period of her life began in 1955, when she was deported from the United States under the Smith and McCarran-Walter Acts for being a thinking and practicing communist. The high point of her British career was her founding of the *West Indian Gazette* (later the *West Indian Gazette and Afro-Asian Caribbean Times*) and of the London Carnival, which since has become the Notting Hill Carnival. The period ends with her death, in 1964. The life of Claudia Jones is relatively better known and documented in the United Kingdom. Indeed, organizations and centers have been named after her in London.[39]

Recovering Claudia Jones has meant, for me, negotiating for and being personally charged with the responsibility of traveling (with trepidation) with her available papers from London to the United States, cataloging them, and delivering them to the Schomburg Research Center in Harlem—in effect, returning Jones to the Harlem she loved.[40] It has meant pursuing her youthful activism and her mature radicalism, finding as much information as is available about her work in the United States. The last and most significant portion of the work took me back to her place of birth, Trinidad, where logically this portion of the research ends.

My search for and recovery of Jones's birth certificate makes possible the full identification of her as a Caribbean woman. I started from Claudia Jones's own words, which identify her place of birth as Woodbrook in Port of Spain, Trinidad. Repeated journeys to the Registry of Births and Deaths in Port of Spain in 2002, queuing in lines with folk who were tracing documents for purposes of travel, land acquisition, rights to family property, and the like, turned up nothing. I was finally referred to church records for Woodbrook, only to be told there that the older records for the period under question are in such poor condition that they have been sealed. Finally, after being given a contact (as often happens in Trinidad) with someone who is a senior worker in the office that handles searches, and with the necessary formal introductions made, I requested a more developed search. I returned, as directed, a week later to learn that a Claude Vera[41] had been found in the Trinidad records of births. "Claude Vera" (her first and middle names) was the Claudia I had been looking for. On the slip of paper that I was handed was written, in red, information about Claude Vera in relation to two of her siblings. Her birthplace was identified as Cazabon Lane, Belmont (not Woodbrook). Her father was identified as Charles Bertrand Cumberbatch; her mother as Minnie Magdalene Cumberbatch, formerly Logan. The birthdate recorded was February 21, 1915, and the record was registered as entry number 505 for the year 1915. This allows me to speculate that the family must have moved from Belmont to Woodbrook during Claudia's childhood and that she was unaware of it or had not remembered the actual location (see chronology).

The reclamation of this radical intellectual-activist as a Caribbean woman allows this black woman to enter history, and in particular the history of Trinidad and Tobago, her birthplace, which includes other important figures such as Sylvester Williams, George Padmore, C. L. R. James, Eric Williams, and Kwame Ture. The facts of Jones's birth were conclusively established in this elusive birth certificate. Another tangible representation of the kind of belonging/nonbelonging that she had as a member of the then colonized Caribbean is her British colonial subjecthood. She had to appeal to Trinidad's prime minister at that time, Eric Williams, who interceded on her behalf, as she sought and finally received a passport; this event also is critical to her Caribbean definition. She is also identified as Caribbean, or as representing the Caribbean, in a number of international forums during her London days. At the end of her life, then, Claudia Jones was operating fully as a Caribbean woman.

Claudia Jones was a person whose politics was practiced in myriad ways, from community organizing to journalism to writing to cultural development. Her final location[42] to the left of Karl Marx, for me, indicates a politics that, by its practice, critiques Marxism-Leninism, though she saw it as her basic orienting politics. Still, accounting for gender, for race, for black communities in migration, for carnival and Caribbean culture was not within the range of positions that Marxists took at the time. And Jones invariably had to do battle to argue for the place of culture in a people's articulation of themselves. In the end, these were precisely the sites of community transformation and conceptual formulation of the Claudia Jones legacy, a politics that advanced well beyond the limitations of Marxism and thereby locates Claudia Jones forever left of Karl Marx.

Chapter 1

WOMEN'S RIGHTS/WORKERS' RIGHTS/
ANTI-IMPERIALISM

Challenging the Superexploitation of Black
Working-Class Women

We can accelerate the militancy of Negro women to the degree with
which we demonstrate that the economic, political and social demands
of Negro women are not just ordinary demands, but *special* demands
flowing from special discrimination facing Negro women as *women, as*
workers, and as Negroes. . . . Yes, and it means that a struggle for social
equality of Negro women must be boldly fought in every sphere of relations between men and women so that the open door of Party membership doesn't become a revolving door because of our failure to conduct
this struggle (emphasis added).

CLAUDIA JONES, "FOR THE UNITY OF WOMEN IN THE CAUSE OF PEACE!"
1951

Participation of increasing numbers of West Indian women side by side
with their men in struggle for national independence and self-governing
will grow because women above all, want a better life, dignity and equality and a better world in which their children will live.

CLAUDIA JONES, IN AN INTERVIEW WITH GEORGE BOWRIN, 1956

Tangible links between women's rights and anti-imperialism
mark the politics and poetics of Claudia Jones and appear
throughout the corpus of her writings. Indeed, we can say with
assurance that she brought an explicitly women's rights orien-

tation to the politics of the Communist Party USA and its organizations, through which she did most of her political work during her years in the United States.[1]

Claudia Jones was a major theoretician for the CPUSA during the 1940s and 1950s. Using her particular ranking position in the party during this period, she wrote nine essays on women, most of them published in *Political Affairs*, the Communist Party's theoretical journal. Additionally, she would run her "Half the World" column, and regularly write other articles on various political issues in the *Daily Worker*.[2] A phenomenal output by any standards, her contribution in all of these various writings is that she brought together theoretically the intersections of race, class, gender, and anti-imperialism. By these means, given her considerable power of persuasion, she challenged the limitations of CPUSA politics as she advanced positions that would influence the subsequent women's movement of the 1960s and 1970s.

Angela Davis describes it this way in *Women, Race and Class*: "Claudia Jones was very much a Communist—a dedicated Communist who believed that socialism held the only promise of liberation for Black women, for Black people as a whole and indeed for the multi-racial working class" (169). In her book *Red Feminism: American Communism and the Making of Women's Liberation*, Kate Weigand explicitly credits Claudia Jones's work with advancing the issues of black women in the CPUSA and thereby informing the party's position on gender and the "triple oppression" logic that would later characterize its ideological orientation (97–113). However, she also recognizes that Jones's work had implications beyond the party. She writes,

> What made the Communist Party particularly unusual among other multi-racial organizations working to improve women's status in this period before the Civil Rights movement burst on the national scene was that it attempted to analyze and respond to the particular problems that burdened black women along with class and gender oppression. This work, inspired by the Party's leading black woman, Claudia Jones, made the Communist movement unique among feminist organizations that existed before the 1960s and shaped the ways that second wave feminists would conceptualize the intersections between race and gender oppression in the 1970s and later. (98–99)

This is a position that Weigand seems to have come to later in her career, for in her dissertation, she had concluded, prematurely it seems, that Jones's contribution was not so independent.[3]

Clearly, Claudia Jones gave to the Communist Party USA as much as she got from it in terms of theoretical orientation. In other words, if the party made Jones, she also made it, at this time. For Jones was definitely and unabashedly a radical black woman, a communist of Marxist-Leninist orientation, willing to pay the price for her political positions. She was also equally clear that she was writing as a black woman, approaching writing as resistance literature. So while one should always use some caution in recuperating historical figures, in order not to make them what they were not, Jones's own writings prove that she occupied this complex position. She put on the table, within the Communist Party, as her refinement of Marxism-Leninism, the particular importance of black women. But she also had other traditions out of which she lived. And outside of the party, she was able to bring some of her party positions to her work in black communities in the United States and United Kingdom.

For some other scholars, it is Jones's Marxist-Leninist politics that remain dominant and through them that one must analyze her positions on women. John McClendon maintains that one cannot read Claudia Jones as feminist in the sense of having a primary gender orientation as a defining politics.[4] For McClendon, "She consistently explained the issues of gender in terms of their connection to class struggle, anti-imperialism, and the battle for peace" (345). His judgment is valid; indeed, it is articulated by Jones herself in her classic 1951 essay "For the Unity of Women in the Cause of Peace": "In this struggle, Communist women, by their leadership among the masses of women, and learning from them to fight for their demands will fuse the women's peace movement under the leadership of the working class, and will thereby help to change the relationship of forces in our land in such a way as to make for a new anti-fascist, anti-imperialist people's coalition, advancing through this struggle to Socialism" (168).[5]

A close reading of this passage reveals that there is a progression in the hierarchy of importance in the stages of the struggle, with the final goal being socialism. Nonetheless, Jones's vision included an anti-imperialist coalition, managed by working-class leadership, fueled by the involvement of women, before socialism will be achieved. Still, all the major ideological components are present and therefore must be accounted for in assessing her politics.

Yet, as in similar analyses from an earlier period that try to bring a female radical subject into a current feminist discourse, one has to make the case from the available published material, through the political positions taken by the subject, as well as from the subject's practice, all of which together provide the feminist equivalence. An example of this would be the work that retrospectively identified Sojourner Truth as a feminist, when that was not how she identified herself in her own time. Contemporary reassessments of other black female historical figures reveal a politics that today would be defined as feminist, with appropriate qualifiers in place, although they personally never described themselves as feminist.[6] Joy James refers to such people as "protofeminist."

While there are several available definitions, generic "feminism" here is defined as a series of political and ideological movements and theories that aim to end all subordination of women in private and public life. Various qualifiers cast particular ideological positionings on this generic definition. Thus, for example, Rosemary Hennessey, in her *Materialist Feminism and the Politics of Discourse*, defines feminism as an emancipatory movement but also as "a set of discourses born out of modernity [, which] has long questioned the master narratives of western knowledge" (1) and which has offered a "long standing and productive questioning of the subject of feminism itself" (2). This "double move between solidarity and critique," she argues, has been perhaps one of the most useful features in allowing space for a materialist feminism.

What we do know about Claudia Jones, and what can be asserted from the outset, is that she was a person able to make linkages between a variety of appropriate political and ideological positions, to identify multiple positionalities and the ways these are interrelated. This chapter identifies her anti-imperialist/women's rights politics from a variety of angles. It makes its case through an analysis of a variety of applicable contemporary feminist/anti-imperialist theoretical positions. The two quotations that form the epigraphs to this chapter articulate an understanding of Jones's role in organizing black women on the domestic level (that is, within the United States), as well as her internationalist role in political organizing of black women in the context of decolonization movements.

Black Feminist Theoretics

Claudia Jones's politics was anchored in the communist struggle for full emancipation of working classes everywhere. But, as a black woman and a communist, she saw black working-class women as absolutely central to that full emancipation.

Jones consistently presented herself as she does in this stream of self-identifications: "[As] a Negro woman Communist of West Indian descent, I was a thorn in their [the U.S. government's] side in my opposition to Jim Crow racist discrimination against 16 million Negro Americans in the United States, in my work to redress these grievance, for unity of workers, for women's rights and my general political activity urging the American people to help by their struggles to change the present foreign and domestic policy of the United States."[7]

Primary among these self-identifications is Jones's identity as a black woman, followed by her origin, and then her range of positions against racism and for workers' and women's rights, followed by a general politics of articulation against state oppression at the national and international level. But clearly, her black female identity was always the primary position, strong enough to lead her other positions, as defined. And her role as the leading black woman of her time in the Communist Party USA gave her the space to advance the specific issues that plagued black women then as they still do now. She was the most prolific writer of her group of women on this issue, and, as a result, we have several essays with which to make an assessment of her positions.

From all accounts, the appearance in 1949 of her essay "An End to the Neglect of the Problems of the Negro Woman" laid this consideration more frontally before the party. Following it, the various "CP [Communist Party] newspapers and journals . . . regularly published essays and articles about the achievements of heroic women such as Harriet Tubman, Sojourner Truth, Ida B. Wells-Barnett, Moranda Smith, Mary Church Terrell, and Mary McCleod Bethune."[8] McDuffie, who defines Claudia Jones as the best-known theoretician on black women's issues in the Communist Party ("Long Journeys," 9), demonstrates that she was still just one of a group of black women communists in this era who were also taking positions that would bring together issues of race, class, and gender. He identifies Louise Thompson Patterson, for example, as the "leading black woman in the American left during the 1930's" (8).[9] To this list of pioneers we can add Maude White, a black communist woman and labor organizer, who articulated the special needs of black working-class women and their superexploitation as early as 1932.[10]

As a prime organizer for women of the Communist Party, Claudia Jones served as secretary of the Women's Commission, which had Elizabeth Gurley Flynn, her friend and comrade, as its president. The only black woman among a group of thirteen communist leaders, Jones was tried with Flynn and incarcerated under the McCarran-Walter Internal Security Act of 1952 during the hysterical House Un-American Activities Committee (HUAC) era. Claudia Jones's relationship with Elizabeth Gurley Flynn is also worth underscoring here in the context of women's rights. Both she and Flynn shared a communist analysis of the problems of women. Both are identified as taking particular positions on women's rights before and after, inside and outside, their incarceration on political grounds. For Claudia, in particular, these positions were always internationalist. While their feminist identifications were ones born of struggle and shared politics of women's rights within the party, their work in the Women's Commission (where the focus was on the particular needs of U.S. women) made them both acutely aware of the specific capitalist interests that located women (and for Claudia in particular, black women) in subordinate economic positions in society.[11]

It is not difficult to argue retrospectively, then, for the identification of Claudia Jones as an early black feminist. She was a black woman, clear about both the condition and the rights of black women and the ways in which these get subordinated to a range of other interests, exploited for financial gain and not allowed to live their fullest. She expressed these ideas publicly, orally and in writing. Indeed, she was aware that she, her mother, and her sisters — all solidly in the black working class — were negatively impacted by these processes. Additionally, since Jones had spent a great deal of time organizing cadres of black women for the CPUSA, she saw black women as one of the party's greatest untapped resources. Her columns in the *Daily Worker* were consistently directed at this black female audience.[12]

The argument made by those, like John McClendon, who see Marxism-Leninism as her dominant position is that her organizing of women was primarily within the context of the advancement of workers' rights, and not women's rights on their own. But in so doing, these commentators fail to understand the links that were being made between black feminism and socialism, expressed often through the intersections between class, gender, and race as systems of domination. Claudia Jones, in particular, made such links. One of the earliest documents in the definition of black feminism, from the black feminist and lesbian activist group Combahee River Collective, articulates a radical politics as follows:

We believe that sexual politics under patriarchy is as pervasive in Black women's lives as are the politics of class and race. We also find it difficult to separate race from class, from sex oppression because in our lives they are experienced simultaneously. . . . Our situation as Black people necessitates that we have solidarity around the fact of race which white women of course do not need to have with white men, unless it is their negative solidarity as racial oppressors. We struggle together with Black men against racism, while we also struggle with Black men about sexism. . . . We realize that the liberation of all oppressed peoples necessitates the destruction of the political-economic system of capitalism and imperialism as well as patriarchy. We are socialists because we believe that work must be organized for the collective benefit of those who do the work and create the products and not for the profit of the bosses.[13]

These are the positions that marked the politics of Claudia Jones and that are expounded in her articles, which constitute early theoretical texts for this line of 1970s black feminism. The fact that Jones belonged to the developing black women's movement is shown by her alliances within a number of black women's organizations and by the support she received from a wide spectrum of these groups at critical moments, particularly during her imprisonment and her deportation. Various newspapers of the time published statements of support from the black women's civil rights group Sojourners for Truth and Justice, the National Council of Negro Women, the black and women's rights activist and publisher of *The California Eagle* Charlotta Bass, and a range of others.

Jones's position on women's rights was always linked to the communist struggle: as a prime organizer for the Women's Commission of the CPUSA, she articulated her black feminist theoretics within a communist framework and context. First of all, her own life as a black woman, and her understanding of why her mother died at the age of thirty-seven from the effects of overwork in her garment industry job,[14] informed her theoretic position and her activism on behalf of all poor, working-class, black women. Two of her sisters, moreover, were domestic workers at some point in their lives. Her particular experience and personal knowledge remained with her throughout her life and were perhaps the most compelling reasons behind her choice to be an activist (she made particular mention of them in the speech she made immediately before her departure from the United States).

That Claudia Jones was also a member of Sojourners for Truth and Justice also supports my argument that there is a link between her positions and current black feminism, especially since the figure of Sojourner Truth has become iconic in the more recent phase of the black women's movement. The Sojourners for Truth and Justice are one of the most important links between the generation to which Claudia Jones belonged and the subsequent black feminist movement. In "Sojourners for Truth and Justice," Erik McDuffie states that "the group anticipated radical black feminist organization of the 1970s and 1980s such as the Third World Women's Alliance, National Black Feminist Organization, Combahee River Collective, and Sisters in Support of Sisters in South Africa" ("Long Journeys"). McDuffie describes the Sojourners as an "all–African American women's progressive civil rights group that sought to give black women an independent voice in the emerging postwar Black Freedom Movement and to build ties of political solidarity with women across the African Diaspora during the early 1950s. . . . The group named itself after Sojourner Truth, the notable nineteenth-century African American abolitionist and women's rights advocate. Inspired by a tradition of African American women's resistance and drawing from the Marxist-Leninist positions of the American Communist Party . . . on racial and gender oppression, the Sojourners developed a radical black feminist program." McDuffie details their politics and their activism:

> The proceedings reveal the influence of Communist Party positions on the "triple oppression" of black women, popularized by Party leader Claudia Jones, who was also member of the Sojourners. The group drafted a constitution, organized a youth auxiliary, and debated strategies to bring black women into the labor movement. The delegates also discussed how to build ties with progressive white women. Sojourners sent letters condemning Apartheid to the South African ambassador to the United Nations. The group took part in anti Apartheid protests in front of the South African consulate in Manhattan. Sojourners also corresponded with female anti-Apartheid activists and labor organizers in South Africa.

Among the Sojourners' most visible activities was an action in Washington, D.C., in which they demonstrated in the Pentagon, in front of the White House, and in the State Department, demanding "civil rights, protection of civil liberties, the end of the Korean War, and the respect of African

American women." The Sojourners had also called for a mass mobilization in the form of a march on Washington, which, however, did not happen, for they too were the subject of U.S. government harassment.

Despite their activism, the Sojourners do not feature prominently in 1980s black feminist understandings, a fact that, in my view, explains why there was no organizational connection to that group from more recent groups, and why appropriate political and intellectual links were not always made. For many in the "second wave" period of black feminism, — and this author is one of them, — there was persistent pressure on black women to justify the need for separate black women's organizing, distinct from the black nationalist movement and any other movement. From all accounts, the Sojourners had already waged a similar struggle.

The Sojourners, Jones included, supported and inspired one another. In her documentary film *Beah: A Black Woman Speaks*, Beah Richards (who was later known only as an actress in the Hollywood motion picture industry) identifies her poem "A Black Woman Speaks of White Womanhood, of White Supremacy, of Peace" as the beginning point of her collaboration with Louise Thompson Patterson (a Harlem civil rights activist and close friend of the poet Langston Hughes). Together the two women issued "A Call to Negro Women" to "Sojourn for Peace." Claudia Jones herself covered Sojourners' activity frequently in her articles in the *Daily Worker*, as we will see in chapter 2, and her coverage helped them reach a large communist readership and many potential participants.[15] Beverly Guy-Sheftall, in her introduction to *Words of Fire*, sees Jones as anticipating a "sophisticated black feminist discourse which was a generation away" and that was reminiscent of feminist-abolitionists such as Anna Julia Cooper (13).

The best and most easily available text for understanding Jones's significant contribution to black feminist theory is her pathbreaking essay "An End to the Neglect of the Problems of Negro Women." Among the essays written on the subject of black women in her time, this essay, "An End to the Neglect of the Problems of Negro Women," is pivotal for the history of black feminist theoretics, as it identifies a much more radical politics and analysis than was available at the time. In this essay, Jones builds a case for the historical role of black women in the family and community. Next, she identifies the specific economic position of black women as women and as workers, giving us her classic definition of what she terms the "superexploitation" of the black woman, in terms of labor given and salary received. She identifies, in this context, the categories of work assigned to black women and their exploitation as unionized domestic workers.

One of the first points Jones makes is that there exists a certain militancy among black women. This militancy, she argues, arises from the particular locations and issues of black women, which, because they are neglected by the Left, limit the full extent of their political articulation. Her major hypothesis, arising from this recognition, is that once black women are radicalized the entire movement will automatically advance: "Once Negro women undertake action, the militancy of the whole Negro people, and thus of the anti-imperialist coalition is greatly enhanced" (28). Clearly directed at a left audience, this statement recognizes black male and white female communists' resistance to this militancy as perhaps one of the biggest barriers to any successful political movement of black and other oppressed peoples. This lack of acknowledgment was rooted in the "neglect" of the black women question. Here we have a dialectical *materialist* connection, where the particular neglect of black women leads to the obstruction of the universal (anti-imperialism and class struggle). Class struggle and anti-imperialism, for Jones, are not materially separated from black women's oppression. Overcoming "resistance" to black women's militancy becomes a matter of struggling to build the anti-imperialist front by addressing black working-class women's needs, among other issues. In her "neglect" thesis, that is, in claiming that there was a neglect of black women's issues, Jones presumes there is resistance among party members to militancy. Such a reading accents how black women's oppression is pivotal to anti-imperialist unity and class struggle. Thus Jones anticipates a later critique given by Angela Davis in "Women and Capitalism: Dialectics of Oppression and Liberation."[16]

Jones's essay "An End to the Neglect of the Problems of Negro Women" makes another major argument: that the black woman "as mother, as Negro" occupies a crucial position in the defense and support of the black family, and that this position is then superexploited by capitalist interests. It is precisely here where the possibilities for resistance lay: the black woman's position renders her both pivotal and vulnerable to struggles; hence her potential for militancy. As Robin Kelley would assert, the "structural position of black people — black women in particular — in the political economy placed them in the vanguard of the revolution."[17] So Jones's view of motherhood was not a romanticized one,[18] as some sort of essential identity, but as a role that can be superexploited. She makes the point that the United States' boast that American women possess "the greatest equality" in the world cannot hold in light of the actual location of black women. In Jones's words, they experience "not equality, but degradation and super-exploitation" (29). Jones makes a point that can be inferred even today from a number of surveys of women's rights internationally, that while the United States claims a certain superiority over other nations at a number of levels, the way that it treats and locates its women, particularly black women, puts it far behind other nations in giving women full human rights.[19] Jones's insight was to locate much of this treatment in the superexploitation of black women as mothers.

Another of Jones's significant contributions in this essay is the link she makes between black women's role in their families and the history of African women in matriarchal traditions. Recent work by scholars like Ifi Ama-diume[20] provides new information on African matriarchy. Jones was clearly aware of the available literature on this subject. In "An End to the Neglect of the Problems of Negro Women," she demonstrates an advanced knowledge of African women beyond the stereotypes and more in keeping with modern African feminist understandings. She insists that the dominant position that women played in their family grouping during slavery was due in part to the conditions of slavery and the destruction of institutions such as marriage, but also to African precedent: these women came from areas in "West Africa where the position of women, based on active participation in property control, was relatively higher in the family than that of European women" (32). Because of these factors, she argues, the role of black women in supporting themselves and their children had to be factored in the understanding of their economic needs and that of the community at large.

Claudia's analysis of the position of black women is one of the clearest available black socialist feminist assertions. This essay and a second one, "We Seek Full Equality for Women," also published in 1949, form the core of Claudia Jones's early and advanced political positions on black women. The best known and most cited is "An End to the Neglect of the Problems of Negro Women" (June 1949). But "We Seek Full Equality for Women" (September 1949)[21] makes a deliberate link with the earlier "struggle of the Suffragists" and contains her classic assertion that the "triply-oppressed status of the Negro women is a barometer of the status of all women, and that the fight for the full, economic, political and social equality of the Negro woman is in the vital self-interest of white workers, in the vital interest of the fight to realize equality for all women" (30). This assertion needs to be much better known, since it is central to understanding the development of black feminist thought.

It is true that as an educator and organizer for the Communist Party, Jones would consistently repeat the larger framing of her understanding of black women's condition within the principles of Marxism-Leninism, that is, that "the position of women in society is not always and everywhere the same, but derives from woman's relation to the mode of production. . . . Hence Marxist-Leninists fight to free women of household drudgery, they fight to win equality for women in all spheres; they recognize that one cannot adequately deal with the woman question or win women for progressive participation unless one takes up the special problems, needs and aspirations of women — as women" (29). But it should also be noted that "We Seek Full Equality for Women" offers Jones's theoretical and political assertion on the location of the black woman in the hierarchy of social and economic positions. For her, these women's rights positions had "profound meaning, both for the Negro liberation movement and for the emerging anti-fascist, anti-imperialist coalition" ("An End to Neglect," 28).

"An End to the Neglect of the Problems of Negro Women" and "We Seek Full Equality" both deal solidly with the specifics of black women as they identify (as she phrases it in the former essay) "the growth of militant participation of black women in all aspects of the struggle for peace, civil rights and economic security" (28) and call for recognition of that fact. Because of the particular history, situation, and politics of black women in political struggle, Claudia challenged the Communist Party to take more serious interest in the cause of black women. "Who more than the Negro woman, the most exploited and oppressed, belongs in our Party?" she asked. "To win the Negro women for full participation in the anti-fascist, anti-imperialist coalition, to bring her militancy and participation to even greater heights in the current and future struggles against Wall Street imperialism, progressives must acquire political consciousness as regards her special oppressed status" (41–42).

Superexploitation and the Black Working-Class Woman

Claudia Jones's best contribution to black feminist thought is her theorizing of the superexploitation of the black woman. The concept rests solidly on Claudia's observation that black women — "as workers, as Negroes, as women" — were "the most oppressed stratum of the whole population." For Jones, "Capitalists exploit woman doubly, both as workers and women. Woman has to face special oppression in every field in capitalist society — as a worker — a wife, a homebuilder and a citizen."[22] While most of her theorizing appears in "An End to the Neglect of the Problems of Negro Women," Jones wrote on the subject also in her column on women's issues for the *Daily Worker*, titled "Half the World," a column that made its position clear in its title, that, in representing women, we are, indeed, representing "half the world."

Using the economic indicators of her time, such as those from the Department of Labor, Jones was able to identify the wage rates of black women in relation to other women and men and found them at the lowest end of the pay scale. The Center for Research on Women at Memphis State University under the leadership of Bonnie Thornton Dill undertook similar analyses and reached similar conclusions in the 1980s. And sadly, recent census data point to a not too different conclusion.[23] In 1948 Jones concluded that "Negro women are still generally confined to the lowest paying jobs," as women of color in general were in 1998: "The super-exploitation of the Negro woman worker," wrote Jones, "is thus revealed not only in that she receives as woman, less than equal pay for equal work with men, but in that the majority of Negro women get less than half the pay of white women" ("For New Approaches to Our Work among Women," 30).

Since black women are often heads of households, entire black communities will remain in poverty if the black women stay underpaid and super-exploited. Jones cites Department of Labor statistics again that show that black women workers were employed primarily in private families as domestics, as cooks or waitresses in a range of other service industries, and in agricultural and clerical work. Professional black women were a small minority. Jones identified domestic work as the kind of "catch-all, fall-back" profession for black women, and in the period after World War II, domestic service was promoted as a desirable job for black women. Ahead of her time, Claudia correctly identifies media representations of black women as one of the sources for maintaining this identification of black women in service roles as well as the work that the "mammy" stereotype did in this process.

From this, and a brief analysis of the historical aspects of black women's existence, Claudia is able to make one of her major challenges:

It is incumbent on progressive unionists to realize that in the fight for equal rights for Negro workers, it is necessary to have a special approach to Negro women workers, who, far out of proportion to other women workers, are the main bread-winners in their families. The fight to retain the Negro woman in industry and to upgrade her on the job is a major way of struggling for the basic and special interests of the Negro woman worker. (33)

Claudia Jones therefore advances the superexploitation thesis to explain the predicament of black women in society. "Superexploitation" for her refers to the ways in which black women's labor is assumed; the way they are relegated to service work by all sectors of society, with the complicity of progressives and white women's and labor interests (including those on the Left). It related to their low salary, compared with the level of work they are asked to give in return.

According to classical Marxist theory, "the extraction of surplus value is the specific way *exploitation* takes place under capitalism." In capitalism, surplus value transforms into profit—it is in fact a source of that profit, which accrues when the working class produces commodities that are sold for more than what it costs to produce them (a large part of that cost being what the workers receive in wages). Workers are paid the value of what they sell—their labor power. The surplus is the difference between the value produced by the worker and the value received as wages. Workers are then doubly exploited, because they have to "sell their labor power and also because they are forced to enter the capitalist production process wherein *exploitation* takes place."[24] Thus, exploitation as a central concept of historical materialism occurs when one section of the population produces a surplus whose use is controlled by another section of the population. Under capitalism, exploitation takes the form of the extraction of surplus value from the working class by the class of industrial capitalists. But other exploiting classes or class fractions share in the distribution of surplus value, for example in the form of rent and interest.[25] Oliver Cromwell Cox, in his 1948 book *Caste, Class and Race*,[26] argues that "the worker's place in the system has been primarily related to production, and has been regarded as an item of cost—that is to say, as both a necessary and important factor of production and as an impediment to the entrepreneur in his basic urge to undersell his competitors. The worker, then was indispensable, but he should be paid only so much as would be sufficient to keep him alive and able to labor — a subsistence wage" (24). The idea, according to Cox, is to keep " 'the worker in a constant state of necessity, which disposed him to labor" (24).

Claudia Jones advances related arguments through her application of this principle to the overworked and underpaid black woman. Her superexploitation thesis rests on the fact that black women, by virtue of being located as they are in society, among the most exploited and most underpaid of workers, tend to be the ones whose value of their labor power various other class fractions (including other exploited workers) benefit from. An example would be the white left women seeking black women as domestic workers, a practice she herself would challenge, and one that would be the source of some contention from white women, who saw Jones's critique as unduly harsh.[27] Black women, in this analysis, are therefore not remunerated in any way equivalent to their labor power nor for the amount of labor they are assumed to deliver voluntarily in and out of their homes. The black woman's labor is therefore multiply exploited (superexploited).

In the 1940s and 1950s, Claudia Jones wrote articles that made this point, framing black women's condition in Marxist-feminist formulations. The masses of black women remain consistently at the bottom in terms of remuneration while there is an inordinate expropriation of their labor. Thus, the superexploitation of black women is imbedded in society's construction of them in terms of race, class, and gender. If they get half the wages of men, their "rate of exploitation" is more than twice that of male workers. Additionally, they are often not represented in trade unions and must face drudgery both in the workplace and in the home.

Jones was clear in her articulation of the economic hardships for black women "as workers, as Negroes and as women" (29–30). For her the "superexploitation of the Negro woman worker is thus revealed not only in that she receives, as a woman, less than equal pay for equal work with men, but in that the majority of Negro women get less than half the pay of white women" (30). Jones would repeatedly make a link between the condition of all women, particularly black women, and the struggle for peace, arguing that the resources used to fund wars could be well applied to ameliorating some of these conditions. She also contended that black women needed to be mobilized for full participation in struggles against imperialism and fascism.

Jones did not come up with her superexploitation analysis in isolation; it is in fact related to a pattern of analysis made by other black activist women.

According to Mark Solomon in "Rediscovering a Lost Legacy," women like Maude White and Louise Patterson, and Jones herself, "shared a belief that racism was nurtured by capitalism, which in their view, sought to gain a huge advantage from the 'super-exploitation of African American labor and from fanning division along racial lines within the working class' " ("Rediscovering a Lost Legacy," 6). These views in fact caused the women various difficulties. McDuffie reports that "the Party's cool reaction to the Sojourners deeply troubled Thompson Patterson. In response she began distancing herself from the American Communist Party." Still, the point remains that black feminist theorizing of the varying interconnections between race, class, and gender were operative in the early determining of a black feminist practice, as it was in the succeeding generation.

The Black Female Domestic Worker and the International Capitalist Economy

The importance of the analysis of the position of the black woman as domestic worker is revealed in many of the other relations of black women to the means of production. Because most black women were located in domestic service, up to the 1950s Claudia Jones felt that a special position needed to be taken in support of the black woman domestic worker. She felt that there ought to be a fight against the relegation of the black woman to domestic service, but simultaneously domestic workers should be organized, like other workers. The trade unions' avoidance of organizing domestic workers, she asserted, had to be dealt with forthwith, as it consigned these women — usually black women — to victimhood and exclusion from the normal social networks and labor legislation (34) that benefited other workers; thus continuing their superexploitation. "It is incumbent on the trade unions," wrote Jones, "to assist the Domestic Workers Union in every possible way to accomplish the task of organizing the exploited domestic workers, the majority of whom are Negro women. Simultaneously, a legislative fight for the inclusion of domestic workers under the benefits of the Social Security Law is vitally urgent and necessary" ("An End to the Neglect," 34–35).

Familiar with the plight of the worker on the lowest rung, as she was with her mother's and sisters' experience (and, indeed, her own experience), she was clear about the details of domestic service: the low salaries, the unending tasks, the undefined though all-consuming duties in the household, and, in some cases, even something akin to enslavement (Jones gives the example of one such worker, "enslaved for more than 40 years"). She writes: "The lot of the domestic worker is one of unbearable misery. Usually, she has no definition of tasks in the household where she works. Domestic workers may have 'thrown in' in addition to cleaning and scrubbing, such tasks as washing windows, caring for the children, laundering, cooking, etc. and all at the lowest pay" ("An End to the Neglect," 34).

This rank exploitation, which continues today, has been well identified by subsequent writers who deal with the experience of the domestic worker, such as Alice Childress in *Like One of the Family* and other writers who have given us a range of life stories of domestic workers who have to live in and be on call, sometimes for twenty-four hours a day, seven days a week.[28]

An earlier treatment of this issue is *The Position of Negro Women* by Eugene Gordon and Cyril Briggs; it specified some of the contours of black women's exploitation as workers. In a section on domestic service, for example, Gordon and Briggs used Women's Bureau and U.S. Department of Labor statistics to show that in 1930 the "largest group of Negro women workers are still to be found in domestic and personal service" and that the "wages of these workers are as low as ten dollars a month. Wages paid day workers — women hired by the day to clean and do the washing, etc. — are as low as fifty cents a day in New York City, and probably lower in other communities" (6). The authors offer an assessment, based on solid information, and articulated as a Communist Party position that is very similar to the one Claudia Jones advances later — that things would be better under the Communist Party; that the Soviet Union offered a shining example of the correctness of the communist program of unity of white and Negro workers; and that in "the Soviet Union, women have been emancipated" (16).

The poor working-class black women whom Gordon and Briggs identify as getting the "dirtiest deal of all times" (14) were clearly an issue for a number of activist "race women" and "racial uplift" women over the years.[29] Francille Rusan Wilson, in her essay on Sadie T. M. Alexander, for example, identifies a domestic women's work bill pending in the Pennsylvania legislature[30] as being a central political issue for Alexander. But the position of poor working women would be a primary agenda of black left women generally and in their work in developing unions such as the Needle Trades Workers Industrial Union. A great deal of the activism of Maude White was in this union, on issues of racism and equity.[31]

In her analysis of black women in domestic labor, Claudia Jones returns us to the "slave auction" model of *day work* that Ella Baker and Marvell Cooke had identified ten years earlier in "The Bronx Slave Market" and that Paule Marshall later described in her *Brown Girl, Brownstones*. Both the article and the novel describe a situation in which white women would come down the streets and take their pick of black women for what was supposed to be day's work but was in reality a week's worth of chores. Her critique of white women who operated within these terms extends similarly to the maid-madam relationship that they instituted. A variety of recent studies of domestic work identifies similar exploitative practices: Jacquelyn Cock's *Maids and Madams: Domestic Workers under Apartheid* provides some comparison in the case of South Africa; Grace Chang's *Disposable Domestics: Immigrant Women Workers in the Global Economy* and the work of Linda Carty on Caribbean domestic workers in the United States and Canada ("Not a Nanny")[32] also provide detailed examinations of this issue. Much of the political and social identifications of transnational labor that inform these works already had appeared in Claudia Jones's formulations and analyses of the superexploitation of domestic workers.

Jones also identified the variety of laws that allowed this superexploitation to continue: laws that limited black women's property rights, miscegenation laws, and laws that "deny the right of choice." Jones felt it important to challenge a variety of easy and trite formulations such as "the battle of the sexes" and the "place of the woman is in the home," which were often deployed as American "commonsense" assumptions. For Claudia Jones, these platitudes ignored the specific location of the black woman, who was not in her home but in someone else's home, who was a participant, not in a "battle of the sexes," but in gender relations complicated by an ongoing struggle for racial emancipation of black people. One of Jones's most insightful positions (which reads like commonplace of 1980s black feminist thought) is the following: "The responsibility for overcoming these special forms of white chauvinism rests, not with the 'subjectivity' of Negro women as it is often put, but squarely on the shoulders of white men and white women. Negro men have a responsibility particularly in relation to rooting out attitudes of male superiority as regards women in general" (37).

Jones is obviously simultaneously aware of what she calls the "double exploitation daily experienced by working-class wives and mothers in present-day society . . . [T]he capitalists exploit women doubly, both as workers and women. Woman has to face special oppression in every field in capitalist society — as a worker, a wife, homebuilder and citizen" ("Foster's Political and Theoretical Guidance," 77). In her essay, Jones analyzes a report by William Zane Foster, the CPUSA chairman, titled "Report to the Party Commission on Theoretical Aspects of Work among Women, August, 1948." Although she also takes the opportunity to argue that the party itself was not fulfilling its responsibilities to women in general, Jones declared that the report was "in the tradition of all great Communist thinkers, recognizing that the fight against women's inequalities is connected with the fight against property relations" (71). Jones sketches out some of the issues that contemporary black feminists and critical race feminists have since elaborated: questions of legal rights, property rights, economic equality, and so on. For example, she is clear about the ways in which a few women are rewarded with government positions in order to camouflage the situation of the larger population. She congratulates some Communist Party initiatives, saying, for example, that the reconstitution of the National Women's Commission under Foster's leadership aided the challenge to male supremacist bourgeois notions, which accompanied a "general neglect of our work among women in industry and in mass organizations" (72). The special conditions of black women, which she showed that Foster was also cognizant of, thereby received attention. At times, in this particular essay, Claudia's own positions superimpose themselves on or underline "Foster's" analyses. There is some suggestion that Jones may have collaborated with Foster in writing the report, a not unusual situation in Communist Party organizing. My own close reading of the report and Jones's response to it support this suggestion. Jones's essay, in the end, clearly takes the party line, that socialism is the framework under which much of this oppression could be alleviated.[33]

Claudia Jones's early writings are a key source for understanding her black feminist politics. Let us look again at her 1949 essay "An End to the Neglect of the Problems of Negro Women," in particular, at a section titled "Key Issues of Struggle" but also at her 1948 article "For New Approaches to Our Work among Women."[34] One of the points taken up in the later essay is the role of the black woman in relation to the family. Jones uses the case of Rosie Lee Ingram (a case also used by the Sojourners) as illustration. Rosie Lee Ingram was a mother of fourteen who faced life imprisonment for defending herself against the indecent advances of a white supremacist. In some ways her case prefigures that of Assata Shakur, who escaped incarceration and has sought asylum in Cuba, as similarly representative of a certain form of black women's resistance. Assata also claims to have had to resist attempted rapes while imprisoned. Through her examination of Ingram's story, Jones highlights the ways that black women have to consistently battle a range of racist and sexist attitudes, insults and oppressive structures present in the larger culture, which become then a central feature of oppression of black people in general.

A second point made by Jones in these texts, and perhaps most surprisingly for someone with her politics, was that white women needed to be clear that the "negro question is *prior* to, and not equal to, the women question" ("An End to Neglect," 38). This perhaps controversial assertion, which is not as straightforward as the "race first"[35] assertion of black (male) nationalism, highlights Jones's position that, to the extent to which the race issue is central to any analysis of women's experience, then the black woman has to be the representative "raced" woman in any of these struggles.

> For the progressive women's movement, the Negro woman, who combines in her status the worker, the Negro and the woman, is the vital link to this heightened political consciousness. To the extent, further, that the cause of the Negro woman worker is promoted, she will be enabled to take her rightful place in the Negro-proletarian leadership of the national liberation movement and, by her active participation contribute to the entire American working class, whose historic mission is the achievement of a Socialist America — the final and full guarantee of woman's emancipation. ("An End to Neglect," 39)

This was not an easy position for Jones to advance, and it exposed her to a great deal of criticism from white women and the charge that she was guilty of "reverse chauvinism." Jones was not directly attacking white women, though she felt that the corporate media was complicit in this representation of white women for all women ("An End to Neglect," 32). But coming from a black woman, a critique like hers would always be interpreted as self-serving. Still, this assertion is consistent with Jones's position that as black women's situation is advanced, so will the entire social structure. As Angela Davis puts it, "White women in the progressive movement — and especially white women Communists — bore a special responsibility toward Black women" (*Women,*

Race and Class, 169). And this, not as charity or goodwill but as a fundamental political position.

The struggle for jobs is another issue that Jones identifies in "For New Approaches to Our Work among Women." She indicates, for example, that the fact that certain government agencies do not hire black people operates synchronically with the larger racist system. Rather than subscribe to the scarcity argument (that the number of jobs is limited) or the competitive argument (that has been used to argue that black women take jobs away from black men), she suggests that getting jobs for black women enhances the entire group's ability to be employed. Therefore, she was critical of "growing trends which show that these postwar employment difficulties are falling most heavily on Negro women, who were the first to be fired in the layoffs especially in the heavy industries" and the fact that "Negro women wartime workers are being forced back into domestic work because no special fight has been put up to secure jobs for them in basic industry by the trade unions" (739). This is important for her superexploitation argument, for it was in domestic work, in her view, that black women faced the highest manifestation of capitalist exploitation.

Another of the key points she raises in these early publications is about organizing for peace; activism for peace becomes an increasingly central principle in Jones's thought and life, as this study will show. This position is linked to the fact that, first, African American soldiers were still experiencing Jim Crow racism, and, second, that several domestic issues pertaining to women (who suffered from the most deprivation during wartime) would be sidelined by the war effort. International in orientation, like the Sojourners, Jones called attention to the struggles of women in North Africa, who had organized a strong peace movement "with 81 million women in 57 nations, in the Women's International Democratic Federation" ("An End to the Neglect," 41). Jones felt that a consciousness of international actions of this sort needed to be brought to the understanding of women in the United States. The support for internationalizing women's struggles was always one of her positions.

Black Women's Leadership

Consistent with her own leadership in the Communist Party, therefore, Claudia Jones felt that black women, more than anyone else, needed to be active in the party and, more precisely, in leadership roles. She saw the socialist alternative for women as the only possibility with which they could enhance their economic situations against U.S. imperialism. In this she felt that both the party and the women needed to be educated.

On the general issue of black women and leadership, Claudia felt it was a waste of resources to allow black women who occupy leadership roles in other situations (church, community, sororities, and so on) not to be utilized in leadership positions once they joined the party. She saw as a model a variety of women who demonstrated progressive women's leadership in struggles for social change and social justice. In her celebrated "International Women's Day and the Struggle for Peace" article she offered a tribute to "heroic women who gave their lives in the struggle for Socialism and freedom" (Elsie Smith, Anna Damon, Rose Pastor Stokes, Fanny Sellins, Williana Burroughs, and Grace Campbell), a list that significantly included Campbell, one of the founders of the African Blood Brotherhood. For Jones, "the present-day struggles of progressive and Communist women merge with the traditions and contributions of such great anti-slavery fighters as Harriet Tubman and Sojourner Truth, of such militant women proletarians as the textile workers of 1848, of such women pioneers as Susan B. Anthony and Elizabeth Cady Stanton, of such builders of America's Progressive and working class heritages as Kate Richards O'Hare, Mother Jones, Ella Reeve Bloor, Anita Whitney and Elizabeth Gurley Flynn" (40).

In many ways, Claudia was a comrade spirit to someone like Ella Baker in her philosophy of organizing communities and political cadres that were egalitarian in nature.[36] Ella Baker would take a similar position in organizational work in civil rights in the U.S. South and in confronting the barriers raised by ministers of the Southern Christian Leadership Conference against women and youth. Baker opted instead, according to Charles Payne, for "group centered leadership," which she sought to apply in the Student Nonviolent Coordinating Committee.[37]

Jones's critique of male supremacy in the Communist Party raises issues like those raised in the 1970s by black women in black power movements, particularly as they relate to leadership. These we already know have been identified as one of the direct reasons for the creation of a black feminist movement. Jones identifies the tendency to relegate "only certain phases of responsibility to women on the assumption that women aren't ready for leadership responsibilities at the policy-making level" ("For the Unity of Women in the Cause of Peace!" 165). She goes on to refute this with actual examples of women's leadership and instead argues for an "elevation of women to policy-making bodies of the Party organization." This is a theme that she would return to consistently and which she makes most clearly in her article "Foster's Political and Theoretical Guidance to our Work among Women." She felt therefore that combating male supremacy should be the task of all, including the men themselves, particularly "the men in our Party who should be more self-critical of these weaknesses, and who must overcome their patronizing attitudes to women."[38]

It is important to note here that Foster himself struggled with this issue. In "On Improving the Party's Work among Women" he accepts that the party had failed "to win the active support of decisive masses of women," but he asserts very early on that this is because "the forces of reaction still have a strong hold on womankind, including proletarian women" (984). He also accepts that there has been neglect, that the theories of male superiority continue to hold sway, and that these are part of the fascist, biologist arguments about master races, which come from reactionary positions that also appear in the Party. He identifies three weaknesses on the part of the party in his essay: first, a "deep-seated underestimation of the need for a persistent struggle ideologically against all manifestations of masculine superiority"; second, "a pronounced reticence in dealing with questions of sex"; and third, a reduction of the issues to the economic while leaving all the other components outside of analysis (987–988).

This last position is perhaps at the core of a "left-of-Karl-Marx" formulation, as it points to what is "outside of analysis" — which then become the grounds for black women's positioning on this issue. Foster's essay also asserts the party line, that "only under socialism can woman become truly free" (984). But, as I have already indicated, what has come down as Foster's position seems to be due to the input of the Women's Commission leadership, which would have included Jones, for Foster also states that knowledgeable women in the party will address the issue more deliberately.

Claudia Jones's analyses have to be seen in the light of this official party position, but they also accompany her ongoing work on black women. In the end, for her it is still a question of economic independence for women. For without this, as she argues, superexploitation continues. In her publications, Jones is clearly speaking back to the Communist Party as well as clarifying her own positions. Thus she asserts that if the party wanted to be a place of equality, then "it means above all fighting for the economic equality of woman, because her economic dependence on men in our society, her exclusion from production, makes for a double exploitation of women (and triply so for Negro women) in present-day society" ("For the Unity of Women in the Cause of Peace!" 166).

Jones, as the major CPUSA theoretician on women's issues, always promoted Marxism-Leninism as the one overarching theory that could generate solutions to solve a myriad problems, and the Soviet Union as the ideal society. The visits of women like Maude White and Louise Thompson Patterson to the Soviet Union, and their reports of the position of women there, must have influenced some of her own understandings as well. Historically speaking, at that time, women in the Soviet Union seemed to have more access to a range of employment possibilities, compared to what was obtainable in the United States and Europe. Thus, Jones's essay "Foster's Political and Theoretical Guidance for Our Work among Women" has to be read as an amplification of her position. It clearly also uses Foster's authority to provide her with the legitimacy she needed to make her own positions explicit within the party structure, and to challenge the party membership to go further. In this article, she takes Foster's positions much further, elaborating on the issues of the "double exploitation daily experienced by working-class wives and mothers in present-day society" (68). To do this she places emphasis on Foster's commentary on his own mother and her life of hardship and drudgery, which in many ways is reminiscent of Claudia's own account of her mother's illness and death. Jones refers also to an earlier work of Foster, which identified what she calls "the barbarous indignities suffered by Negro women in the United States and in Latin America" (69). She sees Foster's position as providing the base that allows her own arguments to have a theoretical space, expanding and developing on his positions throughout her much longer essay.

Claudia's own battles as a woman in her own personal relationships provides another issue related to women and leadership that needs to be identified here. A youthful exuberance and sexuality in the United States clearly defines her in all the photographs we see of her for this early period. There is little information about her brief marriage to Abraham Scholnick, though there are divorce papers available in the Claudia Jones Memorial Collection. There are some suggestions of extramarital relations with one or more Communist Party men. Howard "Stretch" Johnson has suggested, in comments made during a panel discussion at the Schomburg Library, that they had an intimate relationship. Claudia herself indicated plans to marry soon after her arrival in London, though a person is not identified. From all accounts, her association with Abhimanyu Manchanda, with whom she had an intimate relationship toward the end of her life, was a bond of consistent struggle at the personal level. All interviews I conducted in London indicated that their relationship was frequently one of difficulty, competitiveness, and lack of consistent support. Many expressed surprise that Claudia remained with Manchanda. But it is obvious as well that theirs was also a working political relationship. There are wonderful, sensual photographs of Claudia on holiday with Manchanda, away from all the political fray, and there are photographs that show Claudia in relaxed and happy moments with Manchanda and his family, as well as letters that testify to her reliance on him as a working partner. There are also beautifully seductive photographs of her alone at social events in London. Her photographs show someone who aged tremendously while under persecution by the U.S. government but who in London seemed to have "caught herself," as is said in the Caribbean. Always there is evident a consciousness of self-presentation for the future.

Clearly, issues intimate and private to her and those with whom she had relationships are at play here. Nevertheless, her life underscores one position that is often difficult to address on the question of progressive women and the men in their lives. In some ways, this is a matter that has to be addressed at some level in our evaluation of the Jones legacy, for one gets a sense that she was hampered in her London period in her ability to produce at maximum level both because of ill health and inconsistent support. And in a more balanced evaluation, one can observe that, with Manchanda, she came to other kinds of progressive analyses and political decisions, such as changing the name of her newspaper to include "Asian" news and her developing interest in communist China.

This personal dimension of black women's struggles is rarely talked about, except through gossip, consigned always to the personal and private. I think it is important to demystify it here. My point is simply this: black women involved in political, activist, public work that locates them in leadership roles are generally not seen by the rest of society, including their partners, as acting out of positions of possible power for the community, as is assumed for men.

Claudia Jones provides an excellent example of this and in a certain way herself lived out this life of superexploitation. People I talked to in London (January to June 1997) expressed regret, as it seems Manchanda had, at her death, all saying that they wished they had done more for her and the various struggles with which they were allied.[39]

Still, Jones maintained an ongoing activist approach that led to a great deal of support from women's groups when she was threatened with imprisonment and deportation. Her women's rights activism is evident in her organizing work for the National Women's Commission, and several of her articles deal directly with women's issues. Even in her "Speech to the Court" she brings into the public space of the courthouse the article on women referenced as the "overt act" and grounds for her prosecution, which she indicates that the judge himself was unable to cite publicly.[40] In her words, she urges "American mothers, Negro women and white, to write, to emulate the peace struggles of their anti-fascist sisters in Latin America, in the new European democracies, in the Soviet Union, in Asia and Africa to end the bestial Korean war, to stop 'operation killer,' to bring our boys home, to reject the militarist threat to embroil us in a war with China, so that their children should not suffer the fate of Korean babies murdered by napalm bombs of B-29s, nor the fate of Hiroshima" (quoted in Johnson, "I Think of My Mother," 124).

It was out of that kind of consciousness, in which a black female identity is linked to anti-imperialist politics, that Claudia Jones operated and which she continued to advance in England up to her death. The black British feminist orientation, as I indicate in the chapter "Black Women Writing the Critique of Empire" in my Black Women, Writing and Identity, is one that consistently references British imperialism and therefore has embedded a geopolitical orientation. I see Claudia Jones as central to an early formulation of blackness in Britain (including people of African and Asian descent) and thus as the pre-text to current definitions of black British feminism as anti-imperialist in orientation.

Relocating Claudia Jones centrally in particular national or international black/feminist genealogies does not interfere with defining her also as a communist woman. In fact, it means that easy linear historical narratives of any sort have to be disrupted.[41] Her model of accounting for U.S. imperialism (the superexploitation of black women and the variety of internal and external colonial relationships) has a similar orientation to contemporary critiques of corporate globalization.

The possibility of building a nonhierarchical feminism has continued to challenge critical feminist scholarship (the ongoing critique of hierarchy has perhaps, paradoxically, been one of the movement's strengths). How can a discourse built on challenging dominance at the level of gender reinstitute another dominance at the level of class, race, national identity, ability, and so on? A large body of that critique of feminism has been initiated by black women. In terms of 1980s black feminist debates, Audre Lorde said it well in the chapter "Age, Race, Class, and Sex: Women Redefining Difference" in her book *Sister Outsider*: "Now we must recognize differences among women who are our equals, neither inferior nor superior, and devise ways to use each others' difference to enrich our visions and our joint struggles" (122). Numerous feminist scholars of color have spoken of the particular arrogance of academic feminists of a particular class and race orientation who pursue feminist inquiry and make conclusions without any recognition of the realities, histories, knowledges, lives, and political positions of myriad other women who do not then have the space to speak for themselves.[42] Western feminist intellectual production at the outset, as we now know, turned on universalizing assumptions. While many of these women were well-intentioned enough, their particular feminist conceptualizations assumed Euro/American-centric readings of the world. Coming out of their own versions of Western humanist ideology, the universal — as far as their feminism was concerned — was defined by their skewed Western, Euro-American bourgeois experience.[43] When they claimed "I'm every woman," they therefore generalized that experience to all women, thereby creating an essentialist, culturalist logic of a particular flattened gender identity.

This critique of Western feminist assumptions was so pronounced during the 1980s that, throughout the 1990s, it was not unusual to have curricula and research projects that attempted to account for the multiplicity of lives of women, to internationalize women's studies, to expand the bases of theoretical assumptions.[44] Debates on the blind spots in Black Studies and Women's Studies around the issue of gender and race have been similarly mounted. Claudia Jones had already seen that while black and working-class women's leadership in social movements had both to be seen as critical, there was a particular need "to tap deeply the tremendous potential and organizational abilities of our Negro women comrades" ("For New Approaches to Our Work among Women," 742).

Socialist Feminist Practice

Claudia Jones, then, is one of the early formulators of an anti-imperialist/transnational feminism, and a key figure for any study of socialist feminism.[45] That her work may be applied to a variety of feminist paradigms is testament to the extension of her positions across a variety of geographic fields. According to historian Robin Kelley, Claudia Jones has to be credited for "insisting that black women were a decisive group because they experienced capitalist oppression as Negroes, women, and workers, and thus [that] their emancipation would result in the emancipation of all women and men" (*Freedom Dreams*, 55).

Indeed, as Weigand points out, the Communist Party in its publications "regularly used the terms *triple burden* and *triple oppression* to describe the status of black women who were exploited because of their race, class and gender" (*Red Feminism*, 99). Claudia Jones must be recognized among those forging that particular link. One can make the case that the Communist Party's position on race and class needed some refinement — its position on gender even more so — and that all three positions would be greatly enhanced and clarified when Claudia Jones weighed in on the position of the black woman. Making this point even more definitively is Harry Haywood, who states in *Black Bolshevik* that it was

> Claudia Jones's discussion article that kicked off a huge debate in the summer of 1945, attacking Browder's ideological and political stand on the Black national question. Jones contended that Browder's line on self-determination was "based on a pious hope that the struggle for *full* economic, social and political equality for the Negro people would be 'legislated' and somehow brought into being through reforms from on top." Jones upheld the revolutionary position as a "scientific principle that derives from an *objective* condition and upon this basis expresses the fundamental demands (land, equality, and freedom) of the oppressed Negro people." (550–551)[46]

If we follow this argument to its logical conclusion, then Claudia Jones's role in asserting a position that linked race, class, and gender in the Communist Party in the United States is significant and assures her a prominent place in transnational black feminist theoretics and practice.

Claudia Jones was a communist whose many analyses of women originate directly from Leninist positions on women; her insistence on the particular history and experience of black women was her contribution to Marxism-Leninism. She brought as much to the party and to communism as she got from it, and unlike many of her peers, she did not leave the party. This is what puts her, in my understanding, "left of Karl Marx." Jones had read Clara Zetkin's 1920 conversations with Lenin, which Zetkin published as *Lenin on the Woman Question*. It is one of the more heavily underlined and annotated pamphlets in Jones's papers. Zetkin was a German socialist leader who, according to an editorial in *Political Affairs* "at the International Socialist Congress in 1910, made the motion for the establishment of International Women's Day and that March 8 each year be dedicated to fighting for equal rights for all women in all countries" ("International Women's Day," 1). It is thus ironic that Claudia Jones would be indicted for, among other things, an article written to celebrate International Women's Day.

The classic Marxist-Leninist position on women, as argued in Communist Party literature is that "the exploitation and oppression of women [is] as a consequence of class exploitation—today the exploitation of the working class. Women then, are not a class unto themselves but the majority are, in fact, members of the working class as a whole which added exploitation based on sex."[47] Further, in the contemporary period, "monopoly capital benefits from the employment of male and female, reaping all the benefits of labor power provided by the family, as well as added super-profits. Capital has found new ways of super-exploitation and consequently super-profits, while the family struggles for survival under increased burdens. . . . Monopoly can reap huge super-profits by maintaining the wage differential between male and female as it uses lower pay for women as a tool for keeping down the wages for men" (Buxenbaum, "Marxism and the Woman Question Today," 12–13).

While the basic party position on capitalism had served as the underpinning of Claudia's philosophical understanding of the black woman, her personal experiences, that of her mother and her sisters, and the observations of conditions of women such as Rosie Lee Ingram and a host of other women, would ensure that the position of black women be more clearly rethought.

Transnational feminist socialist research, materialist in orientation, has continued in that tradition, analyzing women's work under capitalism and the basic "colonization" of women's labor in international contexts. As Hennessey indicates in *Materialist Feminism and the Politics of Discourse*, this research has proceeded

> on the basis of an argument that Marxism cannot adequately address women's exploitation and oppression unless the Marxist problematic itself is transformed so as to be able to account for the sexual division of labor. With its class bias, its emphasis on economic determinism, and its focus on history exclusively formulated in terms of capitalist production, classic Marxism in the seventies had barely begun to analyze patriarchal systems of power. At the same time, there was a marked tendency in most feminist theory to conceptualize woman in essentialist and idealist terms. In this context, materialist feminism provided a historically urgent ground from which to launch a critical counter knowledge to both feminism and Marxism. (xi–xii)

But there have been other models: Maria Mies et al., in *Women the Last Colony*, use the "sexual division of labor" as a basic orienting principle, arguing, for example, for an understanding of the practice of "housewifization" and the nature of housework: "The woman corresponding to the proletarian or free wage laborer is the life-long, full-time housewife" (174). Another version comes from Raya Dunayevskaya, who, in a paper presented at the conference "Common Differences: Third World Women and Feminist Perspectives" and reprinted in *Women's Liberation and the Dialectics of Revolution*, critiqued Marxist positions that leave out the situation of women. Thus she asserts:

> Feminists of today are right when they separate themselves from Engels' *Origin of the Family* and certainly are right when they refuse to follow the so-called "orthodox" who consider Marx and Engels as one and who stagify the whole question by insisting that we must overthrow capitalism "first" and then, after the revolution, we will be free. . . . They are absolutely right to deny that male chauvinism is a characteristic only of capitalism. The uniqueness of today's women's Liberation Movement, indeed, is precisely that it has illuminated the male chauvinism *within* the Left. (60)

Dunayevska identified the National Black Feminist Organization as affirming in its Statement of Principles the "Half the World" notion embraced earlier by Jones: "We will encourage the Black community to stop falling into the trap of the white male Left. . . . We will remind the Black Liberation Movement that there can't be liberation for *half a race*" (emphasis added, 60). Claudia Jones's work and thinking on this had already underscored this position and in this sense, too, anticipated black feminist organizing of the 1970s and 1980s.

Jones provides another example of a series of women's movements inside, in conjunction with, and also outside of the party. As all researchers on Jones have shown, she became the Communist Party's "principal official theorist on the 'woman question.' "[48] A generation later, Angela Davis's Marxist-feminist politics can be identified as coming out of a context that can be traced to Claudia Jones and to other black communist women organizers.[49] Davis indicates, following Jones, that the "posture of negligence vis-a-vis Black women was one of the unfortunate legacies the Communist Party would have to overcome" (*Women, Race and Class*, 151). In the section on Elizabeth Gurley Flynn in her chapter "Communist Women," Davis credits Flynn's close work with Claudia Jones and Ben Davis as allowing her to understand "the central role of Black liberation within the overall battle for the emancipation of the working class" (*Women, Race and Class*, 164). Davis, like the communist women who preceded her, was therefore clear that black women were caught in a "threefold bond of oppression" (165). Davis continues that this "same triple jeopardy analysis . . . was later posed by Black women who sought to influence the early stages of the contemporary women's movement" (165). Unfortunately her section on Claudia Jones is more a description than an assessment; she does not credit Jones directly for the "women, race and class" analysis, though Davis discusses Jones's "An End to the Neglect of the Problems of the Negro Woman," in which that analysis is explicit.

Claudia Jones's position on black women was radical, to say the least, and caught the attention of the authorities. Although the nominal reason for her arrest was the speech she presented at International Women's Day (and subsequently published), all her organizing work for the Communist Party and all her prior writings are documented in her FBI file as contributing to the case for her trial, imprisonment, and deportation. These positions identified her to the authorities as extreme and radical, and that fact emphasizes the point that more recent black feminists like the Combahee River Collective make, that if black women were organized and able to effect such a challenge on the systems, the entire social order would be challenged, and to belong to the progressive women's movement would be among the most threatening of positions one could take.

Anti-Imperialist Politics

For Claudia Jones, imperialism did not reside solely in its economic-based and international manifestations but in the way it manifested at the domestic and local levels in which black women were the most vulnerable. Claudia's anti-imperialist politics linked local struggles of black people and women against racism and sexist oppression to international struggles against colonialism and imperialism. Thus she saw these as interconnected in a dynamic set of interactions in which the geopolitical operations of capital were central. For this reason, Claudia Jones saw her various struggles, and her role in them, not as contradictory but as elements in an ongoing challenge to imperialist domination at local and global levels.

Perhaps one of the most overlooked essays in the study of American imperialism is Jones's "American Imperialism and the British West Indies." It provides an understanding of some of the central features of her anti-imperialist politics and some of the key philosophical positions that appear in the rest of her work. Written after she leaves the United States, the essay signals her turn to a more Caribbean-oriented politics and allows us also to recover her in Caribbean scholarship. First of all, taking an analytical, Marxist-Leninist, anti-imperialist position, she was clear about the role of U.S. corporate interests in the Caribbean as they related to or were distinct from the British versions. Thus, she is one of an important group of Caribbean intellectuals and activists who were at that time able to recognize the tentacles of U.S. imperialism as they extended into the Caribbean. Written in support of the short-lived West Indian Federation, Jones nevertheless cautioned, as had Aime Césaire in *Discourse on Colonialism*, about the danger of accepting U.S. capital investments. She highlights "the Texaco Oil purchase of Trinidad oil, the growing U.S. investments in Jamaican bauxite and in British Guiana's aluminum deposits" and she concludes, "Clearly the West Indian Federation is already heavily mortgaged to U.S. export capital" (9).

Next, Jones identifies what she terms a "family arrangement" between U.S. imperialism and British imperialism. Her position, which would be borne out by history (witness Grenada, Jamaica, Antigua, Iraq, etc.), was that the outward political responsibility (and cover) remains British but that the United

States controls the economic basis of the society's operations.[50] This is an important distinction for us because, in 1958, much of the decolonization energy was targeted at the British and not the Americans. Additionally, most of the analysts (largely male), who wrote from the anti-colonial paradigm, confined much of their critique and resistance to British imperialism, neglecting the rise of the American colossus. This early analysis of the role of U.S. colonialism and imperialism names "American imperialism" in its title, identifying it for what it is. Thus it is one of the early formulations to which one must turn for an analysis of American imperialism and for the genesis of its particular operations in the contemporary, turn-of-the-century moment.

Not only does Jones's essay specify this American imperialism, as distinct from British imperialism, it also recognizes its ability to camouflage or mask itself. Claudia Jones locates the basis of American imperialism's operation in the establishment, in 1942, of the Anglo-American Commission, renamed the Caribbean Commission in 1946. (This is the same Caribbean Commission with which the historian Eric Williams had worked — and which he would eventually leave — prior to his return to Trinidad to eventually become Prime Minister of Trinidad and Tobago.) But, for Claudia Jones, this commission became the ratifying body for the rapid build up of U.S. capitalist interests in the Caribbean.

The West Indies was identified at the time as a source of cheap food and raw material, a market for U.S. and U.K. products, and, importantly, as a "reservoir of cheap labor." Jones was able to document the importance of the West Indies to business interests from an article in the London *Daily Express*, in which a U.S. State Department official is quoted as saying: "American businessmen look on the Trinidad base as a guarantee of military and political stability for the future." His comment explains the turn toward rapid investment in the Caribbean and to the role of the American bases (such as in Trinidad) through which the US government was and still is able to defend its interests in Latin America, as, for example, the Panama Canal ("American Imperialism and the British West Indies," 10).

This logic of "the reservoir of cheap labor" is what continues to drive Caribbean emigration, in particular domestic labor from the Caribbean, migrant farm workers, and the reservoir of labor in cities, which are the product of a number of waves of migration. So the result is what Jones defined as an "Anglo-American rivalry" but nevertheless a relationship for exploitation.

One of the dangers Jones saw was that the Caribbean leadership, "bourgeois-nationalist" as it was in orientation, thought it could "bargain between the two imperialisms" and, faced with the fact of "resolving economic problems," "look[ed] increasingly to the US for salvation," seeing the United States as an escape from old-style British colonialism (11). Cesaire's point is appropriately recalled here: "I know that some of you, disgusted with Europe with all that hideous mess which you did not witness by choice, are turning — oh! in no great numbers — toward America and getting used to looking upon that country as a possible liberator . . . American domination — the only domination from which one never recovers, I mean one never recovers unscarred" (*Discourse on Colonialism*, 60).

Jones had already come up with the same response and analysis of the United States from personal and political experience, having lived directly within the belly of U.S. imperialism and organized against its practices and also been victimized by it. It is here that the question of Puerto Rico enters, for Puerto Rico had been suggested by some as a possible model for the rest of the Caribbean. Jones saw Puerto Rico for what it was — a U.S. colony. This she had already understood, having witnessed the demise of the Puerto Rican independence movement. Her position on Puerto Rico is clearly identified in her poem "For Consuela — Anti-Fascista," discussed in detail in chapter 3.

A number of significant assertions are made in "American Imperialism and the British West Indies." One is that the struggles of the Caribbean people have advanced along with the "spread of the national liberation movement in the colonial world" (12). Jones was clear about the links to other struggles in various locations of the colonial world (India, Africa, etc.). She mentions trade union activity in Grenada, the then British Guiana (now Guyana), and the Bahamas; the organization of dock workers in Jamaica and workers in St. Vincent, Barbados, and Trinidad in the face of record-breaking profits by "domestic and foreign capital interests" in the sugar, oil, and bauxite industries. She quotes Mao Tse Tung on the flexibility of imperialism to operate in diverse ways as it finds new means to "camouflage its rule" (12), seeing this maneuverability as a response to national colonial liberation movements.

On the establishment of a single Caribbean nation, Jones supported a West Indian Federation, but did not see it as antithetical to self government, as some had. Yet she was cautious that it represented (before its early demise) a kind of half-completed option on the way to full Caribbean empowerment.

Thus, while the federation provided an example of self-government to other islands, it still had to struggle with necolonial leadership. Additionally, she, like John LaRose,[51] saw the struggle for a free Caribbean market as central.

Claudia's four-point suggestion for a single, independent, federated Caribbean nation was as follows:

1. Internal self-government for the Federation entailing a wholly elected Parliament . . . , full cabinet status based on the Party principle with the elected Prime Minister wholly responsible, and restrictions of the Governor-General's powers to representation of the Sovereign as is the case of Ghana, or a republican form of government, as in India, with the Crown as the head of the Commonwealth.
2. Civil liberties embracing the entire Federation including freedom to travel, freedom to organize and to discuss.
3. Protection of rights of minorities for cultural and other forms of development.
4. For full national independence for the West Indies. ("American Imperialism and the British West Indies," 15–16)

Still, as her first point indicates, Claudia seemed unable to go beyond the colonial representatives model, recommending a minimized, symbolic role.

With the demise of the federation, by 1959, much of this possibility of Caribbean unity evaporated. Instead, individual island nation-state assertions became the dominant form of political and economic organizing. The *West Indian Gazette and Afro-Asian Caribbean News*, whose editorials Claudia wrote for that time period, was exhilarated by the Cuban Revolution in 1959. Still, Jones saw labor movements and the trade union organizing as the only saving possibility in the face of a national bourgeoisie being developed by imperialism as a "reliable bulwark to protect its interests for as long as possible even after national independence is won" ("American Imperialism and the British West Indies," 17). But Jones was still hopeful in the development of educational opportunities, the development of scientific approaches to the analysis of current and past realities, and the alliances of progressive and communist forces in Britain.

According to Ranjana Ash, who had worked in one of the political collectives which Claudia organized, and whom I interviewed in England in March 1997, Jones had an amazing ability to link disparate struggles. In her words,

Among her many political concerns was her understanding of the fundamental relationship between imperialist expansion abroad and class exploitation within the metropolis. This inextricable nexus between the national liberation movements then raging in Asia, Africa and the Americas and the working class struggles inside the colonial states be they Britain, France, or the USA, was not often made by trade union or labour movement in general. It was for her a pressing necessity for the metropolitan workers to recognize the signal contribution to their own liberation that was being made by the national wars of liberation against colonial bondage then being fought in Indochina, Kenya, Algeria, Cuba, Cyprus, Malaya, to name a few. ("Remembering Claudia")

Ranjana Ash identifies Claudia's founding of the Committee of Afro-Asian and Caribbean Organisations as significant in this effort, as it brought together in England a variety of solidarity groups that could then be mobilized for rallies, protests, and marches in support of liberation struggles in various areas of the colonial world, including the United States, such as the rally in support of the March in Washington, 1963.[52]

Jones was remembered first and foremost for her anti-imperialist politics: when she died, the *West Indian Gazette and Afro-Asian Caribbean News*, the newspaper she edited, carried the bold caption "Dear Claudia, We Will Hold High Your Banner of Anti-Imperialism." And her gravestone is a permanent marker of her fight against imperialism: "Claudia Vera Jones, Born Trinidad 1915, Died London 25.12.64. Valiant Fighter against racism and imperialism who dedicated her life to the progress of socialism and the liberation of her own black people."

Jones's understanding of colonialism and imperialism as it played out in the United States had already appeared in "On the Right to Self Determination for the Negro People in the Black Belt."[53] In that article, Jones advances the "internal colonialism" argument and characterizes African Americans as an "oppressed nation" within the larger U.S. nation-state structure: "It was our understanding of the Negro question as a *national* question, that is, as the question of a nation oppressed by American imperialism, in the ultimate sense as India is oppressed by British imperialism and Indonesia by Dutch imperialism. It was our knowledge, grounded in Lenin's teachings, that every aspect of Negro oppression in our country stems from the existence of an *oppressed nation*, in the heart of the South, the Black Belt" (69).

Grounded absolutely in Marxism-Leninism, Claudia proceeded to identify the characteristics of a nation, and the qualities of southern African Americans (both rural and urban) that qualify them for oppressed national status.
Additionally, while she considered the push toward integration justified, that
is, integration into the political and economic and legal rights fabric of the
United States, she saw its limitations. So, integration and self-determination
are not synonymous in her understanding, nor is democratic integration synonymous with assimilation: "a struggle for democracy does not divert or
overshadow the working-class struggle against exploitation, it is an aid to it"
(74). Again, the link with other black communist women becomes significant,
for Maude White (who had attended the Sixth Congress of the Communist
International in Moscow in 1928) was an active participant in the debate that
led to the definition of the oppressed "nation with a nation" and the ideological position that U.S. African Americans in the South had a right to self-
determination. According to Solomon, "The theory [of an oppressed 'nation
with a nation'] was important in defining White's evolving ideology" ("Rediscovering a Lost Legacy," 7). White, as previously indicated, was already
prominent in the Communist Party when Claudia became a member, and was
active in the Harlem lecture circuit and various forms of organization. Jones's
argument, then, may be viewed in part as a collaborative position.

Clearly, Jones had precedents for her position. In one of her most direct
challenges to the hegemony of class as a singular definer of the socioeconomic
condition, she indicates that it is impossible to "postpone" the question of
national liberation until socialism is established or to speak solely in general, nebulous phrases about national liberation: "We reject, even if it is
under the name of 'internationalism,' any denial of the right of national self-
determination to the oppressed peoples. For true internationalism, that is,
Marxism-Leninism, places the right of self-determination as a basic program-
matic point" ("On the Right to Self-Determination," 74).

Caribbean Feminism

Caribbean feminist politics would keep the links between anti-imperialism
and women's political rights in a way that these were not kept (or at least,
not consistently) in U.S. black feminist movements.[54] The explanation may be
that decolonization movements in the Caribbean operated with critical labor
movements and women's political organization. As in other anti-colonial
movements, women's participation was often either exploited or utilized pro-

gressively for the political result intended. While I have found no obvious direct political affiliations so far between Claudia Jones and women in political movement in the Caribbean,[55] it is also clear that Jones was well informed about international women's struggles. She was a close friend of Amy Ashwood Garvey, with whom she had initially worked in the development of the *West Indian Gazette and Afro-Asian Caribbean News*, and she engaged in other forms of London activism. Letters in the Claudia Jones Memorial Collection testify to the personal and political nature of Jones's and Garvey's friendship. Mrs. Garvey, we know, had already written "about the evils of imperialism, racism, capitalism, and the interlocking race, class, and gender oppression that black and other women experienced globally, particularly in colonial contexts."[56]

When asked, soon after arriving in London, about her view on the role of women in the West Indies, Jones's response was:

> I have been quite impressed with the activities of the women of the West Indies and their growing participation in the liberation movement as well as the international movement for peace, security and the rights of children. There is no question but that West Indian women represent an indispensable ally in the fight for colonial freedom, because women are triply exploited in the colonies as women, as mothers and as colonials, subjected to indignities and great suffering because of the status of their countries. Participation of increasing numbers of West Indian women side by side with their men in struggle for national independence and self-government will grow because women above all, want a better life, dignity and equality and a better world in which their children will live.[57]

Two books by Rhoda Reddock (*Women, Labour and Politics in Trinidad and Tobago* and *Elma Francois, the NWCSA and the Workers Struggle for Change in the Caribbean in the 1930s*) show how two other Caribbean women, Christina Lewis and Elma Francois, developed similar positions, linking anti-imperialism to feminism. Francois was one of the founding members of the NWCSA (Negro Welfare Cultural and Social Action), which was also responsible for the formation of three major trade unions. The organization took active positions on international issues relevant to the black community such as the cases of the Scottsboro Boys and Angelo Herndon, and Mussolini's invasion of Ethiopia. But significantly, "from its very inception, the NWCSA set out to attract women members . . . The organisation took the position that women and men should cooperate in the development of their collective political consciousness. It rejected the separation of women into "women's arms" or "women's auxiliaries" (*Elma Francois*, 17, 18).

Indeed, for Reddock, this is perhaps the basis of any definition of Caribbean feminism.[58] Parallels between Claudia Jones and Elma Francois are striking. For example, Reddock reports, that "in February 1938 Francois became the first woman in the history of Trinidad and Tobago to be tried for sedition" (33–34) and "Francois, unlike other defendants, undertook the greater part of her own defence herself" (34). She includes in the book Elma Francois's speech in her own defence at her sedition trial (35–36). Francois's speech is very similar to Jones's speech before Judge Dimock, and it reveals as well a series of internationalist/pan-Africanist connections similar to those that Jones espoused. For example, when asked to define "world imperialism and colonialism" Francois "described the relationship between the ruling classes of the world and the exploited workers of the colonies" (37).

Claudia Jones shared many of these positions on women's activism and involvement in political struggle.[59] A case can also be made for identifying Jones with Francois as central contributors to our understanding of Caribbean feminism. For Reddock and other scholars in the Caribbean, one of the distinctive features of Caribbean feminism is its anti-imperialist, labor orientation, which sees women's economic rights as central to any fulfillment of their human rights in general.[60] In this sense then, Claudia Jones's anti-imperialist feminist, socialism belongs also in this other genealogy — Caribbean in geographic and cultural identification and anti-imperialist in orientation, linking labor, black, and women's rights.

Jones shows, by her example, a way of maintaining her political positions and affiliations and advancing others, beyond Marx's theoretical positionings and benefiting from Lenin's advances on the issue of imperialism and the national/colonial issue. While being an avowed Marxist-Leninist, she continued to assert the primacy of black women as an analytical category, subject to society's "super-exploitation," but still active subjects, potential leaders, and, by her example, also thinkers. Her ability to link race, gender, geography, and labor in the context of the situation of black women internationally, along with her internationalist, anti-imperialist approach, provided a more advanced reading of both the conditions of and the possibilities for resistance by black women under imperialism.

Jones's article "International Women's Day and the Struggle for Peace" documents the activities of a range of women activating for peace and therefore against imperialism. In it, Jones presents the work of the Women's International Democratic Federation as offering the possibility of an international, anti-imperialist women's organization. In defining situations that would later be identified in feminist theory as the feminization of poverty, she assesses the conditions of women across the United States as workers ("working women, farm women, workers' wives, Negro women, women of various national origins"), impoverished and underpaid, seeing them as providing the best cohorts for building a local and global movement: "When we deal with the situation of women workers," she wrote, "we do so, not only to protect the most exploited section of the working class, but in order to rally labor-progressives and our own Party for work among the masses of women workers, to lead them into the emerging anti-fascist, anti-war coalition" (37).

In this context, Claudia offered a nuanced position on the Equal Rights Amendment proposed at the time, suggesting that while it seemed on the surface of benefit to women, as written, it would eliminate whatever safeguards women had. Very critical of bourgeois feminism, she felt that those early feminists held on erroneously to a notion that "women's oppression stems, not from the capitalist system but from men" (44). From this position, she proposes several measures for the party: continuing analysis of the oppression of women; the assignment of cadres to work among working-class women "on a mass and Party basis"; more education in general and, in particular, on Marxist-Leninist teachings on the woman question; further analysis of where the party was on the woman question; and action based on the understanding that "the long neglected problems of Negro women must become an integral part of all our future work among women" (44). Claudia was concerned, it seems — and rightly so — that these would become the dominant modes of women's movement politics. The chapters that follow will detail the mechanisms through which she articulated these concerns.

Chapter 2

FROM "HALF THE WORLD" TO THE WHOLE WORLD

Journalism as Black Transnational Political Practice

We affirm, like other great African and Asian peoples, our spirits too have caught the contagion of national independence. And that nothing less than that achievement will satisfy us.

The *West Indian Gazette* supports Federation. In common with the vast body of West Indian opinion, we see this step as a first, halting but unfailing new step towards national independence for the Federation and a complete self-government for its units. We urge Dominion Status in five years and an end to all restrictive practices towards minorities, an extension of civil and cultural rights and freedom of movement between the islands.

CLAUDIA JONES, "WEST INDIES FEDERATION," 1958

Journalism as Political Praxis

The life and work of Ida B. Wells, who had run her own paper and publishing house and linked a politics of black resistance directly to journalistic writing, is particularly illustrative of Claudia Jones's own trajectory as a journalist. Much like Wells, Claudia Jones practiced her activism and communicated her political positions through the medium of journalism. Herbert Aptheker describes Wells's work in a way that is suggestive of Jones.

Ida B. Wells's first published piece — in a church paper in 1887 — was an account of her battle against the Jim Crow railroad company. This attracted wide attention and a demand developed for more articles. Wells soon entered upon her journalistic career which was to last until after the First World War. In 1888, she joined the staff of a small Memphis paper, the *Free Speech and Headlight*; soon she was editor and part-owner. Her attacks upon the scandalous conditions provided in Memphis for the education of black children led to her dismissal from the school system in 1891.

She now turned all her attention to journalism, shortening the name of her paper to the *Free Press*. Arming herself with a pistol to help keep it free, she began to travel about the country as a kind of roving reporter and her stories were reprinted throughout the Negro press of the time. When, early in 1892, three black men were lynched in Memphis itself, she published in her paper scathing attacks upon this barbarism and the city's elite who condoned and permitted it.[1]

Claudia Jones too would begin her primary career as a journalist, make her way through the various editorial levels of communist party organs, and finally found and manage the London black community's first major newspaper, the *West Indian Gazette*. Indeed, journalism, as I will show, was one of the ways in which Jones's anti-imperialist politics were always articulated. Her journalistic skill and experience, honed from her early years with Communist Party newspapers such as the *Daily Worker* (as writer, associate editor, then editor) would, in fact, continuously serve as her basic mode of transmitting her ideas. According to Jones's own autobiographical recounting, when she joined the Young Communist League she had already been working with a black newspaper and had also worked with community publications and written for at least one national black newspaper in Harlem.[2] Thus she had the kind of journalistic skill to do political education in England and to found the *West Indian Gazette* (later the *West Indian Gazette and Afro-Asian-Caribbean News*). Away from the United States, having been deported to England, she was able to give full articulation of her positions on U.S. imperialism. Editorials in the *Gazette* (generally written by Claudia herself) pursued a range of issues linked to Caribbean community advancement, pan-Africanism, and critiques of imperialism.

Claudia's own self-identification as a journalist is perhaps more relevant to this chapter's assertion about the uses of journalism for transnational black organization. In her passport, the assigned professional descriptor "typist" is consciously crossed out and replaced by "journalist" (see figure 2). Clearly a conscious professional identitarian renaming, in the feminist sense, the word "typist" with all its connotations is embedded in her passport, as in her FBI file, as the definition the state gave to her. Ironically, the same FBI file makes the case for her arrest, trial, imprisonment, and deportation using her journalism as evidence.[3] Still, this deliberate self-identification as journalist[4] simultaneously challenges a patriarchal assignment of women to subordinate roles and allowed Jones to reclaim her own life space to do the kind of activist work for which she had been known. She describes her career in the United States as follows:

> During this period (1935–1936) I worked on a Negro Nationalist newspaper where I wrote a column (circulation about 4–5000 copies) and had a weekly column called "Claudia's Comments." My job consisted there also of writing precis of the main editorial comments on Ethiopia from general commercial press, Negro workers trade union press etc. During the next ten years from 1936–1946/7, I was active in the YCL and the youth movement. Served as organizer of the YCL in Harlem for a year. 1937 was sent to a six-month National Training School of the CP. On my return was elected to National Council YCL and became associate editor of the *Weekly Review*. . . . Later I became editor of the *Weekly Review* (1938–40). During 1943–45, became editor of *Spotlight*[5] national publication of American Youth for Democracy. . . . Worked from 1945–46 as editor of Negro Affairs *Daily Worker*. . . . Elected full member National Committee 1945 Convention CP. . . . Arrested June 29, 1951 with 17 working-class Communist leaders, including Elizabeth Gurley Flynn, under the infamous Smith Act for writing an article which described the forward movement of Negro and white women in opposition to the fascist bent world domination US foreign policy.[6]

Claudia Jones's career as a journalist moves from early articles in black newspapers to her work in the Young Communist League's *Weekly Review* and indicate a steady movement through the journalistic and party hierarchies. In each of these cases, her work as a journalist paralleled other political positions and served as a means of public education and organizing. Her work on the *Weekly Review* accompanied her service as education director of the

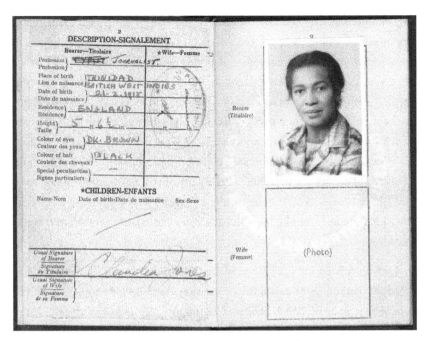

2. Claudia Jones's last passport, showing the profession "typist" corrected to "journalist." From the Claudia Jones Memorial collection.

Young Communist League for New York State. Her subsequent work on the *Daily Worker* paralleled her position as secretary of the National Women's Commission of the Communist Party USA (CPUSA). Even while under direct surveillance, awaiting her trial under the Smith Act, she traveled around the country with Elizabeth Gurley Flynn and enrolled over forty-eight new members to the Communist Party.

Significant in this context of feminist socialist organizing would be her writing of the column "Half the World" in the *Daily Worker*. A fairly advanced formulation for its time, the column allowed her to actualize both her journalist practice and feminist/socialist organizing. All of this journalistic activity would culminate in the United Kingdom, in her development of her own paper, the *West Indian Gazette and Afro-Asian Caribbean News*. This paper brought together a great deal of her philosophy on community education and organizing and became an important forum for anti-imperialist politics and a tangible exercise of her growing commitment to pan-Africanist and third world politics, all leveraged through her own brand of communism.

The importance of journalism in transnational black organizing and for communicating anti-imperialist politics is the backdrop against which one can view Claudia Jones's activity in this field. For Jones was not unique in this way. Journalism was a significant way in which black activists historically were able to articulate resistant positions and easily reach their audiences. Radical black intellectuals saw themselves as communicating directly with the public through newspapers. Robert Chrisman, in his preface to Theodore Vincent's *Voices of a Black Nation*, identifies the importance of radical black journalism — called at one point "the greatest single power in the Negro race" (20) — in this way.

> There were reasons why black journalism was the most liberated of black institutions involved in political expression. The press, like the comparatively nonpolitical church and fraternal orders, was created by blacks to serve black society. The black press, from its inception in the 1820s, had avoided competition with white newspapers and magazines by concentrating on issues affecting black people. . . . At the turn of the century there were roughly two hundred organs of the black press, both newspapers and magazines. In the early 1920s there were close to five hundred. Today, even with the radical press revival, there are no more than two hundred. (23)

The portability of newspapers for international circulation allowed the carrying of messages of organizers such as Marcus Garvey and the Universal Negro Improvement Association to places like Brazil, the rest of Latin America, Europe, Australia, and Africa. Penny Von Eschen, in *Race against Empire*,[7] shows how a transnational black press and its communicating of political positions, accompanied the activism of decolonization and anti-racist struggles of that time. And there are other examples throughout history of the development of newspapers to accompany the political and social life of black communities. Examples range from the early *Freedman's Journal* of Frederick Douglass to Henry Bibb, who ran the first abolitionist newspaper, the *Voice of the Fugitive* (1851), in Canada, and Mary Ann Shadd, the first newspaper woman in North America, who ran the *Provincial Freeman* in Toronto (1854–1857). Later ventures include the journal the *Crusader* from the African Blood Brotherhood and, in Harlem, the *West Indian American*, which fulfilled a similar role as the *West Indian Gazette* would later. In the process, a very literate and informed audience was developed. But the black press was not the only source of information and education: Reddock describes, for example, how the *International Negro Workers Review*, later named the *Negro Worker*, published by Comintern (the Communist International, also known as the Third International, the organization founded by Lenin and the Russian Communist Party), was brought to Trinidad and Tobago with the aid of seamen such as those who would later form related unions and organizations like the Seamen and Waterfront Workers' Trade Union and the Negro Welfare Cultural and Social Association.[8]

Today, as corporate journalism, embedded reporters, and mass media control via television have become the dominant modes of communication, the absence of more radical media is noticeable. But up to the mid-twentieth century, activist journalism allowed a rapid transportation of ideas throughout black communities and abroad, helped, as in the example just given, by sailors and longshoremen. Perhaps the Internet and related news systems can be similarly identified today, but now, because these are technology-driven, with their own particular access politics and given that the black press is no longer vibrant, various political ideas and theoretical positions do not reach black communities in the same way that radical black journalism did at the start of the twentieth century up through the 1950s. It was in this activist sense of print journalism as a direct communicator of political information that Claudia Jones's work was most significant.

In *Communists in Harlem During the Depression* Mark Naison locates Claudia Jones within a community of black members of the Communist Party USA, highlighting her particular professional identification in this way.

> Claudia Jones, of West Indian background, was a skilled journalist and public speaker; Howard "Stretch" Johnson had been a dancer at the Cotton Club and an actor in the Negro People's Theatre, and Angelo Herndon, now a permanent Harlem resident, was a former political prisoner who held national office in the American Youth Congress, a predominantly white student organization. Sophisticated, confident and personally attractive (Jones and Johnson were strikingly good-looking people) they gave the left an almost glamorous aura that contrasted with the tough "proletarian" image that it sought once to project. (201)

The glamour that Naison seems to revel in notwithstanding, there was a consistent level of political commitment and service among this group of activists, both to communism and to black social and political advancement not seen in later groups of activists. Jones and her colleagues were also great writers. William Maxwell, in *New Negro, Old Left*, notes that "the gallery of black literary intellectuals variously affiliated with Communism in the 1920s and 1930s makes a fair who's who of African American writing from the same decades" (2). For this group, I would add that progressive journalism in particular was a branch of writing that marked their praxis. Claudia Jones, "skilled journalist" that she was, and located within the leadership of the Communist Party USA, would be absolutely central to this politics throughout the 1930s, up to and through her deportation to London in the mid-1950s.

Jones's Early Journalism: From "Claudia's Comments" to "The Political Score"

One of the most significant points in the development of Claudia's own journalism is that she identifies her father as having been a journalist for one of the black newspapers in Harlem.[9] She indicates a very early sense of having herself a career in this field and its link to political expression. She describes herself as working from 1935 to 1936 for a black newspaper in Harlem and writing a weekly column, "Claudia's Comments."[10] (This preceded her involvement in the Communist Party.) Jones describes herself as critical of the newspaper and its leadership when she discovered that the summaries she wrote on black issues were used by the editor as his own. Her entry into the Young Communist League (YCL) accompanied the offer of a position as a journalist in one of the party's youth organs.

The copies of the YCL's *Weekly Review* that I have examined document a consistent and steady building of journalistic credentials, starting as a writer for the *Weekly Review* and rising through associate editor and editor to editor-in-chief, the position she reached March 1943. Jones also wrote interesting essays for the *Weekly Review*: one of her earliest pieces, "The Story of Bigger Thomas," was a review of Richard Wright's *Native Son* paired with an article by Everett Loomis about the black South, "Native Sons Strive for Freedom." The *Weekly Review* also reports on her organizational career: she is reported as attending the Second World Youth Congress held at Vassar College, along with Harry Winston, both in the capacity of members of the Young Communist League; later, she is mentioned in articles as the New York State education director and then as chairman of the Young Communist League. During my research, I was particularly excited to suddenly come upon one of the most striking and beautiful youthful images I have seen of Claudia Jones, in the *Weekly Review* of October 1938.

Throughout this period, Jones developed both her journalistic skill as well as her Communist Party ideological orientation. Assessments of Jones in this early period are that her writing adheres closely to Communist Party positions. The most substantial proof of this is that she changed her position on the Second World War in keeping with the party's ideological shifts, as we see in her essay "New Problems of the Negro Youth Movement" and her two booklets on the war, *Jim-Crow in Uniform* (1940) and *Lift Every Voice — For Victory*. Typical of criticism of Jones in this period is that "her adherence to the Party's line on the war compromised her writing, preventing her from critically commenting on racial discrimination and issues vital to black communities."[11] In the process it seems she also challenged some of the leaders of black national organizations, such as Walter White and Roy Wilkins of the National Association for the Advancement of Colored People (NAACP), but also the more left-leaning W. A. Domingo and A. Philip Randolph. Taking the party position does not seem to me surprising for somebody like Jones, who developed through and spent the most important parts of her youth working within and for the Communist Party. That this approach would continue throughout her years as editor of *Spotlight* (1943–1944) is also not as difficult to understand as McDuffie indicates ("Long Journeys," 347). Here was a young woman in her early twenties trying to study ideological positions and learn and utilize some practical skills, but also to make her way professionally.

My examination of Jones's work in the *Weekly Review* identifies a growing number of positive representations of black athletes and other figures. The concern with ending Jim Crow would occupy a great deal of newspaper space, and must have been the background source of one of her early pamphlet *Jim-Crow in Uniform*.

In the *Review*, besides articles on various subjects, Jones ran a weekly column titled "Quiz," in which she provided answers to a range of commonly asked questions. For example, in the September 23, 1941, issue, the question "We know that the Nazis persecute the Church but doesn't the Soviet Union also suppress religion?" was followed by a detailed response that laid out the facts about religion in the Soviet Union and in Communist Party ideology, as identified in its constitution. A later column called "The Political Score," responding to current political and social events, ran throughout her period as editor-in-chief. Yumeris Morel, in her master's thesis on Jones, offers an assessment of the number of her articles of that time period; she concludes that "Jones exhibits a black nationalist dimension to her perspective through the issues that she chooses to bring to light. This is particularly evident in 1942, a year in which twelve out of fifteen of Jones' journalist pieces focused on race issues and the concerns of African Americans" (51). Morel also finds that all of Jones's major pieces of writing from 1938 to 1955 deal with "the black struggle" (52).

From all accounts, Claudia Jones was a journalist very much at the center of CPUSA informational structures and one of the critical workers in the execution of its programs. She had been trained as a youth in the party and moved through its various levels with comrades like Benjamin Davis, very much part of a cadre of black communist activists in the 1940s and 1950s. Claudia became a leading woman in the Communist Party, but one with substantial links to black communities in New York. Her entry as an editor of "negro affairs" for the *Daily Worker* in 1945 would also provide the opportunity, as revealed in her political essays, to focus on issues pertaining to black women.

Half the World

"Half the World" was the title of a column that Claudia Jones published throughout the early 1950s in the Woman Today section in the Sunday edition of the *Daily Worker*, in the magazine section. The context of her work as an organizer of women for the Communist Party is significant in terms of the development of this column. Jones had served as the secretary of the Women's Commission from its inception in 1947, with Elizabeth Gurley Flynn as chairperson. Together they had traveled across the United States speaking, lecturing, and organizing women's sections, and, in the end, both were political prisoners incarcerated in New York and later in the women's prison in Alderson, West Virginia.

"Half the World" was targeted, first, at reaching and organizing an audience of women and, second, at raising what the party called "the woman question" to a significant level. Claudia's position was that women, in particular black women, needed to have their consciousness about their position in American society raised significantly, as they often bore the brunt of the culture's economic and social exploitation. This is well laid out in "An End to the Neglect of the Problems of Negro Women" and "For New Approaches to Our Work among Women," as I have already shown. In the latter piece, for example, she argues:

> To begin with, women represent over half of the nation. Moreover, there are nearly sixteen million women wage earners, one fifth of whom are heads of families. Thirty-seven million women are housewives in cities or farms. Eight per cent of these are working mothers. There are forty-seven million women eligible to vote in the United States, over a half million more than men! As regards their degree of organization, nearly 30 million women are organized in various clubs and national women's organizations which are, in the main, bourgeois led. (738–739)[12]

The logic of "Half the World" carried the essential materialist-feminist assertion that women make up half the world's population and as such need to be similarly represented in terms of resources, access, and identification. Today, it is not unusual for agencies like the United Nations to operate on this basis in identifying women's human rights, but at that time period it was the Communist Party that carried that assertion forward as a basic principle.

The column itself, in presentation and content, communicated information on various women's organizing activities, such as the Sojourners for Truth and Justice. It also provided commentary on various political and social developments that had to do with women at both the local and international levels; served as a vehicle for Jones's own political positions on some issues aimed at raising her audience's consciousness; and promoted women's activities for peace.

We can contrast the "Half the World" column with others in the *Daily Worker* at that time. For example, Elizabeth Gurley Flynn ran a frequent column called "A Better World," which had as content a wide range of political issues, not directly targeted at women. A number of other columns dealing with labor, trade unions, black liberation, and international issues consistently appeared in the *Daily Worker*. The significance of the "Half the World" spot which Claudia wrote for the Sunday edition was that, as part of the "women's issues" section, it used that space specifically for the political education and organizing of women.

One of the strengths of Claudia Jones's writings is that in each piece she often provided analyses of a range of contemporary intellectual, political, and social issues. She was not afraid to use the column to challenge bourgeois intellectual theory and practice. In one of her "Half the World" columns (April 23, 1950), she directly challenged the ideology of male superiority and female inferiority in the ideas of Walter Lowenfels, who, it seems, had just written a provocative piece on the position of women that had circulated in national newspapers. Claudia recognized that these ideas also circulated uncriticized among party members. Consistent with her own Marxist-Leninist ideology, she saw the "theory" of women's inferiority as a feature of capitalist society that would change under socialism; her mission, then, was to critique any theories that would damage women in the interim. She critiques Lowenfels and simultaneously identifies the intent of "Half the World" as follows:

> The practical aim of this "theory" besides that of upholding and perpetuating conditions most advantageous for the unbridled exploitation of the working people in general and of women in particular, is to exclude women, *who comprise half of humanity* (*as this column is paraphrased*) from public and political activity and struggles. The bourgeois idealists realize that the larger becomes the section of exploited people who take part in active political struggles, the more acute will these struggles become, and all the more reason will there be for misgivings about the fate of capitalism (emphasis original).

A women's rights position, based on the principle of the representation of the interests of "half the world" would not be so boldly articulated in subsequent women's movement initiatives — those, say, of the 1970s and 1980s. The premise of "half the world" is more solidly located now in women's rights activities and the United Nations initiatives and conferences that try to represent women's rights as human rights. But in Jones's articulation the important point is that no attempt to move society forward is possible if half the population remains unaccounted for. In this analysis, societies lose the contributions of half the world, literally, when a large proportion of their populations, totaling in the millions, are shut out from active political involvement in pressing issues that directly concern them. Thus with at least "half the world" not directly involved, we are assured the continuance of various forms of capitalist oppression.

The "Half the World" column carried the subtitle "In the fight for peace, equality, security in the home, on the job, in the nation." In the November 4, 1951, issue the column occupies top and center of the page. The rest of the page is devoted to "A Checklist of Books on Women"—an annotated bibliography that provided information for those who wanted "to learn about women in other countries and how they are fighting for peace and socialism . . . to brush up on the history of Negro and white women in our own land, their heroic struggles for liberation, for trade union organization, for suffrage . . . to marshal convincing arguments and Marxist theory against male supremacy." The recommended books ranged from biographies of Sojourner Truth, Harriet Tubman, and Lena Horne to the *U.S. Department of Labor Handbook of Facts on Women* (1950), books on women in China and the Soviet Union, *Aptheker's Documentary History of the Negro People in the U.S.* (1951), and the selections from Marx, Engels, Lenin, and Stalin in a book entitled *The Woman Question*.

Since the aim of the column was to educate the general readership of the paper on the "woman question," it ran side-by-side the ideas raised by Claudia Jones and Elizabeth Gurley Flynn and the Women's Commission, and put into practice one of the ideas Jones had suggested in her essay "An End to the Neglect," that is, community education for transformation. So "Half the World" was also meant as a forum for women to communicate and circulate their ideas and experiences. Several columns ended with requests for readers to write in response, to send updates on organizing activity, and to communicate generally to each other and to the editors.

It is here that the antiwar and women's peace movement political links are made most directly, and clarified repeatedly. Several columns would be as specific and clear as the one titled "You Can't Have Guns and Butter Too" (September 2, 1951), which asserted that "millions of American homemakers are learning" this essential fact. The rest of the column was an analysis of the relative income of American families, citing the *1950 Joint Congressional Committee on the Economic Report* and from the National Social Welfare Assembly's report, *Making Ends Meet on Less than $2,000 a Year*, a compilation of one hundred family case histories across twenty-seven states and the District of Columbia. The column identifies how health, food, schooling, and day-to-day survival and general well-being are impacted when the government emphasizes war rather than people. Particular attention is given to the report's findings on black, Mexican, and Puerto Rican families who often lived in poverty. The column ends by saying "Let *Woman Today* hear from its readers on what you are doing in your community: (1) to demand an end to the wage freeze and for immediate wage increases; (2) for immediate price and rent control; (3) for a cut in taxes of low-incomed people."

Several other "Half the World" columns were directed at informing the readers about international and grassroots organizing of women against the war, some of it focused on collecting signatures for the World Peace Appeal. A column on August 13, 1950, identifies antiwar activity by the Women's Committee of the African Democratic Rally, Dutch women, and rallies in Côte d'Ivoire, Vietnam, and Korea. The attention of this particular column, though, was mainly on Eugenie Cotton, a French scientist and president of the Women's International Democratic Federation and head of the Union of French Women, who had recently been arrested by the French government. It provided addresses to which letters of support for her should be sent.

On the U.S. domestic level, several columns identified some of the peace work being initiated. "If enough women unite, together with the growing legions of peace fighters all over the world, we can save the peace," begins a July 30, 1950, column about the women's delegation to the United Nations, which named itself American Women for Peace. It met, the column tells its readers, on July 13, "to raise their voices for a peaceful settlement of the Korean conflict" and to announce a National Delegation for Peace to Washington, D.C., on August 9. Another column, on June 4, 1950, shares information received in a letter from a "British sister," which reports, "Among other things that incense British women is that the burdens of the Cold War are being placed on the backs of the British working class," and also describes the high price of goods in Britain, which had led to various boycotts. Most "Half the World" columns closed with a characteristic pithy statement; in the case of the June 4, 1950, column it was about the need for "uniting British and American women" to help expose the governmental level propaganda.

The fate of children in general and women's concern for them would be a central theme in these columns and an obvious and identified way of reaching a cross-section of the population of women. An interesting column in the October 8, 1950, issue shows a U.S. military policeman frisking a Vietnamese child. This image had also appeared in the *New York Times* and the *Daily News*. Jones, clearly adept at seizing the image and the moment to make a political statement, begins her column with the question "Who can look at the picture *Woman Today* prints on the page — and not feel the revulsion that every mother, every woman, man and child must feel at glancing at it?" The picture, she says, cries out to us "WE MUST STOP THIS NOW!" The rest of the column is dedicated to organizing work in support of the World Peace Appeal and has a characteristic closure: "Only we, labor-progressive women, women from churches, Negro, Jewish, trade-union American women can fulfill this basic responsibility to our sisters and to our own families."

Other "Half the World" columns deal with issues of education, the cost of food, the "fascist-like indoctrination of children," various (mis)statements of Dean Acheson (then secretary of state) on the war effort, the ideological campaign being waged through women's magazines to ready women for the war effort, and the link of the war to racism at the national and international level. Claudia understood the ways of the "capitalist press," as she called it, in how it presented black issues selectively, and the larger ideological orientation which it represented well: "The rarity of capitalist news coverage as concerns the Negro family stops at the water's edge as to the solution of real problems, the problems of life and death for Chaneta Holden, victim of Jim Crow housing conditions and national oppression. Only struggle and unity of Negro and white to change the society can guarantee her a life of peace and a happy childhood."[13] Other articles written by Claudia Jones in the *Daily Worker* were similarly devoted to pursuing the issue of the challenge to the war and the assertion of a women's peace movement.

The wide publicity Jones gave to the projects of the organization Sojourners for Peace and Justice would be one of her major contributions to an understanding of the formulation of support for black feminist practice and would guide and orient an important aspect of Claudia Jones's journalistic activity. The "Half the World" column for September 20, 1951, is a notable example. In it she writes a fairly long article titled "Call Negro Women to 'Sojourn for Justice.'" She names the initiating committee of "Negro women leaders," with Beulah Richardson, poet and actress of Mississippi, as acting secretary. Many of this group's members were already significant as black women organizers, writers, actresses, and activists. Including Richardson, the committee comprised Mrs. Charlotta A. Bass, of California; Mrs. Alice Childress, New York; Miss Shirley Graham, New York; Mrs. Josephine Grayson, Virginia; Mrs. Dorothy Hunton, New York; Miss Sonora B. Lawson, Virginia; Mrs. Amy Mallard; Georgia; Mrs. Rosalie McGee, Mississippi; Mrs.

Bessie Mitchell, New Jersey; Mrs. Louise Patterson, New York; Mrs. Eslanda Robeson, Connecticut; Mrs. Pauline Taylor, Ohio; and Mrs. Frances Williams, California. It is significant that Claudia Jones is not on the initiating committee, although she was a member of the Sojourners and a friend and colleague of many of its members. Her role for the group seemed to be specifically as a leading champion and supporter of its activities and as a philosophical ally, for she clearly shared its perspectives and had already argued them in Communist Party platforms.

"Sojourners for Truth and Justice," an essay by Jones devoted to the group, was identified as a Negro History Week contribution in the Woman Today section of the *Daily Worker* (February 10, 1952). It reported that the Sojourners for Truth and Justice were recognized for their contribution to black advancement. The article began with the prominent statement "Peace and Freedom. Negro women are in the forefront of this fight. And some of the biggest steps along the path is the advancement of the fight for full social, political and economic equality of Negro women." It continues: "A group of 14 women leaders last fall initiated a CALL TO NEGRO WOMEN to convene in Washington in a SOJOURN FOR TRUTH AND JUSTICE. In less than two weeks, over 132 Negro women from 15 states responded. These Negro women met in Washington, D.C. to voice their protest against the aborted effort of the government to imprison the great intellectual and Negro leader W. E. B. Du Bois."[14]

Based, in naming and political intent, on the historic activism and legacies of Sojourner Truth and Harriet Tubman, the Sojourners for Truth targeted poverty, loneliness, drudgery, disease, the lynching and execution of black men, the reviling of black civil rights leadership, the reasons why young black men were imprisoned or "poured into foreign wars" while they were "denied equality on the battlefield and at home," the rape and degradation of young black women, and the absolute and overwhelming fact of segregation and discrimination in the United States. As an earlier article in the *Daily Worker*, dated September 20, 1951, had already announced, "There is no state in the whole of the 48 in which we can eat, live, work, play, rest, or breathe free of segregation and discrimination, and when the greatest voice we have produced dares sing out against these indignities, his passport is recalled and he is denied the right to earn a living."[15]

The range of issues that the Sojourners for Truth and Justice embraced extends far beyond the narrow gendered formulations that appeared later in the mainstream feminist movement and was more in keeping with agendas in the black movement and black women's movement, pursuing issues to do with advancement of the entire community. Claudia Jones clearly saw the value of the Sojourner movement, and her "Sojourners for Truth and Justice" column locates it in the context of larger historical movements of black women organizing in the United States. She closes the article by linking the Sojourners to other movements of "colonial women" around the world: "The growing struggle of Negro women for freedom and peace can be strengthened a hundred fold if we bring to our country and to these emerging movements a greater consciousness of the magnificent strength of the colonial women's movements in Korea, the Far East, in Latin America and in Africa, affiliated with the Women's International Democratic Federation." Characteristically, Claudia Jones saw all these people's movements as linked, and the movement of black women as essential to realizing the "full potential" of the black liberation movement as well as the women's movement.

On women's issues, then, the "Half the World" columns indicate a maturing of Jones's position on the place of women's rights. It is in this period that we see Claudia, as active journalist, able to advance a series of positions on women and for peace simultaneously. Her earlier understandings of Jim Crow racism and her positions on women are sharpened and come together in her work on black women in general.

The *West Indian Gazette*—Journalism and the London Experience

Claudia Jones's founding and editing of the *West Indian Gazette* in 1958, three years after her arrival in London, would be the culmination of a life of journalist activity that she knew well. In the entire scheme of her journalistic work, the *West Indian Gazette* period (she worked for ten years on the paper) was short, but it was the most important period in her long journalistic career. Though brief, it was nonetheless important, because it allowed her to bring her skill, experience, and politics together again, this time directed at a black British and Afro-Caribbean community, the development of its readership, and the assertion of a black British culture.

According to Donald Hinds, who learned journalism and politics from Claudia Jones and became one of the *Gazette*'s most loyal reporters, Jones's journalistic experience proved invaluable to the London community, which benefited from the fact that, in his words, "She was a trained journalist and she had been actively engaged in working for improvement in black people's condition in the United States before she was expelled. The Committee [editorial committee organized to publish the paper in late 1957] could not fail to have been anything less than impressed by her credentials" (*Journey to Illusion*, 126). Hinds defines the *Gazette* as the "parent of all the other journals . . . an entry in the chronicle of the West Indian story in Britain" (149).

Edward Pilkington, in *Beyond the Mother Country: West Indians and the Notting Hill White Riots*, identifies the *Gazette* as a Caribbean community paper from its inception, "allowing West Indians to express their uncertainties and confusions in the wake of the riots. Their British identity had been jolted by the riots, for how could they call themselves British after being treated like unwanted strangers? This left a vacuum to be filled. . . . Out of the ashes of the 'Mother Country' a new vision was born. The riots marked the dawn of a new West Indian identity for black people living in Britain" (143–144).

Harry Goulbourne, writing about Caribbean publishers and diasporic communication in his book *Caribbean Transnational Experience*, sees Jones as critical to the birth of radical black journalism in the United Kingdom. A later vehicle for the radical black voice, in a medium that reached beyond the world of books, would be the *Black Liberator*, which Goulbourne describes as "the leading black and Caribbean journal in Britain," but confirming that "the work of this publication has attracted no attention in the academic literature" (81). The *Black Liberator* and its editorship becomes important also to this discussion of Claudia Jones, because Alrick ("Ricky") Cambridge, the founder of this journal, was best positioned to carry on Jones's legacy, having been Jones's last assistant before her death.

Goulbourne places Claudia Jones in the context of two major subsequent publishing efforts that would take off in the 1960s: New Beacon Books and the related activities of John La Rose and Bogle L'Ouverture Publications, run by Jessica and Eric Huntley. Both these publishing initiatives continued the advancement of African diaspora publishing in London, with a series of books by scholars and writers of African descent across the world. The Third World and Radical Book Fair that they organized throughout the 1980s, the republishing of critical novels in Caribbean history, and the publishing of the work of historian and political activist Walter Rodney would continue that early radical tradition, and would provide subsequent writers with an avenue for the publishing of their work. Significantly, all of the important actors in this process knew, interacted, and were affiliated in various ways with Claudia Jones, even if they were not part of the same organizations. One can say clearly that London continued to be a site of tremendous African diaspora activism at various levels from the time of Claudia Jones and through the 1980s and 1990s, though less so after that period.[16] "Whilst Claudia Jones brought to Brixton and the emerging Caribbean communities springing up in England her immense experience from the United States, the other publications were largely experimental, produced on extraordinarily messy Gestetner printing machines in often damp and unhealthy basements and terraced houses both north and south of the Thames" (137). The *Gazette*'s predecessor, the *Caribbean News*, even though it had a limited left audience, was, like the *Gazette*, professionally printed, but only because the management had a connection with someone with a printing shop, who printed the paper as a favor to a fellow comrade.[17]

Claudia Jones's opening editorial for the *West Indian Gazette*, "Why a Newspaper for West Indians?" (March 1958), clearly spells out the answer in terms of the intended audience and the political issues they faced. Its aim was to accompany the Caribbean community in London as it began to encounter the particular challenges that living in the colonial capital presented. Hinds reports that a poll was conducted prior to the monthly paper's launching, which indicated that "there would be support for a paper which would not only bring the news from back home, but would also report on the many communities in the 'mother country.' There was little doubt that the paper aimed right from the start to take a strong line against racial discrimination" ("The *West Indian Gazette*," 149). Thus the paper was justified in opening with the statement "There are least 80,000 good reasons why we believe a West Indian newspaper is necessary and will be welcomed. They are the 80,000-odd West Indians now resident here. Together we form a community with its own wants and problems, which our own paper alone would allow us to meet" (1).

Anti-imperialist in orientation, pan-Africanist in politics, feminist in its leadership and concern for women, the *Gazette* followed the developments in the various anti-colonial struggles around the world during the key period of the 1950s and is a key source of information for anyone studying transnational social movements and politics of that time. The paper suffered from attacks from London right-wing racist groups such as the London Branch of the Ku Klux Klan of Britain, which sent a letter to the editor in August 1958.[18] From the outset, the newspaper saw the tackling of British racism as one of its central issues. Thus, it was an important organizing tool during the Notting Hill riots of 1958, as was Claudia's electrifying presence as an orator who recognized well the foundations of racism and was clear about the differences in its manifestation in the United States and in the United Kingdom. All her editorials at this time articulated these positions. As a communist, however, she saw "imperialism as the root cause of racialism. It is the ideology which upholds colonial rule and exploitation. It preaches the 'superiority' of the white race whose 'destiny' it is to rule over those with coloured skins, and to treat them with contempt. It is the ideology which breeds Fascism, rightly condemned by the civilized people the whole world."[19]

The *West Indian Gazette* also saw itself as accompanying the developing West Indian Federation. Jones's essay on the West Indies Federation (*Gazette*, March 1958), which I quote from in the epigraph to this chapter, makes the case clearly: "Last March it was Ghana. This March, 1958 — still another new nation — the West Indies Federation will be born." Jones continues, "Just what does it mean? To begin with, similarities to a politically independent Ghana are fewer than the differences. Federation in the Caribbean is the first of a series of great steps required to ensure full national independence for the West Indies as a whole and self-government for its units" (2). In *Journey to an Illusion*, Hinds notes that the paper came into being at the same time as the "possibility of a federation" and the parallel "new excitement among West Indians not only in the United Kingdom, but also in the Caribbean" (150) about understanding and representing Caribbean history, culture, and heritage.[20]

The *Gazette* was comparable in scope and appearance to other papers. My investigations found that it was similar to earlier papers on which Claudia Jones had worked — the *Weekly Review* and the *Daily Worker* — in format, size, appearance, and content; all three carried film and book reviews, sports news, popular information, major political news and analyses, and an editorial page.

The journalistic work of the *Gazette*, together with some of the struggles that occurred at its founding and its economic difficulties, are described by Donald Hinds in his essay "The *West Indian Gazette*." Hinds feels that the paper's economic woes are explainable by the difficulty of developing a readership and of paying contributors in the Caribbean. The struggles of the *Gazette*, one can conclude, were no different from that of other newspapers of similar intent, history, and date.

In this writer's view, though, journalism for Claudia Jones was a means or — more precisely — a medium; the political and ideological positions were the message. The urgent political and cultural needs of the Caribbean community in England became paramount. Claudia Jones's last published essay, "The Caribbean Community in Britain," which was written for the celebrated Caribbean issue of *Freedomways*, is also in many ways an assessment of the contribution of the paper. After talking about the Commonwealth Immigrant Act of 1962 and its effect on black people in Britain, she describes the paper as follows:

> A major effort designed to stimulate political and social thinking has been the launching, six years ago, of the progressive news-monthly, the *West Indian Gazette*. This newspaper has served as a catalyst, quickening the awareness, socially and politically, of West Indians, Afro-Asians and their friends. Its editorial stand is for a united independent West Indies, full economic, social and political equality and respect for human dignity for West Indians and Afro-Asians in Britain, for peace and friendship between all Commonwealth and world peoples. (354–355)

In the first instance, the education of the community is seen as a priority, as it was in all of the other journalistic activity in which Claudia Jones was engaged. But its anti-imperialist, pro-black community position remained clear. Again from the *Freedomways* article:

> Whether against numerous police frame-ups, to which West Indians and other colored migrants are frequently subject, to opposing discrimination and to advocating support for trade unionism and unity of colored and white workers, WI news publications have attempted to emulate the path of progressive 'Negro' (Afro-Asian, Latin-American and Afro-American) journals who uncompromisingly and fearlessly fight against imperialist outrages and indignities to our peoples. The *West Indian Gazette and Afro-Asian Caribbean News* has served to launch solidarity campaigns with the nationals who advance with their liberation struggles in Africa and in Asia. (355)

In this context, of journalism as political praxis, we see Claudia Jones in a new political light. All her editorials in the *Gazette* took a position on some aspect of international or local politics. Here, the needs of the Caribbean community and their links with other communities and nations of Afro-Asian, African, and Latin American peoples necessitated a politics even more internationalist in scope than was possible in her prior journalistic endeavors.

From all accounts, the *West Indian Gazette and Afro-Asian Caribbean News*[21] always had a difficult passage, from the struggle at its inception to its consistent financial woes and its ending after Claudia's passing. But this is not unusual for a newspaper of its type, which tried to identify and develop a Caribbean (and then Afro-Asian) readership and serve as an independent voice for the black population in Britain. Robert Chrisman, in his foreword to *Voices of a Black Nation*, identifies this problem as common also in the United States. Theodore Vincent asserts, "Almost all black newspapers, even in the heyday of the New Negro press, were in constant and serious financial difficulties. The turnover among the smaller ones was enormous" (28). Their difficulties are attributed to the "paucity of advertising," among other things, from a black population still in dire financial straits. Today, of course, there are several newspapers created specifically for the Caribbean and/or black community, in London and elsewhere, but back in the 1950s, there was a virtual absence of print communication links. Donald Hinds details well the various aspects of the *Gazette*'s financial problems ("The *West Indian Gazette*," 134–138), some of these anatomized by Claudia Jones herself (136), such as the high cost of production, the questions of regular circulation, its being a people's paper dependent on support from the immigrant population themselves, and the management's inability to "establish a working team that takes responsibility for every aspect of the paper's growth, circulation and editorial work" (136). As a result, some say the paper came to be too identified with Claudia Jones herself. Correspondence between Manchanda and Jones (October 1962), particularly when he served as general manager in her absence, are very stark about the problems of staffing the *Gazette*. A letter from Jones to Manchanda, dated September 17, 1964, a few months before her death and written from the Soviet Union while she was in hospital there, tells him, "Please let me know if you have been able to assuage our creditors. Are you OK? Where is WIG [*West Indian Gazette*]? Love Claudia."[22] A postscript says, "Sad about Gurley Flynn isn't it," and adds a comment on Moise Tshombe of the Congo who was implicated in the demise of Patrice Lumumba, Congolese Prime Minster in 1961. A post-postscript adds, "The retail news vendor in the Station (L junction) near the office has agreed to take our papers over a month ago . . . Try him with September's, OK? Are you getting additional help? Donald? George? Others?"

In the initial issue of the paper, then titled simply *West Indian Gazette* and subtitled *A Periodical of WI News and Opinion* (March 1958), Jones's article "Why a Paper for West Indians?" referred to the census figures for the number of Caribbean people in Britain at that time. A beautiful photo of two smiling Caribbean children accompanies the article, with a caption underneath "A bright future belongs to them." The opening editorial identifies the desire for news from home, but adds a rider: "As a WI nation comes into being we want more news and fuller news from home. But we also want news about fellow countrymen here." Other topics that the editorial says the paper will cover are reports of conferences and actions that would have impact on the Caribbean community, debates about restrictions of Caribbean immigration, and general information on developments of relevance to Caribbean peoples and in the academic world. Above all, it ventures a question: "How many know why we're truly here — some to study, some to escape frightful colonial poverty?" Claudia identifies the work of the West Indian Workers and Students' Association, which had surveyed the Caribbean community to identify its needs, one of them being a paper. The editorial ends with a call for the community to write, to respond, and above all to subscribe.

In the back section of this first, two-page issue, a feature titled "West Indian Federation" compares the birth of the nation of Ghana to the birth of a West Indian Federation as "another new nation." "Federation in the Caribbean is the first of a series of great steps required to ensure full national independence as a whole and self government for its units," announces the piece. It closes as follows:

> We associate ourselves with the ancient dream of West Indian stalwarts and
> fighters for West Indian Federation who hoped to found a strong, united
> progressive West Indies, playing a role on national and international af-
> fairs. We call on the talented sons and daughters among our workers and
> students to lend their skills so we may hold fast to this dream. We affirm,
> like other great African and Asian peoples, our spirits too have caught
> the contagion of national independence. And that nothing less than that
> achievement will satisfy us. (2)

The sentiments identified here are consistent with those put forward by a variety of activists for Caribbean decolonization at the time, that is, a wish not for separate, independent, and small island nations but for an integrated Caribbean nation.[23] The *West Indian Gazette* begins then by taking a political stand, even as it supports the development of its readership. On the same page as this editorial, it asks for advertisements and the paper includes, in fact, advertisements for furniture and book sales, coach excursions to Hastings, and a gala Federation dance to be held in Peckham.

By the October 1963 issue, the *West Indian Gazette and Afro-Asian Caribbean News* is twelve pages long, with advertisements for real estate, hairdressers, Caribbean grocery items (Enco brand products like West Indian Hot Pepper Sauce, for example), chemists, the Indian astrologer Pundit Sinjin for readings and diet advice, hair products, jazz clubs, travel agencies, employment agencies, furniture shops, and accommodation agencies. Intellectual and political content remains strong. The front-page story is the impending resignation of Sir Learie Constantine from the post of high commissioner of Trinidad. Other news from across the pan-African world includes stories from Kenya ("Kenyatta Expresses Confidence in Kenya Victory"), Nigeria ("Nigeria Becomes a Republic," a story accompanied by photographs of two young Nigerian women), and the United States ("American Negroes Demonstrate in Memory of Schoolgirls Killed" [in Alabama]). There is also information about Africans on trial in South Africa and specific island news from across the Caribbean. Two articles are on cultural topics: "The Negro and Cinema" by Clinton Jones and a review of Baldwin's *The Fire Next Time* by Jones. Significantly, the proceedings of the Socialist Party of Jamaica are included (they were serialized in prior issues and summarized in this issue of the *Gazette*).

The role of the *West Indian Gazette and Afro-Asian Caribbean News* in advancing Caribbean culture is evident both from its initial editorial intent and its subsequent content and practice. Bill Schwarz came to the same conclusion in his own study of the paper, which he writes about in his essay "Claudia Jones and the *West Indian Gazette:* Reflections on the Emergence of Post-colonial Britain."[24] Schwarz also makes the following interesting observation:

> Much of the originality of the *Gazette* was to be found in its attempt to connect the local with the global: to link, say, the specific neighbourhood concerns of its readers in Notting Hill to the wider global world of anticolonialism and the Civil Rights movement. . . . The experience of dias-

pora which the *Gazette* strained to voice, turned the polarities of the local and global inside-out. . . . By extension, the local which the *West Indian Gazette* brought into being was, resolutely, a black local. (270–271)

According to Schwarz, the carnival and the *Gazette* were the two institutions whereby the Caribbean community was made "conscious of its history . . . . on British soil" (273). Schwarz sees the *Gazette* as having therefore a central role in creating the postcolonial Caribbean community in London and, further, that "the conditions of a diasporic locality" can itself be identified in the *Gazette* (282).

The *West Indian Gazette and Afro-Asian Caribbean News* would indeed have a foundational role in developing the Caribbean diaspora in London. The paper benefited not only from Claudia Jones's professional journalistic skill but also from her knowledge of the role of the *West Indian American* in Harlem, on which it seems her father had worked. It would have a critical role in a series of secondary community activities, among which the sponsoring of the Caribbean Carnival would be one of the newspaper's important contributions — but there would be others. The newspaper's offices were situated in the middle of Brixton, in the borough of Lambeth in south London (at 250 Brixton Road), above a Caribbean record shop. Thus it was physically at the heart of the then developing Caribbean community in Brixton. The Caribbean Carnival souvenir programs identified the carnivals as events organized by the *Gazette*: Jones, in the 1959 program, for example, credits the "Caribbean Carnival Committee 1959, set up last November under the sponsorship of the *West Indian Gazette*." She continues: "May the aim of our mutual efforts be to help build the *West Indian Gazette* and above all in that endeavour help to extend the already acknowledged cultural influence of the Caribbean throughout the Commonwealth."[25]

Significantly as well, as *The West Indian Gazette* expanded its title to incorporate "Afro-Asian Caribbean" news, no doubt as a manifestation of the related development of a larger understanding of what constituted the "black community" in Britain. This change in the definition of the black community would later lead to the formation of the Committee for Afro-Asian Caribbean Organizations (1962), which was organized as a lobbying group for these communities, as well as related politics in their home contexts. The new understanding of black community in London as also incorporating the South Asian community became an integral part of the organizational logic of these bodies. This, as we know, is quite different from the U.S. definition of "black community." The wider, British definition is due to the various migratory patterns of a range of third world peoples to Britain and their early encounters with racism, as well as the fact that British racists saw these communities as a homogenous group of foreign immigrants. Still, it is important to recognize this political move that Jones made both at the personal and political level. This incorporation of the struggles of the peoples of the South Asian subcontinent and Africa would also run through the politics of many similar political movements in the Caribbean.

The *Gazette* would also be a place where Caribbean artists and cultural workers were given space, as it simultaneously served as a site for announcements about their activities and appearances, such as at the annual carnivals. The Mighty Sparrow, Lord Kitchener, Dixieland Steelband, Boscoe Holder, and other performers from Trinidad, for example, are identified in various issues of the *West Indian Gazette*, as were a range of Caribbean writers in London. The *Gazette* thus served, in Schwarz's words as "the house-paper for a generation of Caribbean intellectuals who had made the journey to London" ("Claudia Jones and the *West Indian Gazette*," 280). Edward Pilkington, in *Beyond the Mother Country*, sums it up best, saying that the *Gazette*, under Claudia Jones's direction, would serve as a "mouthpiece for the new associations which were being formed" and play a role in the redefinition of Afro-Caribbean identity in Britain, as it changed from the earlier "British colonial subject" identity that many of the immigrants carried with them to that country. It is significant that writers and artists had a major role in this process, as many of the writers who emerged in the 1950s were then resident in London. The *West Indian Gazette* was clearly a medium through which their writings and ideas could reach a larger community, and it has to be credited in much the same way that the British Broadcasting Corporation is credited for its role in the development of a space for Caribbean arts to develop. Many cite a Jan Carew essay on the definition of the West Indian as germinal in this process ("British West Indian Poets and their Culture"), because it spoke directly to, and allowed contemplation of, the creation of a West Indian identity outside of the earlier British subject definition. The fact that the *West Indian Gazette* is so named is also important here as well.

The *Gazette* acted as a forum for debate, allowing West Indians to express their uncertainties and confusions in the wake of the riots. Their British identity had been jolted by the riots, for how could they call themselves British after being treated like unwarranted strangers. . . . Out of the ashes of the "Mother Country" a new vision was born. The riots marked the dawn of a new West Indian identity for black people living in Britain and the beginning of a search for a common black ancestry, which culminated in the 1960s Black Power movement. (143–144)

According to Donald Hinds, "It is perhaps somewhat misleading to separate the *Gazette*'s social from its political activities, as the 'social' always had a political purpose" ("The *West Indian Gazette*," 138). Hinds's perspective is important because, as a writer for the *Gazette*, he is able to provide valuable details on the struggles of the paper — its financial, staffing, and space problems — and its relatively short-lived but impressive role in the Caribbean community in London, leading the way for the now numerous papers that inform and represent the community. But in the 1950s the *West Indian Gazette* was the most influential (and perhaps the only) organ, following the demise of its predecessor, the *Caribbean News*. The *Gazette* wanted to reach and serve the larger community in various ways; thus its social activities included not only sponsoring the carnivals and various other cultural shows but also supporting political organizations like the Afro-Asian and Caribbean Conference and, of course, the larger community in its various editorials and coverage of the range of black and third world events. Hinds identifies philanthropic causes as well, such as a benefit concert for the victims of hurricane Flora (140). Hinds, incidentally, provides one of the few accounts of a joint endeavor of the Trinidadians C. L. R. James and Claudia Jones: "The benefit Concert Committee members included Nadia Cattouse, Claudia Jones and CLR James and the sponsors were Edric Connor, Peal Connor, George Lamming, Dr David Pitt, Andrew Salkey, Sam Selvon and the Rev Dr Donald Soper" (140).[26]

In a sense then, the *West Indian Gazette and Afro-Asian Caribbean News* was much more international than pan-Africanist (it served an audience larger than the African-descended communities) in its geographical scope and reach, though pan-Africanism seemed to be one of its critical elements. By means of this paper and its allied activities, Claudia Jones, through her London move, accessed the international reach of socialism that was initially envisaged in some ways in the CPUSA and not fully realized in the *Daily Worker*, which covered only briefly some of the items that the *Gazette* could give full and frontal attention.

Connecting the London black community to the various activities, creative and political movements, struggles, and figures of U.S. black community would also be another critical achievement that Claudia Jones was able to bring off because of her extensive connections in the United States. Perhaps Paul Robeson best symbolizes this shared connection—as a personal friend of Jones, he did benefit concerts for the *Gazette*. As we have already seen, he and his wife, Eslanda Goode Robeson, were members of Jones's Harlem community and maintained connections with Claudia throughout her time in the United States and United Kingdom. But Martin Luther King Jr. also visited and was interviewed, W. E. B. Du Bois appeared in the *Gazette*, and there were constant reviews of black writing from the United States and United Kingdom, Claudia's review of James Baldwin's *The Fire Next Time* among them. The march organized by the *Gazette* to parallel the March on Washington would be another of those symbolic events. Clearly, Claudia Jones and the *West Indian Gazette and Afro-Asian Caribbean News* is the part of the larger missing Caribbean subject in any understanding of "the Black Atlantic"—one that is absent from Paul Gilroy's interpretation of this concept.[27] Jones's contribution to developing an African diaspora consciousness nevertheless comes through, as did Marcus Garvey's earlier newspaper *The Negro World*, that is, not only through music and books but through journalism and a politics of resistance.

As I have shown, the connections forged by Jones would extend beyond the United States and, under her leadership, the *Gazette* provided information on and connected the entire black world, with a heavy emphasis on the Caribbean, which was the target of the paper and its developing Caribbean diaspora scope of coverage, but also on decolonization movements internationally.[28] In this way and by these means, Claudia Jones had the perfect platform and location to more accurately articulate a positive anti-imperialist, anticapitalist, international approach, which had the potential of building an important transnational network of disenfranchised peoples. Through journalism, Claudia Jones was able to move from the specific space she carved out in the United States—via the *Daily Worker* and related community organizing, and thereby to broaden the scope of her socialism beyond its CPUSA beginnings into a more fully international paradigm, more in keeping with, but also extending, her Marxist-Leninist ideological orientation.

3. Claudia Jones, on the cover
of *Young Communist Review*,
October 1938.

4. One of Claudia Jones's "Half
the World" columns. From the
Daily Worker, November 4,
1951.

Half the World
by Claudia Jones

Women Should Protest War Incitements

A SHOCKING EXAMPLE of the growth of war propaganda and war incitement was the recent Collier's Magazine issue which devoted its entire contents to a series of articles entitled "Preview of the War We Do Not Want."

Using slick journalistic techniques, the editor, Louis Ruppel, former Hearst newspaperman, gathered up a cure of leading conservative writers and outright reactionary spokesmen to write articles based on the assumption that we (the UN) have devastated and now occupy Europe and conquered the Soviet Union. This is glorified "police action" on a world scale. Conscious of the overwhelming peace sentiments of the American people, Collier's editors in brazenly advocating this path, emphasize that such a war, supposed to start in 1952 and end in 1960, will lead to the establishment of the "free enterprise system" all over the world.

A mere indication of the kind of racist philosophy which will govern this "better era" which Collier's editors hold will surely come by such devastation, death and a fearful cost of human lives, is one of the cartoons by Bill Mauldin. Mauldin draws an American soldier who leads before him a Russian soldier with a gun butt in his back asking: "Is that ALL you have to say for yourself buddy —What about the lynchings in the South?" Here is not only an effort to whitewash the widespread criticism of the fruits of the jimcrow "free enterprise" system for millions of Negro citizens, but to leave the impression that concern for lynchings is merely "Communist propaganda." Collier's asks its readers to believe that the seven Negro fathers in Martinsville who were legally lynched or the legal murder of Willie McGee is inconsequential either for the Negro people, or for labor. Is it possible that this is one of the reasons not a single Negro writer was asked to join this series?

Despite their title, "Preview of the War We Do Not Want," there is not one word by the men or women who write (among whom are Sen. Margaret Chase Smith and Marguerite Higgins, Herald Tribune reporter, who covered the devastation on the Korean war front) about how we can prevent war by negotiation of outstanding differences between nations for peace. Instead this is a vicious attempt to whip up a war psychology based on the ideology of worldwide military victory led by the U. S. and "a better era." *

This is the kind of fancy that Hitler, in his vain dream of world conquest, spinned to the destruction of millions of people, including the German people whose cost in destruction and lives were equally great. This kind of thing simply couldn't happen in the Soviet Union or the New Democracies, because in these lands there are laws prohibiting propaganda for war. Mothers, and women particularly, should be among the first to condemn this and all other examples of war incitement, so that editors and writers will think twice before so easily rousing war fever which is designed to make people fearful instead of expressing their true sentiments which is for peace, friendship and trade between nations on the basis of respect for their independence and sovereignty.

*

THIS WAR INCITEMENT, evidenced in the spectacle of American children who are wearing "dog-tags," is part and parcel of the wave of war hysteria now prevalent in the country. I recently came in possession of an excellent leaflet handed to me on the streets on this issue. The leaflet, issued by Mt. Eden Women for Peace in the Bronx County of New York City, asked: "Dog Tags —What Future for Our Children?" It challenges the idea perpetrated by the Board of Education that our children will feel more secure with a "dog tag" around their necks. "Should we mothers," the leaflet asked, "feel more secure knowing that we will be able to identify a charred body or part of one? We say that there is only one real way to protect our children and that is through Peace." Urging letters of protest to Superintendent of Schools William Jansen in New York, 110 Livingston St., N. Y. C., the mothers urge that "we put our energies in avoiding death by banning atomic weapons instead of preparing for war by issuing identification tags to our already bewildered children." They call on the Board of Education to use these desperately needed funds for the growth and development of our children into healthy and upstanding citizens.

*

THE SAME CRY has come from the Great Northwest, where a group of mothers in Tacoma, Washington, calling themselves "Cold War Mothers," are circulating a petition to President Truman telling him that they need not "dog tags tags, but peace." The petition of the Tacoma mothers reads:

"Every day the papers are full of talk of using atomic weapons in Korea. Here in Tacoma we mothers are receiving forms to fill out with the necessary information for the dog tags being issued to our children.

"We ask you, Mr. President: Will dog tags save our children's lives? No! They will only make it easier for us to identify the lifeless, mutilated bodies. We don't want our children to die!

"If our leaders would get together with other countries to ban the use of atomic weapons instead of contemplating the use of them in Korea and elsewhere, our children would not need dog tags.

"As long as the war in Korea drags on and political and military leaders consider using atomic weapons and other 'fantastic' weapons, the danger of total war increases."

The fate of the peace, the stopping of all war incitement would take a qualitative leap if mothers everywhere let the officials of every state, every Board of Education, every Congressman and Representative hear from them in unanimous chorus: "The only real security for our children is peace!"

5. Cover page of the first issue of the *West Indian Gazette*, March 1958.

6. "Claudia Jones Memorial Issue" of the *West Indian Gazette and Afro-Asian-Caribbean News*, February 1965.

Chapter 3

PRISON BLUES

Literary Activism and a Poetry of Resistance

Barbed wire fence surrounds me
And the fog rolls slowly in
The elms stand tall and stately
And the maples crowd them in
CLAUDIA JONES, FROM "THE ELMS AT MORN," N.D.

Elizabeth Gurley Flynn, Claudia Jones and Betty Gannett are scheduled to be transferred to the only U.S. women's prison, at Alderson, West Virginia, Monday, according to US marshal Thomas J Lunney. They will be taken by train, arriving there Monday night, he said. The Communist national leaders have been in the city's Women's House of Detention, 10 Greenwich Ave, jail since January 11. . . . Miss Flynn faces a three-year sentence on the Smith Act conspiracy frame-up; Miss Gannett, two years, and Miss Jones, a year and a day. . . . Recent visitors to the Greenwich Ave Institution, however, reported [that] Claudia Jones, only Negro woman Smith Act defendant, had been confined in the jail's infirmary ever since she was jailed. . . . [T]hroughout her trial in 1951, she was plagued with a heart condition, and shortly after conviction entered a hospital here for a prolonged stay.
DAILY WORKER, JANUARY 21, 1955

The links between incarceration and certain forms of creativity have already been made in a variety of literary studies and histories. Barbara Harlow's *Resistance Literature* offers perhaps some of the best definitions. She identifies a range of creative acts, which, in their articulation defy an oppressive state's attempt to silence and contain political actors. In these cases, a creative individual, committed to art as to progressive social transformation, uses the space and time of incarceration to make known a set of political positions or perhaps to document the experience autobiographically, possibly to reflect on the social and personal. Often, writing becomes a way of keeping the political consciousness alive even in times of most intense state policing. Harlow identifies resistance poetry, narratives of resistance, and prison memoirs as the three primary categories of such creativity. Much of the material for her analysis comes from communities that have had what she terms epic resistance to domination: the Palestinians, the South Africans, the Algerians, "the national liberation struggles and resistance movements against Western imperialist domination of Africa, Central and South America, and the Middle and Far East" (4).

The 1998 movie *Slam*, which starred performance poet Saul Williams, develops well the context of spoken-word creativity in incarceration. In this case, the spoken-word poetic form provides the mechanism for critiquing one's social, racial, and economic conditions, as it also allows a space for creativity and connection. The film itself signaled the rise of a new generation of spoken-word activists, which has given oral literature new life in the wake of hip-hop culture's reassertion of the "word" as primary. It has allowed forms that have marked the continuity of expression of spoken-word dynamics to have new ascendance. Jamaican dub poetry and the work of the Last Poets combine with a range of voices as the spoken-word movement exploded everywhere in the 1990s.[1] June Jordan's "poetry for the people" formulation had created a similar, outward movement in the public use and creation of poetry in the 1980s and 1990s, a style in which Jordan similarly presented her own work.

The poetics of the hip-hop movement is also beginning to be documented by a new generation of scholars. Greg Thomas at Syracuse has developed readings of the erotic/poetic wordplay of popular but misread figures such as Lil' Kim within the context of "lyrical gun" formulations articulated by Carolyn Cooper.[2] Imani Perry, in *Prophets of the Hood*, also provides extensive examination of the aesthetics and politics of hip-hop poetic creativity.

Yet another category of resistance writing, dealing primarily with the work produced by women, also in resistance to a range of dominations, needs separate identification. The work of Claudia Jones fits into a range of overlapping categories, and women's creativity is certainly one of them. In the case of creative women, geopolitical contexts mark the terrain, as they do for other resistance artists, though for women other, gendered geographies must be delineated. For if some women function in a variety of locations as doubly colonized, then the resistance literature of women similarly challenges foreign domination but also the internal struggles against patriarchal domination and class oppression.

For Claudia Jones, poetry was one of the ways that she was able to articulate some of her deep emotions, to write herself sometimes out of state restrictions on her life. Audre Lorde's assertion that "poetry is not a luxury" but indeed the way that we give "form to our feelings"[3] is rightly invoked here. Lorde's assertion has already guided a succeeding generation of writers. But it is also applicable retrospectively to the way that Jones gave form to her feelings.

Prison Blues

The poetics of the blues resonates similarly and is the aesthetic in which I want to locate my discussion of Claudia Jones's creativity in poetry. Angela Davis's *Blues Legacies and Black Feminism* focuses on the work of Ma Rainey, Bessie Smith, and Billie Holiday, one of its aims being to "demonstrate that there are multiple African-American feminist traditions" (xix) "helping to forge other legacies — blues legacies, black working-class legacies — of feminism" (xx). Davis includes a fair selection of blues lyrics as an appendix and identifies the recurring theme of imprisonment in both female and male blues. Examples include "Jail House Blues," "Work House Blues," Sing Sing Prison Blues," "Send Me to the 'Lectric Chair," and "Chain Gang Blues," which most incisively and realistically address this omnipresent fact of life in the black community (given the machinations of the prison industrial complex) (102). The convict lease system and the chain gang system, we learn, did not exempt black women "by virtue of their gender" (103). Bessie Smith's "Jail House Blues," for example, includes lyrics that capture the isolation of prison even as it speaks its resistance:

> I don't mind bein' in jail, but I got to stay there so long, so long
> I don't mind bein' in jail, but I got to stay there so long, so long
> When every friend I had is done shook hands and gone. (302)

For Claudia Jones, creative output in poetic form communicated some of the political positions, journeys, and emotions that she had experienced and asserted. For under imprisonment, she wrote in the manner of the prison blues, expressing both pain and resistance. Her contributions to the form are but another expression of her poetics—a poetics that also contributes to our understandings of other legacies—blues legacies, black working-class legacies—of feminism, in the way that Angela Davis defines it above.

To speak of Jones's poetics is to refer to the entire range of her creative and intellectual assertions, in a variety of contexts and genres, but in this chapter I will focus on her interpretations, in verse, of very difficult situations. In my view, in those periods of her life in which she experienced the most intense pain or the most intense joy, poetry became the only means of succinct articulation of deep and complex positions and pain — both physical and emotional. I will include as well a few poems that honor Claudia Jones. These serve as emotional clarifications at certain points or as emotionally reciprocal counterpoints that capture in poetic form the meaning of her life and contributions in ways that she could not express herself.

For the purposes of this discussion, we can identify three types of "prison blues" literature. First, there are the works produced by the already recognized writer, incarcerated for political views, writings, and positions, who, upon and after incarceration writes poetry, political treatises, and reflective autobiography that deal with the condition of incarceration and the larger social and political issues that resulted in his/her imprisonment. Ken Saro-Wiwa[4] of Nigeria was representative of this group: a challenging creative writer and political activist voice, protesting the environmental degradation and exploitation of his community (the Ogoni people) for the benefit of huge corporate oil interests; he was put to death by the Nigerian government on charges of treason despite world outcry. Barbara Harlow, in *Resistance Literature*, also provides a discussion of a large group of such writers, all political prisoners who have produced prison memoirs across the world.[5] Another notable example is Nawal el Saadawi, incarcerated on various occasions by the Egyptian government for her political views, who continues to have to defend herself against the Egyptian state for taking critical feminist positions in a context in which women should be silent. She has written *Firdaus, or Woman at Point Zero*,[6] which organizes well the structures of incarceration, the thresholds between inside and outside, and the concentrated location and meaning of the cell within the prison complex. The story of her fictional character Firdaus is told, from within the death row prison cell, by a woman on the verge of being executed for killing a man who exploited her. The rest of the novel shows how society at large also functions as a prison for this young woman, curtailing her ability to be fully in the world at every point of her life. In the end, prison becomes a kind of liberated, creative space for Firdaus.

A second category of prison writing is the autobiographical writing of the political activist who uses the space of incarceration and the time of detention to reflect on the conditions of being incarcerated, the political conditions of the state, and the nature of the human condition and his/her life up to that point. Examples are political activists who, like Jomo Kenyatta, Assata Shakur, Nelson Mandela, Winnie Mandela, George Jackson, Angela Davis, Kwame Nkrumah, and Domitila Barios de Chungara, document an oppressive state's actions and their will to resist it and to simultaneously initiate new frameworks.[7]

A third identifiable category of prison writing (since oral production is understood here as oral literature) is unquestionably the creative individual (blues singer, hip-hop artist, spoken-word poet), also imprisoned by the state for crimes that have to do with living and surviving in oppressed communities, who upon incarceration reflects in lyric form on the condition of imprisonment and the nature of his/her community's condition. A range of blues singers communicate in this "prison house blues" genre. Spoken-word poets and lyrical artists such as Tupac Shakur[8] also contribute to the articulation of this particular mode of creativity.

It is interesting to note that Billie Holiday did time in Alderson Prison just before Claudia Jones was sent there. While there, she also demonstrated her own resistance to institutional mandates. Elizabeth Gurley Flynn, in *The Alderson Story*,[9] reports as follows:

> The most famous addict prisoner, who had been there before we came, was Billie Holiday, a Negro woman, who was one of the greatest blues singers. She served a year and a day in Alderson on a narcotics charge. While there she endeared herself to the inmates by refusing to sing for a party of guests at the Warden's residence, saying under her contract she was not allowed to sing free. But she could sing for charity, so she offered to sing for the inmates which was refused. (166)

Claudia Jones is an important addition to the long list of political prisoners in the second category of writers, and thus to any consideration of such intellectual and creative production. As an activist-intellectual, she also fits the definition of "imprisoned intellectuals" articulated by Joy James: "public intellectuals" who are denied freedom because of political activism (*Imprisoned Intellectuals*, 3). Jones also attained a symbolic role as a black female heroic figure in prison, having a stature among black inmates in the same category as Billie Holiday. Says Flynn: "Claudia Jones was greatly respected by all the Negro inmates. They were proud of her achievements, her talent and her bold independent spirit, as they had been proud of Billie Holiday" (*Alderson Story*, 178). We see examples of Jones using her influence to educate young women about the politics of sexuality/race intersections in American history; the workings of these politics affected all prison women, including of course black women, who were at a disadvantage in prison reproductions of the exploitation of women by men.

Joy James's important documentation of voices of political prisoners in the United States in *Imprisoned Intellectuals* must be recognized here.[10] In her preface, she identifies the distinction between writing about prisoners and writing by prisoners as the fundamental impetus for her collection of their writings. Significantly too, she delineates the voices of "progressive political prisoners" as intellectual voices in the Gramscian sense,[11] referring to the ways in which their creativity is expressed through critiques of state-generated oppressive systems. Claudia Jones is listed here along with C. L. R. James, Emma Goldman, and Marcus Garvey, but none of her writing is included in Joy James's collection, though she is identified in James's preliminary discussions of the construction of a new category of "political prisoner awaiting deportation" (12).[12]

The following discussion brings to the fore the creativity of Claudia Jones, sometimes reflective, sometimes speculative, sometimes narrative, always lyrical. I am using the blues metaphor for obvious reasons, since blues is associated with a certain creative resistance in spite of pain, and thereby becomes one of the ways by which one's humanity is asserted in conditions that seek to deny or negate that humanity. What I refer to as Claudia's "prison blues" in this chapter then has an aesthetic affinity with that genre of the blues which deals with incarceration, also called prison blues, a concentrated reflection on the nature of the human condition put under stress, contained by powers larger than itself.

A letter written by Claudia Jones while she was in Ellis Island in 1950 sums up well the intent of her creativity under incarceration. Written to John Gates, editor of the *Daily Worker*, the entire text is worth quoting here, as it is captures well the emotions surrounding her incarceration, as it does her awareness of the reality of "political imprisonment."

> Ellis Island
> Saturday afternoon
>
> Dear Johnny,
> In thinking about the collusion of the "free press" with the ruling circles' attack on American democratic liberties, I decided to write to you. Of course, if I attempt to write descriptively, it will only be because, while I know you (and I) hold brevity to be the soul of wit, description should not be the second-class citizen so here goes my letter:
> Homing pigeons gather aimlessly in the large yard on an island which lies in New York's great harbor. Occasionally a pigeon flies in from the bay dotted with white caps and the pigeons scatter.
> They either gather in a solid mass and noiselessly fly away together, or, with loud grace, flap their wings and soar away. . . . One flapped his wings 31 times before he ascended to fly over the massed brownstone buildings with numerous windows.
> If one looks closely, it is obvious this is not just a haunt of homing pigeons or seagulls. The windows on all buildings are all wired with criss-cross light iron bars. Others are heavier. . . . Around the huge yard, barbed-wire way beyond the height of a man, towers and outdoor lights, as on a baseball diamond, are spaced with regular frequency. . . .
> Look even closer. . . . Men in shirtsleeves or rough lumber jackets peer out from occasional windows on the right end of the yard, looking out on the bay, where now and then, on this foggy, rain-swept day, foghorns cry their warnings to occasional vessels. . . . Some of the ships are more beautiful than others. There are tugs and passenger ships. . . . Coastguard cutters and barges are anchored to the pier on the left of the island, which barely commands our view.
> It is not too foggy to see the towering skyscrapers which beckon beyond the bay, on the other shore, on the mainland.

One cannot imagine the mainland without its wealth of men, women and children of many lands, who for centuries — and likewise today — toiled in mine, mill and factory and the endless plain — all the stretch of these great green states to make America.

From this view, another famous island, that so many ships and their passengers from five continents have eagerly nodded to, throughout the last 300 centuries, cannot be seen. Bedloe's Island, home of the Statue of Liberty, gift of the descendants of Joan of Arc, lies on the left of this shore. . . . And well it does — for this woman, with liberty's torch, still stands proudly aloft her earthy home. . . . And literally stands with her back to Ellis Island.

Here, on Ellis Island, it would not be well for her shadow to grace the newly established wing of the Attorney General of the U.S. — or as the 17 imprisoned inmates of this wing call it — "the McCarran Wing." In this wing, are 17 men and women — a virtual United Nations in composition. Oh yes, and the guards — one woman guard and two men guards.[13]

The letter, poetic in its own right, offers a detailed view of the place of imprisonment, Ellis Island, paradoxically, the entry point into "freedom" in the United States. So the images of freedom are deliberate — birds able to fly; homing pigeons at times captive, at times free. The birds and flight contradict starkly with the images of captivity. For the subsequent images are of window bars crisscrossing and thereby imprisoning the buildings' inhabitants. Another juxtaposition that Jones makes in order to emphasize the contradictions in the delivery of U.S. freedom is the projection of the image of the Statue of Liberty against the prison. The statue is of course itself symbolic of freedom — a gift from the people of France, "the descendants of Joan of Arc," a woman also persecuted for political positions; in Claudia's account, she is deliberately set "with her back to Ellis Island." What is behind this statue and its representation of freedom carries additional significance — the "McCarran Wing" (so called because the prisoners housed there were imprisoned under the McCarran Act) contained numerous political prisoners of international composition, who were therefore, in her words, a "virtual United Nations." But more important to Jones are the communists; of the seventeen arrested and tried, thirteen had been sentenced and were now political prisoners of the United States because of their ideological commitment to communism. A third image of freedom that Jones invokes is that of the ships at a distance, able to come and go, different types of sea vessels with a variety of functions. Her description is reminiscent of Frederick Douglass's *Narrative*, in which he describes his recognition of freedom in the free movement of ships and birds. These contrast well with images of barbed wire and iron bars and of men peering out behind these, unable to be free, as those ships and birds outside are free.

Typical of Claudia Jones's rhetorical style is the opening jab at the nature of the U.S. press and its inability to be fully free in its reportage. Thus, her letter written for the *Daily Worker*, with its decisively left/liberal readership, becomes the only place where voices like hers can have full public recognition. But she also takes the space to weave into her narrative commentary on capitalist America's urban and rural landscape and the contrasts between its beauty and its oppression of its working poor, toiling in "mine, mill and factory and endless pain." These for her are the "wealth of the mainland."

Doing Time in Alderson

The infamous Alderson Federal Prison for women in West Virginia would be home to a number of resisting women over the years. Like the "McCarran Wing" of Ellis Island, Alderson became a place at which a number of politically active women would be incarcerated at the same time. And Claudia Jones would be one of that prison's most illustrious prisoners, spending the most sustained portion of her imprisonment as a political prisoner in the United States there. Sentenced to a year and a day, Claudia Jones faced tremendous difficulty in prison because of ill health — as reported in the newspaper article quoted in the epigraph to this chapter; she was eventually released early on those grounds. Elizabeth Gurley Flynn reports that Claudia "had developed a painful condition in her feet in September and spent 25 days in the hospital. Whether the ailment was due to working loom with her feet or the cement floors in the craft shop or both, the doctors could not determine" (*Alderson Story*, 116–117).

Claudia Jones left no account of her stay in Alderson, but Flynn's *The Alderson Story* documents some of the conditions at this prison farm:

> Betty, Claudia and I were now en-route to a federal prison. It ended one ordeal of four years and commenced another. . . . The Federal Reformatory for Women is located in a remote southeastern corner of West Virginia, in a mountainous region. We three women went from New York in

two Pullman compartments, made into one. We were accompanied by a man and woman, federal marshals. They occupied the upper and lower berths on one side, while I occupied the lower and Betty Garnett and Claudia Jones were crowded into the upper on the other side. (22–23)

Flynn describes their arrival at Alderson and the imposed solitary confinement. It was only after her release that she learned that Claudia had been sent to the hospital on the day of their arrival, suffering from "cardiac asthma and had been in the hospital several times in New York. This had probably influenced Judge Dimock to give her a one-year sentence in contrast to Betty's two years and my three" (30). Flynn provides extensive details about the geography of Alderson, the racial conditions there, and the daily experiences of a political prisoner in that type of prison facility.

With reference to Claudia again, she provides details of some of their initial experiences there: "Claudia Jones had been delayed by hospitalization and remained in orientation. Later, she was assigned to a segregated 'colored cottage' and to work in the craft shop, which was then in the basement of the Auditorium Building" (43). Jones technically integrates Alderson at this point. Flynn described the joy she felt when she learned that Claudia Jones would be moved closer to her, even though that meant that she would now be in a maximum-security unit. This moment of integration is described this way: "But the silver lining to my cloud was that Claudia Jones was now moved from a segregated cottage to 26 . . . assigned to a vacant room two doors from me" (77).

> I can never forget my joy at seeing her in the doorway, with friends helping carry her things. It changed my life in prison for that period. She worked days in the craft shop weaving. She made over 30 beautiful colored tablecloths for the staff dining room. She became interested in all the crafts taught there — ceramics, pottery, metal jewelry, wood carving, and leather work. Miss Helen Smithson, in charge of the craft shop, refused to be classified as a custodial officer and was officially designated as an occupational therapist and teacher. She told me later that Claudia was the most talented pupil she ever had. It was remarkable, since Claudia had never done any of those things before. (77)

That Claudia was brilliant and creative is noticed by the teacher and even by Flynn, but it is clear from Flynn herself that Claudia was determined to make the best out of even this very difficult situation: "She even set up a loom in her room and wove a centerpiece and matching place mats of white and gold, which won a prize at the local county fair. . . . Claudia taught several girls in our cottage to model in clay and another to play the piano" (78).

An entire chapter of *The Alderson Story* is devoted to Jones's departure, and it is here that we learn of her concern about maximum-security incarceration.

> As the time approached [for her departure in October 1955], she became increasingly concerned about leaving me in Cottage 26. . . . She knew from experience that life was easier elsewhere. . . . Claudia was very indignant that I had been kept in maximum security for so long. . . . [On leaving] Claudia gave each cottage inmate a gift which she had made — a ring, pin, ashtray, and the like. They tearfully bade her farewell at lock-up time. In the early dawn, the officer who came to dress her . . . opened my door for a hurried "Goodbye." My window faced the roadway, and I was able to see her leave. She turned to wave — tall, slender, beautiful, dressed in golden brown, and then she was gone. (115–116, 117–118)

Jones herself refers only briefly to the Alderson portion of her life in her autobiographical reflections to William Foster. She reduces the experience to skill development: "January 11, 1955 entered prison serving a year and a day sentence at the Federal reformatory at Alderson W. Va. Got 72 days off, serving 9 months and 18 days for so called 'good behavior' . . . won First Prize Blue Ribbon at August State Fair of W.A. for women skills learned there."[14]

The Poetic Output of Claudia Jones

It is not surprising that Claudia Jones wrote poetry in prison. For Claudia, all writing was directed at revelation. Hers was a poetry written by an activist who uses the space of incarceration and the time of detention to reflect on the conditions of being incarcerated itself, the political conditions of the state, and on the nature of the human condition.

Imprisoned four times for her political activism, Jones responded to her condition each time with poetry. Her collected papers, and the newspapers I have been able to examine, yield fifteen poems, but we can safely assume that there are more awaiting recovery. A sizable portion of this poetry was produced during Jones's stay at Alderson. Elizabeth Gurley Flynn writes that Jones prepared for her departure by memorizing the poems that she had created and destroying the papers on which they were written, saving out one she had written to Elizabeth. On the way to New York by train, Jones wrote down the memorized poems while they were still fresh in her mind.[15] "Claudia had written a number of poems, but she doubted if the prison authorities would clear them and return them to her. So, she memorized every one of them and recited them all to me, while I checked her text. Then she destroyed all but one, addressed to me, which she gave me. She was letter perfect, and Mrs. Kaufman told me Claudia wrote them all out again on the train, en-route home. Several were subsequently published."[16]

The context of Claudia Jones's poetry is thus one of maintaining the beauty of creativity in the face of oppression. Incarceration in Alderson was clearly a low point in the life of Claudia Jones, but her poetry reveals, as do the reports of her activities there, that she was determined to make the best of her situation, to learn from it, and not let it defeat her. This determination reveals itself in her successful creation in other art media: sculpture, weaving, music, and letter writing. Her poetry reflects on several themes: solidarity with other activist women, the meaning of the Atlantic, human existence, political commitment, and exile and placelessness.

Solidarity with Other Activist Women

A political solidarity with other activist women communicates Claudia Jones's own anti-imperialist feminism, as I noted earlier. Claudia was very purposeful about which women she wrote about in verse, and the poems were few but very significant. The most striking among these is one dedicated to the Puerto Rican activist Blanca Canales Torresola, who served a four-year sentence in Alderson. I will quote the entire poem here as it provides, in verse form, many of the ideas I see operating in Jones's essays on imperialism:

"FOR CONSUELA — ANTI-FASCISTA"
It seems I knew you long before our common ties — of conscious choice
Threw under single skies, those like us
Who, fused by our mold
Became their targets, as of old

I knew you in Jarama's hills
Through men and women drilled
In majesty, whose dignity
Rejected shirts and skirts of dimity.

I heard you in Guernica's songs
Proud melodies that burst from tongues
As yet unknown to me — full thronged
With Liberty.

Anti . . . Anti-Fascistas!
That was your name
I sang your fame
Long fore my witness of your bane of pain

I saw you in the passion-flower
In roses full of flame
Pure valley lily, whose bower
Marks resemblance to your name.

Oh wondrous Spanish sister
Long-locked from all your care
Listen — while I tell you what you strain to hear
And beckon all from far and near.

We swear that we will never rest
Until they hear not plea
But sainted sacrifice to set
A small proud nation free

O anti-fascist sister — you whose eye turn to stars still
I've learned your wondrous secret — source of spirit and of will
I've learned that what sustains your heart — mind and peace of soul
Is knowledge that their justice — can never reach its goal.[17]

Though there is no independent confirmation of the fact, from internal evidence it seems indisputable that "For Consuela — Anti-Fascista" was written from Alderson. Certainly, it is Jones's clearest statement in poetic form of the link between feminist and anti-imperialist politics.

This poem makes one of the first substantive points I have noted in Jones's anti-imperialist feminism, which was that it was truly international in nature. Jones was able to make decided links because of her anti-imperialist position vis-à-vis other women struggling for liberation. Jones's own personal autobiography is implicated in this poem, in her transnational approach and her links with another Caribbean woman revolutionary. This sense of Caribbean identity and migratory subjectivity had been developed in her formative years in the United States, This early experience would clearly inform the way she understood the world and is clearly evident in the way the poem evolves.

The chapter "The Politicals in Alderson" in Flynn's autobiography provides an extensive account of encounters with the female Puerto Rican political prisoners, including Lolita Lebrun, who were all imprisoned in Alderson at the same time she and Jones were there. Flynn had encountered what she described as a "stout little white-haired woman, who spoke with a Spanish accent. She smiled and smiled at me with such cordiality that I felt she must be someone special. When I described her to Claudia she said: 'That's Blanca, one of the Puerto Rican nationalists.' I had often heard Claudia speak of this woman, whose beautiful face resembled Dolores Ibarruri of Spain, known as La Pasionaria" (*Alderson Story*, 140).[18]

Blanca Canales Torresola had headed the 1950 uprising in the mountains of Puerto Rico in the country's struggle for independence from the United States. She was significant to the uprising for her leadership role, particularly as a woman. Additionally, it was she who proclaimed "la republica de Puerto Rico in Jayuya" during the nationalist insurrection in 1950. Referring to her in the poem's title as "Consuela," seems to be, perhaps, a way to conceal at that time the identity of the person for whom she was writing, as her real name is given in the note that Jones added later. "Consuela" means "counsel" or "advisor" in Spanish, but also "comfort." In the fifth stanza, Jones links her name to the passionflower and to the lily of the valley.[19]

"For Consuela — Anti Fascista" recognizes the power of women in leadership positions in the political struggle for radical social change, a theme that runs through other work by Jones. One could perhaps find no finer embodiment of Jones's sense of female leadership, militancy, and revolutionary fervor than Blanca Canales Torresola. Jones identifies herself with "Consuela" as an identity of "conscious choice" and says that she had basically already known Consuela intuitively and politically before they were thrown "under single skies." The poem further indicates that Jones wants this information to be known and that she and others with her vision saw the liberation of Puerto Rico as a laudable political goal. There is also an identification that is fully Caribbean (beyond language and colonial boundaries) in nature, as it presents "Consuela" as kin — in Jones's words, "Spanish [i.e., Spanish-speaking] sister," Caribbean sister. Another point they have in common is their joint desire for an independent Puerto Rico, a link to the self-determination of other Third World peoples against colonizations of various sorts. Thus, a politics of decolonization similarly appears.

Another poem significantly related to "For Consuela — Anti-Fascista" is the one dedicated to Elizabeth Gurley Flynn, which Jones wrote as she left prison in Alderson in what was to become her last known personal encounter with Flynn, since she was headed toward deportation and Flynn would stay in prison almost two years longer. It resonates with the permanence of Flynn's impact and their friendship. Jones and Flynn had worked together over the preceding years, organizing women across the United States in the Women's Commission. They had gone through the trial of the communists together and were sentenced together to Alderson as two women in a group made up largely of men. They had been incarcerated together both at the women's prison in New York and at Alderson. Rosalyn Fraad Baxandall speaks about their relationship in *Words on Fire*:

> In Alderson, [Flynn's] only companion was Claudia Jones, a black Smith Act victim. Given the tradition of segregation — the prisons had just been integrated — their companionship made an important political state-ment to the Alderson population as well as providing Flynn with a close friend. When Jones's sentence expired eighteen months prior to Flynn's, the latter was left without anyone who shared her past or who cared about what she read or heard from outside. This little poem marked her despondency:

> The longer you are gone, my dearest friend,
> The harder are the lonely days to bear,
> Eight months have passed — and you so far away;
> I have no one my thoughts and dreams to share,
> I long to see your warm and pleasant smile,
> To hear your words of comradeship to me
> As your swift hands flew at the loom, the while.

> Your days are marred by sorrow at my fate,
> My days are solitary and they harder grow,
> But we can hope — the dawn is never late,
> And we will meet again, dear friend I know.[20] (*Words on Fire*, 63).

Flynn spent a total of twenty-eight months in prison, most of them after Jones's release. Jones's own poem to Flynn is understated and dwells more on the consistency of memory in preserving friendship. The poem, given to Flynn as she left prison, reveals her own sadness at the situation, even as it carries the hope for a better future. It begins "I think I'll see you everywhere" and continues to identify links between various times of day when nature reveals itself: "At morn—when sunlight's radiance bathes all things like verse." This is followed by the identification with new birth:

I'll see you in young shooting sprouts
That sneer at weeds—age-gnarled in doubt
Of users who defile in epithet
A life well-lived in service built from strife.

The identifications of Flynn with the sun at its height at noon is the deliberate center of the poem, linking the sun's healing of hurts as also ushering in renewal of courage. The third identification of her memory of Flynn with twilight as with night completes the poem's temporal linkages. The closing stanzas repeat the poem's theme:

I'll think of you forever
And how your spirit rings
Because your faith leaps as a flame
Sweet nurture to all things.

Finally, she identifies a constant communication with each other that they will share:

Of all the times I'll miss you most
Is when I'm least aware
Because you will intrude I know
Upon my inner ear
Beloved comrade—when from you I tear
My mind, my heart, my thoughts you'll hear!

Claudia would be deported within three months of giving the poem to Flynn, and Flynn, still imprisoned, would not have additional contact with her. Ironically, they would die within months of each other in 1964, Flynn dying a few months before Jones.[21] The intent of the government's actions, we already know now, was to destroy the communication links within the Communist Party and to deliberately separate its organizers in the hope that this would then destroy the party's organizing network. Claudia's deliberate ending, with its promise of a possibility of communication, in a way, challenges instinctively that intent. She suggests a more interior communication between them, just as she did to Blanca Canales Torresola in "For Consuela," in saying that she had somehow known of her Puerto-Rican counterpart's activism even before they had met.

Several months before she wrote the poem "A Friend (To Claudia, June, 1956)," at the time Claudia was released from Alderson, Flynn had written "Farewell to Claudia" (October 24, 1955). The poem captures well the infectious optimism that Claudia obviously had communicated to Flynn. More important, it suggests that Claudia was too big in spirit to be contained by Alderson: "Sometimes I feel you've never been in Alderson," writes Flynn. Flynn links Jones to sun, to radiance, to joy, to active movement and describes a distinct pride that Claudia carried at so many levels.

Nearer and nearer drew this day, dear comrade,
When I from you sadly part,
Day after day, a dark foreboding sorrow,
Crept through my anxious heart.

No more to see you striding down the pathway,
No more to see your smiling eyes and radiant face.
No more to hear your gay and pealing laughter,
No more encircled by your love, in this sad place.

How I will miss you, words will fail to utter,
I am alone, my thoughts unshared, these weary days,
I feel bereft and empty, on this gray and dreary morning,
Facing my lonely future, hemmed by prison ways.

Sometimes I feel you've never been in Alderson,
So full of life, so detached from here you seem,
So proud of walk, of talk, of work, of being,
Your presence here is like a fading fevered dream.

Yet as the sun shines now, through fog and darkness.
I feel a sudden joy that you are gone,

That once again you walk the streets of Harlem,
That today for you at least is Freedom's dawn.

I will be strong in our common faith, dear comrade,
I will be self-sufficient, to our ideals firm and true,
I will be strong to keep my mind and soul outside a prison,
Encouraged and inspired by ever loving memories of you.[22]

Flynn captures an aspect that marked Claudia Jones, and that I define as "beyond containment," in the line "Sometimes I feel you've never been in Alderson." She sees herself at first as unable to match Jones's optimism and vitality. Her despondency is clear at this point, feeling the effects of incarceration, and clearly manifesting her own "prison blues." But she feels encouraged and happy for Jones, who was then reclaiming her freedom.

Claudia Jones's optimism, in my view, came from her confidence in her political position and the history of black people — of black women in particular — surviving with dignity the various societal abuses visted on them, but it came also from her always open possibility of living "elsewhere." For her part, Claudia Jones felt a similar respect for Flynn. Besides her poem to Flynn, she wrote also a newspaper piece entitled "Her Words Rang Out beyond the Walls of the Courthouse," in which Claudia had written about Flynn's heroic stance there, which Claudia would later herself emulate. It begins: "With head erect, she stood magnificent at the left end of the counsel table in the packed courtroom at Foley Square. It was our beloved Elizabeth Gurley Flynn addressing the court in her own behalf of the sacred working class principle that 'an injury to one is an injury to all.'"

Jones offers an analysis of Flynn's speech to the court and ends with "It was a day for our history books. It was a day that will live, made memorable by the words and actions of a proud woman, a communist leader defending the traditions of her Irish ancestors, of the working class, the Negro people and all who cherish peace, democracy, brotherhood." Claudia Jones clearly saw Flynn as a communist sister of great stature, and their friendship was consistent and solid: "One could not be objective — and I speak as a co-defendant, comrade and co-worker with Elizabeth Gurley Flynn — as one sat in the courtroom. Deep pride in the courage, self-sacrifice and dignity of this towering working-class leader filled one's breast."

Therefore, her poem to Flynn as she leaves prison comes from strong connections, a personal history of shared struggle and mutual respect and admiration. Jones's memory of Flynn, which she evokes in the words "I think I'll see you everywhere" then is not just of the person, Elizabeth Gurley Flynn, but—as in the Blanca Torresola poem—all that Flynn represented: sisterhood, pride activism, organizing, dignity, political commitment born of Flynn's "40 year fight for the welfare of her people, of labor, of her country" ("Her Words Rang Out," 3). It is significant, too, that Flynn also was offered deportation. According to Baxandall, Flynn engaged in a good-humored rep- artee with Judge Dimock, who had at one point made her the unprecedented offer that it could be arranged for her to spend the rest of her life in Russia as a substitute for prison if she would be interested. Flynn, at age sixty-two, of course rejected the assumption implicit in the judge's question, that America did not offer ideological plurality. "I am an American. I want to live and work in the United States of America. I am not interested in going any place else and would reject that proposition" (*Words on Fire*, 60). Claudia Jones, of course, did not have the option to stay in the United States.

Claudia Jones wrote another poem, "To a Dear Friend on Her Birthday," written, according to a note, at the request of "FSS" (whom I have not yet identified). It is a less intense poem about communication and deals more with the "ties" that bind them, of the "thoughts, the plans in life we dare / To share." It is a more pessimistic poem, linking nature and close attachment with pain:

Under a shroud of rain
To remind us that sometimes pain
Is consequence of ties held all too close
In heart — or — mind — or brain.

Jones on the Atlantic

A piece written to her father, titled "Ship's Log: Paean to the Atlantic," written aboard the *Queen Elizabeth*, at 10:45 p.m. (ship time) on December 10, 1955, speaks to Jones's positions on her exile from the United States. In the text preceding an accompanying poem, she refers to her condition as "my exile for my independent political ideas" and speaks with fondness of the "land I belong to and know and its people with whom I have worked and struggled for social progress." Jones, however, shows her adeptness at trans- forming pain into a more positive emotion: she soon turns the "ship of exile" into something more like a cruise liner, which would carry her to "marvelous places" that would beckon and excite her. That she called the piece a "paean" is important, for "paean" means a song of praise, joy, or triumph; a religious or festive hymn of invocation. Thus, in this move, at the level of language, she effects a reconception of her experience and thereby shifts the pain of deportation into the possibilities of diaspora.

Claudia describes her first "transatlantic crossing" as occurring on a "magnificent ship" and details the elaborate cuisine of "English lamb roast, mint juice or sauce, iced pineapple, salad, a fat baked potato, vanilla ice cream." What I have also found in this text, though, is that through it she communicates her ongoing optimism and her willingness to take on the space of the unknown in a transformative way, to consistently make something out of nothing, as has been done by many black women before her and after her.

First, there is her awe of the Atlantic Ocean itself and what it means in terms of its natural beauty, an awe of nature, the Atlantic's vastness and power. Second, there is its meaning as a conduit full of "rising promise of international visits, exchange and cultures for the world's people." The Atlantic in this second formulation is not a racially coded Atlantic but an Atlantic that challenges national limitations — an Atlantic that was also the major path of the development of a global capitalistic network, and also an Atlantic that serves as a possible "bridge," a path to new modes of being. Third, there is a clear reversal of the direction of migration and thus the "coming to America and freedom" narrative. Her trial, imprisonment, and deportation from the United States, for her ideas and political affiliation, had already spoken powerfully to her of the contradictions embedded in this "land of the free" mythology. Fourth, her "Atlantic" includes sadness at separation from her family and her friends. She speaks of "memories crowding (as they will continue I know) on me. Long after more than 50 of my closest colleagues and friends/neighbors, Negro and white, and their children, my father, my sister and others left, the room was full of their presence." Fifth — and more important to the theme of this chapter — Jones turns her exile via the Atlantic into an opportunity for new connections. "Tomorrow — the first morning of my exile," she writes, and ends with a rhetorical question from one of her telegrams, which said, "What is an ocean between us, we know how to build bridges."

The poem that is included in "Ship's Log" is titled "Paean to the Atlantic." It is almost a meditation, undoing the narrow meaning of exile as it prepares her for the new life ahead:

To watch your ceaseless motion
Your foam and tideful billows view
Is but to glean your beauty
Of immemorial hue

Oh, restless wide Atlantic
Path of nations old and new
Asylum path of peoples
Bound to social progress true

I stand awe-struck before you
As swiftly league on league
You cradle us to lands — accrue
Of mankind's search for freedom's clue

To understand your motion
Is to reason why like you
Millions move towards ascension
Nurtured by your ancient dew.[23]

For Claudia Jones, as she departed the United States — the place she had emigrated to with her family as a little girl of eight, where she came of age, her home for thirty-two years, the place of her educational and political formation — for an unknown future, the Atlantic is revealed as the contradictory route of exile/route of asylum, a path for progress as it is a path for separation: "Path of nations old and new / Asylum path of peoples / Bound to social progress true." The Atlantic is, among other things, a vast space of possibility that has served as a conduit of numerous peoples, of all types, in both directions. Claudia is able to locate herself in her own "transatlantic" crossing as just *one* of them. There is no heavy and deliberate consciousness of the Middle Passage in this formulation of the Atlantic, even though clearly it would have been embedded at the level of African diaspora or "race memory." Here instead is a black, activist woman on a transatlantic ship bound toward organizing at a different locale, ready to hit the ground running, and knowing that comrades were going to be meeting her upon her arrival.[24] For this exile, home is not so much a final location but as Michael Echeruo has described it, the place to which one is able to identify some traceable descent.[25] The commitment to return always remains a possibility, which marks the difference between the exile, properly speaking, and the mere wanderer or the purposeful recreator of herself. In Claudia Jones's piece about the Atlantic, the implications of deportation and exile are deliberately linked to the creation of diaspora, and then connected to a creativity that is a direct response to state repression. The so-called immigrant figure is targeted by a series of Immigration and Naturalisation Acts, which work only unidirectionally. In my analysis, Claudia Jones's life work is one of a number of missing gendered black Atlantic texts, missing in Gilroy's "Black Atlantic" formulation, being one who figures not in terms of his "crisscrossing" model but in a crossing as a deliberate relocation and self-creation in activism.

According to Alrick Cambridge,[26] Claudia's political orientation and education had prepared her for the fact that if you are a militant, there are different sites of struggle, and that if you define yourself as a world revolutionary, then circumstances may determine that you may be located at a different geographical site. A new geographical location then is not punishment but rather a different strategic location. So, in one way hers is a "Black Atlantic" in the sense that Paul Gilroy means it, among those who crossed the Atlantic, "not only as commodities but engaged in various struggles towards emancipation, autonomy and citizenship" (*Black Atlantic*, 16). But hers is a "Black Atlantic" and more. Claudia in this context allows herself to be caught up in the awesomeness of the Atlantic to manage her own distress at separation and her pain at being deported. Her own sufferings, then, become but one aspect of some larger and grander set of historical actions, beyond the specific realities of black existences.

Harry Goulbourne asserts, within the context of an examination of black transnationalism, "For Caribbeans, particularly those of African backgrounds, the central problem is likely to be a continuing one: how to effect equality in access to, participation in the enjoyment of available material resources."[27] This would be a concern of Claudia Jones, who uses the Atlantic crossing in the geopolitical sense now, for a deliberate and purposeful migration and for a specific set of reasons as identified by the various communities (United States and United Kingdom) with which she worked.[28]

Lessons from Nature

Claudia's poetry uses nature effectively to communicate meaning and address life conditions. Her poems "Elms at Morn" and "Storm at Sea" were written during periods of isolation and pain: the first while imprisoned at Ellis Island, the second while she was hospitalized in Yalta in 1962. "Elms at Morn" accompanied the letter to John Gates, editor of the *Daily Worker*, quoted above (November 8, 1950). The poem identifies the harsh reality of her confinement. It begins with a stark, concentration camp image: man-made negativity contrasted with nature:

> Barbed wire fence surrounds me
> And the fog rolls slowly in
> The elms stand tall and stately
> And the maples crowd them in.

Here fog accompanies the barbed wire image and the stately elms remain imperious, seemingly untouched by what surrounds them and also by what "crowds them in." The image in the next stanza is of the work that accompanies imprisonment and the women who are near to her:

> The mops are on the porch my dear
> And Frances sits beside me
> Lois smokes a cigarette
> I am in an awful net.

The last line of the poem repeats the incarceration of the first, and implies a likeness to a captive butterfly or fish, perhaps. Though the "net" is a less brutal image than "barbed wire," the effect of containment is the same.

"Morning Mists" is more hopeful. It begins:

> Deep in my heart I know beyond the mists
> Lies Morning — that full blown with morn
> Will waken free from list of rest
> That comes with dawn.

Jones sees the cycle of the rolling in and receding of mists as paralleling the nature of human existence. Still, instinctively, the mind rebels against incarceration, as she sees a future beyond the prison and its constriction of her body, though not her mind.

> While this I know, my heart rebels
> At screens that shut off sunlight's beams
> My thoughts rise too like tinkling bells
> To welcome shafts of light in seams.

Ere as I write bright rays peep through
Their fiercer power pierce this dew
Strength born of atoms held at bay
Simulation of men's will to cast all doubt away.

These last two stanzas of the poem capture the resolve that obviously sustained her in prison. Sunlight always pierces through the fog, and nature provides the answer she needs about the human condition and its role in nature. There is a power in nature, as in the storm, as also in the sun, and it can conquer adversity.

"Storm at Sea" marvels at the delightful fearfulness and power of nature in this manifestation. Like the "Paean to the Atlantic," it captures the movement of a body of water:

Today I saw a storm at sea,
A choppy fearful sight,
T'was if it were besides itself
And running from some fright.

The poem ends

Today I saw a storm at sea
Its bilious white and black
It spent its forces as if it knew
The power of its back. (October 8, 1962, Yalta, Crimea)

Two other poems complete this group. "Radiant Season" deals with the meaning of autumn — its beauty linked to pain and change, the transience of human existence. Although fall is beautiful as a season, it is only temporary. It is as though nature shows its best in order to foreshadow the impending betrayal:

How fickle is your radiance
Unseemly this bright dalliance
Your tang is false, your garb's untrue
Smile of your beauty's full of rue.

But Jones's instinct is to return to the theme that nature can teach us lessons. For fall is linked to maturity, knowledge, a leaning toward the natural cycles of life:

And yet this much I've learned from you
Though costly is my pastime new
That riches lie in store for those
Who gaze on changeling, transient pose

For your's the time that bids all things
Retire unto winter's wings
You Autumn — known as radiant season
Is really knowledge come to reason.

In general, the poems in this group deal with human existence, and are born of reflection on nature but always illuminated by a consistent political commitment. "Radiant Season" seems to be written as a mature response to her life, and in a way foreshadows Jones's sense of her life as transient. Another poem in this reflective vein is "There Are Some Things I Always Remember." What Jones identifies in this poem is a sequence that begins with "the hurts," "the cruelty of cruelness, the harshness of reality." But she raises them to dismiss them, suggesting that as one remembers them they should also be forgotten: "Staunch the hurt, mend the rip of heartbreak." It reminds one of the sentiment of Angelina Grimke's "Letter to My Sister"[29] but — significantly — does not go as far as Grimke to suggest silencing oneself.

An assertive response to dealing with the insurmountable through sheer force of personal will is revealed. Still, memory betrays as one "remembers till it hurts remembering too . . . / the plans, the buds of / forgotten dreams." There is a memory of youth there and of the dreams one conjures up for the future that seem to be betrayed by "the fleetness of summer and / the suddenness of autumn." Aging and memory come together in this poem. Claudia was conscious that she was entering her mid-life. Although she would die before her fiftieth birthday, it was a life rich with activity that she lived. She accomplished much that she intended, but there is also in this poem the sense that she knew she would never be able to achieve *all* that she had intended. Nature teaches again, but it is a painful lesson, and though she does not seem to want the hurt and the pain, in a personal and political sense, to dominate, they seem to do so in this poem.

Politics and Revolution

More energetic poems, full of explicit resistance, are relatively few in number in the small collection that comes down to us. "Lament for Emmet Till" is a bold poem that begins with the exhortation "Cry lynch-murder!"[30] The stanza ends with "Raise fists — in more than anger bands!" It has the same energy of resistance as Claude McKay's classic poem "If We Must Die."[31] Jones wants her readers to resist lynching and racial oppression, to organize and resist and not be passive victims of racist terrorism.

> People, people, you who swore
> Vengeance for this brutal hour
> Make your unity soar above strife
> To swiftly avenge Young Emmet Till's life.

She identifies this vengeance as coming from the people themselves — "you who swore / Vengeance for this brutal hour." So it is less an assumption of any direct confrontation than a call for a unifying movement that would deter the kind of racist terrorism that Till's murder represented. The issues of Jim Crow racial segregation had haunted Claudia's life in the United States and was one of the sources of her great pain and disappointment with the United States: its rank injustice and seeming inability (up to the 1960s and the civil rights and black power movements) to change. Ironically, Claudia would die before seeing the emergence of the youth movement of the Student Non-violent Coordinating Committee, which she would have supported and nurtured, as Ella Baker did. The Black Panther Party and the existence of young Trinidadian and African American activists like Stokeley Carmichael (Kwame Ture) and others who would frontally challenge American racial oppression would have excited her, particularly given Stokely's common Trinidad origin. In many ways, the murder of Emmet Till became another turning point in black activism in the civil rights movement, itself a youth movement in many ways.

Another fascinating poem written by Jones in Alderson is "Clay Sculpture." Writing about a created object allows her to make commentary about the potter's art and its meaning, the fact that the art object, once made, enters time. Elizabeth Gurley Flynn reports that Claudia learned clay modeling in prison: "Her absorption in many projects helped pass the time more quickly. Even in hospital, she did clay modeling. . . . She also taught several girls in our cottage to model in clay, and another to play the piano enough to encourage her to take lessons from the music teacher."[32] "Clay Sculpture" has an experiential though historical theme:

How nature hid in tablets here
Past History in its prime.

But most of all when turning 'round by hand this property
I turn the lock on all mankind's recorded history
For here lies proof supremely clear that bold humanity
Can storm all doors through toil and will — if
they but see!

In the art object then, she sees both human labor and human ability in the connections between the lessons of art and of political transcendence. Claudia would make this point about art again later, in her interpretation of the Marxian axiom "A people's art is the genesis of their own freedom" in the context of Caribbean Carnival, as described in chapter 5.

Another poem in this vein is "Paean to Crimea," written on October 11, 1962 while she was in the Rossia Sanatorium in Yalta. It is another song of praise to the place, its geography, its long history, which stand out through its dignified mountains which link well in her consciousness to the "people's system-rare." The memories she acquires here in her mind will sustain her.

My heart will fill with thoughts of you
My brains and mind will fashion, too,
Memories, long to inspire me,
In climes and lands — so unlike thee!

A narrative version of this poem is published as "Visit to the U.S.S.R." in the *West Indian Gazette* (December 1962) with a photograph of Claudia in Yalta and a group photograph with a range of Soviet people — the Russian cosmonauts and their families but also including her old ally from CPUSA days, Henry Winston, identified in the caption to the photograph as "blinded in U.S. McCarthy jails." The article is a travelogue, describing her joy at fulfilling her life's dream of visiting the Soviet Union and begins with a reflection: "I wanted to see for myself the first Land of Socialism; to meet its people, to see for myself the growth of its society, its culture, its technological and scientific advance. I was curious to see a land which I already knew abhorred racial discrimination to the extent of making it a legal crime and where the equality of all people is a recognized axiom." This desire was fulfilled. The rest of the essay described Moscow, free education, women doctors, happy children, and the availability of education for people from around the world, with language training at the Patrice Lumumba Friendship University. Such a short visit, nevertheless, we know would not produce a full and objective study of those desires identified above. Instead, we get her assessment based on her stay there and, particularly, her vision of their medical system; having been hospitalized for a period during her visit, she would have firsthand knowledge of it.

A more detailed and energetic poem about socialist reconstruction is "Yenan — Cradle of the Revolution," written as she returned from a two day visit to Yenan, China, August 28, 1964. It is one of her last poems (she died in December 1964), but it captures well her faith in socialism and the way that she saw the Chinese revolution as manifesting some of the dreams that socialists share for a better society. She sees the people of China as living out the dream of "bright thought — for mankind's future." So she defines them as neither academic dreamers nor idle dreamers. Rather they are people who use their landscape, their history, their climate to fashion themselves a better future, one that defied their better armed oppressors.

What then turned the tide?
What organised the people
Simple in their aspirations
And desires, into a fighting fist
To crush forever their Chiangs
Their war-lords, backed
By the imperialist might of
U.S. dollars and many-flagged guns.

Her response to her question "What then turned the tide?" is that their own innate abilities allowed the Chinese to create, organize, and challenge seemingly superior forces. This is perhaps the most explicit poem of her understanding of socialist revolution through Chairman Mao's teachings, and in particular what unity can do for a people oppressed.

The fight to win and
Change the mind of Man
Against the corruption of centuries
Of feudal-bourgeois, capitalist ideas
The fusion of courage and clarity
Of polemic against misleaders

She sees the place, Yenan, as heroic, demonstrating man's ability to "transform Nature, and, so doing / To transform society and Man himself." Thus she brings the poem to a close with a stanza expressing the poem's theme:

No idle dreamers these—
and yet they dared to dream
The dream—long-planned
Unfolds in Socialist China.

Yenan becomes significant because it was here, in Claudia's words, "in the Kiangs mountains, where Chairman Mao Tse Tung brilliantly applied Marxist-Leninist principles to evolve the strategy and tactics of the armed struggle against China's chief enemies securing victory over imperialist intervention in China's affairs, defeating its puppets and establishing China's socialist power."[33]

In retrospect, and with our current knowledge of what has become now of the Chinese Revolution, we may come to a different judgment, but in 1964, when this was written, it was a heady poem, excited about actually witnessing a socialist revolution in process, something Jones had only up till then written about or called for. One feels a sense of happiness for Jones in this instant; her joy is infectious, although the poem itself is very polemic. But this is a committed communist witnessing the creation of a communist state. This is as far as one can get from "Lament for Emmett Till." Claudia never managed to write all her reports about her experience with socialist China. Much of it remains in notebooks difficult to decipher because they are rapidly written, with peculiarities of handwriting and individual note taking—much of it having the appearance of scribbled notes, taken for minutes of a meeting.[34] However, this poem—the first draft written on August 25, 1964, "on the plane returning from a two-day visit from Yenan to Peking"—captures the moment, as poetry does, and locates Claudia Jones in time.

Jones's poetic oeuvre is small, relative to her journalistic output and to the output of a person whose single interest is poetry. Rather, hers is a creative output linked to articulation of feelings (in the sense in which Lorde identified it), and within the blues tradition of creativity out of oppression. Clearly, Claudia Jones was not a poet in the traditional sense, nor did she claim this as an identity. However, she was absolutely a creative person, and this creativity facilitated her poetic expression. Above all, like the blues, her poems reflect that doubled sign of pain and of transcendence of that pain. Audre Lorde's poem "For Assata" is similarly evocative here.

> I dream of your freedom
> as my victory
> and the victory of all dark women . . .
> Assata my sister warrior
> Joan of Arc and Yaa Asantewa
> embrace
> at the back of your cell.[35]

In the midst of her struggles with the United States government, a poem appeared in the *Daily Worker*. It was called "A Ballad to Claudia,"[36] and is a fitting way to conclude this chapter on Jones's poetry. The poem sums up well the issues of struggle and African American history that is her legacy and situates her as well within a group of fighters for black liberation.

> There's a woman who walks this mighty land
> With a queenly grace goes she
> In her struggles she never stands alone
> For look at her company.
>
> Harriet Tubman is at her side
> "Good cheer, Claudia," cries she
> "The slavers also wanted my head,
> But our brave people still fought free."
>
> John Brown is with her wherever she goes
> And his voice rings clear as a bell
> "I died to uphold the spirit of equality.
> Defend it till the freezing of Hell."
>
> And the martyred Nat Turner is here with her too,
> Staunch Nat with never a doubt.
> "I staggered the slavers of my day, Daughter
> Defeat yours and knock them out."
>
> And gaunt and tall against the wall,
> Denmark Vessey speaks out his mind.

"I defeated the cruel masters of my day, Daughter,
Finish off their modern kind."

Fred Douglas and Garrison are here with her too,
And the people of every land
Stand shoulder to shoulder with Claudia Jones
She speaks . . . and they understand.

Chapter 4

DEPORTATION:
THE OTHER POLITICS OF DIASPORA

"What is an ocean between us? We know how to build bridges"

There are, under our present immigration laws, numerous aliens who have been found to be *deportable*, many of whom are in the subversive, criminal, or immoral classes who are free to roam the country at will without supervision or control.

INTERNAL SECURITY ACT OF 1950 (MCCARRAN ACT) PUB. L. NO. 831, CHAPTER 1024, pp. 984–986

Definitions
. . . . (8) The term "publication" means any circular, newspaper, periodical, pamphlet, book, letter, post card, leaflet, or other publication.
(9) The term "United States" when used in a geographical sense includes the several States, Territories, and possessions of the United States, the District of Columbia, and the Canal Zone.

INTERNAL SECURITY ACT OF 1950 (MCCARRAN ACT), PUB. L. NO. 831, CHAP. 1024, P. 987

The imprisonment and deportation of Claudia Jones for being a communist prefigured contemporary strategies of incarceration and deportation in what has been defined as the war on terrorism. Following the April 1997 passage of what some consider to be a brutal Illegal Immigration Reform and Immigrant Responsibility Act, the U.S. Immigration and Naturalization Service (INS) showed a 70 percent increase in deportations in the last quarter of fiscal year 1997. In their words, "In fiscal year 1997 (which ended in September), the INS deported more than 113,000 people and the agency has set a goal of 127,300 deportations for fiscal year 1998." Thus, the number of deportations, or as they more dramatically refer to them — expedited removals — from the United States, more than 32,000 for 1998, increased by nearly 50 percent over the previous year.[1] And since the combination of FBI and INS lists, under the Department of Homeland Security, incarceration and deportation is a much more common experience.[2]

The result of this massive deportation activity for places such as Trinidad, Jamaica, and the Dominican Republic, for example, is an upsurge in "returnees" (as they are called by INS), many of whom had left home as young children and who were deported back to the Caribbean as adults, sometimes with no close or visible relatives left there. Pedro Noguera's helpful analysis of what he calls the "overrepresentation of Caribbean and central American immigrants among the ranks of the deported" ("Exporting the Undesirable") provides a series of charts that show the geographical spread and island representation in the ranks of the deported. Caribbean immigration officials argue that these designated returnees are actually U.S. nationals who had spent all their lives in the United States (i.e., came to the United States as children, were schooled, socialized, and in effect were products of the United States system; many have children and other family members who are U.S. citizens living in the United States, jobs, houses, and apartments and otherwise complete lives there) and are then effectively relocated to a "home" that they do not know, where they have either no family or one with which they maintained little connection. The crimes of these returnees range from prostitution and drug offenses (sometimes only teenage smoking of marijuana) to the more serious ones of rape and other physical violence. One consulate official calls it a "policy without care." Often deportees are sent without warning, or attention paid to the types of crimes committed, to the "home countries," which often do not have the type of social services to accommodate their needs. Technically, anyone convicted of crime is deportable; indeed some are deported without completing sentences in the United States.[3] At times, according to one consular official, deportation is used retroactively for people who had committed crimes in their youth.[4]

In other words, deportation became an alternative to long-term incarceration in the United States for a range of offences. However, it is not strictly an alternative to imprisonment, as many of the deportees serve some prison time prior to deportation. The framing of deportation in terms of criminality in the United States masks the fact that deportation is one of the ways that all states use to construct the citizenship they desire. This policy of "expedited removal," as well as prolonged detention, in some cases pending deportation, has begun to be challenged legally, both by the receiving states, in terms of international law and within the United States. Cases such as Zadvydas v. Davis, 533 U.S. 678 (2001), and Donald Seretse-Khama v. John D. Ashcroft, 215 F. Supp. 2d 37 (D.D.C. 2002), began to make their way through the courts. In the latter, Seretse-Khama (who had been living in the United States with his family from the age of eight and had lived there consistently since then) had been detained pending removal for close to three years because of a number of technicalities, including the Liberian government's refusal to issue him travel documents.[5]

Following the terrorist attacks on New York and Washington, D.C., on September 11, 2001, more sweeping legislation, via the USA Patriot Act of 2001 (Uniting and Strengthening America by Providing Appropriate Tools Required to Intercept and Obstruct Terrorism), has produced numerous violations of civil rights and numerous deportations, some of which have been effectively challenged and overturned by federal courts.[6] Additionally, in December 2002, the National Security Entry-Exit Registration System was developed by the Justice Department in which tens of thousands of male foreign nationals from targeted "Middle East" countries were registered, fingerprinted, photographed, and questioned. Of the 82,000 Arab Americans asked to register, nearly 14,000 of those registered were placed in deportation proceedings, and only approximately 150 of these registrants had committed any crimes.[7] According to the immigration attorney David P. Rowe, immigration law has become confusing and contradictory since 2001, as the continuing "War on Terror" has had a "chilling effect" on First Amendment rights of aliens and citizens.[8]

Key constitutional rights have been suspended or infringed by the U.S. government in the post-September 11, 2001 period, under the pretext that this is a nation "at war." A number of citizens and residents, defined as potential terrorists by the state under the USA Patriot Act of 2001, have faced — and continue to face — incarceration and deportation. In some cases, minor immigration violations are treated with the heavy punishment of imprisonment and deportation with their concomitant separation from family, friends, property, and livelihood.

A similar set of targeting activities took place under the Smith Act of 1940 and the McCarran-Walter Act (the Immigration and Nationality Act of 1952, written by Senator Pat McCarran, a Democrat of Nevada, and Francis Walter, Democrat of Pennsylvania), which criminalized communism. The similarity between the policies and actions of 1952 and those put in place after 2001 is a point taken up by Alicia J. Campi, in an Immigration Policy Center immigration policy brief "The McCarran-Walter Act: A Contradictory Legacy on Race, Quotas, and Ideology." In it, she says, "The Act . . . redefined the ideological grounds for the exclusion and deportation of immigrants. Most of these provisions were formally repealed by Congress in 1990, but many were resurrected by the USA Patriot Act of 2001."

One of the stipulations of the Internal Security Act of 1950 (the McCarran Act), operating through the Subversive Activities Board, that resembles clauses in the Patriot Act, was the requirement that all communists register with immigration authorities and local police. Elizabeth Gurley Flynn, who had herself been targeted and imprisoned for membership in the Communist Party, has an analysis of the McCarran Act in which she explains: "Title I is Subversive Activities Control. This deals with enforced Communist registration; denial of passports; the defining of defense facilities where employment is restricted; the labeling of publications as Communist; naturalization regulations and registration; *deportation of aliens*; *and more stringent amendments to laws dealing with the foreign born*" (emphasis original; *The McCarran Act*, 2).

Thus, contemporary antiterrorist actions and their negative implications for immigrants and the civil liberties of American citizens in general have a precedent in the way that communism was criminalized in the 1940s and 1950s. During the era of McCarthy and the House on Un-American Committee's Activities, an almost identical set of practices prevailed. Indeed, an examination of the *Daily Worker* from the 1950s reveals the documentation of a consistent practice of deportation following passage of the McCarran Act. Elizabeth Gurley Flynn reported on this practice in an article titled "Miss Liberty's Torch Grows Dim":

> Among those sent to Ellis Island were fathers of families, and older people who came here as young children, including three women. The women are Claudia Jones, executive secretary of the Women's Commission of the

Communist Party and my closest co-worker, Betty Gannett, educational director of that party, and Rose Nelson, an executive officer of the Emma Lazarus division of the Jewish People's Fraternal Order. . . . The deportees are held in special quarters on Ellis Island, now known as the McCarran wing. During the war it was used, I am told, for German Bundists. So when the torch of the Statue of Liberty lights up every evening, the rays shine over a newly-made concentration camp for American political prisoners, a strange and terrible sight for our country. (8)

Referring to the criminalization-deportation issue, and the particular case of Claudia Jones, Flynn continues: "These political deportees are not criminals. They are charged with ideas, not crimes. Claudia Jones came here as a child from British Trinidad, grew up here, went to school here, and made fruitless attempts to become a citizen" (8).

In any assessment of Claudia Jones's contribution, her fate as a political prisoner and then as a deportee has to be centrally located. Furthermore, this condition and its relation to others suffering similar fates have to be elaborated. Indeed, the Communist Party USA, realizing that many of their membership were being subject to incarceration and deportation, filed suit to void the McCarran Act. In a piece captioned "17 Foreign-Born Jailed under McCarran Act. 107 File Suit to Void McCarran Act" it is identified as "the Justice Department's deportation dragnet of progressive non-citizens . . . extended . . . in seven major cities."[9]

A range of artists, intellectuals, and activists began to be targeted. An April 28, 1952, *Daily Worker* article with a beautiful photograph of the dancer Pearl Primus, also from Trinidad and Tobago, in her classic "dance-flight" routine, indicated that because of her position in support of peace, "a few hours before her Los Angeles recital, Miss Primus was visited by a representative of the State Department. Her passport was picked up 'because of the delicate international situation.' The passport revocation, unless reversed will cause Miss Primus to abandon plans for an international tour with her troupe." Several clergymen, among others, protested the attacks on the "foreign born," which were aimed at both naturalized citizens and noncitizens, signing their names to the article, which declared that "a host of new crimes have been created against naturalized citizens making it possible for citizenship to be taken away at any time."[10] The article reported that "non-citizens can be arrested for deportation at the merest suspicion by any agent so designated by the Attorney General" and can be "held without bail indefinitely."[11] Jones herself, along with Ferdinand Smith and four other Communist Party members, petitioned the United Nations under Articles 2 and 9 of the Universal Declaration of Human Rights (1948), asserting that their rights were being violated by the U.S. government: "Human rights are abrogated, our freedom of conscience violated and our right to think outlawed" and "no one shall be subjected to arbitrary arrest, detention or exile." The petition continues:

> It is mandatory that the United Nations, on the basis of its character, investigate the manner in which immigrants in the United States are being treated by agencies of the United States government. If we can be denied all rights and incarcerated in concentration camps, then trade unionists are next, then the Negro people, the Jewish people, all foreign-born, and all progressives who love peace and cherish freedom will face the bestiality and torment of fascism.[12]

There is no indication that the petition went very far.

The criminalization and deportation of Claudia Jones prompted my consideration of deportation, in relation to a number of other figures, for political activity. In doing so, I identified a pattern within the larger context of the deportation of "aliens" identified above: one in which the state treated radicalism and communism as equivalent, for all politically active figures. At the heart of the matter, according to immigration attorney David Rowe, was a legal question that had to be wrestled with: The Constitution's guarantee of freedom of speech does not legalize treasonable conduct, so the question becomes, "If communism or Marxism-Leninism is a political doctrine, should not the First Amendment protect those who wish to discuss this doctrine and/or advocate it as a political position?" Further, "Does one who so adheres to this politics and or organizes around it automatically become a criminal?"[13] The courts answered this second question affirmatively in cases such as the United States of America v. Elizabeth Gurley Flynn, et al. (216 F.2d 354) and related cases and appeals.

In the case of immigrants, under naturalization law, advocating the overthrow of the U.S. government by force or violence, orally or otherwise, is a basis for denial of an application for naturalization. Communism was defined in that period as doing just that. Indeed those applying for U.S. citizenship, even today, must answer questions still in their formal application about current or prior membership in and association with communist organizations. So active membership in the Communist Party became criminalized and therefore the basis of exclusion and removal of all aliens as well as a denial of legal permanent residence and naturalization.[14]

Almost none of the literature on diaspora has dealt in any substantive way with this issue of deportation and/or the "other politics of diaspora." The major texts in African diaspora studies tend to focus on diaspora as a product of separation from Africa via transatlantic slavery in relation to the larger issue of pan-Africanism and have made a great deal of headway in specifying the terms of diaspora discourse. *Global Dimensions of the African Diaspora*, the collection of essays edited by Joseph Harris, set the terms for this model of African diaspora studies. The actual movement in and around the Caribbean and the Americas, inside Africa, to Asia and Europe remains to be developed.

Deportation, clearly the other side of immigration, also creates another dimension of diaspora. A different construction of diaspora, beyond the home-exile dialectic, but with an understanding of a variety of globally interconnected communities, reveals some more practical issues.[15] Recognition that one is always a "deportable subject" can impose a certain set of disciplines in the general population. These disciplines will affect specific choices in terms of activism, political identification, and so on, unless one chooses deliberately the life of the sojourner or the African returnee who exercises his African diaspora citizenship, as, say, W. E. B. Du Bois or Kwame Ture (Stokely Carmichael) did.

That Claudia Jones's deportation was an earlier version of the criminalizing and parallel conferring of statelessness on those with political positions who are deemed radical by the state is noted by Gerald Horne, in his *Black Liberation/Red Scare*. The treatment of a range of other black civil rights activists such as Martin Luther King in the 1960s and all black militants under the Counter Intelligence Program (COINTELPRO) in the 1970s and 1980s seem then nothing less than a continuation of policies applied to the Communist Party in the 1940s and 1950s. Dhoruba bin Wahad in *Still Black, Still Strong* is very good in documenting some of these actions on activists of the 1960s and 1970s.[16]

In Claudia Jones's case, this sense of statelessness under deportation had the result of creating an international identity in diaspora. Jones's writings reveal that she was very clear about her membership in the Caribbean diaspora, as she was clear about her identification as an African American under the oppression of U.S. racism. Still, beyond ethnic identification, Claudia Jones identified herself solidly as an American, being denied rights due to incidental legal manipulations: "No law or decree can whittle away or pierce by one iota our convictions and loyalty to America's democratic and revolutionary traditions. We are Americans, each and every one of us, similarly persecuted, not by accident of birth, but by choice. We yield to no one in laying claim to being true patriots."[17]

Following her trial, conviction, and indictment for communist ideas, Jones faced both incarceration and then deportation. The convergence of the McCarran Act (Internal Security Act of 1950) and the McCarran-Walter Act (Immigration and Nationality Act of 1952) with the Smith Act (Alien Registration Act of 1940) created a wedge that isolated those the U.S. government wanted to terrorize. The Smith Act, chap. 1024, is clear on this issue.

> Amending Section 20 of Immigration Act of February 5, 1917
> Sec. 20 (a) That the deportation of aliens provided for in this Act and all other immigration laws of the United States shall be directed by the Attorney General to the country specified by the alien, if it is willing to accept him into its territory; otherwise such deportation shall be directed by the Attorney General within his discretion and without priority of preference because of their order as herein set forth, either to the country from which such alien last entered the United States; or to the country in which is located the foreign port at which such alien embarked for the United States or for foreign contiguous territory; or to the country which had sovereignty over the birthplace of the alien at the time of his birth; or to any country of which such an alien is a subject, national or citizen; or to the country in which he was born; or to the country in which the place of his birth is situated at the time he is deported; or if deportation to any of the said foregoing places is impracticable, then any country which is willing to accept such alien into its territory.

Following the final deportation decision, a series of pleas and suits, based on her ill health, were mounted on Claudia's behalf. For example, the January 26, 1955, issue of the *Daily Worker* reports that "motions to suspend the sentences of Claudia Jones and Jacob Mindel on the basis of their health were filed on their behalf in the U.S. District Court here yesterday."

Filing of the motions by attorney Mary M. Kaufman, followed by a day the departure of Miss Jones, Elizabeth Gurley Flynn and Betty Gannett for imprisonment in Alderson, W. Virginia. Affidavits of physicians testified to the worsening of the condition of Miss Jones . . . since sentence was imposed February 3, 1953. . . . Miss Jones offered, through an affidavit of her attorney, to take all steps to facilitate her departure to another country if that were made a condition of the court's suspension of the remainder of her sentence of a year and a day. . . . The Negro Communist leader is under a deportation order now. A final order was entered against her six months ago, the government vindictively pressing the deportation procedure after the Smith Act conviction. . . . Miss Jones was in an infirmary while imprisoned with Betty Gannett and Elizabeth Gurley Flynn for two weeks in the Women's House of Detention here prior to their departure by train Monday night. (2)

An interesting article that underscores the defense action on her behalf, is Richard Boyer's "Why Six Negro Leaders Defend Claudia Jones."[18] In it, Boyer argues that the leaders felt justified, because they believed that

"The Smith Act indictment against Claudia Jones is part of a concerted government attack on the whole Negro people, as well as upon the West Indian people in the United States. . . . [The leadership in her defense included] Cyril Phillips, a New York businessman, Mrs Charlotta Bass, former publisher of the *California Eagle* and chairman of the Sojourners for Truth and Justice, William Cheravez, New York attorney, Hope Stevens, also a New York attorney and a leader of the West Indian people in the United States, Miss Louise Jeffers, acting secretary of a provisional committee defending Miss Jones, and Mrs Rosa Lee Gray, president of the Manhattan Young Sojourners for Truth and Justice. Miss Jeffers declared yesterday that one of the objects of the brochure was the formation of a National Defense Committee for Claudia Jones.

Challenging the action against Claudia Jones as against the Caribbean Community, Miss Jeffers makes an important link with the way the entire community was treated at the time and in a sense continues to be treated by current deportation actions.

The 100,000 people from the West Indies in the United States are particularly familiar with deportation proceedings, being a favorite target of the immigration bureau. They resent Senator McCarran's proposal to limit West Indian emigration to the United States to only 100 persons a year. (5)

The National Defense Committee for Claudia Jones, which had created the brochure listing her political actions and linking it to the harassment of other leaders, from Du Bois to Benjamin Davis and other black activists, is an important document in identifying the links between Caribbean and U.S. African Americans as far as the issue of the denial of rights are concerned. These concerted efforts on Jones's behalf were able to release her from imprisonment in Alderson on grounds of ill health.

Jones's health was certainly precarious, and incarceration was making it worse. One article captioned "Claudia Jones Denied Diet Prescribed for Heart Illness"[19] reports that she had written to her father from Alderson that she was unable to obtain the salt-free diet prescribed her. "In one letter she revealed that before she had been in the women's federal prison a month, she had been set to scrubbing floors, which had brought on a swelling of the ankles related to her heart condition." In the Jim Crow prison facilities, the harsh diet and the physical labor took a toll on her physical condition; the reports support the contention that the state's treatment of her was a major contributing factor to her early demise.

But leaders from many communities mounted an active assault on what seemed to be the system's intention, for her to die in prison. So in a sense her release was a huge victory for the African American and Caribbean communities in that it spared her life. But it could not save her from deportation.

The Communist Party position, as articulated by William Z. Foster, was that the deportation of Claudia Jones was "inconsistent with justice and our democratic tradition":

Since 1951, the government of the United States, through its immigration officials, has been attempting to accomplish the deportation of Claudia Jones. This deportation threat was first issued while Miss Jones was defending herself and her Party from the lies of informers and the hysteria of a Smith Act persecution. . . . Claudia Jones was released from prison on October 23. Since then she has not known a day free from harassment and petty persecution despite the fact that she has been hospitalized, stricken down by the effects of a heart ailment which became aggravated while she was in prison. Now in this condition she is to be forcibly separated from her friends, uprooted from her home and familiar surroundings, in middle life driven out into a country she has never known, to begin her life all over again without the health and youth that she gave in the service of the American people. This is what is meant by "deportation" — the respectable name for the medieval punishment of banishment that has long since been abandoned in every other civilized country.[20]

The FBI file for Claudia Jones reveals that her crime was identified as practicing the ideas of communism and that this made her an enemy of the state. Several of the articles that she had written were used as evidence for her conviction and are reproduced in their entirety in the files. The relevant law (Pub. L. No. 831, Chap. 1024, p. 1002, of the Internal Security Act of 1950), under which she was indicted reads as follows:

(G) Aliens who write or publish, or cause to be written or published, or who knowingly circulate, distribute, print, or display, or knowingly have in their possession for the purpose of circulation, publication or display, any written or printed matter, advocating or teaching opposition to all organized government, or advocating (i) the overthrow by force or violence or other unconstitutional means of the Government of the United States or of all forms of law; or (ii) the duty, necessity, or propriety of the unlawful assaulting or killing of any officer or officers (either of specific individuals or of officers generally) of the Government of the United States or of any other organized government; or (iii) the unlawful damage, injury, or destruction of property; or (iv) sabotage; or (v) the economic, international, and governmental doctrines of world communism or the economic doctrines of any other form of totalitarianism.

Following a failed appeal (May 10–11, 1954; decided October 14, 1954), Jones was sentenced to prison followed by deportation: "The appellants were convicted of conspiracy under 18 U.S.C. 371 to violate the Smith Act, 18 U.S.C. 2385, making it an offense to advocate forcible overthrow of the government" (216 F.2d 354). Petitions to release her from prison before the completion of her sentence were finally heard because of her grave health. Once released, she attempted to fight the deportation order and be cleared of any crime, but in the end, her ill health made her decide to opt for exile. With looming deportation and having already identified her opposition to U.S. practices and policies, having been arrested, tried, jailed, and then placed under an order of deportation, Jones and her legal and political team were able only to shift the designation of deportation to a kind of voluntary departure to England, rather than a deportation to Trinidad. Articles in the *Daily Worker* at that time indicate that the plan was to eject her immediately upon her release from prison to Trinidad. Since she was ill, having — according to one account — suffered a heart attack two days after release, she and her lawyers were able to negotiate a delay. A series of articles recount several brief stays of deportation: one-day or one-week stays, and so on. In the end, it seems, Claudia decided to become more proactive about where she would be and the conditions of her departure. One final news item in this period summarizes her decision to leave: "Claudia Jones Will Go to London; Too Ill to Fight Deportation Order," gives the following account: "Claudia Jones, victim of the Smith Act and the Walter-McCarran Immigration Act is scheduled to leave December — under so-called 'voluntary departure' for London it became known yesterday. . . . Miss Jones had been forced by ill health, itself aggravated by government harassment, to drop her court challenge of the deportation order."[21]

Though the distinction between "exile" and "deportation" may seem negligible (indeed, it is one that both the Communist Party and subsequent reviewers conflate), my concept of "migratory subjectivity" allows me to read the linguistic and procedural shift from one to the other in ways that make a difference. While one definition of "exile" is linked to being forced to leave one's home, another allows that leaving to be voluntary, even if induced. Thus this redefinition allowed her to step out of the dominant discourse surrounding her and into her own discourse. It also technically allowed her to claim her African American identity. So while black political and social groups, black women's organizations, and the Communist Party challenged her deportation and organized against it,[22] Jones herself was clear on the meaning she would give to her departure; her own personal (self) re-definition was already in progress.

If this view of Claudia's departure holds, then her journey to London on the *Queen Elizabeth* (ironically) became a possibility for the creation of a new identity. Her work in England bears this out, for her orientation became more directly pan-Africanist and also internationalist, under the terms of a Marxist-Leninist construction of world revolution. Claudia Jones had already had substantial experience of that kind of pan-Africanist organization in New

York and at the highest levels of the Communist Party USA. According to one account, her home and the building in which she lived were always a prime location for all sorts of black artists, activists, and political figures from the United States and elsewhere.[23] London would provide the opportunity to put this internationalism into operation. A large segment of the Anglophone Caribbean intellectual, creative, and political communities also saw London (the colonial center) as a site of political incubation of ideas and action for decolonization. For example, the Trinidad Independence Party, which had urged the release of Claudia Jones, had as its general secretary John La Rose, who would eventually be central to the organizing of intellectual and creative activity in London and in the Caribbean.[24] That Jones would, upon leaving the United States, became one of the prime organizers of the Afro-Caribbean community and a key point person for all black activists, political figures, writers, and entertainers from all over the world as they arrived in England was not an unimagined possibility.[25]

Jones's activism, as I have already shown, was also manifested in her consistent use of journalism for community organizing. In London, this is demonstrated in the *West Indian Gazette and Afro-Asian Caribbean News*, which she edited. My surveys of the newspapers indicate that all issues carried coverage of the African world, the Asian world, particularly decolonization struggles, but also specifically coverage of the Caribbean in the larger translocal sense.[26] Articles on Cuba, for example, were prominent and insightful. Africa Unity House also became a site for a great deal of her organizing activity.[27] And her coalition of Afro-Asian organizations functioned as a lobbying group for issues critical to the African, Caribbean, and Asian diaspora.[28] In many ways Claudia's activism in London supports her father's position that "wherever she goes, Claudia will do her best."[29]

In one of her early interviews in London, Claudia Jones offers her famous summation on why she was deported.[30] A number of factors are identified, which I would like to individuate:

> I was a victim of the McCarthyite hysteria against independent political ideas in the USA, a hysteria which penalizes anyone who holds ideas contrary to the official pro-war, pre-reactionary, pro-fascist line of the white ruling class of that country.
>
> I was deported from the USA because as a Negro woman Communist of West Indian descent, I was a thorn in their side in my opposition to Jim

Crow racist discrimination against 16 million Negro Americans in the United States.

[I was deported for] my work for redress of these grievances, for unity of Negro and white workers, for women's rights and my general political activity urging the American people to help by their struggles to change the present foreign and domestic policy of the United States.

I was deported and refused an opportunity to complete my American citizenship because I fought for peace, against the huge arms budget which funds should be directed to improving the social needs of the people.

I was deported because I urged the prosecution of lynchers rather than prosecution of Communists and other democratic Americans who oppose the lynchers and big financiers and warmongers, the real advocates of force and violence in the USA.

In her characteristically clarifying way, Claudia was able to identify all the specific rationales for her deportation but all of which came down to the fact that she, a black woman assumed the identity of being a communist, as did Angela Davis two decades later, namely someone who struggles through an organized Communist Party effort to bring about an egalitarian society free from class, race, and gender injustices. Her political identity as a communist, added to her identification as Caribbean, complicated even further, in the view of the INS, her rights to U.S. citizenship.

This ongoing denial of citizenship rights speaks most strongly to what citizenship in the United States constituted, and still constitutes, for black people. Other examples of the denial of citizenship rights (constitutional rights) to the black population as a whole have been evident throughout U.S. history: consider, for example, the Fugitive Slave Act, the Supreme Court's decisions in *Dred Scott* and *Plessey v. Ferguson*, and the need for the Fourteenth and Fifteenth Amendments to the Constitution creating for African Americans the possibility of citizenship:

[Amendment 14, sec. 1 (1868)] All persons born or naturalized in the United States, and subject to the jurisdiction thereof, are citizens of the United States and the states wherein they reside.
[Amendment 15 (1870)] The right of citizens of the United States to vote shall not be denied or abridged by the United States or by any state on account of race, color, or previous condition of servitude.

Neither of these amendments has removed the loophole of imprisonment, by which a technical denial of citizenship and imposition of slavery remains in effect: Amendment 13, sec. 1 (1865) stipulates: "Neither slavery nor involuntary servitude, except as punishment for crime whereof the party shall have been duly convicted, shall exist within the United States, or any place subject to their jurisdiction."[31]

Technically the United States functions as a "multination state," with African Americans historically being treated at times as equivalent to, or often worse than, foreign nationals. Supreme Court decisions such as *Brown v. Board of Education* (1954) and critical assessments of that case (for example, Charles J. Ogletree's 2004 study) make a similar argument. Thus black identity and being born outside the United States (as in the cases of Marcus Garvey and C. L. R. James, both ending in deportation) come together to create a dual sense of not belonging; when this is linked to the hated communist identity, as in Jones's case, the effect is multiplied.

So an Afro-Caribbean woman seeking U.S. citizenship — as she had for close to twenty years — with those specific political identifications in place, further transgressed the given black identity in the United States at that time.[32] Jones's choice of Britain as her destination following her "voluntary departure" created another paradox. On the one hand, the British felt it would be easier to accommodate her politics in Britain than in the Caribbean, where decolonization and labor struggles were being fiercely waged at the time. In addition, this was the beginning point of the large groundswell of Caribbean migration to the United Kingdom, which is traditionally recognized as having started in 1948 with the immigration of Caribbean workers aboard the MV *Empire Windrush*. At that time as well, because of their colonial status, Caribbean nationals had British passports and were technically British citizens. On the other hand, while London was Jones's place of choice for health reasons, the possibility of belonging to, returning to, and engaging the Caribbean as an adult was not guaranteed.

In my examination of the Claudia Jones papers, I found a few items that identify her administrative identification as a Trinidadian national. In one extended two-year period in which she was denied a British passport for travel to the Soviet Union, Claudia wrote a letter dated July 23, 1957, to Eric Williams, then prime minister of Trinidad, asking him to investigate why her passport was being withheld and expedite the issuing process. Williams himself responded and referred the matter to the colonial secretary for action, who sent a reply to Claudia; eventually she was able to obtain a passport. Her letter to Williams says, in part:

> I sought on the second day after arriving in England to secure a passport since I wanted to evade the rigors of the English winter in my health's interest, suffering as I do from a chronic heart ailment. My passport was not granted to me at that time, with no reason given me by the Passport Office. Later, in February of last year, 1956, I again applied while hospitalised with a heart attack at which time I received a communication from the Passport Office that they saw no reason why they should grant me a passport although they stressed they would happily give me a travel document to return to Trinidad. Besides carrying a strong hint of the "colonial go home" approach, they also gratuitously suggested that insofar as my health needs were concerned the Caura Sanitorium in Trinidad might be the place to cater to my health. . . . Now, the Passport Office has broadly indicated that the fly in the ointment is not here — but in Trinidad, since being a subject of Trinidad, permission must be granted there. Besides being questionable, this seems to be a case of discrimination against me personally and as a citizen of Trinidad and the UK. If my assumptions are invalid as regards discrimination, then now that my qualification of residency has been met, and I have secured a prominent recommender, my own physician, certainly there should be no difficulty in what ought to be a routine matter. If it is a question of political views, this would not apply if I were of English birth since such people of all political persuasions, including Marxists, are not denied the right to travel out of England, because of their political views. Am I then to conclude that this special discrimination holds against me solely as a West Indian woman?[33]

This is one of the first instances in which Jones identifies herself as a Caribbean woman. Still, even at a time when Trinidad was politically independent, being born in Trinidad did not necessarily translate into guaranteed citizenship rights in the Caribbean, for one was still administratively a "British subject." There are several cases of threatened or attempted deportations and incarcerations in Trinidad itself, also for political views. C. L. R. James was placed under house arrest by prime minister Eric Williams and his People's National Movement government, and later Kwame Ture (Stokely Carmichael) was barred entry during the black power period of the 1970s. These various denials of entry, denials of right to vote, deportation, and incarceration make the point that citizenship for black people anywhere is a very fragile and mutable condition.

Being a communist was then, as it is now, often regarded by states wary of radical thought as one of the most hateful of identities. Claudia's applications for U.S. citizenship (she had initially applied at age twenty-three and again while married to a U.S. citizen) were held up for over fifteen years and finally denied. These struggles testify to the significance of citizenship in relation to a state that has already defined what constitutes an appropriate citizen. Clearly, length of residence (almost an entire life in Claudia's case) or birth are trumped by race and political affiliation. As we know now, incarceration by the state is equivalent to the denial of citizenship rights. By the time Claudia Jones had left the United States she had experienced both.

The Smith and McCarran Acts and the Legalization of the Denial of Rights

Michael Hanchard, in his essay "The Color of Subversion: Racial Politics and Immigration Policy in the United States," identifies how "state monitoring of U.S. African-American movement and migration has been from the outset related to broader fears of racial and ideological subversion in national political cultures" (1). Thus, the political histories of "immigration, racial politics and political repression are not so separate and discrete" as U.S. African Americans are often wont to make them. Hanchard notes that an important aspect of this situation is that African Americans in the United States have routinely also been denied basic "citizenship rights" throughout history (1–2). Indeed, historically, their struggle in the United States has been to get those rights in their country of birth. Pettis Perry, in an analysis that resonates with the Hanchard article, offers a summation in his *Catholic Worker* article, "The New 'Alien and Sedition' Law." In it he argues that "any attack upon the foreign-born in any way whatsoever is an attack upon the Bill of Rights and the Constitution and upon the democratic rights of all Americans."

By the end of 1950, deportation was such a common occurrence that each issue of the *Daily Worker* named who was next on the list: people such as Rose Nelson Lightcap, vice president of the Elma Lazarus Division of the Jewish People's Fraternal Order; George Siskind, Marxist educator; and Alexander

Bittelman, Marxist theoretician and political-economist are all identified. Harry Raymond called the practice an "Illegal Gestapo Build Up by the FBI against the Foreign Born."[34] By December 1950, a series of pleas were issued as Christmas appeals to President Truman to end the "cruel and needless" deportation drive. Bishops and ministers from all across the United States were signatories to this appeal. This effort would lead to a large-scale nation-wide action to fight the deportation drive, in the form of a national conference to defend the Bill of Rights. The conference was covered by the *Daily Worker*, which reported: "The delegates who represented unions, fraternal, women's church, educational, political and professional organizations in cities from Massachusetts to California" asked "to repeal all provisions of the Mc-Carran police state law which strikes at the civil rights of the citizen and non-citizen alike. . . . The conference designated March 1951 as 'Fight Deporta-tion Month' called for 'mass conferences during the first week of March in local communities in defense of the rights of the foreign-born.' Much of this activity would be spearheaded by what developed in the wake of McCarran, the American Committee for Protection of Foreign-Born."[35]

The politics of incarceration in the late twentieth and early twenty-first centuries, and the resulting denial of voting rights (plus the frailty of the Voting Rights Act), are continuous for large proportions of the African Amer-ican population in this ongoing denial of citizenship rights. It is in this context that the practice of deportation in the case of Arab and other Islamic people must be located. As the Claudia Jones experience reveals, incarceration and deportation are the twin ways that the U.S. state has dealt with its "unde-sirables." Hanchard makes the point that "deportation and imprisonment of African-American (Afro-U.S. and Afro-Caribbean) political activists during the first half of the twentieth century, the tensions between black politi-cal activism and state restriction made sojourners of many U.S. African-Americans and black West Indians residing in the United States" (2). The revocation of passports for black figures with activist identification, such as W. E. B. Du Bois, is worth recalling here, as it becomes an analog for the deportation that was Jones's lot, and equivalent to the "house arrest" that was C. L. R. James's in Trinidad.

The Smith Act, or by its official name, the Alien Registration Act (18 U.S.C. 2385) of 1940, was designed "to prohibit certain subversive activ-ities; to amend certain provisions of law with respect to the admission and deportation of aliens; to require fingerprinting and registration of aliens; (basically already criminalizing aliens) and for other purposes." Title 1, sec. 2(a) says:

It shall be unlawful for any person

(1) to knowingly or willfully advocate, abet, advise, or teach the duty, necessity, desirability, or propriety of overthrowing or destroying any Government of the United States by force or violence

(2) to print, publish, edit, issue, circulate, sell, distribute or publicly display any written or printed matter advocating advising, or teaching the duty necessity, desirability or propriety of overthrowing or destroying any Government in the United States by force or violence

(3) to organize or help organize any society, group or assembly of persons to teach, advocate or encourage the overthrow (40)

The punishment for such acts was prison, fining, and deportation.

But, deadlier than the Smith Act was the McCarran Internal Security Act of 1950, which required Communist Party members to register with the attorney general; the subsequent McCarran-Walter Immigration Act (1952) lay the foundation for immigration checks, deportation, harassment of African Americans, and even "authorized concentration camps for emergency situations."[36] In section 22 of this far-reaching act, under which Claudia Jones was deported, a variety of aliens are identified as inadmissible or deportable for offences such as teaching revolutionary information. Updating, revising, and tightening the Immigration Act of 1917, the McCarran-Walter Act, along with the Smith Act, served as the basis for state surveillance and the well-known activities of Congress's House Un-American Activities Committee (HUAC) throughout the 1950s and later.

The singer Paul Robeson also became known in this period as one of the most popular resisters to HUAC machinations. He also had his passport and right to travel revoked by the U.S. government from 1950 to 1958, and there were numerous succeeding denials of requests for travel and reinstatement of his rights to own his passport. In one instance, in August 1955, it was suggested to Robeson that he would be issued a passport if he signed a noncommunist oath. Robeson, of course, refused. Challenging the notion of U.S. borders, Robeson, at the height of the denial of his right to travel, like the runaways ahead of him, used Canada as sign and staged a concert on May 18,

1952 at the "in-between" space of the Peace Bridge between Canada and the United States.

It is noteworthy, as well, that Claudia Jones and Paul Robeson and his wife, Eslanda Goode Robeson, were close friends in New York and continued that friendship in London. Robeson, we learn from the Claudia Jones papers, was meant to serve as her executor following her death but was himself too ill to travel to London; he sent a message, however, to be played at her funeral.

The link to discourses of "unbelonging" in Britain are clear, especially since Claudia Jones ended her days in England. Indeed, one of the triggers for Claudia's continuing activism and early struggle was against the similar kind of denial of rights that she witnessed in London. She felt the looming Commonwealth Immigration Act and the treatment of blacks in Britain paralleled the denial of rights for African diaspora peoples in the United States.

The Incarceration/Deportation Nexus

The U.S. case for the deportation of Claudia Jones was made in starkly clinical terms, as we see from her FBI file (NY100–18676).

> The subject was arrested on January 20, 1948 on a warrant issued by the INS on charges that the subject "entered this country at New York City on the ninth day of February, 1924, and has been found in the United States in violation of the immigration laws thereof and is subject to be taken in custody and deported pursuant to the provisions of the Act of October 16, 1918 as amended, in that she is found to have been, after entry, a member of the following class, set forth in section one of said act: An alien who believes in, advocates, and teaches the overthrow, by force or violence of the Government of the United States, and writes and publishes and causes to be written and published any written or published matter advising, advocating, or teaching the overthrow, by force or violence, of the Government of the United States.
>
> The subject was arrested a second time by the INS on October 23, 1950 as an Alien Communist in violation of Section 20 of the 1917 Act as amended by the Internal Security Act of 1950.
>
> The subject was ordered to be deported to her native country, Trinidad, British West Indies on the completion of hearings held at the INS, 70 Columbus Avenue, New York City, on December 21, 1950. It was found that as an Alien Communist she was in violation of Section 20 of the 1917

Act as amended by the Internal Security Act of 1950 and as such was deportable.

The deportation of the subject is at the present time pending and she continues to reside at 504 West 143rd Street, Apartment 6-A, New York City. (sec. B, Naturalization, pp. 3–4)

Claudia Jones was indicted, finally, for an article "Women in the Struggle for Peace and Security" that she wrote for International Women's Day. This article, also published as "International Women's Day and the Struggle for Peace," is included in the FBI file. But what is revealed from a study of the file is that it is the cumulative body of her writings that provided the documentary evidence the state used to argue for her deportation. Additionally, there were several attempts to arrest and deport her preceding the final action.

The logic of "un-American" behavior and its link to U.S. ideologies of patriotism, capitalism, and racism still has to be carefully unpacked in discourses of American identity, as they have lingering implications. These are often repackaged and reused whenever U.S. dominance has to be invoked worldwide, such as during war efforts like the U.S. invasion of Iraq and national elections like those of 2004, in which the politics of fear was used on the population at every level. Fascism, we already know, is one of the highest forms of a state's expression of its nationalism and patriotism in the need to advance state interests. African Americans such as Paul Robeson and U.S. American communists of European descent and those merely suspected of "un-American behavior" were therefore policed by the state for not living up to particular nation-state patriotism expectations. (In one of his exchanges with the HUAC investigators, Robeson told them that *they* were the ones who were un-American.)[37]

The Internal Security Act of 1950 (amending section 20 of Immigration Act of February 5, 1917), spells out the justification for the legislation of the denial of civil rights, and defines the terms employed:

(1) There exists a World Communist movement which in its origins, its development, and its present practice, is a world-wide revolutionary movement whose purpose it is, by treachery, deceit, infiltration into other groups (governmental and otherwise), espionage, sabotage, terrorism, and any other means deemed necessary, to establish a Communist totalitarian dictatorship in the countries throughout the world through the medium of a world-wide Communist organization. (987)

Claudia Jones had not only boldly and proudly identified her membership in a communist organization but was involved in countereducation processes, even seeking to educate the judge or at least set a public record on the definitions of communism.[38] At her trial with twelve other communists, the argument they offered was a denial "that the principles of Marxism-Leninism, as taught by them, have anything to do with the overthrow or destruction of the Government of the United States by force and violence. These principles as taught by them, they assert, form a unified whole, and are a true social science."[39] Communism for them was an ideological position; a social, cultural, intellectual, and political practice.

For her part, engaging largely in a defensive rhetorical exercise with the judge, Claudia Jones offered her own interpretations admitting very early that this was the case.

> Quite candidly, your Honor, I say these things not with any idea that what I say will influence your sentence of men. For even with all the power your Honor holds, how can you decide to mete out justice for the only act to which I proudly plead guilty, and one, moreover, which by your own prior rulings constitutes no crime — that of holding Communist ideas; of being a member and office of the Communist Party of the United States? ("Speech to the Court," 121)

In an analysis based mostly on the deplorable condition of the African American population in the United States, Claudia Jones challenged the judge that he too was circumscribed by the terms of the dominant discourse and chided him for not being able to even read publicly any of what she had written and was technically arrested for, that is, the text of her speech "Women in the Struggle for Peace and Security" because "it urges American mothers, Negro and white, to write, to emulate the peace struggles of their anti-fascist sisters in Latin America, in the new European democracies, in the Soviet Union, in Asia and Africa to end the bestial Korean war" (124).

We know that the activities of a number of strugglers for rights against racist domination were identified as subversive and were always linked to communism; from this, we can conclude that the state ideologies and definitions of communism (as identified, for example, in the *Congressional Record*, one of the main sites of this nation's self-definition) were also making important links between state repression and racism. All strugglers for human justice, for liberation of various kinds, because they challenge the nature of U.S. policies and practices, became technically "deportable subjects."[40]

In her letter written from Ellis Island to John Gates, editor of the *Daily Worker*, and published November 8, 1950, Claudia Jones identifies deportation as a weapon of the state. Her detailed description of the group of individuals being held there under the McCarran Act is therefore fundamental to identifying the international nature of the movement. Describing the group of seventeen as "a virtual United Nations," and not forgetting to mention the three prison guards, she writes:

> Among our company of 17 is a Slavic-American, the brawn and brain of whose people are forever merged with the great industrial achievements of America's working people — the miners of Pittsburgh, the auto workers of Detroit, the anthracite and copper miners on the Messable range of the Minnesotas.
>
> Here is a Finnish American, who sat four years in a similar detention jail, when another attorney general, Palmer by name, sought to impose Alien and Sedition raids and laws, defeated by the mass protests of Americans of an earlier day.
>
> Here are trade unionists from fur, electrical and maritime industries, who smile their firm greetings of approval when, from shops and locals, wires or letters come, telling of actions taken on behalf of American liberty. Here is a Negro man from the British West Indies whose people's blood mixed with Crispus Attucks, on that early day on Boston Commons when West Indian warriors, of the strain of Toussaint l'Ouverture, fought in the American Revolution. Second-class citizens, like 15 million Negro Americans, whose sons serve in Jim Crow units in Korea, they are no strangers to the second-class, Jim Crow justice likewise meted out to West Indians of foreign birth.
>
> Here are women, Negro and white, whose lives, like those of Emma Lazarus and Harriet Tubman, are a refutation of women's inequality in any field of endeavor; women, whose lives from early youth was [*sic*] pursuit of truth and, once learning, applied that truth learned in American homes and schools to help guarantee life, liberty and the pursuit of happiness in devotion to the American people and to future generations of children by participating in the struggles of our people.
>
> Here too, are leading representatives of the vanguard party of all the

toiling people — Communist leaders. One of the women, as you know, was confined for over a week to solitary confinement and was under constant surveillance.

All 17 here are examples of devotion to the strugglers of the labor movement, in the fight for Negro rights, against discrimination and lynching, in the fight for democracy, in our efforts on behalf of the peace and security of the people. And some hold beliefs that only under a Socialist society can these rights be finally secured!

There is a Spanish-American, a Ukrainian-American, an Italian-American, a Greek-American, and Jewish Americans. Descendants of Haym Solomon and Guiseppe Garibaldi, and of the people of Simon Bolivar and La Pasionaria, Sam Martin, they are proud and honored descendants of these heroes and heroines.

The diversity of subjects identified for deportation is deliberate. The phrase that Jones used to describe the group, "virtual United Nations," encapsulates her rhetorical intent to speak for the range of people victimized by the McCarran Act. The seventeen incarcerated are described as representative of people from Eastern Europe and the Caribbean and a range of "hyphenated" Americans and are multiplied into the thousands of people they represent from a variety of U.S. communities and around the world. Within the group of prisoners were those who had taken positions on behalf of black rights and workers' rights, as well as women's rights. Gender identification is central to this description, for she identifies women whose political practices have precedents, and who have mounted a "refutation of women's inequality in any field of endeavor."

Jones is clear in articulating the reasons given for their incarceration and threatened deportation. She asks, "Why are we here — on this notorious 'Island of Tears' — so close to Liberty's statue, where we have always been in mind, spirit and action?" and supplies the answer:

The majority of newspapers tell you that we are here because we are awaiting deportation hearings. That is a foul lie. Like many others now incarcerated, we have been out on bail for various periods of time pending disposition of deportation proceedings launched against us.

Many of us have had no hearings or legal examinations of any kind. We have never been confronted with any evidence, or made familiar with any crime, alleged or charged against us. Nor have any of us been informed or charged with the slightest infraction of the terms of our release on bail. . . . Nevertheless the government has re-arrested us without due process of law, and seeks to assign us to a virtual life-long imprisonment on Ellis Island.

We are threatened by the government with becoming the first inmates of America's concentration camps, the direct victims of the mad drive of the ruling circles to fascism at home and atomic war abroad.

Others like U.S. Attorney Irving H Saypol, who fought our plea for a restraining order against illegal re-arrest and who argued against the writ of the 11, already here nearly two weeks, for bail (which has already been substantially place on all our heads), claim that the U.S. Attorney General used his discretionary powers under the unconstitutional McCarran Act to deny us bail. This too is a foul lie.

The ridiculous part of it is that the American people are supposedly asked to believe that we are "awaiting deportation hearings" — a "normal procedure," and hence the Attorney General so uses his discretionary powers that he first illegally re-arrests people, already out on bail, then asks the court to give him time to ascertain whether he was discreet about the use of his discretionary powers. But Lincoln once spoke of the basis on which people can be fooled.

The truth, of course, is, that this is a clear violation of the American Constitution, the Bill of Rights, both of which guarantee the right of bail and the right of habeas corpus. That Judge F. McGohey ruled on the government motion on postponement first, and not on the right of bail, is a clear violation of this time-honored right.

I feel and I'm sure all the rest do likewise, that legal struggles, important as they are (and we feel our attorneys and the American Committee for Protection of Foreign Born are doing a heroic job) are incidental to the mass struggle to free us. We can and must win the right to remain free on bail. We must and can win the right to our citizenship — the onus of which legal lack is on the Department of Justice and its Immigration Service, who denied us naturalization, purely on the grounds of our conscience, our belief and our ideas.

Here, Claudia speaks of issues that are strikingly familiar to us in the period after 9/11 and the institution of the USA Patriot Act: the discretionary powers of the attorney general, violation of rights under the U.S. Bill of Rights such as habeas corpus, detention without bail, the absence of hearings, and the similarity to concentration camps. The entire situation of deportations, incarcerations, denials of freedoms of mobility and full citizenship rights, bring into sharp relief the frailty of rights under nation-states that purport to protect those same rights.[41]

Elizabeth Gurley Flynn, in *The Alderson Story*, summarizes how events played out for her comrade Jones:

> The last period of [Jones's] stay was one of further anxiety as to what would happen on her release. There was an outstanding order of deportation against her. We knew of women who had been picked up at the gate by immigration officials and shipped to Cuba, Mexico, and other Latin American countries. Claudia was born in Trinidad in the British West Indies. She was brought here as a small child by her parents. A representative of the British government came to see her shortly before her sentenced expired, and she requested to be allowed to go to England. Finally, Mrs. Kaufman arranged a nominal bail and for Claudia's release in her custody. (117)

Following her release from Alderson, on October 23, 1955 and her hospitalization at Mt. Sinai Hospital, Claudia Jones commented on her deportation in a way that linked her ideas to her American schooling:

> The fine talk about the free flow and exchange of ideas internationally and about freedom of speech in the US rings false when placed against this desperate attempt to deport me because of my political views. I am proud of my political views because I learned them in American schools. The traditions of democratic struggle exemplified by Franklin, Lincoln, Jefferson, Frederick Douglass and Sojourner Truth are the ideas that inspired me in my views. Why are they so frightened about the political view of one Negro woman? (*Daily Worker*, November 10, 1955)

Ironically, at the same time that Claudia Jones was fighting deportation, a jury refused to indict the kidnappers and murderers of Emmett Till. The Till case served as the front-page story of the *Daily Worker* issue in which Claudia's article appeared. In contemplating the vigor with which her political ideas had been persecuted, it was not lost on Claudia that equal energy was not spent in attacking U.S. racism.

Claudia Jones's farewell address at the party in her honor at the Hotel Theresa on 125th Street, New York, ended with "a poem to Elizabeth Gurley Flynn with whom she had shared imprisonment at Alderson, West Virginia . . . dedicated to all of her friends and comrades here."[42] According to the report, she spoke to a filled auditorium about her early years in Harlem and the influence of her parents, and how it felt to be exiled from her country after thirty-two years living there. But she also voiced her confidence in the "restoration of the principles of freedom." Jones was clear about the meaning of her exile as she left the United States, but as always she was optimistic that social change would come. William Patterson's "Remarks on the Eve of the Deportation of Claudia Jones" is similarly optimistic and points to the possibility of internationalizing connections:

> Claudia goes as a deportee, but as Frederick Douglass once left our shores carrying a message describing the crime of slavery, as William E. Burghardt Du Bois once went to Europe to denounce the monstrous crimes inherent in racism, Claudia Jones will show the racist rulers of America now threaten all mankind. Then on the other hand she will testify to the fact that growing insoluble contradictions plague the American enemies of freedom-loving peoples. Claudia will say that the ever-growing unity of the American people around the cause of civil liberties and civil rights testifies to who will best whom in the United States. Claudia's words will strengthen our allies.

In the piece "Ship's Log" that Jones wrote for her father aboard the *Queen Elizabeth*, her positions on her exile from the United States are clearly set out. She refers to her condition as "my exile for my independent political ideas" and of the United States as the "land I belong to and know and its people with whom I have worked and struggled for social progress." But Jones, as I noted in chapter 3, where I discuss this piece, transforms her pain into a positive emotion, turning the "ship of exile" into a vehicle that will take her to "marvelous places." In so doing, she transforms her punishment into an opportunity to carry her activism into the further reaches of the diaspora. By naming her experience exile, Claudia was able to play with the idea of citizenship and belonging. In the basic dictionary definitions, an *exile* is one who is separated from his or her own country, often, as a result of banishment (*New Webster's Dictionary*, 331). "Deportation" overlaps with "exile" in that it refers to "the lawful expulsion of an undesired alien or other person from a state or

Daily Worker

Vol. XXVIII, No. 64
(12 Pages) Price 5 cents

New York, Thursday, March 29, 1951

WHITE HOUSE PICKETED ON DEPORTATION ARRESTS

—See Page 2—

7. The response to deportation arrests. From the *Daily Worker*, March 29, 1951.

8. The *Queen Elizabeth*, on which Claudia Jones traveled to England.

Cunard R.M.S. "Queen Elizabeth"

country." Claudia had lived in the United States from the age of eight. It was her home. The shifting of the sense of "deportation" to a discourse of "exile," and beyond that to "purposeful migration," "internationalism," and "diaspora" becomes part of her resistance to nationstate constructions of the desirable citizen because it challenges the condition of "being deported."

Claudia's Caribbean Diaspora

Claudia Jones had already understood and participated in the earlier creation of what is now identified as a Caribbean diaspora, which by extension, because of the older history of African enslavement in the Caribbean, was part of the larger African diaspora. She had already been aboard a ship bound for the "land of the free." She had come to the United States as a child, accompanied by her aunt and three sisters, to join her parents in New York, arriving in Harlem in the middle of all the political and cultural activity of the Harlem Renaissance. As a young girl, she had experienced the poverty of urban black America but along with that partook of the experience of being an immigrant in the United States and the developing U.S. Caribbean diaspora of the 1920s.

Jones's FBI file describes the family's entry into the United States as follows: "According to Manifest #7888, page thirteen, line six, the subject arrived in New York City from Port of Spain, British West Indies, aboard the SS *Voltaire* on February 9, 1926. She was accompanied by an aunt, ALICE GLASGOW, and three sisters: LINDSEY CUMBERBATCH, age three, IRENE CUMBERBATCH, age five, and SYLVIA CUMBERBATCH, age nine" (3).

Claudia's own account of her family's migration expresses it in this way:

As a child of eight I came to the United States from Port of Spain, Trinidad, British West Indies. My mother and father had come to this country two years earlier, in 1922, when their economic status . . . had been worsened as a result of the drop in the cocoa trade from the West Indies which had impoverished the West Indies and the entire Caribbean. Like thousands of West Indian immigrants, they hoped to find their fortunes in America where "gold was to be found on the streets" and they dreamed of rearing their children in a "free America." This dream was soon disabused. Together with my three sisters, our family suffered not only the impoverished lot of working-class native families, and its multi-national populace, but early learned the special scourge of indignity stemming from Jim Crow national oppression."[43]

9. Flyleaf of Claudia Jones's passport.

10. Inside page of Claudia Jones's passport showing identification information.

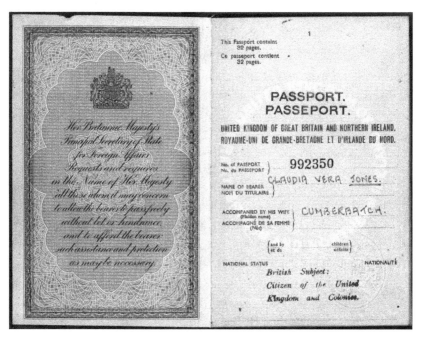

11. The Russian entry visa and stamps in Claudia Jones's passport.

12. The China entry visa and stamps in Claudia Jones's passport.

The basic details of arrival are the same. But Claudia's version describes what life was like for the black working-class family in the United States and her own belonging, through the family's participation in the same conditions that faced U.S.-born African Americans of the period. Some of that *energy of return* that people like Patterson identify emerges when one combats the erasure of Claudia Jones and the deporting of the "radical black subject," as I have aimed to do in this book, But this effort speaks as well to the need for a more complicated understanding of what "black community" means beyond nation-state circumscriptions and class meanings. The black community can certainly move beyond these historical definitions, as Jones and her contemporaries already knew. "So sure as the sun will rise again, so sure is it that we shall pave the way for Claudia's return. . . . We are certain that tomorrow there will be no more deportations, when passports will not be needed to ensure the right to travel nor visas to gain entry into another country. Claudia will return to us."[44]

The exiling of Claudia Jones to London effected the deporting of the radical black female subject, as I have argued. If deportation means relocating someone outside the boundaries of a given nation-state, then this end was achieved. The only possible recuperation of that subject exists in a recognition of diaspora discourses that challenge specific nation-state limitations. Claudia's politics were radical because of her ability to link decolonization struggles internally and externally and create for herself an international black subject identity.

One way of seeing deportation is as the limbo-like existence of unbelonging. But Claudia Jones's life proves that it can also be read in terms of the deliberate use of transnational movement to create diaspora, as the larger African population has done worldwide. So, after deportation, for Claudia Jones is a life full of organizing, travel, struggle and hardship, and new friendships, culminating with her death in December 1964, nine years after she left the United States. Testament to this is the way she was identified by the London Caribbean community at her death. A letter from the Afro-Caribbean Organization, dated April 1, 1983, says in part: "We see the memory of our dear Sister Claudia belonging to all conscious black people. We believe that Claudia's contributions to our struggle and the struggles of all oppressed people, is one of the most outstanding of contributions of a black Communist. Second only to Paul Robeson. We name our home for Homeless

Order Claudia Jones Deported Under McCarran Law

By Harry Raymond

Claudia Jones, outstanding Negro woman leader, was ordered exiled to the British colony of Trinidad under provisions of the McCarran Law yesterday at the conclusion of a temporary-style deportation trial.

Her "crime": She neglected to be born in the U.S.A. and since her arrival here 20 years ago she has been a nationally recognized leader in the struggle for Negro liberation and women's rights.

The deportation order against Miss Jones was announced orally by Immigration Hearing Officer Joseph J. Mark. Mack admitted the government had been unable to present evidence that the respondent had, as was originally charged, been a member of an organization advocating overthrow of the government by force and violence. He ruled her deportable on testimony of two Mikol paid government informers, Paul and Sylvia Crouch, who said they "knew" her as a member of the Communist Party.

An hour after the "trial" of Miss Jones concluded, Hearing Officer

CLAUDIA JONES

13. The McCarran Law crushing Liberty, with Labor trying to protect her. Note the dying flame in Liberty's torch. From a 1950s *Daily Worker*. Photograph by author.

14. The deportation of Claudia Jones. From the *Daily Worker*, December 22, 1954.

Your presence is requested at a

FAREWELL RECEPTION

for

CLAUDIA JONES

(On the Eve of her Departure)
For Britain

Wednesday, December Seventh
Nineteen hundred and fifty-five
Eight-thirty P. M.

Skyline Ballroom — Hotel Theresa
Seventh Avenue at 125th Street
New York City

Cultural Program — Social Dancing — Refreshment
No Admission Charges — — — Contributions Welcome

Your Hosts:

Mr. and Mrs. William L. Patterson   Louise Jeffers
Mr. and Mrs. Howard Johnson   Cyril Philips
Mr. and Mrs. James W. Ford   Mary Morgan
Mr. and Mrs. Robert Fogel   Leon Wofsy
Ramona Garrett   Herbert L. Wheeldin
Alec Jones   Mrs. Helois Robinson

Mildred McAdory Adelman

15. Copy of the invitation to the farewell reception for Claudia Jones, 1955.

16. Claudia Jones in the company of three other travelers aboard the *Queen Elizabeth*, 1955.

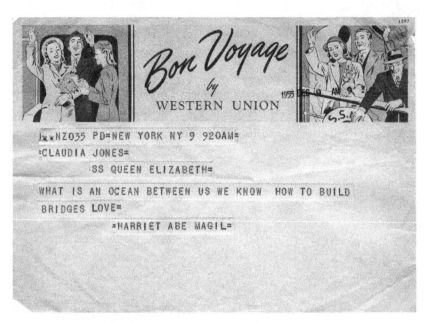

17. Harriet Abe Magill's telegram to Claudia Jones on board the *Queen Elizabeth*.
Claudia Jones Memorial Collection.

Black youngsters, Paul Robeson House for the same reason as we intend to honour Claudia Jones."[45]

A women's liberation magazine, *Journal of Women's Liberation Front* (London) carries a Peking Meeting Tribute (along with others from Latin America) which speaks of her work in London in a similar vein.

> Claudia Jones was also identified with that other great movement of our time, the struggle for national liberation. For years she was a leader of the liberation struggle of the American Negroes. In Britain, she was the champion of the West Indian people, and of Asian and African people as well, in their struggle against racialism. She worked hard informing links between the national liberation struggle in the Caribbean and those in Africa and Asia. . . . Thus, she did her part in the urgent task of building a worldwide united front against the common enemy, U.S. imperialism. Claudia Jones was never in doubt that the enemy was imperialism and that its leader was U.S. imperialism."[46]

An internationalist, diaspora framework recovers the radical black female subject that Claudia Jones represents and begins a process of relational work, combating the imposed erasure that was attempted by the U.S. government.

For Claudia Jones in this context, diaspora certainly meant pain and separation from family but it also meant a host of other things: recreation of community, the love of life, struggle, and public organizing, creation of communication mechanisms such as a newspaper, organizing of forums and actions such as the march on London in 1963, the bringing together of black scholars and artists across the diaspora, beauty pageants, and last but not least, carnival.[47]

Chapter 5

CARNIVAL AND DIASPORA

Caribbean Community, Happiness, and Activism

A people's art is the genesis of their freedom
CARIBBEAN CARNIVAL 1959, SOUVENIR PROGRAM

The intellectual, cultural, and political work of Claudia Jones, in my estimation, offers one of the best models of African diaspora activism available. For Jones, who emerged as a leading member of the developing London Caribbean community in the 1950s and early 1960s, carnival carried, in its cultural practice, resistance to Euro-American bourgeois aesthetics, imperialism and cultural hegemony, and political and racial oppression. Carnivals, in the African diaspora tradition, demonstrate the joy that its people experience in "taking space." A number of scholars have identified the generating elements of Caribbean carnivals generally.[1]

In her essay "The Caribbean Community in Britain," written for a special issue of *Freedomways*,[2] Claudia Jones provides one of the earliest detailings of the historical, political, and sociocultural experiences of the Caribbean diaspora in the United Kingdom. Beginning with Louise Bennett's famous concept of "colonization in reverse" as a poetic representation of what Caribbean migration entailed, Jones cites some demographic statistics from the early 1960s in order to talk about immigration from the Caribbean and the controls the British were instituting. In this context, she cites specifically the Commonwealth Immigration

Act (1962) as the culmination of the heightened racial prejudice in Britain. From there she assesses some of the common problems facing Caribbean immigrants, ranging from housing and work to other social conditions and cites the role of the *West Indian Gazette* in community organizing in Britain.

Claudia Jones was well positioned to assess the conditions of Caribbean peoples in the United Kingdom in relation to the rest of the colonial world and of course to the United States. Doubly or triply diasporized, twice a migrant herself (to the United States as a child and then to England), as a political activist and journalist, and as editor of the *West Indian Gazette and Afro-Asian Caribbean News*, the first major Caribbean newspaper in Britain, Jones ushered in the development of a Caribbean readership that paralleled the formation of this Caribbean diaspora in Britain.

Caribbean Diaspora/Caribbean Activism

The early assessment of the London Caribbean community that Jones provided in "The Caribbean Community in Britain" makes it also a founding text of what would become a "black British" discourse. Since then a number of other texts have detailed various aspects of the London black community. Among these, Paul Gilroy's *There Is No Black in the Union Jack* sought to present some of the aspects of the experience of black Britains as they confronted racism and developed their own cultural formations. Winston James and Clive Harris's *Inside Babylon: The Caribbean Diaspora in Britain* dealt more directly with the experience of Afro-Caribbean peoples in Britain from a variety of angles: migration and identity formation, racism, black women's organizing, carnivals, and the state.[3] Of relevance to this study of Claudia Jones is the fact that the James and Harris book *Inside Babylon* is dedicated to "Kelso Cochrane, Antiguan carpenter, killed by racists in the streets of Notting Hill, 16 May 1959, aged 33 and Claudia Jones, (21 February 1915 to 25 December 1964) who fought oppression and exploitation on both sides of the Atlantic."

Sociologist Harry Goulbourne's book *Caribbean Transnational Experience* begins by seeing a larger project of "the development of theoretically relevant and empirically informed knowledge about the living connections between Caribbeans in Britain and their links to a wider world across the Atlantic" (vii). He makes some important distinctions between concepts of diaspora and transnationalism making it clear that although these are conceptually intertwined, having migration as their base, "a diaspora can come into existence without there being any significant increase or development of either transnationalism or globalisation" (7). For Goulbourne, the future of the Caribbean diaspora has to remain an open question as we locate its formation, identify some of its contours, and examine the "lived lives of real people" (207). Goulbourne provides important details about the nature of Caribbean transnationalism, following the Jones essay (of the 1960s) and the intervening four decades since then. In the 1990s, for example, the work of cultural studies provided a great deal of understanding of the nature of identity formation within the context of the postmodern. Stuart Hall is identified as offering the most dynamic theoretical leadership in this process, coming to terms with the mobility of black identities and their modes of articulation.

In a related vein, the projects of Alrick Cambridge and the Race Policy Unit in Brixton produced a series of workshops and study groups on this question and at least two texts that specified the nature of antiracist politics and the related issue of belonging in England.[4] Claudia Jones's essay on the Caribbean community ("The Caribbean Community in Britain") was also republished in the journal the *Black Liberator*, which Cambridge edited and which in many ways carried forward the legacy of Claudia Jones to a new generation. Cambridge, who had worked with Jones as her last assistant before her death, is identified by Donald Hinds as "the new boy on the block, [who] was alone and answering the phone at the offices of the WIG [when he broke the news to Hinds]. He turned with the saddest face imaginable: 'Claudia is dead!' he said."[5] From all accounts, it would not be a death of Claudia Jones's vision. Cambridge's work in the formation of black political organizations and related movements in the 1970s was able to move the political culture forward and influence a subsequent generation, including creative spoken-word artists like Linton Kwesi Johnson.[6] The continuing contributions of John La Rose of New Beacon Books and Jessica and Eric Huntley of Bogle L'Ouverture publications, along with a variety of other publishers such as Amon Saba Saakana of Karnak House and Buzz Johnson of Karia Press, advanced into the twenty-first century a literature and culture of the Caribbean diaspora that Jones in many ways had stimulated.

As she entered the London leftist community, Jones realized right away that the close and respected central relationship she had with the Communist Party USA and her various comrades in the party there would not develop in

London. Marika Sherwood details the nature of the Communist Party Great Britain (CPGB) and its failed relationship with Claudia Jones, and above all its shortsightedness in not using her skill and organizational talents.[7] Beyond the initial, obviously deliberate, lukewarm reception she received from the CPGB, and the larger racial and gender discrimination that accompanied it, there were a series of petty bureaucratic challenges (such as for missed meetings), which alienated her from the party. (These are documented in the Claudia Jones Papers in the Schomburg Research Center.) These difficulties are traceable to the English brand of racism manifesting itself within the party, but also with sexism from the left, that she had fought against so strongly in the United States. Unable to work with the CPGB and witnessing the growing needs in the migrating Caribbean community firsthand, she turned her skills and attention to advancing the interests of this community and established, simultaneously, more definite pan-Africanist positions.[8]

The first major ship voyage from the Caribbean, which ushered in Caribbean migration to England, occurred in 1948, barely seven years before Jones's arrival. So she was, in effect, at the beginning point of what would become the flourishing Caribbean community in London. On that ship, the MV *Empire Windrush* there were at least three major calypsonians and a variety of other entertainers from other parts of the Caribbean. Others would join the London Caribbean community later.[9]

Jones clearly still had sufficient memory of the Caribbean to interact with its community and to access its culture. Her birthplace, Belmont, and childhood home, Woodbrook, in Port-of-Spain, were two of the prime urban centers of carnival production in Trinidad. She was part of the first wave of Caribbean migration to the United States and was raised in a Caribbean immigrant family in New York, living Caribbean culture in migration on a daily basis.

Perhaps a more significant connection in her understanding of the nature and functions of Caribbean culture in diaspora and of carnival as one of its prime manifestations is that during the time that Jones lived in New York, there had already developed the first Caribbean carnival in a major metropolitan area. Dale Byam reports that following the first wave of Caribbean migration to New York in the 1920s, there began the process of cultivating a carnival. Much of it resembles what happened in London under Jones's leadership.

The beginnings were auspicious, immediately attracting popular attention through the dances that defined the event. These dance hall parties — carnival fetes — introduced the "idea" of carnival with the street parade a later addition. Caribbean immigrants such as Hubert Lucas and Daphne Weekes organized the dances to reconstruct their country's annual festive celebrations (held concurrently with the carnival festivities in Trinidad during the pre-Lenten season) by providing Caribbean music and masquerade bands in these dance halls. . . . The dance hall parties constituted the full extent of carnival in New York up to 1946. Up to that time the formal street parade was virtually non-existent except for an impromptu parade which took to the street after the dances, but winter limited that outdoor revelry. . . . In 1946 the first formal Caribbean parade took to the streets of Harlem, New York as one section of a Labor Day marching band. The event created new meaning and new responsibility as revelers revealed Caribbean culture to the wider mainstream culture.[10]

Byam reports that the carnival in New York coincided with the resuming of carnival in Trinidad after the war and that it was also seen as a way of bridging cultures at a time of "growing interest in human and civil rights in the United States."

Jones was well aware then, at the experiential level, of the nature of carnival in diaspora, as the event took place in Harlem throughout the 1930s and 1940s.[11] But in my estimation, and given her politics, she would have been critical of the fact that there was no link to the lived realities of African American and Caribbean peoples in the New York version. For her, the trials of poverty and migration, and of the difficulties of living in a large, cold, and impersonal metropolitan site, as well as her political involvement in the Communist Party from an early age, produced a different approach to culture. She would implement this link between politics and culture in her own development of the London Carnival as she brought all of these experiences to her work in London among the growing number of Caribbean immigrants. All of her London activity was therefore organized to enhance and advance the lives of her Caribbean people in Britain.

So, Jones began to engage the London location as another site of struggle, in an affirmative response to the pain of separation from family, friends, and community in New York. Thus upon her arrival in England, despite suffering from a heart condition exacerbated by her nine and a half months in prison, she almost immediately began organizing the London Caribbean community, using as one of the major tools of mobilization the founding of the *West Indian Gazette*.[12] The *Gazette* was founded in 1957 and launched in March 1958, just twenty-seven months after her arrival in the United Kingdom. As we have already seen, the newspaper itself became one of the defining forces of the Caribbean community of the 1950s and 1960s, communicating news on the gains of the various independence movements, pan-Africanism, anti-apartheid and anticolonial struggles, sports, and culture. By 1958 when the first issue was published, the Caribbean population numbered 80,000.

Jones describes the newspaper herself as a "major effort designed to stimulate political and social thinking" (354). So it is significant that the newspaper was the prime sponsor of the first London Carnivals. The "WIG," as Jones called it, was meant to be a primary information organ for the Caribbean community and to serve the role of political educator for a community that was beleaguered, scattered, uninformed, and subject to racial oppression, including racial violence. Glaring examples of this violence were a series of racially motivated attacks in the Notting Hill area, and in particular, the murder of Kelso Cochrane in May 1959, the victim of a gang of white youth following the Notting Hill race riots of 1958. Most of the people I interviewed,[13] as well as scholars of that period, agree that this series of incidents provided the catalyst for putting in place a more self-directed and culturally and politically aware community.

On the *West Indian Gazette* itself and its impact on the development of Caribbean culture in London, Donald Hinds reports that "some of the best Caribbean writers have written for the journal. Perhaps no other Caribbean journal other than BIM has ever had such a collection of writers. One of the most quoted articles the *Gazette* has published was novelist Jan Carew's great definition of the West Indian. Also the poetic prose of George Lamming has appeared from time to time" ("The *West Indian Gazette*," 151–152). Events such as the establishment of a Caribbean Carnival in London was but one of the cultural end-products of this organizing and one which Jones self-consciously employed to heal a racially divided community in the aftermath of the 1958, racist-motivated, antiblack attacks.[14] Edward Pilkington similarly assigns the riots and the rise of the *West Indian Gazette* this role, suggesting that "the riots marked the dawn of a new West Indian identity for black people living in Britain and the beginning of a search for a common black ancestry which culminated in the 1960s Black Power movement" (143–144). He also cites Jan Carew's article as part of the attempt to define Caribbean cultural values and identity.

In *Beyond the Mother Country*, Edward Pilkington suggests that the *Gazette*, under Jones's direction, would serve as a "mouthpiece for the new associations which were being formed" and play a role in the definition of Afro-Caribbean identity in Britain, replacing the earlier "British colonial subject" identity that many of the immigrants carried with them to the United Kingdom.

> The *Gazette* acted as a forum for debate, allowing West Indians to express their uncertainties and confusions in the wake of the riots. Their British identity had been jolted by the riots, for how could they call themselves British after being treated like unwarranted strangers. . . . Out of the ashes of the "Mother Country" a new vision was born. The riots marked the dawn of a new West Indian identity for black people living in Britain and the beginning of a search for a common black ancestry, which culminated in the 1960s Black Power movement. (143–144)

Pilkington also identifies the link between the riots, which were directed against the presence of Caribbeans in the Notting Hill area of London, and the decisions of those same Caribbean people to assert their presence culturally and politically. It is here that Jones was able to utilize her experience in organizing for the benefit of the community. Accordingly, among her many contributions, says Pilkington, she worked with Norman Manley to create a "fund to help pay the fines of black people arrested during the disturbances" (143). "The task of all these organisations was to create something positive out of the destruction of the riots. . . . Four months after the riots she (Claudia Jones) organised, as a gesture of black solidarity and of inter-racial friendship, the first Caribbean Carnival in London, forerunner of the Notting Hill Carnival" (143).

Bill Schwarz offers another insight into the function of the London Carnival, seeing it as also conducting the Caribbean community in London into Caribbean nationhood, identifying them therefore as an important component of the Caribbean diaspora. "Carnival may have been inspired by the particular conditions of London, following the Notting Hill riots, but it was also conceived as an organic part of the movement for colonial independence, and of the ambitions to transform the West Indian Federation into an active, living cultural reality" ("Claudia Jones and the *West Indian Gazette*," 273).

It may be useful therefore to identify at least six movements in Jones's activism in London. First is her tentative work in the Communist Party, comprising membership in two subcommittees of the CPGB and various other sporadic work in rallies and other activities. The second major movement includes her work in the Notting Hill area: the antiracist work surrounding the white riots and various other manifestations. The development of the *West Indian Gazette and Afro-Asian Caribbean News* and her extensive journalistic contributions to the formation of the paper and its related activities and events would constitute the third movement. The founding of the London Carnival and the other related cultural projects such as talent shows would be the fourth. The fifth is the formation of the Afro-Asian Conference and the subsequent development of the Committee of Afro-Asian and Caribbean Organizations, which had much to do with the mobilization of the African and Asian communities of Britain and involved work with Africa House and the African community in London. The sixth movement would clearly be the intellectual work that went into the definition of anticolonial and anti-imperialist theoretics. In the same vein, Jones was also involved in the formation of social and political organizations of white and black people, with antiracism at the center.

Claudia Jones's Position on Carnival and (Caribbean) Culture

The London Carnival has had perhaps a greater impact than any other initiative or event in making Caribbean culture central to the British experience. From all accounts, Jones struggled against comrades who felt that carnivals and beauty contests were trivial in light of the larger issues of struggle for rights in the United Kingdom. But Jones clearly felt that Caribbean traditions had much to offer the world in terms of creating a culture of human happiness over the ignorance and pain of racism, and indeed that it was a people's culture that provided them with the basis for acquiring their freedom.

Jones always acted from the principle that economics, politics, and culture were inextricably linked. She was, for example, critical of the "cultural barriers" that the Communist Party instituted and that, therefore, did not allow access for the people who deserved the relationship the most. This was one feature of her critique of racial exclusions in the Communist Party USA, which would become more salient in London and in the CPGB, with its inability to respect black women of her experience, much less to recruit black women from the community.

According to Lydia Lindsey, Jones's stance was unlike that of other black spokespersons of the Communist Party USA, which often did not understand that these three elements — economics, politics, and culture — worked together.[15] This position would similarly be a source of struggle for her in her relationships with some of her black left comrades in England.[16] Several of them scoffed at the idea of having carnival, dances, and beauty contests as means of doing political work, and Jones was forced to defend her ideas on using culture to create community on several occasions.[17] In the specific case of the Caribbean community, which she had already identified as suffering from day-to-day struggles in the unwelcoming administrative center of their colonial experience, Jones determined that culture, as a series of normative practices, was an important tool in the community's development as in larger political and economic struggles as a whole. It was through this vision of culture, she felt, that the various black British communities would be educated about each other while developing self-awareness of their own cultural histories.

It is as if the vividness of our national life was itself the spark urging translation to new surroundings, to convey, to transplant our folk origins to British soil. There is a comfort in this effort not only for the Carnival Committee and the *West Indian Gazette*, for the fine artists participating in our Carnival who have lent of their talents here, but for all West Indians, who strain to feel and hear and reflect their idiom even as they strain to feel the warmth of their sun-drenched islands and its immemorial beauty of landscape and terrain."[18]

Far from being a "culturalist" in the sense of celebrating culture for its own ends, Jones instead saw culture in materialist terms. Still within the context of Marxism-Leninism, therefore, Jones was drawn to those aspects of culture that lent themselves to community joy and social transcendence of the given conditions of people's experience, that is, their material culture. Thus putting in place the celebratory, in this case, was an act of cultural affirmation.[19] This is true also of the historically important celebrations of black women's beauty, even if Jones did use a format that 1960s and 1970s bourgeois feminists would later reject, namely the black beauty contest.

Jones's signature piece, "A People's Art Is the Genesis of Their Freedom," in the souvenir booklet of the first carnival in 1959, spells out her position in detail. In this statement, Marxist in its formation, she applauds the rapid response from the work of the Caribbean Carnival Committee, which had been set up the prior November (1958) by the *West Indian Gazette*. Become now something of a progressive Caribbean nationalist, in the sense of arguing for a united Caribbean people,[20] Jones asserts: "If, then, our Caribbean Carnival has evoked the wholehearted response from the peoples from all the Islands of the Caribbean in the new West Indies Federation, this is itself testament to the role of the arts in bringing people together for common aims, and to its fusing of the cultural, spiritual, as well as political and economic interests of West Indians in U.K. and at home."

Clearly the joy in coming together as a community can be defined as one of the prime energies behind carnivals abroad. I have written about this elsewhere, responding to the Miami Carnival as follows: "The genesis of these carnivals carries the intent of resisting, on some level by Caribbean migrants, the otherwise alienating conditions of life in North American/Puritan based culture: to carnivalise in 'postcolonial' intent these landscapes with some of the joy and space commensurate with Caribbean Carnival."[21] In the case of the London Carnival, Jones herself says: "The vividness of our national life was itself the spark urging translation to new surroundings" ("A People's Art"). However, the political history that led to the carnival, the murder of Kelso Cochrane, is not lost. "There is of course another cause to be assessed to their response to those who have filled St. Pancras Town Hall. That reason is the event of Notting Hill and Nottingham — an event which was the matrix binding West Indians in the United Kingdom together as never before — determined that such happenings should not recur" ("A People's Art").[22] Jones makes the links between the cultural phenomenon of carnival, landscape, history, home, and the politics of struggle for social change. Yet the connections are not limited to Caribbean culture, but extend to engage international cultural expressions. For Jones, then, Caribbean culture, because it is multiracial and multidimensional, should provide the example, "helping the universal quest to turn the instruments of science everywhere for the good of all mankind, for the freedom of all the world's people, no matter what the pigment of their skin for human dignity and friendship of all peoples everywhere" ("A People's Art"). For Jones, as the title of her article indicates, art and culture, if linked deliberately to human freedom as fundamental aspects of human self-assertion and expression, provide the impetus for human liberation: A people's *culture* is the genesis of their liberation! (My emphasis.)

It is significant to note as well that the Caribbean Carnival was just one of the cultural events that Jones and her associates organized. A variety of concerts, such as those that featured Paul Robeson, talent shows, and other cultural events were frequently sponsored by the *West Indian Gazette*. Additionally, there were forums on the West Indian Federation and on particular countries in Africa and the Caribbean; the forum "China, the Bomb and Disarmament," chaired by a noted authority on China; and marches against racial discrimination and apartheid, organized by the Committee of Afro-Asian and Caribbean Organisations. The *Gazette* itself became an informational network, connecting a variety of political and cultural communities with information about the various countries and advertisements from local businesses and social clubs. In a sense, the advertisements themselves provide an insight into some of the dynamic developments of the community at that time.

Place, Time, Space (Inside/Outside), and the London Caribbean Carnival

The first London Carnivals were organized to coincide with the Trinidad Carnivals, so they tended to be held during the winter months (January through March). Carnivals were held annually from 1958 up to Jones's untimely death in 1964. Several of these were televised by the BBC and aired in the Caribbean. The obviousness of naming should not be lost in all this. The carnival initiated by Jones was called the "Caribbean Carnival." The implementation of a structure of carnival in diaspora is, I have been arguing, one of Jones's major contributions; and the major structures of the carnival that she founded were identical to ones found in Trinidad-style carnivals everywhere.

Claire Shepherd in "Who Controls the Notting Hill Carnival?" takes it back further to the influx of carnival-knowledgeable folk in London:

Among the *Windrush* passengers were two calypsonians from Trinidad — Lord Beginner (Egbert Moore) and Lord Kitchener (Aldwyn Roberts) — they were a part of the vanguard to the whole calypso culture in Britain.

Three years later, more steel pan players arrived in Britain, among them Philmore Gordon Davidson — nicknamed "Boots," hailed as "the father of the steelband culture in this country. In 1951, at the age of 22, he led the Trinidad All Percussion Orchestra (TAPSO) in an unprecedented six-week tour of England as part of the Festival of Britain, with Sterling Battencourt, Russ Henderson and many other pan players. . . . Henderson stayed in Britain with a few of the other pan men when most of the band returned to Trinidad after the Festival and played at venues such as Victory House, Leicester Square, a popular centre for "West Indian dances." He was joined by Claudia Jones, Selwyn Baptiste, Andre Shevington, and still later by Ashton "tailor" Charles, Byron Rock, Rolph Webster and many other pan players. . . . The London Carnival began as a mode of artistic and cultural expression. (3)

The carnivals that Jones and the *West Indian Gazette* organized therefore served as an early template for carnival in diaspora: a model, a condensed version of a successful carnival — the Trinidad Carnival — which only had to be opened up and executed in the creation of the now internationally known Notting Hill Carnival. In that connection, it is important to identify a few of its features. First of all, the carnival was a popular response to the racially motivated riots and attempts at intimidating Caribbean people in Notting Hill and Nottingham and in particular to the murder of Kelso Cochrane. The initial aggression might then be likened to the initial impetus for African-based carnivals in the Caribbean, the *cannes brulées* and emancipation origins of carnival, as distinct from the European pre-Lenten festivals. According to Pilkington:

> Every year at the end of August, carnival is celebrated on the streets of Notting Hill. Unlike the carnivals that used to take place in the Caribbean under British rule, the Notting Hill festivities have no imperial undertones. No reference is made to Queen Victoria liberating black people from slavery, and instead of Union Jacks, stallholders sell posters of Marcus Garvey or Haile Selassie. Today's carnival, which attracts over a million people, is a symbol both of the growing self-confidence of Britain's black community, and of greater inter-racial mixing. It is also a commemoration of the 1958 riots, being held each year on their anniversary, an irony which escapes most carnival-goers. (*Beyond the Mother Country*, 153)

The extent to which this political link is actually broken or set aside by those who study or organize the carnival is of course debatable. Nevertheless, the history of the carnival is well documented, as are the ongoing struggles of the Carnival Development Committee, including a series of near riots and confrontations with police that have taken place over the years.

Cecil Gutzmore in "Carnival, the State and Black Masses in the United Kingdom," identifies the variety of prohibitions that the state has consistently tried to enforce and the various forms of resistance to these. He also argues the link between the Notting Hill Carnival and the Notting Hill race riots of 1958 and subsequent carnivals such as Carnival 1976, in which excessive state policing led to open resistance. Before 1958, he indicates, there were no attempts by the state to confront or suppress "any major cultural activity of the black masses" (212). But the white racist riots changed all that. Gutzmore sees the carnival as a cultural form, organized in a street version, and solidly in resistance to and in the face of state repression, though with all its various contradictions in place.[23]

The relationship between inside and outside, and the logic of taking place, or, more precisely, "taking space," are as central for the performance of carnival[24] as are other key components like music, dance, and costume. The first Caribbean Carnival took place indoors (though there are reports of people taking the London Underground in costume to go to the carnival, who thus created a public presence outside of the limits of the hall space).

The only distinction that can be made between the first and later manifestations of the London Carnival is their inside or outside dynamics and therefore the issue of scale and time, based on the fact that the first carnivals were indoors. Still, given the season (winter) when the first carnival was held, an indoor carnival was the only logical possibility. This would also be the case in a number of the early carnivals in the United States, particularly the university-based versions held indoors, and the subsequent decisions to hold the carnival during the summer months (Toronto, New York, and Hartford, Conn., and Washington, D.C., for example). The changing of the time of the year for the Caribbean Carnival, after Jones's death allowed an outside version to develop in more elaborate style, as is typical with outdoor festivals.

To execute that initial carnival, Jones as editor of the *West Indian Gazette*, the prime sponsor of the event, organized a Caribbean Carnival Committee to decide the nature of the celebrations and produced its various components.

Essential elements in the first London Caribbean Carnivals included masqueraders, steelband musicians (Trinidad All Stars, Dixielanders), live brass bands, calypsonians (Mighty Terror, Sparrow, and Lord Kitchener).[25]

Another important element of the carnival was the carnival queen competition, and the crowning of the carnival queen. There were also Caribbean dance companies such as Boscoe Holder and Troupe, bongo dancers, tambour bamboo, limbo dancing, and a "jump-up." The carnivals were recorded by the BBC and transmitted to the Caribbean, and televised coverage still marks carnival celebrations in the Caribbean. Photographs reveal huge dancing crowds of attendees.

Clearly Jones and her Caribbean Carnival Committee condensed the extended period of the Trinidad-style carnival into one night in which all the various elements could take place. A distinguished panel of judges selected the carnival queen, and a production team of well-known exponents of Caribbean culture, such as Edric Connor, provided leadership. In the spirit of "working with what she had available," Jones was able to produce a carnival of distinction, given its time and place. Pages of the *West Indian Gazette*, for months before the carnival, advertised its various events and deadlines, and announced who would be participating, reportage that also served to increase its readership.

Claudia Jones's central role is corroborated well by Colin Prescod, whose contribution benefits from the oral histories of those (including himself) identified as being in the company of family members who were friends of Jones. Additionally he quotes Trevor Carter, who said that "the spirit of the Carnival came out of Claudia's political knowledge of what to touch at a particular time when we were scared, we were people in disarray."[26]

Exactly who founded the London Caribbean Carnival that became the Notting Hill Carnival has been a subject of debate, though the facts are well documented. Errol Hill in his classic, well-respected text, *The Trinidad Carnival*, for many still the definitive study of carnival, explains Jones's role in the founding of the London carnival in the introduction to the 1997 edition as follows:

> The Notting Hill Carnival, now attracting an estimated 1.5 million spectators, claims to be the biggest street festival of popular culture in Europe. It is a two-day celebration taking place on the last Sunday and Monday in August, a bank holiday weekend. This Carnival was initiated largely as an

annual indoor event (with occasional outdoor sorties) by the Trinidad-born journalist Claudia Jones in an effort to reinforce the Caribbean community following the Notting Hill race riots of 1958. After her untimely death in 1965, a street carnival organized by London-born community leader Raume Laslett was, by 1970, decisively being run by West Indians under constant scrutiny by the London police. (xxiii)

Extensive research carried out by noted ethnomusicologist Geraldine Connor (the daughter of Cedric Connor, one of the members of the carnival committee) for her master's thesis, "Culture, Identity and the Music of Notting Hill Carnival," identifies a variety of sources that corroborate the information about Jones's role in London Carnival's origins; she cites the London-based Caribbean academic John La Rose, the black leader and carnivalist Darcus Howe, and Paul Oliver, a specialist on black popular music styles, as confirming that carnival has been celebrated in Britain "in some form or fashion since 1959" and that it began "under the auspices of political activist and writer Claudia Jones."[27]

The argument, advanced by Abner Cohen in *Masquerade Politics*,[28] that ascribes the carnival's origins to Rhaume Lazlett, a British social worker, misses the point. Clearly, Ms. Lazlett, without knowledge of carnival, can be credited (if there is still a need for any such credit) for simply tapping, as any good social worker should, into the preexisting sociocultural structures and working with the various community practitioners of carnival, who clearly knew what they were doing. Claudia Jones, by contrast, was not only Trinidadian but also a skilled and knowledgeable community organizer who organized the London black community on various fronts, carnival being only one of them.

In each of these scenarios though, it is impossible to disempower the community by attributing ownership of something as large as a carnival to one individual. Carnivals are attributable to community, led by an organizing team, that is, of those who know and understand the nature of the elements of masquerading, and this was the case in the first London Carnivals, as it would be in the subsequent Notting Hill Carnivals. The structures of carnival and, additionally, the organizing work require a variety of individuals to produce the event. Thus it makes sense that a Notting Hill Carnival Committee was founded, in the 1970s, to manage and develop the London Carnival. Its origins can be traced to the mid-sixties, in the adventure playgrounds in the

Tavistock and Golbourne areas of Notting Hill, and it took shape with the intent of enabling "the West Indian Community to feel at home in a country to which it is historically and spiritually tied." Its constitution identifies one of its aims as being "to use the ambiance, pleasure and social spirit of Notting Hill Carnival as an instrument for the advancement of better race relations in North Kensington generally."[29] This basic impulse is, of course, identical with the initial aims and vision that Jones advanced for the London Caribbean Carnival. All of the contributors to the 1996 Claudia Jones symposium at the Institute for Contemporary Arts[30] spoke to the links between the outdoor carnival and the initial indoor versions that Jones and the Carnival Committee managed.

A 1996 newsletter for the Association for a People's Carnival[31] supports the connection between the early London Carnival associated with Jones and the later Notting Hill ones in another way. It comments on a proposal to erect two statues in the Notting Hill area — one of Jones and one of Kelso Cochrane, murdered in the race riots there. The carnival exists in Notting Hill largely because of these two figures. Referring to Cochrane's death, the article notes:

> This death was the mobilising force for Claudia Jones, editor of the *West Indian Gazette* and her Carnival Organising Committee who purposely started a carnival that same year. Claudia Jones and the Carnival Organising Committee believed that a Caribbean-style Carnival would, firstly, bring together the West Indian peoples together building upon unity of purpose they used to defeat racists during the riots. Secondly, it would show the British people the creative and artistic contribution West Indian people could produce to enrich British culture. (5)

It is not surprising that the Notting Hill (street-based) Carnival started in 1965, the year after Jones's death.[32] The fact that her death ended the indoor carnival is significant, in that her passing created a vacuum that could only be filled by the outdoor development, which happened and which becomes a living testament to the memory of Jones, who was loved, honored, and respected by the entire London Caribbean community.[33] In other words, carnival represents precisely what Jones suggested it was — the "spirit of a people that cannot be contained, that which therefore contains the genesis of their own (self-articulated) freedom."

Seeing the carnival as part of the long history of African peoples to empower themselves, Claire Shepherd identifies it as carrying the same legacy of self-articulation that is the tradition of carnival in its Afro-Caribbean origins. "The Notting Hill Carnival remains carefully confined and patrolled, yet carries with it the many stories of the will of African peoples to adjust to new environments, to survive and thrive" ("Who Controls the Future of the Notting Hill Carnival?" 3). Claire Holder, a chairperson of Notting Hill Carnival Limited, identifies it in terms that echo Jones's early articulation of culture and art as expressions of freedom: "Carnival is a celebration of our liberation. . . . [F]or us as a people, carnival is spiritual — the embodiment of our sense of being and purpose."[34]

Fortunately, the children of some of these early committee members are around and old enough now to articulate what they experienced — at times in their own homes — of the history of London Carnival. Their accounts constitute important first-person documentation of important cultural history. David Roussel-Milner, the son of Carmen England,[35] an early member of the Caribbean Carnival Committee and one of its organizers, has given us an invaluable resource in his "False History of Notting Hill Carnival." In it, he challenges the ascription of the founding of the carnival to Rhaume Lazlett. Instead, he sees the Notting Hill Carnival as a "fulfillment of Claudia's promise to demonstrate to frequently racist, native Londoners that Caribbean people possessed a great culture and artistic ability which they would be happy to share with their neighbours" (9). He says that, in the various meetings of the Carnival Committee, many of which he attended, "One question always in our minds was how to move our Carnival onto the same streets of Notting Hill where Black blood had been spilt by the racist murder of Kelso Cochrane" (11). Omitted as well from the official history, he finds, is the black struggle for carnival, the various committees that worked incessantly to make sure that such an event would happen. So, he concludes, "Following Jones's tragic death, the planned 1965 February indoor Carnival event was cancelled, but in August that same year a steelband was moving through the streets with its supporters winding behind" (11). Thus, there was no hiatus in the London Carnival initiated by Jones, *The West Indian Gazette*, and the Caribbean Carnival Committee, simply a moving of locale and time and thus a more deliberate assertion of a political public presence of Caribbean people in London.[36]

The announcement about the cancelation of carnival in 1965 came in the *West Indian Gazette* (February 1965):

NO CARNIVAL THIS YEAR
On account of the death of Miss Claudia Jones,
founder and editor of the West Indian Gazette
and Afro-Asian Caribbean News, there shall be no
Caribbean Carnival this year. (4)

By virtue of being clearly identified as such, the "Caribbean Carnival" is enshrined even in its absence and therefore assured continuity. For those familiar with the spirit of carnival, nothing should "stop the carnival." So a suspension to honor Jones's passing, and because much of this was her work, would have indicated the break that did occur. But after the mourning, the transformation.

Intellectual Property Issues in Assignment of Origins of London Carnival

Claudia Jones, in her own detailing of the "super-exploitation of black women,"[37] in many ways reveals that she herself fell victim to this same super-exploitation. The kind of massive labor output donated without recompense that is one of the characteristics of superexploitation was required of her and undoubtedly contributed to her early death.[38] In a sense, the erasure of black women's work and ideas, that is, their intellectual output, can be read as instances of this same superexploitation. An example from India is the development of traditional beauty products by women, which are then marketed by Western business enterprises with no recompense to the women who developed them (a practice challenged by Indian women's organizations). Under the rubric of what has been defined as intellectual property rights, legal arguments are used to challenge the false ownership, theft, or expropriation of ideas and cultural approaches to personal care, style, food, and so on, that are generated from and by a community and that are then given a market value from which those same people receive little or no rewards. This theft of intellectual property has been a constant, with the appropriation of black community products internationally from blues singers, calypso singers, and other creative artists and scholars and from inventors of products and ideas. One has therefore to consistently reassert the strategic location and ownership of this intellectual property, the ideas of black women in particular histories among them, otherwise they remain erased.

Such is the context in which this discussion of Jones and the London Carnival is intended.[39] In the case of Jones, where there was a deliberate attempt by the U.S. government to erase her from U.S. history, and in the case of the British to minimize her role and presence, Jones's own ideas and works persist and cannot easily be erased. Indeed, part of the imperative in my assessment of her work and life is to maintain the record and to accord her some of the intellectual property rights that she is owed in terms of her placement in a series of histories. We know already about C. L. R. James, but there has to be a similar consistency to the knowledge of all our cultural workers and thinkers and certainly Claudia Jones was one of the stellar ones. Carnival is a movement of the people and its development is often one that advances relative to the personnel, availability, time, space, occasion, and initiative of the knowledgeable practitioners. In this case, we have an accomplished organizer, a Trinidadian woman who took the initiative — based on childhood memories of carnival and its structures, a knowledge of the early New York version of carnival, knowledge of political organizing and journalistic skill — and the input of other Trinidadians like Edric Connor, who were resident in London at the time. These attributes and connections combined with her respect for culture, people, and social change and political justice. Thereby were created the conditions in which there could be the beginnings of carnival organizing in Britain. Geraldine Connor has in fact suggested that the Notting Hill Carnival be renamed to honor Jones.[40]

The early work by Jones in the Caribbean community in England was one of the early building blocks in the formation of the Caribbean diaspora.[41] An argument I make elsewhere is applicable, that "taking space"[42] is central to carnival and in each context, the space — physical, emotional, cultural — gains are what mark the development of carnival. The initial move by Jones to assert a presence and to challenge racist violence and racist constructions of the community is the first level of that movement, as is the initial Caribbean Carnival that she mounted. The outward movement could only come after a more assertive public and political presence was negotiated by a series of activists, prominent among them being Jones. The internationalist focus and orientation of her *West Indian Gazette and Afro-Asian Caribbean News* and the

18. Paul Robeson at an event organized by *West Indian Gazette*, London, 1960. Claudia Jones is to the right of Robeson.

19. Claudia Jones as editor of the *West Indian Gazette*. WIG photo.

20. Claudia Jones on the microphone at an event. WIG photo.

21. Claudia Jones as a practicing journalist in London. WIG photo.

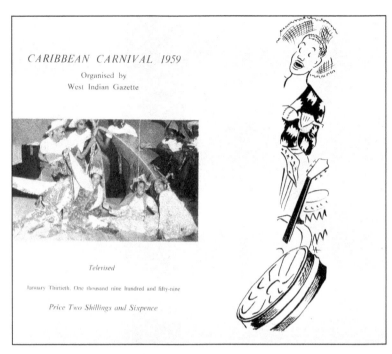

22. Cover of the program of the Caribbean Carnival, London, 1959.

23. Inside cover of Caribbean Carnival program, London, 1959.

A Peoples' Art is the Genesis's of Their Freedom

RARELY have the creative energies of a people indigenous to another homeland been so quickly and spontaneously generated to such purpose as witness the work of the Caribbean Carnival Committee 1959, set up last November under the sponsorship of the *West Indian Gazette*.

It is as if the vividness of our national life was itself the spark urging translation to new surroundings, to convey, to transplant our folk origins to British soil. There is a comfort in this effort not only for the Carnival Committee and the West Indian Gazette, for the fine artists participating in our Carnival who have lent of their talents here but for all West Indians, who strain to feel and hear and reflect their idiom even as they strain to feel the warmth of their sun-drenched islands and its immemorable beauty of landscape and terrain.

There is of course another cause to be assessed to their response to those who have filled St. Pancras Town Hall. That reason is the event of Notting Hill and Nottingham — an event which was the matrix binding West Indians in the United Kingdom together as never before — determined that such happenings should not recur.

If then, our Caribbean Carnival has evoked the wholehearted response from the peoples from all the Islands of the Caribbean in the new West Indies Federation, this is itself testament to the role of the arts in bringing people together for common aims, and to its fusing of the cultural, spiritual as well as political and economic interests of West Indians in U.K. and at home.

A PRIDE in being West Indian is undoubtedly at the root of this unity, a pride that has its origin in the drama of nascent nationhood, and that pride encompasses not only the creativeness, uniqueness and originality of West Indian mime song and dance — but is the genesis of the nation itself.

It is true to say that pride extends not only to what the West Indians have proudly established in the culture of the Caribbean but to the treasury of world culture.

In midst of our revelry let us remember that it is a world on eve of conquest of Space — tribute to man's unconquerable quest for adventure, achievement and mastery over Nature and himself. Our multi-racial culture should be the fount, helping the universal quest to turn the instruments of science everywhere for the good of all mankind, for the freedom of all the world's peoples, no matter what the pigment of their skin, for human dignity and friendship of all peoples everywhere.

By
Claudia
Jones,
Editor,
West
Indian
Gazette

If our Carnival is a triumphal success, it is not only as a result of the inspired spirit that has permeated its preliminary activities but from its inception, but also the moral and material support given generously by our friends and neighbours in the British Isles representing tangible evidence of their goodwill.

FOR me, and for the management of West Indian Gazette, and in all of the Carnival Committee I say a deep thank you. It would be unfair for me not to tell you that we have still another determination, that is, to make the *W.I.G. Caribbean Carnival* an annual event. In that endeavour, we know we can count not only on — the artists, the decor, the committee bends, our friends and neighbours but many who we have not yet reached.

May the aim of our mutual efforts be to help to build the West Indian Gazette and above all in that endeavour help to extend the already acknowledged cultural influence of the Caribbean throughout the Commonwealth. And may that by the leaven to weld still more firmly the brotherhood and unity of West Indians and other peoples of colour, as well as the friendship for all peoples that will be the fruit of this cultural exchange.

24. Claudia Jones's statement on the importance of the Caribbean Carnival, Caribbean Carnival 1959 souvenir program booklet.

development of pan-Africanist activism along with and/or in place of carnivals carry that politics of diaspora.

We can conclude that as far as Claudia Jones and the British version of the Caribbean diaspora are concerned, it is not simply "dispersal" that is at the root of diaspora, but the political and cultural contributions that are part of the transformative, reelaborative energies that mark African and Caribbean diaspora cultures and peoples at home and abroad.

Chapter 6

PIECE WORK/PEACE WORK

Self-Construction versus State Repression

For over 300 years the best fighters of our people have had a price on
their heads.

CLAUDIA JONES, *BEN DAVIS*, 1954

You dare not, gentlemen of the prosecution, assert that Negro women
can think and speak and write!

CLAUDIA JONES, "SPEECH TO THE COURT," 1953

Instant report contains a large amount of material from subject's
writings which largely concern the equal rights of women as well as
equality for Negroes.

CLAUDIA JONES FBI FILE, LETTER DATED SEPTEMBER 8, 1951

On the left is a black woman, determined to articulate political and ideological positions that would contest the boundaries of freedom of speech as defined by American bourgeois
democracy. These boundaries, while ostensibly "real" rights
such as freedom of the press and habeas corpus[1] nonetheless
carry limitations, which keep the individual within the structures
that define the modern market economy and the definition of the
ideal American citizen.[2]

On the right are the institutions of the U.S. government such
as the FBI, determined to discipline those rights within its historical project of the rise of capitalist freedom. Thus, while American democracy would seek to position itself as the ideal democ-

racy and as the major exponent of international human rights, challenges to this claim continually emerge internally from a range of cultural and political activists, like Claudia Jones, as well as from the global political movements of decolonization.

When I requested the FBI file on Claudia Jones I received the following answer:

Request No.: 0964081–000
Subject: Jones, Claudia

Dear Requester:

This acknowledges receipt of your Freedom of Information request. Information you requested has previously been released to other individuals. In an effort to expedite your request, 807 pages are available in the same form as it was released in the past.

Pursuant to Title 28, Code of Federal Regulations, Section 16.11, there is a duplication fee of ten cents per page for every page released over 100. To receive these documents, please send a check or money order payable to the Federal Bureau of Investigation, in the amount of $70.70. Your material will be copied and forwarded to you as soon as we receive this payment. If we do not receive this payment within sixty days your request will be closed. Remember to place your FOIPA number on your check or money order so we can identify your Freedom of Information Act (FOIA) request.[3]

The relatively cheap cost of obtaining the FBI file and the perfunctory nature of the response do not disguise the expense, detail, and seriousness with which the state built up its case and attempted to destroy the lives of Claudia Jones and similar activists. For the FBI file on Claudia Jones is a massive, two-volume compilation close to a thousand pages long, which took many years to assemble. Much of it is blacked out, that is, still classified, particularly names of informers and other sources through which information was gathered, such as names of covert and active agents, places of surveillance, and the like.

Interestingly, visibly named sources of information include, in the Claudia Jones case, the New York Public Library and librarians of the Library of Congress, but important as well, all the published articles of the subject herself. The irony of the library as a place of acquiring information, but also for the formal gathering of intelligence which the state can then use against the individual, highlights the conversion of these public institutions of information gathering to the repressive objectives of the state. Documentation and individual writing, both of which are foundational to individual freedom and knowledge production, become sources of information gathering, and acts of individual creation become weapons of subversion of the same individual freedom in the interest of the overall management of the state.[4]

The FBI is, famously, a huge bureaucracy, created to sustain the U.S. government and its various state apparatuses. Its excesses are similarly well known. The FBI's surveillance of black activists, writers, and cultural workers of all political affiliations has been well documented.[5] Its propaganda machinery made all activism for black rights in effect equivalent to communism and therefore antithetical to the interests of the U.S. state. Its more public aggressive role against radical movements for social change, such as its activities under J. Edgar Hoover in COINTELPRO (Counter Intelligence Program), which had as its mission the destabilization and/or destruction of civil rights and black power leadership, has been identified in several studies.[6] Dhoruba bin Wahads identifies the targeting of militant black liberation movements by the U.S. government, through the FBI, and cites as an example: "Documents that surfaced under the Freedom of Information Act subsequently showed that George Jackson was a target of the Counterintelligence Program aimed at the Black Panther Party."[7]

In the contemporary period, numerous excesses, inadequacies, and misidentifications have been revealed in the U.S. state responses following the massive September 11, 2001, terrorist actions against the World Trade Center in New York City and the Pentagon in Washington, D.C., and the intelligence failures that followed. The FBI has been given an even more powerful protective role in the maintenance of United States security, in accordance with the preemptive foreign policy that marks George W. Bush administration. The monitoring of the general public has been further legitimized by the Patriot Act of 2001, which moves activities of repression into the center of the legal and administrative branches of the state. And youth of the hip-hop generation are suspicious of some of the ways in which its leadership is targeted by the range of state and national policing machineries in a kind of hip-hop COINTELPRO.

But it is the FBI's prior role in the criminalization of communism and of

Claudia Jones that is the more immediate context in which this particular discussion is located. This period — the well-known McCarthy period, with its House Un-American Activities Committee, noted for its witch hunts, and the rise of J. Edgar Hoover — is recognized for the FBI's active role in the destruction of the Communist Party USA as a central part of the United States's international declaration of its war against global communism and its internal manifestations. The use of a range of paid informers, as well as rampant misuse of the judicial system,[8] became taken-for-granted stratagems as the state launched these projects. This is the time period and machinery under which Claudia Jones suffered the harshest repressions and reprisals: trials, several incarcerations, and deportation.

This chapter takes the Claudia Jones FBI file as the finished product for the framing mechanism, through which the U.S. government would seek to deny Jones individual agency and reconstruct her as an enemy of the state. Often, as in this case, an FBI file is a detailed (excessive and repetitive) compilation of information for the benefit of the state, allowing the state, in this case the Federal Government of the United States of America, to use its already pre-conceived political conclusions as legitimate judicial premises for indictment of radical political practices. For Claudia Jones, who was under surveillance under both the Smith and McCarran Acts for communist activity, the state was able to amass a huge document in order to make its case for her imprisonment and deportation.

Claudia Jones, like the other communists indicted and convicted, was clearly a political prisoner in the full sense of the term: one incarcerated by the state strictly for her political views and actions. When Jones was arrested for the second time on June 29, 1951 (her earlier arrest came in 1948 under the McCarran Act), the ground for this action was a Supreme Court decision that upheld the Smith Act. The decision in Eugene Dennis v. the United States, 341 U.S. 494 (1951), which targeted the leadership of the Communist Party USA, was handed down in June 1951. It upheld the criminalizing of communism, continuing to define it narrowly as teaching or advocating the violent overthrow of the United States government. A few days thereafter Jones was among another group of communist leadership incarcerated. The second group of communists, among which Claudia Jones was finally a defendant, was "convicted of conspiracy under 18 U.S.C.A. 371 to violate the Smith Act, 18 U.S.C.A. 2385, making it an offense to advocate forcible overthrow of the government" (216 F.2d 354).

Fact patterns for this case, as available in legal archives (such as the electronic database Westlaw) indicate that the state under the Smith Act could prosecute individuals for conspiracy on the basis of the implied meaning of their membership in the Communist Party, that is, their individual culpability within the broader aims and objectives of membership in the Communist Party:

> In prosecution for conspiracy to violate the Smith Act making it an offense to advocate forcible overthrow of the government, relationships of defendants and of others acting in concert with them, defendants' positions of responsibility in the Communist Party, their activities in carrying forward the objectives of the Communist Party, and the nature of those objectives were all matters to be considered on the intent of any particular defendant. (216 F.2d 354).

Conspiracy to overthrow included theoretical exegesis such as discussing, writing about, and advocating Marxism-Leninism. Thus, having ideas contrary to the U.S. state's dominating capitalist ideology was also criminalized. So, during and after the demise of the Communist Party, black and women's activism for civil rights was also deemed as against the state, often defined as communist, and similarly targeted and criminalized by the U.S. government. The immediate objective was the destruction of communism. But engaging in a broader ideological and national struggle, all ideas that did not advance dominant state ideology could be criminalized as anti-national and anti-U.S.[9] In the process, those deemed as enemies of the state, defined then as members of the Communist Party USA, could be jailed or deported. This allowed the United States to erase their presence and destroy the growing prevalence of those ideas. According to Ellen Schrecker,

> Central to the campaign were the criminal prosecutions and deportation proceedings directed against individual party leaders and key activists. The direct consequences of these proceedings — the jail sentences or deportations that were visited on these people — put them out of commission and thus deprived the party of their services. At the same time, the proceedings themselves, which invariably involved years of litigation, forced the party to devote most of its dwindling resources to its own defense. Moreover, criminalizing the Communist party as these initiatives did was a powerful way to marginalize it.[10]

Thus was provided the evidentiary basis for the government's case against leading members of the Communist Party USA. The same approach would be used later in the active dismantling of subsequent political movements that ran counter to the state's ideology. The FBI as an institution would be absolutely essential in this assault, as it would subsequently be in the case of the Civil Rights and Black Power Movements because its function in the state apparatus was, so to speak, to protect the boundaries of loyalty and subversion. To run afoul of such a massive machinery as the United States government, whose various legal and administrative branches complemented each other, was a dangerous location for Claudia Jones — as, indeed, it is now, for those defined as "enemies of the state" anywhere.[11] But Claudia Jones was willing to rise to the task of defining her ideas, politics, and positions as a subject without rights, and therefore in contradistinction to the state's definitions, for her. Thus "peace work" was the framework utilized by her as an organizing theoretical and tactical strategy for embracing her position as a black communist woman. I shall examine her autobiographical statements and essays, which contain political assertions in the cause of peace. I aim thus to use Claudia Jones's own voice to counter the state's indictment: her self construction to the state's already fixed construction. As Schrecker also notes in *The Age of McCarthyism*, the accusation against Communist Party members had necessarily to be as theoretical as Communist Party activity itself, especially since the "prosecution relied on literary evidence" (50). But literary interpretation as methodological device became dangerously applied here. And though flawed, as it was in this case, it ends up being misused as the basis for the state's presentation of its understanding of the intellectual thought and political activities of a black communist woman.

> The Communist party's revolutionary ardor was obviously theoretical and none of the defendants had ever called for violence, let alone begun to gather guns. As the excerpts from the transcript of the trial reveal, the prosecution relied on literary evidence — on those passages from the works of Marx, Lenin, and Stalin that advocated revolutionary violence against the bourgeois state. To link the individual with the incriminating texts, the government enlisted an assortment of professional ex-Communists and FBI informants. These witnesses testified about their experiences in the party, describing the instruction they had received in the party's schools and the books they read. (50)

That there were opposing narratives and interpretations needs to be taken into account in any reassessment of the case, for the FBI file is little more than the extensive documentation of everything Jones had ever written, published, and spoken, marshalled to make a certain kind of case of ideological criminality. The publication of her ideas was what constituted her criminal offense. Now that the material is all available to us, we can see that in its use of "literary evidence," the state's case rested on literary misinterpretation, flawed and biased analyses, and deliberately superficial critical reading.

Autobiographical Assertions

I was impressed by the Communist speakers who explained the reasons for this brutal crime [the Scottsboro Boys frame-up] against young Negro boys; and who related the Scottsboro case to the struggle of the Ethiopian people against fascism, and Mussolini's invasion. Friends of mine who were Communists, although I didn't know it then, seeing my interest, began to have frequent discussions with me. I joined the Party in February, 1936 and was assigned to work in the YCL shortly there after.
CLAUDIA JONES, "AUTOBIOGRAPHICAL HISTORY," 1955

Subject, under the name CLAUDIA JONES, is a member of the National Committee, CP USA; Secretary of the Women's Commission, CP USA, and Negro affairs editor of the "Daily Worker." She is one of the most prominent of the younger leading Negro Communists. In view of the foregoing important positions held by Claudia Jones, the New York Office considers [her] to be a top functionary in the Communist Party, therefore, necessitating that continuous, active investigative attention be given to this case.
MEMORANDUM TO THE DIRECTOR OF FBI FROM SAC, NEW YORK, APRIL 28, 1947

The interviews that I conducted with people who knew Claudia Jones well indicate that she had been engaged in writing an autobiography up to the time of her untimely death.[12] Many were surprised that a full autobiography was not available and some even suggested that an autobiography might have been among the documents seized by those who had access to her apartment at her death.[13] No definitive autobiography has so far appeared in her papers, nor is one mentioned in any of the available archives. So my conclusions made in this chapter remain as always preliminary and open to expansion if and when additional material becomes available.

So far, five written texts that can be defined as autobiographical in nature have been identified: one was prompted by a request from William Z. Foster, the head of the Communist Party USA, and is dated 1955; another is a letter Jones wrote to John Gates, from the prison on Ellis Island, which was published in the *Daily Worker*, November 8, 1950; the third is her 1953 speech before Judge Dimock and the court in her defense upon conviction; the fourth, the interview she gave to George Bowrin in 1956, soon after her arrival in England;[14] and the fifth, a hand-written reflection about six pages long, written about six months before her death and dated June 1964. To these can be added Jones's pamphlet in defense of the Harlem councilman Benjamin Davis, which reveals much about her own positions, and which I regard as another autobiographical source.

One can easily argue that all written output is autobiographical to a certain extent. In other words, experience consistently informs the creative and intellectual process. As I showed in chapter 3, a great deal of the poetry Jones wrote from prison was also self-reflexive in nature. In this chapter, however, I limit the discussion to statements that are deliberately autobiographical and those which seemed to be written in order to articulate her personal self in the context of political praxis.

So let us take first the most substantive autobiographical piece written by Claudia Jones, which is also the first self-construction that is offered in her own voice. It is a letter addressed to the Communist Party leader, William Z. Foster ("Comrade Foster") and dated December 6, 1955, just a few days before her departure for London. Claudia herself identified it as "autobiographical history" at the start of the letter, and it is clear that it was solicited by the party: "Dear Comrade Foster: The following is the autobiographical (personal, political, medical) history that I promised to forward to you." She begins chronologically, with the personal and family history that describes her migration to the United States as a child "from Port-of-Spain, Trinidad, British West Indies," in 1924. She describes her family's economic status and the lure of migration to the United States in search of the American dream of wealth and freedom. Jones details the ways in which this dream became nightmare as urban poverty and racial oppression and its indignities ensued. (In recounting these details, the letter also becomes an important document of the first major wave of Caribbean migration to the United States, which took place in the 1920s.) The rest of this first section develops the details of her early education in the United States and how it led her to question the nature of "wealth and poverty; why there was discrimination and segregation;

why there was a contradiction between the ideas contained in the Constitution and the Bill of Rights."

Because the letter is brief, the elements she selects for presentation are critical. An obviously pivotal event, and absolutely central to her formation is her mother's death: "My mother had died two years earlier of spinal meningitis suddenly at her machine in a garment shop. The conditions of non-union organization, of that day, of speed up, plus the lot of working women, who are mothers and undoubtedly the weight of immigration to a new land where conditions were far from as promised or anticipated, contributed to her early death at 37."

It is significant that this event is recounted in such detail and so early in the autobiography, an event that would of course escape, or not be at all important to, state constructions. Jones's mother's death becomes one of the formative experiences in her life, allowing her later on to see the connections between their family's singular struggles and those of "millions of working class people, and negro people [who] suffered this lot under capitalism." Encounters with American racism for the immigrant Caribbean family would similarly be significant. So, Claudia goes on to describe racism within the U.S. educational system itself and the ways that the family's poor economic situation was related to institutional racial structures. This for her would be another important and constitutive element.

Another important detail in terms of the Caribbean immigrant community but also in terms of her becoming a journalist subsequently, is that she identifies her father as "an editor of an American-West Indian newspaper." This would contribute solidly to the construction of an inherited family political/professional praxis and could indeed make a counterargument to the state's definition of her writing as simply ideological and therefore usable in its case against her. And it also identifies the development of Caribbean American institutions like newspapers, which marked a new Caribbean diaspora.

The family's economic woes and poor living conditions in the United States would also be directly linked to Jones's subsequent ill health. She learned after many years that the dampness in her room was the direct result of the fact that an open sewer flowed past their apartment; the poor housing conditions clearly led to her contracting tuberculosis and being hospitalized in a New York sanatorium at the age of seventeen. Her subsequent assembly line work became her practical experience for analyzing the conditions of poor working women. This personal story is juxtaposed with the Ethiopian War and the development of black nationalism, and street corner meetings and rallies during the Scottsboro Boys trial. She found that she was most impressed by a communist speaker's explanations about this trial and the Ethiopian War and of the economic conditions of African Americans under U.S. racism, and so joined the party in February 1936.[15] Jones then identifies her activism in a variety of organizations, social clubs, and youth movements from her teen years onward.

Her beginning trajectory as a journalist, through her first assignment (writing her weekly column "Claudia's Comments") is also central to her self-construction and therefore figures prominently in this autobiographical history. Jones identified her profession as journalism. This was not just self-definition, but an argument against conviction. For if freedom of the press was an important pillar of democracy in the United States, she reasoned, how then could someone, especially a journalist, be prosecuted for her writings?[16]

In this short "autobiographical history," Jones also details her active work for the Communist Party, particularly, as she says, her organizing in a variety of "national women's movements." She explains her peace work as being "for peaceful coexistence between nations, for peace, national dignity, full equality for women and the equal rights of women." She recounts her various bouts of ill health, her hospitalization for coronary heart disease, and the leaves she had to take from her organizing work for recuperation.

Jones also identifies various arrests until she was served with deportation orders: her first arrest on January 28, 1948; another arrest on June 29, 1951, under the Smith Act, as one of a group of seventeen communists, in her words "for writing an article which described the forward movement of Negro and white women in opposition to the fascist-bent world domination US foreign policy"; a third arrest in October 1951, under the McCarran-Walter Act, with eighteen working-class and communist leaders. The third arrest led to a brief incarceration in the "McCarran Wing" of the prison on Ellis Island and is described in some detail. She ends the letter with an account of her fourth and final incarceration, on January 11, 1955, in Alderson, West Virginia, and from where, she says, she "was to be summarily deported straight to the Caribbean from prison on October 23 [the] day of release of this year but for protests here and abroad and intervention of British authorities."

Claudia Jones included in her account not only the significant details of her life but also a closing note about the various drugs (digitalis, nitroglyc-erine, supercil) that she had been prescribed and the diagnoses given her while in prison. Significantly, her marriage to Abraham Scholnick,[17] her di-vorce, and her plans to remarry in England within the next few months appear only in a postscript in the document. A second postscript notes that she had applied for U.S. citizenship at the age of twenty-three but had been denied it, and that she had been politically active from the age of eighteen.

While it is clear that the autobiographical history had been solicited by Foster, Claudia's detailed account provides the most significant documenta-tion of her life, political trajectory, and medical and social history available. In autobiographical writing, we know, details are selected depending on what aspects of her or his life the writer wants to give meaning to and bring to the knowledge of the reader. But nothing in Jones's life is hidden in this account. The FBI's copious file simply fleshes out this bare-bones history.

The second autobiographical source that I want to consider is the letter written by Jones to John Gates, editor of *the Daily Worker*, which was pub-lished in that paper November 8, 1950. The letter begins by identifying the nature of the corporate press as an arm of the state: "In thinking about the collusion of the 'free press' with the ruling circles' attack on American demo-cratic liberties, I decided to write to you. Of course, if I attempt to write descriptively, it will only be because, while I know you (and I) hold brevity to be the soul of wit, description should not be the second class citizen." The rest of the letter details the conditions under which she and many others were incarcerated on Ellis Island, including the composition of those residing in what they called "the McCarran Wing." In specifying this community of detainees, she returns to a familiar theme, one that would run consistently through all her own self-articulations, that she was one of a group of people imprisoned because they challenged some of the most oppressive features of the state: "All 17 here are examples of devotion to the strugglers of the labor movement, in the fight for Negro rights, against discrimination and lynching, in the fight for democracy, in our efforts on behalf of the peace and security of the people. And some hold beliefs that only under a Socialist society can these rights be finally secured."

Another significant aspect of this letter is its corrective against the propa-ganda being unleashed by the government and supported by the press: "The majority of newspapers tell you, that we are here because we are awaiting deportation hearings. That is a foul lie." And, in a situation that has repeated itself in the detention of a number of suspects in the United States following the September 2001 events and onward, "Many of us have had no hearings or legal examinations of any kind. We have never been confronted with any evidence, or made familiar with any crime, alleged or charged against us. Nor have any of us been informed or charged with the slightest infraction of the terms of our release on bail. . . . Nevertheless the government has re-arrested us without due process of law, and seeks to assign us to a virtual life-long imprisonment on Ellis Island."[18] She spends some additional time describing her counteranalysis of the state's actions: "The truth, of course, is, that this is a clear violation of the American Constitution, the Bill of Rights, both of which guarantee the right of bail and the right of habeas corpus. That Judge F. McGohey ruled on the government motion on postponement, first, and not on the right of bail is a clear violation of this time-honored right."

She insists that they are due those rights as Americans: "No law or decree can whittle away or pierce by one iota our convictions and loyalty to America's democratic and revolutionary traditions. We are Americans, each and every-one of us, similarly persecuted, not by accident of birth, but by choice. We yield to no one in laying claim to being true patriots."

The letter to Gates, while deliberately self-reflexive, is also communal autobiography, in the sense that Jones uses her journalistic skills to document the experience for all those who were in prison with her; what their roles, national identities, status, and politics were, and what the physical surroundings were like. The autobiographical "I" is used in this case, as is often done by those involved politically, to represent a larger cause, to express a community's condition. Within this letter, Claudia creates a deliberate distinction between the state's construction and her reality via her correction of the biased media representation of those incarcerated. Claudia, as journalist, as she had throughout her career, allows her writing to re-present her self and her community.

The definition of "the self synonymous with political struggle," is an important variant of political autobiography. One sees it operating in the South African antiapartheid movement and the African decolonization struggles, as well as in African American autobiography of abolition and the Civil Rights and Black Power periods. Black women's autobiography, as I have demonstrated elsewhere,[19] often has a similar orientation in these contexts, but more definitely inserts the personal and familial into the narrative: "The act of autobiographical writing itself, for the African woman writer, therefore fulfills a range of personal requirements: it allowed her to order, to make sense of painful experience, to articulate herself, to write her self, to deliberate on the position of women, the poor, of African people."[20] These conclusions can clearly be applied to the corpus of Claudia Jones.

The entire process of autobiographical writing, we know, moves the self from the margins of discourse to the center, takes authority over the discourse. According to Sidonie Smith, "Women who do not challenge those gender ideologies and the boundaries they place around woman's proper life script, do not write autobiography. Culturally silenced, they remain sentenced to death in the fictions surrounding them."[21] Claudia Jones is a classic example of the woman who refuses to be silenced.

The paucity of autobiographical (as well as biographical texts) on black communist women remains a cause for concern.[22] The larger attempts by the state to silence these women along with the relative "neglect" in the identification of these texts present the false picture that black radical women were — and still are — lone, brave, Promethean figures. My research reveals that there are clearly a number of black women who can always be identified also as radical black female subjects.

Jones's statement[23] to Judge Edward J. Dimock before she was sentenced to imprisonment for "a year and a day" is probably the finest example of her self-articulation, and is the third of the autobiographical texts that I will consider. It begins with a clear and deliberate attempt to have her voice heard, to not be silenced, to have the whole context of freedom of speech and freedom of the press be positioned centrally: "Your Honor, there are a few things I wish to say. For if what I say here serves even one whit to further dedicate growing millions of Americans to fight for peace, and to repel the fascist drive on free speech and thought in our country, I shall consider my rising to speak worthwhile indeed."

In her statement to the court, then Claudia continues to assert that this was a trial of the ideas of Marxism-Leninism. She concludes that it was they, the defendants, who were "morally free, and conversely it was the prosecutors and the Court itself that [stood] naked before the Bill of Rights and the Constitution and people of our country." Her argument is a classic reversal. For while the state's case was based on prosecuting these defendants for their political positions, these were positions known and accepted by many. Thus, it was clear that the judge himself and the state's legal apparatus were the guilty parties. "We feel no guilt" was the conclusion, for "it is not we Communist defendants who tremble at this final stage of these trial court proceedings, but the very prosecutors of our ideas." It was easy from this point then to pick apart the state's case, full of bias and trumped-up charges as it was, and witnesses without any credibility.

Perhaps the most critical component in this self-assertion and defense is that in bringing forward the so-called evidence (numerous articles and pages from her work) and not reading a line of them, the prosecution was in fact caught in its own sexist and racist bias. Claudia goes to the heart of the institutional sexism and racism that flourished prior to 1980s discussions of silencing: "You dare not, gentlemen of the prosecution, assert that Negro women can think and speak and write!"

Claudia Jones was able to seize the moment to reinsert herself and her ideas publicly by speaking back in one of the key centers of U.S. power, its courts. Thus she references the article for which she was indicted and relays its intent, even as she indicates the reasons why it could not be read:

> It cannot be read, your Honor — it urges American mothers, Negro women and white, to write, to emulate the peace struggles of their anti-fascist sisters in Latin America, in the new European democracies, in the Soviet Union, in Asia and Africa to end the bestial Korean war, to stop "operation killer," to bring our boys home, to reject the militarist threat to embroil us in a war with China, so that their children should not suffer the fate of the Korean babies murdered by napalm bombs of B-20's, or the fate of Hiroshima.

In the rest of her presentation, she describes learning about the ideals of liberty as she studied it in American history in U.S. public schools and of her existence in the United States since she was a child of eight — and of having at the same time "experiences which are shared by millions of native-born Negroes — the bitter indignity and humiliation of second-class citizenship, the special status which makes a mockery of our Government's prated claims of a 'free America' in a free world for 15 million Negro Americans."

These experiences, she indicated, led her to try to find answers to this working-class poverty and the concomitant racism, and the Young Communist League became her source of clarifying information. Claudia Jones would return to this theme many times in all her accounts, and so make the links between black empowerment, her empowerment, and participation in the Communist Party, which she did not see as antithetical to that empowerment but as powerfully collaborative with it.

She makes the same point in her June 1956 interview with George Bowrin following her arrival in London, when interviewed about why she was deported. In it she reports:

> I was deported from the U.S.A. because as a Negro woman Communist of West Indian descent, I was a thorn in their side in my opposition to Jim Crow racist discrimination against 16 million Negro Americans in the United States, in my work for redress of these grievances, for unity of Negro and white workers, for women's rights and my general political activity urging the American people to help by their struggles to change the present foreign and domestic policy of the United States.[24]

The text of this interview, as it appears in Buzz Johnson's "*I Think of My Mother,*" is the fourth autobiographical text I identified above.

Still, in the range of deliberate defensive countervoicing, another publication needs also to be identified within the context of self articulation. Though not autobiographical in the standard sense, of it being her own story, Jones's 1954 written defense of the Harlem councilman Benjamin Davis becomes also her own defense and also fits that model of telling a communal story. *Ben Davis: Fighter for Freedom* is a booklet written to defend Davis, who was among the first group of communists leadership sentenced for their ideas in the state's process of destroying the Communist Party USA. All of the arguments raised in the Ben Davis booklet seem to foreshadow Jones's own impending trial with her group of thirteen communists. Each of the sections in *Ben Davis* begins with a heading and statements from black historical figures who were involved in the struggle for African emancipation in the United States — Harriet Tubman, Sojourner Truth, David Walker — or selections from the Bible and from resolutions on McCarthyism issued by the National Association for the Advancement of Colored People (NAACP).

Claudia begins by laying out the fact pattern in the case against Benjamin Davis, locating it in a long, three-hundred-year history of injustice to black people in the United States — slavery, lynchings, Jim Crow racism, housing, segregation, bombings of political facilities, attacks on scholars such as W. E. B. Du Bois, incarcerations of the innocent, and trumped-up trials. Her summary was: "For over 300 years the best fighters of our people have had a price on their heads" (quoted at the beginning of this chapter). Jones goes on to summarize what the state's charge against Davis was, telling us forthrightly that "Ben Davis is in jail because books he believes in — books which contain the science of his beliefs — known as Marxism-Leninism–are considered dangerous by McCarthy and the warmakers" (17). She spends some time explaining the nature of the Communist Party and its operations and links it to her central theme, the role of black leadership in teaching their community and how it is being impacted by the Smith Act:

> One of the main threats the Smith Act represents to our crusade for equal rights as Negroes in this country is that it *censors speech, thought, teaching and advocacy of social change.*
>
> Now, as Negroes, we have got to "teach and advocate" change in the many Jim Crow laws and practices of federal, state and government agencies.
>
> But the threat is: that any Negro citizen or organization advocating such changes runs the risk that some paid informer will appear in court or some government hearing to lyingly testify that one's intent — *deeds and acts to the contrary* — is to overthrow the U.S. Government by force and violence.
>
> The Smith Act further makes it a "criminal conspiracy" to teach or advocate or circulate almost any idea which hired stool pigeons can testify imply "intent" to overthrow the government by force and violence, even though as in the case of Ben Davis and his co-workers — *not a single act or deed can be pointed to as showing such attempt at overthrow, simply because there aren't any.* (20)

Claudia was clearly aware that she too was facing a similar fate to Benjamin Davis. She refers to the trial of thirteen communist leaders, for example (she being one of them), toward the end of the booklet (44). The defense of Benjamin Davis becomes a defense of the entire party and its projects and thereby a defense of herself as well.[25]

Benjamin Davis, for his part laments, in a subsequent letter to Claudia, written while she was resident in London, that he was not able to put up the fight needed to keep her in the United States largely because of his own challenges from the state, especially his incarceration. He says on one occasion: "It seems to me you're an American not a 'British citizen.' This is where you spent your life and made your contributions to American democracy — they were very important contributions. Only in the technical sense — frankly, not even that — are you a 'British citizen.' Then if you're an American, you should be here, not there, except on a trip like any other American."[26]

The state's legal case against Claudia Jones was based, as we have already seen, on "literary evidence" — that is, on her writings. It used ideas in a process of flawed interpretation, as there was no factual evidence that she or her comrades were in any way involved in overthrowing the U.S. government by force, as was charged. In some cases, Jones's FBI file itself spoke to this absence of evidence, asking its agents to seek out more revolutionary statements, as all the state had for its case was a collection of essays on the need for the equality of black people and women. The fact that this was the extent of their "evidence" reveals how a weak case can be made strong, if constructed with all the state's machinery behind it. Thus, throughout the two-volume FBI file, all we find are (helpful) bibliographic identifications of essays and articles by Claudia Jones, giving the places they were published, times, and other details; the documentation itself proves if anything the contrary of what the state was trying to prove. Paradoxically the FBI becomes Claudia Jones's amanuensis, providing one important means by which Claudia Jones's own works can articulate their own positions.

The entire intellectual corpus of Claudia Jones's work becomes the single and most important countervoice to the massive compilation that the FBI used to make a case against her. In the end, her FBI file became, ironically, one of the most significant of her biographical documents. In a strange turn of events, the FBI also becomes the mad bibliographer. Since the evidence they compiled was literary and their case was based on her writing, the file contains an archive of the most significant body of materials (some of it unavailable elsewhere). The file (particularly volume 1) corroborates many of the details that Claudia herself gives, providing specific dates, the names of associates, clubs and organizations, positions held, and so on.

In a sense, even though the FBI file sought to contain the life of Claudia Jones, the material itself is so powerful and so honest that it transforms these same files into a massive documentation project, producing instead of destroying its subject. Much of this material had already been articulated by Claudia herself in her various published articles and speeches. The brevity of the purely autobiographical material, compared to the massive compilation of data in the FBI file, is also an obvious recognition of the imbalance between the state's massive machinery and documenting process and an individual black woman armed with only her intellect and her communication skills (that is, her defined ability to think, speak, and write). Thus history, following the famous axiom, is now able to judge whether these essays and her activities justified the state's reprisals: jailing, deportation, harassment. The answer is clearly in the negative. Indeed, subsequently in *Yates v. United States* (354 U.S. 298 [1957]) just two years after Claudia had been deported and many other lives destroyed, the Supreme Court limited conviction to direct action to overthrow the government and not to ideas; that is, it decided that teaching communism was not equivalent to plotting to overthrow the government. The harassment that Jones and her fellow plaintiffs experienced was therefore unjustified, even by the state's own standards — but by the time of the *Yates* decision it had already happened. The salient distinction of course was the intent ascribed to those materials. Claudia for her part was clear about how she described her project — it was "peace work." The U.S. government clearly understood this intent, but was determined to make a case for the opposite.

The FBI File on Claudia Jones

The prosecution also cancelled out the overt act which accompanied the original indictment of the defendant Jones entitled, "Women in the Struggle for Peace and Security." And why, your Honor?

CLAUDIA JONES, FROM "SPEECH TO THE COURT, FEBRUARY, 1953"

In this article ["Negro People Are Joining the Party that Leads Struggle for Equality," April 7, 1946], she championed the Communist Party as being the Party for the negro people, stating that it was a Party for the oppressed people because the Communist Party is the Party not only of the negro people "but of all the oppressed," and went on to point out that the Communist Party had pioneered in bringing about equality between races in all phases of life.

CLAUDIA JONES FBI FILE, ENTRY DATED SEPTEMBER 24, 1946

Two major items were identified in November 1, 1946, in the then developing case against Claudia Jones, as grounds for "continuing investigation" by the FBI: "Subject's Party membership and affiliation" and "Subject's knowledge of the Party's revolutionary aims and purposes."

An early entry, dated February 2, 1942, sets up the terms as follows: "Claudia Jones, a negress, said to have been born at Lawrenceville, Va, 4/17, has been active in N.Y. State YCL for last several years. Member of Natl. Council of YCL. Is also Educational Director, YCL and has written for Weekly Review, organ of YCL. . . . This case is predicated upon information developed regarding subject during the course of investigation of the case entitled 'Young Communist League; Voorhis Act' " (New York file 102–9). It continues by identifying the various communist organs such as the *Daily Worker* in which she is either mentioned or her writing appears, and the meetings she attended.

The basic biographical facts are what we have encountered in other sources, except for the identification of 1917 as her year of birth and Lawrenceville, Virginia, as her birthplace (this appears to be self-protective disinformation, as was her use of the name Jones).[27] We learn later that she adopted the name Jones in place of her family name Cumberbatch, perhaps for protective purposes.[28] The name change worked in her favor, as the FBI investigators were unable to make the link between the "Claudia Vera Cumberbatch" and "Claudia Jones" for at least five years.[29]

The FBI files are also definite about naming her in its own terms. Volume 2, for example, consistently refers to her as Claudia Scholnick. All indications are that Claudia never referred to herself by this name, though she identifies her marriage to and divorce from Scholnick in the "autobiographical history" she wrote for William Foster, where it is relegated to a postscript.[30]

The FBI's intent at this time was to investigate the Young Communist League and to prove them as oppositional to the U.S. government's interests. Several entries are titled "Claudia Jones: Internal Security — C." Another entry (June 23, 1943) to the Special War Policies Unit, recommends her for "custodial detention in view of the existing emergency," and a custodial detention card was prepared but not issued. Another entry, dated August 30, 1943, from the legal attaché of the American Embassy in London, mentions her in the same file as Paul Robeson.[31] The entire entry remains classified, blacked out to public access.

An entry dated September 24, 1946, interestingly also identifies her as a lecturer in the "Labour College" circuit for 1945, speaking on "The Role of the Negro in American Life," and as a participant in a symposium, *New Novels about the Negro*, at the Jefferson School of Social Science, on February 17, 1946. The file indicates that her various articles "follow the Communist Party line and are centered around the negro." For example, the September 24, 1946, entry from which I quote above is detailed in its analysis of a range of her published essays. It cites one of these essays published on April 7, 1946, "Negro People Are Joining the Party that Leads Struggle for Equality," quoting her assertion that "the Communist Party" was "the Party for the negro people," because "it was a Party for the oppressed people because the Communist Party is the Party not only of the negro people but of all the oppressed." The link between racial oppression and activism against that oppression of course does not matter to the state. So her final assertion that "the Communist Party had pioneered in bringing about equality between races in all phases of life" would obviously be ignored in FBI-style analysis. Hers was the kind of assertion frequently made by creative thinkers of the time and one that Claudia Jones herself would return to repeatedly. But the FBI was selective in the "literary evidence" it used in its case against Claudia Jones. Its faulty literary analysis was a hallmark of the case.

The file turns up some other points worth noting. In documenting Jones's party membership and affiliation, it provides detailed and useful information of the various leadership positions that she had held in the Communist Party. Significantly, there is no information in the part of the file devoted to immigration that she was ever naturalized. The proof of Jones's knowledge of the Communist Party's revolutionary aims and purposes comes from essays dating from August 1945 onward, published in *Political Affairs*, with quotations from specific articles that tell us what the FBI evaluators understood of the case. Indeed, it becomes clear that the FBI directed its venom at Claudia Jones because she linked the struggles of African Americans to her understanding of issues of inequality as theorized through Marxism-Leninism. Thus her "Pre-Convention Discussion Article" and her article "On the Right to Self-Determination and the Black Belt" became key evidence in the state's case against her. An informant quotes her as saying, in the Plenum of the National Committee of the Communist Party, "We urge a strong fight against white chauvinism which must be reflected in our press, theoretical organs, and above all, our struggle." The prosecution of Claudia Jones for her Marxist-Leninist positions slides easily into a prosecution for her position against racism.

Proving that the political intent of her persecution by the state overrode the facts of her politics is a letter mailed September 8, 1951, from the FBI official in New York supervising her case (I quote it in the second epigraph to this chapter). It says, in part:

> Instant report contains a large amount of material from subject's writings which largely concern the equal rights of women as well as equality for Negroes. In some instances the articles, or portions therefrom, are duplicated in different sections of the report. Care should be taken to avoid such duplication in the supplemental report. . . . A strong effort should be made to locate data which would bolster Sections 3 and 4 of the report which can be testified to by live sources. Particularly there should be obtained revolutionary statements made by the subject showing advocacy of the overthrow of the Government by force and violence. . . . Testimony concerning subject's teachings in Communist Party schools which would reflect her adherence to Marxism-Leninism should be included in this report. (1)

Later in the same letter we read, "In view of the subject's present position and past history in the Communist Party movement, it is felt that a much stronger case exists than is presented" (2). These quotations make it clear that the FBI struggled to make its case against Claudia Jones and in the end decided to stretch the facts to fit the case that they built.

Claudia Jones, for her part, remained honest about her activities, challenging at times the legitimacy of the laws that were being created to restrain the party. So Jones's alien registration forms for the same period (included in the file) indicate that she had listed all her Communist Party affiliations, as well as her professional name and her various activities, truthfully. Still, the FBI continued to monitor and amass its "literary evidence" against her, much of it repetitive, asking periodically of its director if some action should be taken.

A highlight of one of these surveillances was a radio debate, transcribed in the file, with Jones, a Judge Gunther, and a Colonel Irwin (July 18, 1947), the subject of which was the policy of universal military training. As the interview progressed, the real surveillance purpose became evident to Jones, in that the debate began to be centered around the Soviet Union and communism and her support or understanding of its principles. At one point she queried: "Colonel Irwin, under discussion here on this radio debate, as I understand it is whether a policy of universal military training serves the best interests of our nation." She characteristically attempted to reorient the discussion to its purported theme and her own position: "Will such a policy contribute to peace? I maintain that such a policy will not contribute to peace because it is not disconnected with other policies which our State Department and War Department are pursuing."

In the end the "overt acts" for which Claudia Jones was accused included her 1946 report "On the Right to Self-Determination for the Negro People in the Black Belt" and the resolution on this subject made December 1946; a draft resolution of 1948 and the statement adopted at the 14th National Convention of CPUSA, August 1948; party directives made while she was a member of the National Committee of CPUSA; her 1950 International Women's Day statement, made when she was secretary of the National Women's Commission of CPUSA;[32] and finally, her report to the 15th National Convention of CPUSA, December 1950.

To the extent that the Communist Party held theoretical principles that assumed in the end a transformed state, "a dictatorship of the proletariat," by which means the capitalist ordering of society would give way to communism, then a literal reading of Claudia's communist positions would indeed produce the assumption of an overthrow of the U.S. state. But the articles identified here contained ideological positions, political arguments, and community organizing rhetoric that challenged racism, sexism, and class domination and worked peacefully toward the creation of a new and egalitarian society.

Peace Work

From 52–53 worked on National Peace Commission giving leadership to peace centers, to peace struggle namely around Korean war for the program registered at Geneva for peaceful coexistence among nations, international friendship in a world of peace.

CLAUDIA JONES, FROM "AUTOBIOGRAPHICAL HISTORY, 1955"

"The Daily Worker" of March 12, 1953, page 8, column 3, carried an article entitled "CLAUDIA JONES Cites Women's Fight for Peace." The article stated that the subject declared that peace is the central thread of our dedication of International Women's Day in 1953 and that the subject called on leaders of the labor-progressive movement to "grasp the significance of the tremendous peace ferment among American women." The article further stated that Miss JONES spoke at this International Women's Day forum at the Jefferson School of Social Science.

CLAUDIA JONES FBI FILE, NY 100-18676, ENTRY DATED AUGUST 27, 1953, UNDER HEADING "COMMUNIST ACTIVITIES"

In assessing the intent of the poetics and politics of Claudia Jones during the last years of her stay in the United States, the formulation "peace work" gives us perhaps the most significant overarching and organizing moral framework in which to locate all of her positions. It accounts for and describes her various contributions to a range of struggles for human justice. The most salient feature of her peace work is the ways she linked women's rights to anti-imperialism and black rights to labor exploitation. According to Gertrude Elias, Jones said that it was her writing in this area of women's rights, linked specifically to her position against the Korean War, that was one of the causes for her arrest by the FBI on June 20, 1951.[33]

Claudia Jones, though she had earlier supported the war against Hitler, was generally an advocate of peace, a position informed by her understanding that war efforts had as their goals the expansion of capitalist and imperialist interests and, in the case of wars waged by the United States, entailed at the same time the subordination of black people and women domestically. "The burdens of the crisis are increasingly being placed on the backs of women workers" ("International Women's Day," 36) and the working class as a whole is affected. Jones develops these arguments well in her "Half the World" columns, as discussed in chapter 2.

Black political women on the left, both within and outside the Communist Party, were key players in the fight for peace. Citing one well-known black woman activist, Charlotta Bass, Norma Chase reports, "In 1950 Bass went to Paris and to Prague as a member of the Peace Committee of the World Congress. There she supported a ban on the atomic bomb. She attended the World Student Congress in Prague and visited the Soviet Union. *Soviet Russia Today* published her article praising the Soviet Union and its lack of racial discrimination.[34]

Bass's position was shared by many, and became a commonplace of 1960s peace activism and still marks late-twentieth- and early-twenty-first-century antiwar sentiments globally (on the first Gulf War and the war on Iraq, for example). Jones's short book *Jim Crow in Uniform* (1940) argued the antiwar position well, making the point that black soldiers had to deal with racism during and after their service — a point raised before and since by countless other activists, scholars, historians, and literary critics. (See for example, Claude McKay's poem "If We Must Die," published in response to the 1919 "Red Summer" of race riots that occurred throughout the United States.)

According to George Lamming and Jan Carew, who knew Claudia in

London, any identification with peace struggles in the United States during the 1940s and 1950s, branded one as anti-U.S. and therefore a communist.[35] Fernando Claudin notes that in fact "the peace movement . . . was reduced to a chameleon disguise for the Communist movement and its offshoots" (*The Communist Movement*, 582). It was an era of war and patriotism, not unlike the current war on terrorism, in which anyone who took a position against the "war" was suspect and identified as unpatriotic. A case in point is W. E. B. Du Bois; the specifics of the state's treatment of him are developed well by Gerald Horne in his book *Black and Red*, and Robin Kelley links that treatment to the peace movement, saying that Du Bois "was arrested in 1951 for his involvement in the Peace Information Center and charged with treason and conspiracy" (*Freedom Dreams*, 57). Du Bois's bitter experience had a lot to do with his eventual repudiation of the United States and his adoption of Ghana, then a newly independent African nation, as his final resting place.

Peace work was, by all accounts, a Communist Party position. One can identify two tendencies. On the one hand, the Soviet position was, according to Fernando Claudin, "to mobilize all 'supporters of peace' against the danger of a third world war" (*Communist Movement*, 577). The World Congress of the Intellectuals for Peace in fact officially launched a peace movement in 1948, which included seventy-two countries, but, continues Claudin, "in the rest of the world, with some variation, the 'fighters for peace' were reduced to the members of the Communist parties and of the mass organizations it controlled (trade unions, women's youth, and cultural organizations)" (577).

The category "fighters for peace" would represent the kind of movement to which someone like Claudia Jones would belong and represents the second tendency in the peace formulation. One therefore has to give some credit to the initiative of black and women activists who saw peace work, as Claudia did, as a viable way of confronting the inequities in U.S. domestic policies and its international/imperialist desires. The *Daily Worker* for this period reports groups like the Sojourners for Truth and Justice organizing and protesting on the treatment of black intellectuals, and activists like Du Bois simultaneously organizing, lobbying, and marching for peace.

It is significant therefore that it is her International Women's Day article that was cited in her indictment as the "overt act" that led to her arrest, trial, incarceration, and final deportation. What seems clear, from a study of the entire political development of Claudia Jones, is that both the arrest and the text itself are culminations of all her political activity and writings over the years in the United States. The FBI file itself identifies several related speeches and publications as justifications for her arrest.

Several of Jones's publications deal directly with the "Struggle for Peace." "International Women's Day and the Struggle for Peace" describes efforts to make the 1950 celebration "a day of demonstrative struggle for peace, freedom, and women's rights" (32). "For the Unity of Women in the Cause of Peace," seems innocent enough. But on close reading, it is obvious that the article's aims were first, to document and elaborate on the "growing surge for peace among women of our country" and the fact that women were becoming more vocal in their protest against the war ("For the Unity of Women," 151, 153–154); and second, to identify the political strategies that advanced that movement in relation to the advancement of Marxism-Leninism and related party activity internationally.

To her credit, Claudia saw the U.S. war activity as always linked to U.S. imperialist intentions, comfortably using "the sons of American mothers as 'blue chips' in their vicious plot of world conquest, fascism, war and death" ("For the Unity of Women," 151). Making a point she had made earlier in her "Half the World" columns in the *Worker*, Claudia saw war as placing additional burdens on working-class and black mothers, destroying their families and linked somehow to "general male supremacist attitudes prevailing toward all women workers" (152). These include similarities to the Nazi policy, which was willing to draft all sources of labor (including women) into the war machine. For this reason, she felt that all progressives needed to "fight for the demands of women workers; to guarantee their integration into the unions; to eliminate the age-old wage differentials and secure equal pay for equal work; and to take special measures to protect the rights of the triply-exploited Negro women workers . . . to fight for special social services for women workers and to wage a struggle for the promotion of women trade unionists to posts of union leadership" (152–153).

Perhaps what was most troubling to the authorities was Jones's call for, and organization of, women, as a "distinct women's peace movement." This is something that Claudia had consistently tried to articulate, that is, that there was a need for some form of independent women's movement to take care of women's issues — an idea that she had argued within the party itself. She felt that the conditions of life and work for women necessitated a way in which a "specific approach to the women, as women," could be addressed. The Party could thus "give leadership to this wide peace sentiment expressed by women, to transform that sentiment into a mighty movement for lasting peace and defense of the needs of the children!" (156).

Claudia Jones articulated this understanding of peace elsewhere, in terms that would now be defined as feminist transnationalism. For example, she identifies "a new phenomenon of worldwide identification and sisterhood of women — [which] grew out of the years of boundless suffering by women under fascism":

> Women in the technically advanced countries, suffered outrageous degradation. They learned and experienced the lot of their sisters in the colonial and imperialist oppressed countries. Coupled with this was the uprooting of all bourgeois-democratic relationships involving women, the extermination of whole families and generations of families. It was these and other costly experiences that gave rise to the new determination of women throughout the world that never again would they allow the use of their sons for the imperialist slaughter of other nations and peoples. (157)

Jones notes that "American women bear a heavy responsibility to the millions of our anti-fascist sisters in the world camp of peace, precisely because the threat to world peace stems from the imperialists of our land" (157).

The authorities must have been particularly concerned that Jones saw the possibility that, with this new international women's movement, if it were well nurtured, "the struggle for the equality of women will merge with the general class struggle of the working class which understands and defends the needs and demand of the masses of women" (157).

In Claudia Jones's understanding, women's organizing was not an end itself but an important and essential component in any kind of internationalist organizing of peoples against oppression and fascism. In her justly famous article, she pointed to the role of the German communist leader Clara Zetkin in the designation of March 8 as International Women's Day. Claudia was already well versed in Zetkin's ideas on women and explained them in her speech, easily linking women's rights with rights to full emancipation. Jones felt at the time that the people of the Soviet Union had the promise of this equality in their hands. She critiques bourgeois feminism for blaming men for women's oppression rather than the exploitative system of capitalism.

Some of the strategies put forward by Jones to achieve this emancipation included support for the developing Women's Peace Center, particularly for its role in organizing women's peace activities and "stimulating and organizing women's peace committees on a community level." Claudia felt deeply that "Communist and progressive women everywhere must give leadership to women in their communities, and their organizations" on a range of issues, from war activity to taxation and inadequate supply of services that would benefit women and their families.

Another related position to which she would consistently return was the role of black women in the struggle for peace. In all of her discussions, Claudia felt that black women were constantly denied a significant place (even in the party), largely because of racism. Her position was clear: "we must once and for all overcome the gap between the influence of the triply oppressed Negro women, expressed in their own mass organizations and in the Negro people's movement generally, and their role in the organized peace movement" (159).

Claudia saw black women, so affected by war activity, as essential to any women's peace movement. She viewed the failure to involve black women at the highest organizational levels as a major one and one of the greatest weaknesses of the movement. Thus, she urged: "We must multiply a thousand fold the leadership of Negro women in the fight for peace" (159). Claudia blames this tendency not to involve black women on the "white chauvinist hesitation to raise the Negro question in the broad labor and people's peace movement, particularly in the context of America's imperialist aggression against the colored people's of Asia" (160).

Black women, who were active in their communities, recognized the links between external aggression and internal oppression. Jones felt that if this understanding could be kept in the forefront, one could have a broad people's movement: "the merger of this anti-imperialist current with the broader labor, people's, women's and youth peace movements, [and this would] greatly strengthen the peace camp as a whole" (160). Looked at this way, unity becomes a radical strategy against both masculinity, racism, and imperialism. This is what the government recognized as dangerous — the linking of these disparate struggles into a unified movement for social justice, thereby producing a politics more radical than communism.

Claudia, for her part, saw no disconnect between the struggle for jobs for black women, the need to organize black women workers, housing and school rights, and the international peace movement. Indeed, she felt the need to link these disparate struggles as central to any communist organizing activity. For her it was a fundamental question of which interest should prevail, and the need to constantly make the connection apparent between women's "immediate demands and the struggle for peace." Thus: "The cost of a single battleship could provide 325 family-sized dwelling units. Shall this money be used for a false national emergency in which 70 billions are being spent for bombs or shall the money be spent for housing projects and homes?" (163).

Claudia Jones summarized the particular questions as far as women's peace work as the necessity to build a distinct women's peace movement, the rooting of that movement among working women and the wives of workers, and the special necessity to bring the fight for peace to the Negro women (162).

She saw women's movement as not simple but complicated and multileveled. And the issue of women's leadership was critical: "Winning this struggle also means defending the principle of the right of Communist women to work among, and earn leadership among the masses of women, in order to help dissolve the foul tissue of lies about women's capability and leadership in women's struggle for peace and progress" (164).

Claudia felt above all that the party had a responsibility to help move all of these preliminary and/or spontaneous movements at the local level to the national and the international levels. This, she felt, also had implications for the relationship and attitudes to women in the party itself: "The new level of work achieved by our women comrades, and the new currents stirring among the masses of women, must be reflected in our Party's new level of understanding of the woman's question. This goes for our entire leadership and membership" (164).

The aim was clearly, in this formulation, to help move the women's peace initiative into a movement that would be much larger and able to merge with other similar movements internationally. The way that this becomes a significant feminist text is her awareness of male supremacy as being the major obstacle to this organizing, both inside and outside of the party: "Overcoming these male supremacist notions means to recognize moreover that our Party, as distinct from those who hold petty-bourgeois equalitarian notions, fights for the true equality of women. What does this mean? It means fighting for the right of women to enjoy every right and privilege enjoyed by men. Many shout equality in general, but in practice show lack of understanding of the special aspects of equality" (165–166).

The rest of the article outlines some strategies for advancing the movement of women. These included advancing an ideological campaign throughout the party on the specifics of women's issues and educating about the Marxist-Leninist approach to women in society; using the Women's page of the *Worker* to reach women; and the promotion of women to leadership positions.

Claudia's Communism

We Communists adhere to the fundamental belief that complete and lasting equality of imperialist oppressed nations of peoples can be guaranteed only with the establishment of Socialism.

CLAUDIA JONES, "ON THE RIGHT TO SELF-DETERMINATION FOR THE NEGRO PEOPLE IN THE BLACK BELT," 1946

For even with all the power your Honor holds, how can you decide to mete out justice for the only act which I proudly plead guilty, and one moreover, which by your own prior rulings constitutes no crime—that of holding Communist ideas; of being a member and officer of the Communist Party of the United States?

CLAUDIA JONES, "SPEECH TO THE COURT, FEBRUARY, 1953"

Claudia Jones offered a consistent and unabashed identification of herself as a communist, as Marxist-Leninist, even in situations when she was in grave danger from the state's punitive mechanisms. Her courtroom speech is explicit in making her philosophical and ideological positions clear in a public and official place; it was not a plea for leniency, but a demonstration that black women were also thinkers, held ideological positions, and could assert them.

Claudia Jones joined the Communist Party USA in her youth because it provided her with the best interpretation of her experience of racism and because it explained best the larger social conditions which she had experienced. The Communist Party at that time was actively engaged in the Scottsboro Boys case,[36] defending them from possible lynching and in the process providing examples of black men and women who were activists and committed communists. Claudia entered a visible black left community. She says: "I was, like millions of negro people, and white progressives and people stirred by this heinous frameup. I was impressed by the communist speakers who explained the reasons for this brutal crime against young Negro boys; and who related the Scottsboro case to the struggle of the Ethiopian people against fascism, and Mussolini's invasion" ("Autobiographical History," 5).

The "communist speakers" she identified were black communists in Harlem. From this early involvement, at age eighteen, Jones experiences a rapid rise through the party hierarchy and as a journalist in Communist Party organs, developing and enacting specific party positions as she advanced. She consistently upheld the positions of the Communist Party USA, though she modified and innovated them in light of her views on race and gender issues, as I have shown throughout this work. The larger ideological framework for her analyses always remains Marxist-Leninist.

My intent here is not to reevaluate the principles of Marxism-Leninism; there are numerous works that already claim to do this.[37] Rather, my concern is to show how Claudia Jones used her understanding of communism to analyze the conditions in which she saw black people, especially black women, subordinated. Many of her essays do not go into detail about what communism is,[38] though she does provide definitions and repeatedly identifies herself as a communist of Marxist-Leninist orientation. Marx, we know, provided both a theory of society in which there would be a movement from feudalism through capitalism to socialism and an analysis of the nature of class exploitation under capitalism, and a sketch of the larger principles of a socialist society. Lenin would advance these ideas further, and would add issues of colonialism and imperialism and an analysis of women in society, thus summarized: "The major components of Marxism-Leninism are dialectical and historical materialism as a method of analysis, political economy as the study of the class relationships to the means of production and the level of productive forces, and the theory of scientific communism (the structure and process of communist societies). More narrowly defined, Leninism is that tendency within Marxist thought which accepts the major theoretical contributions of Lenin to revolutionary Marxism."[39]

In "On the Right to Self-Determination for the Negro People in the Black Belt" Claudia Jones demonstrates her understanding of the applicability of Leninism to the colonial question and, in particular, how it is linked to the definition of black people in the U.S. South as an oppressed nation, internally colonized, citing an unfinished 1913 essay by Lenin on the national and colonial question.[40] Having specified the nature of the contours of the black community in the U.S. South and how they fit the definition of a nation in terms of language, territory, economic life, and common culture, Claudia challenged the revisionist perspective of Earl Browder[41] as it related particularly to black self-determination, insisting: "It is only by helping to interconnect the partial demands with the right of self-determination, that we Communists, in concert with other progressive forces, can contribute guidance to the struggle for complete equality for the Negro people" (74). The application of the communist notion of self-determination to the situation of black people in the South constitutes for Jones an uncompromising stand against imperialism and for socialism, which she saw as the only ideology operable at the time by which any state could guarantee full equality for all its people.

Within her ideological framework, particularly while she was still living and working in the United States, the Soviet Union seemed to be the site for the most advanced human relations for women; she saw it as demonstrating the truth, as advanced by William Foster and others, that only under socialism would the human being be liberated. In her 1951 essay "Foster's Theoretical and Political Guidance to Work among Women," Jones had indicated that "the emancipation of woman is possible only under Socialism": "Under Socialism, full enjoyment of equal rights by women is *guaranteed* by the very nature of a society in which classes and exploitation are abolished" (78). In hindsight, we can see that this was an idealistic position. While it is true that at that time Soviet women were being offered opportunities in employment not open to women in the United States until the women's movement of the 1970s, full emancipation of women in the USSR remained elusive, as subsequent studies would show.

From some angles, Jones's positions can be read by some as ones informed largely by Communist Party literature and indoctrination and idealism. Her writings, however, never defend hardline Stalinist programs. Jones was well read in Leninism, and recognized that Lenin had advanced views on the colonial question, as he did on the woman question. She would therefore have found Stalinist positions untenable, even though she would have supported the Communist Party's links with the Soviet Union, which dated back to the Second World War. The violence of Stalinism and its strong dictatorship alienated many communists in the 1950s, even as they struggled to understand and represent Communist Party official positions on Stalinism. Khruschev's "secret speech," "On the Cult of Personality," which denounced Stalin, would be delivered in 1956, a year after Claudia had left the United States and several years before her own visit to the Soviet Union in 1963. Claudia Jones, then, was not a Stalinist; but she also did not see Stalin as the problem — for her, the enemy was not Stalin but growing U.S. imperialism.[42]

Harold Cruse's[43] controversial position that black activists in the Communist Party were unimaginative and followed the communist line "without deviation," and that the Communist Party USA was too pro-Soviet therefore pro-Stalin has been challenged by numerous scholars. When he was writing his critique (first published in 1967), Cruse felt, among other things, that black activists were unable take what was applicable from back-to-Africa Garveyism and Marxism in order to "lay the foundation for a new school of revolutionary ideas" (*The Crisis of the Negro Intellectual*, 151). He claimed that by toeing the line to defend communism and repressing internal critique of the Soviet Union, the Communist Party USA became a conventional Communist Party.[44] Cruse's argument would have perhaps been more nuanced had he examined some of the ideas of black activists of the time, especially women like Claudia Jones.[45] A number of black women, while participating in communist party theoretics, attempted nonetheless to create a political praxis that brought together an assemblage of positions hitherto defined as disparate. This assemblage of related positions into one theoretical framework would be the basis for the definition of black feminism in the generation following Claudia Jones.

Claudia's work in England and her visits to the Soviet Union and China provide another layer to an understanding of her communism and of her own practical interpretations of communism. But unfortunately Claudia died soon after these visits and was not able to leave us any detailed account of them; we therefore do not have the kind of information that would have enabled a more complete analysis. Nonetheless, since for many it was axiomatic that if one were pro-Soviet then one could not be also pro–Maoism, Claudia's visit to China and her growing appreciation of Chinese communism, advances another feature of her special brand of (left of Karl Marx) communism.

Another interesting summary of this position is that "Jones was fiercely loyal to the Party and yet she was not a blind advocate of all CPUSA positions. She was a classical Marxist who supported the idea that the working class/the proletariat would bring about social and economic change."[46] In this regard,

Jones was not unlike a range of African American, African, Caribbean, and other third world intellectual-activists who saw in Marxism-Leninism an interpretive framework for understanding, resisting, and redefining their colonial situations. Jones herself makes this point as she recounts how she came to join the Communist Party. Her outspoken support for the Cuban Revolution is indicative of her leanings on these issues, which came to the forefront when she moved to London.[47]

The invitation that Jones received from the editors of *Soviet Women* (a women's magazine) to visit the Soviet Union offered her another opportunity to move beyond the "woman question" of the party to a fuller understanding of the roles of women and to a more direct and personal association with them. Claudia May sees her as being "inspired by the progress made by the Stalin administration to create programs that placed women and workers at the center of domestic policies" ("Nuances of Un-American Literature(s)," 4). But nowhere in Jones's numerous articles is there any obvious defense of Stalinist excesses. Instead, Jones's communism, Marxist-Leninist in orientation, became the analytical and political tool that she used to analyze the conditions of black people and women in the United States and subsequently to critique British racism and understand the decolonization movements around the world.

Cedric Robinson, in *Black Marxism*, sees the limits in Marxism precisely in its inability to deal with racism, which in his words "ran deep in the bowels of Western culture" (82): "Marxists have often argued that national liberation movements in the Third World are secondary to the interests of the industrial proletariat in the capitalist metropoles, or that they need to be understood only as the social efflux of world capitalism. . . . What is least defensible though, is how scant the attention paid to intra-European racialism has been" (84).

The lukewarm reception Jones received from the Communist Party of Great Britain (such a contrast to the resounding sendoff from the Communist Party USA) is absolutely pivotal in understanding her shifting political orientation and practice in London. Claudia had already experienced and struggled against racism in the United States, and in the Communist Party USA in particular. She would have to begin the struggle all over again in the United Kingdom. Gertrude Elias reports that when she met Jones, soon after her arrival, she remarked that Jones must be busy going all over the country, lecturing and so on, for the Communist Party. Claudia replied that as far as the Communist Party of Great Britain (CPGB) were concerned, she might as well be dead.[48] Trevor Carter in *Shattering Illusions* describes both the attraction of the Communist Party to West Indian workers in London, but also their disillusionment with it: "Racism within the communist party, both at the theoretical level and in practical and personal terms, added its weight to the growing disillusionment and frustration of many of the black comrades in the fifties and sixties" (59). Carter describes efforts by black comrades to raise the issue within the CPGB (60–61). He indicates as well that another major upset to many Caribbean party members' understanding of the aims of communism was "Khrushchev's speech to the 20th Congress of the CPSU [Communist Party of the Soviet Union] in 1956, where the political crimes of Stalin were announced and denounced." Still, as he describes it, "Many of those who were in the party at the time say that it was not so much the British Party they felt they had joined, but rather the international Communist movement. . . . The Soviet Union was at the heart of that international movement and had been seen to play a key role in the anti-colonialist and anti-imperialist struggles of which the black Communists in Britain were a product and a part" (59). It was into this context that Claudia Jones stepped, when she arrived in Britain in late December 1955.

Carter reports, though, that for the black communists in London at that time, Claudia's knowledge and example would play an important role: "Many of us who got frustrated and grumbled were sustained in our political faith by the encouragement of Claudia Jones" (61). And in the end, her political experience and background would be vital. Thus, in dealing with the racist bases of immigration, "the Communist Party, for all its imperfections, [was] the only British political party in complete opposition to quotas and controls for Commonwealth immigration" (70). It is significant that Carter uses Claudia's analysis of this to make this point (70–71), for in other places he discusses her ability to use astute analysis to get at the heart of relevant political issues.

The Caribbean leftists, many of whom had been or continued to be members of the Caribbean Labour Congress and the Communist Party, saw her as providing new leadership. So while she was an important member of a cadre of black and white communists in the United States that struggled within the Communist Party against racism in its ranks and in the larger society, in London, there was no equivalent functioning grouping. Jones became instead the leader of a Caribbean communist community outside of the party, which broadened its alliances to include a range of other allied activist groups. The space for the kind of work she was skilled at doing and the kind of cadre with which she could work would have to be created. So, while she remained a Communist Party member, it was in the international communist movement sense, and that could also mean for her organizing outside of Communist Party structures and directly in black and working-class communities in England.

Thus, ironically, deportation and London provided the opportunity for the kind of distancing that would allow her to develop a fuller pan-Africanist and Caribbean community orientation. Technically, Jones was always a communist first and foremost. Thus, Billy Strachan, an ardent Communist Party member, in his discussion of Claudia's relation to the party, states that there were no gaps in her relationship with them: "There was no difference between the Communist Party and Claudia at that time."[49] In other words, Claudia would never disavow the Communist Party and her commitment to a socialist reordering of society that is at its base. What one observes instead is an operational distance, as far as her own conduct is concerned.

It is here that the issue of her relationship with her fellow Trinidadian, C. L. R. James, enters, for James was an avowed Trotskyist, pan-Africanist, and advocate of the decentered state,[50] who critiqued the practices of the Communist Party, saw Stalin as a betrayer of the principles of communism, and the Soviet Union as a failed communist state; he provided his analyses in "Notes on Dialectics."[51] This is the basis of the operational gap that is noticeable between Jones and James. There is no indication that they ever collaborated closely in London, though each lent distant support to the other's positions, and their political responses would be similar on some issues; Donald Hinds identifies them as being on the same panel once, in London as a benefit to hurricane victims in the Caribbean, and they are both included in the *Freedomways* 1964 special issue on "The People of the Caribbean Area."

Claudia's visits to both the Soviet Union and China toward the end of her life provide the final elements we can use in an assessment of her communism. It is significant that her visit to the Soviet Union was sponsored by a Soviet women's group. She was clearly impressed by the achievements of women there, and with the history and strength of the Soviet Union that she witnessed there, as well as the excitement, as a communist, of having finally made it to Russia. She reported back with satisfaction that she had been able to see structures of management and talk with people who were participating in continuing socialist transformation.

Jones seemed, however, more excited about the possibilities opened up by the Chinese Revolution. Her poem "Yenan — Cradle of the Revolution" (see chapter 3) is a critical text in our assessment of her still evolving communism and lifelong practice of learning. Operating fully from a third world position, she uses the poem form to express her admiration for what was happening in China. An allied response would also come from Shirley Graham Du Bois, as reported by Gerald Horne in *Race Woman*. Du Bois, too, was impressed with China and supported its revolutionary programs. Horne notes that "when signs of the rift between Moscow and Beijing first became evident, she was reluctant to take sides and instead, tried to bring the two sides together" (226). Meeting Chairman Mao, as Jones did (with a Latin American delegation) was clearly a high point in Claudia's life as a communist,[52] as was her interview with some of the leading women in the Chinese Revolution.

Jones's article about that meeting, "First Lady of the World: I Talk with Mme Sun Yat-sen," begins with an amplification of the bold claim in her title: "Madame Soon-Ching-Ling, Vice Chairman of the People's republic of China, and widow of the famed Sun Yat-Sen, President of the First Democratic Republic of China, may properly be termed the First Lady of the World." The article itself develops a conversation "about the great achievements in Socialist re-construction in the New China based on its policy of Self-Reliance in the field of agriculture and industrialization in light and heavy industry." Claudia was impressed that Madame Soong Ching Ling was familiar with her imprisonment in the United States and of her work in the *West Indian Gazette* and related Caribbean organizations. The conversation covered a range of issues, from Claudia's impressions of China to Madame Soong Ching Ling's speech in Ceylon, which "by its clarity and profoundity inspired anti-imperialist fighters enhanced by this confidence in the anti-imperialist, pro peace struggle." The "peoples' communes" also occupied a large portion of their conversation, with included details of their development from the early days to the present. Claudia indicates that her travels confirmed "Mme Soong's confident claim that 'Peasants have become masters in our own land — not like before. Yes, everywhere the land is luxuriant. We adhere very strongly to our policy of self-reliance for our Socialist Construction.' " In the end, Jones suggests to Madame Soong that anyone seeing the developments there would not consider the "Peoples Communes as having been initiated 'too swiftly' for China's socialist development."

The trajectory of Jones's career in London, with its opportunities to direct her activism in new directions, indicates a shift away from a Soviet communist party line toward a third world communist position that celebrated the accomplishment of national revolution. She would debate these issues with her companion, Abhimanyu Manchanda. In a letter to Manchanda dated September 7, 1964, she says, for example:

> I had just returned from a few days ago from the great industrial north—east in Shenyang and Anchan—one of the heavy industrial bases of the People's republic. It's an exciting experience to visit and meet, learn and observe the numerous innovations in China's heavy industry, metal and machine tool plants and to visit my second People's Commune. How much clearer I understood the rather complex (no sense of political emphasis) inter-relations of agriculture and industry. But we (peace delegates to Tokyo 10th world conference) had benefited from a splendid lecture earlier by a brilliant economics professor who also is vice chairman for the promotion of foreign trade. After seeing some light and heavy industry and then another People's Communes the questions thoroughly explored and answered, asked by me and others present—came to life as one saw under hot sun, the acres of green fields, rice, tall sorghum, corn and other harvests to comes. Best of all was interviewing the families—at random.[53]

The path taken by Maoist China would fundamentally challenge the Soviet logic of evolutionary steps toward communism. Claudia would see in China a national revolution rooted in the people, in particular the peasantry. So, she writes excitedly about these visits to Manchanda. Unfortunately, because she dies relatively soon after these trips, we never see an unfolding of her new understandings of these different approaches in communism.

This experience in China contrasts greatly with an earlier letter from the Soviet Union, dated August 21, 1962. While she was excited about being in the Soviet Union, where she was hospitalized briefly, and talked about how impressed she is with women's roles in the Soviet Union, the letter deals largely with her concerns about the *West Indian Gazette* and its operations. She indicates, though, that she was well taken care of and spoke about Yalta.

Her poem "Paean to the Crimea" written October 11, 1962, from Rossia Sanitorium is much more sober and reflective

In which earth's crust were your depths probed
To fill your breasts with blue-green seas
That tough the shores of ancient lands
And is milieu for echoing changes,
Of peans of praise to you, Crimea.
And to your people's system-rare

Jones was obviously writing this while hospitalized. Still, in no way does it carry the obvious excitement that subsequently comes through about her experiences in China, and especially in her poem to Yenan, which is much more optimistic in tone.

Much of her attention in this time, and therefore her expressions of her communism, was focused on her application of these positions to an understanding of British and U.S. imperialism. Communism was the means by which she could advance her anti-imperialist and internationalist work. A beautiful and happy photograph of Jones amidst a group of Chinese children was used as her holiday greeting card that December. And at her death, wreaths and statements from China, the Soviet Union, Cuba, a range of African and Caribbean countries, and a variety of organizations worldwide testified to her numerous connections.[54] A parallel memorial ceremony was offered for her in China, as well, after her passing.

Conclusions: Pan-Africanism, Feminism, Communism, and More

Will you measure, for example, as worthy of one year's sentence, my passionate adherence to the idea of fighting for full and unequivocal equality for my people, the Negro people, which as a Communist I believe can only be achieved allied to the cause of the working class? . . . It is this, your Honor, that explains the not-so-strange reason that you yourself observed that we feel no guilt.
CLAUDIA JONES, FROM "SPEECH TO THE COURT, FEBRUARY, 1953"

Pan-Africanism, feminism, and communism are all ideological constructs, intellectual positions, analytical categories, conceptual and theoretical frameworks; as terms they may be used to define, locate, or understand someone like Claudia Jones. Though these are concepts that in themselves could be containing or limiting, for one who moved easily and confidently through an assemblage of positions, they were not so. Instead, Jones was able to make the connections. The pan-Africanism of Claudia Jones is clear in her various assertions of linkages with African people's globally and in her political work to make this a reality. Although she is never identified as participating in any of the official pan-Africanist organizations, her friendship and political work with Amy Ashwood Garvey in London is well documented, and there is evidence that they knew each other in New York as well. Mrs. Garvey was on the editorial board of the *West Indian Gazette*, and they worked together for the community following the Notting Hill riots and maintained letter communications when not in the same place. Jones would maintain an ideological link between pan-Africanism and Communism. Jones is identified as having influenced pan-Africanists — such as Nkrumah — from the standpoint of bringing Marxist-Leninist views to bear on their pan-Africanist thinking.[55]

Claudia identified W. E. B. Du Bois as her "teacher," in the sense that he was someone she had learned from about black political life, knowledge, and activism.[56] It is interesting that Jones said this, after Du Bois had left the Socialist Party of America. Du Bois was not the only influential black activist working on issues central to Jones's mission who was neither a communist nor a member of one of the major parties. Several other black activists (Hubert Harrison and Claude McKay, for example) had also left formal party structures, dissatisfied with party positions on racism, even if they kept socialist positions ideologically. A number of them remained socialists even as they supported independent black radical organizations. Examples are Cyril Briggs and Grace Campbell of the African Blood Brotherhood, who defined themselves as black Bolsheviks; they had earlier been linked to party communism more via ideology than to specific state operations.[57]

Many black leftist activists decided that an independent black political movement would be more successful than party activity in the realization of black rights and black liberation in the United States. Activists like George Padmore, identified as one of the founding figures of pan-Africanism, would similarly operate from a solidly internationalist position. Indeed, the logic of a black, international, pan-Africanist, working-class movement would be fundamental to organizations like the Council of African Affairs and the early Negro World Unity Congress, founded in 1935. According to Brent Hayes Edwards, in *The Practice of Diaspora*, this activity "represents an earlier effort to think in such international terms, extending the impulses of Du Bois's Pan-Africanism, and Garvey's Back-to-Africa movement in the 1920's"; "calls for a Black International were not uncommon even earlier," he notes (276–277).[58] Linked to decolonization struggles in the third world, this "black international" would carry power, especially given the recognition of the black people in the United States in general as an oppressed nation. Black internationalism would emerge from international communism, though it would be separate from it and at the same time pan-Africanist in practice and orientation. With clear demands for self-determination, particularly in the black belt, it was a position already taken by Claudia Jones within the Communist Party and it would be be central to resolutions and human rights petitions outside of it, as, for example, before the United Nations.[59]

John McClendon makes the argument that C. L. R. James (unlike the later Padmore) did not see pan-Africanism as an ideology but rather as a movement; in James's view, Marxism-Leninism was an ideology and pan-Africanism a movement that could realize the goals of ideology (9–15). James argued that this distinction between black internationalism and international communism does not ideologically collapse into the principle of self-determination. Self-determination is a practical question, not an ideological question. Padmore had a different perspective. He held that pan-Africanism was an ideology, as was communism, and that one had to choose one or the other. Padmore did not develop this view until after his break from communism, yet he supported the principle of self-determination, as had other Marxists, including Lenin. McClendon's view is that even though C. L. R. James, a Trotskyist, argued for self-determination and pan-Africanism, he also upheld proletarian internationalism; it is therefore entirely consistent that James and Jones, even given their differences over Trotsky and Stalin were on the same page when it came to the black international.

In her London experience, Claudia Jones seems to have carried forward her own version of this position of self-determination for the third world, given the recalcitrance of the Communist Party of Great Britain in embracing her and her positions. Most of her London organizing activity was outside of the party and linked specifically to Caribbean and Afro-Asian communities.[60] It was not unusual for the *West Indian Gazette and Afro-Asian Caribbean News* to carry articles that highlighted the connections within the pan-African world — the Caribbean, Africa, the United States of America, and, of course, Europe. London provided an important vantage point from which to witness and participate in these developments. Jones's work in the *Gazette* precedes the Caribbean Artists Movement (1966–1972) in giving voice and space to the writers in a forum of their own. Many of Jones's meetings and other activities were held in Africa House in London. In her files are letters that maintain an ongoing commentary on various developments in Africa and their impact on the rest of the colonial world. And significantly, the memorial ceremony for Claudia Jones, held February 27, 1965, in the St. Pancras Town Hall, Euston Road, was chaired by Raymond Kunene of the African National Congress, with introductory remarks by H. E. L. Khelifa, ambassador of the Democratic Republic of Algeria.

Claudia had consistently throughout her writings in the United States challenged the Communist Party to keep in the forefront a consciousness that black liberation was fundamental — in her terms, "prior" — and that black women were an index to our understanding of the conditions of the society as a whole. Indeed, her position that African Americans constituted an oppressed nation and so were deserving of protection by the United Nations would link her to a number of other black activists who would take this position over the years. In the 1960s Malcolm X would make this argument, and as recently as 2004, black political representatives were seeking protection for their constituents from a repeat of what happened in the 2000 presidential election and its aftermath, when African Americans in Florida were denied voting rights.

This early assertion of an internal colonialism[61] (which highlighted the links between the diaspora and African and other nations involved in decolonization struggles) is made manifest in concrete ways in a range of pamphlets about the experiences of African Americans in the United States, the legacy of Jim Crow, and continuing exploitation and the nature of the black condition in both urban and rural areas. From all reports, Jones's political and personal circle of friends and acquaintances were conscious of these links. Her close friendship and organizational work with Amy Ashwood Garvey speaks eloquently and symbolically about pan-Africanist and feminist linkages. But beyond the historical link between African peoples was the context of decolonization struggles and women's movements working internationally for peace, which provided tangible examples of people breaking the yoke of imperialist oppression worldwide.

A letter to Claudia from Benjamin Davis, the black Harlem councilman, makes this point and affirms her position: "All of your remarks on the national and colonial questions are pertinent and sound, in my judgment. The deterioration of the colonial system, and its effects on the whole question of peaceful co-existence, on economic issues, on the whole political struggle — is the biggest thing in the world picture. We have yet to deal with that question fundamentally over here."[62]

Claudia Jones's position on women's rights and women's movement, the organizing of women for empowerment, the challenge to male supremacist tendencies inside and outside of the party, defines hers as an anti-imperialist feminist position, as described in prior chapters. But as always, her position as a leading communist is articulated frontally and unflinchingly.

A Marxist-Leninist ideologically, she remained nevertheless "left of Marx" in her constant challenges to the limitations of party frameworks, as of communist theoretical positions. Her intent was to use Marxism-Leninism as an analytical tool,[63] that is, to understand the conditions of a range of subordinated peoples at a time when many black, creative, and intellectual figures left the party over what they saw as its limited positions on race. Sylvia Wynter has an allied "left of Karl Marx" position in her own critique of Marx, which says that Marx's argument about the consequences of ownership of the modes of production was only partially right. In other words, it is true that a system in which the modes of production are owned by individuals (i.e., capitalists) cannot deal with the poor and impoverished and only functions for the well-being of the global middle classes. But what is produced is not just the material conditions we live under but also the very conception of what it is to be human.[64] Claudia in many ways struggled with that very challenge to her humanity.

In her practice, Claudia Jones remained left of Marx, a diaspora subject, a migratory subject, a radical black female intellectual-activist, complex and multifaceted in the end, able to move beyond the inadequacies of Marxism, to arrive at a theoretical and practical position in which she could articulate many of the practical issues that her communities faced and that Marxism had not touched. The position she represented so well, left of Marx, becomes then a location and an ideological orientation that a range of radical subjects occupy in response to mistreatment by a dominant capitalist or socialist state or ideology.

As always, as one comes to the end of a project as formidable as this one, there are always new revelations to be made, additional information to be factored.

I see this project as reopening even as it closes. Perhaps a piece from Jones's final piece of autobiographical writing, a draft of an essay among her papers dated June 18, 1964, is the way to bring this phase of my study of Claudia Vera Cumberbatch Jones and this discussion to tentative completion. It captures Jones in a reflective mood, imagining what life would be like in the future. She reflects poetically on some of her own emotions, identifying herself as always forthright and unrelenting, fighting weakness and never openly sympathizing with it. She wonders why she has these tendencies, and answers herself in this way: "Is it because a lurking fear exists that capitulation to manifested weakness in others (even when not self-imposed) may in turn impinge on what I regard as essentially impermissible?" In the end, what has remained constant, she says, is her belief in the "Loom of Language and in the Family of Man." Her unwavering faith in the permanence of words is clear, as is a commitment to our ability to live the best of our humanity.

In the decades that followed Jones's death a major peace movement would be launched in the United States, with reverberations everywhere around the world. Civil rights, black power, and youth movements would challenge entrenched systems of racist terrorism. Decolonization movements would struggle to liberate colonized African, Caribbean, Latin American, and Asian countries from imperialist domination. A feminist movement would challenge the subordination of women. A black feminist movement would put together theoretically the major principles and programs that Claudia Jones advocated, and include as well the experiences and struggles of black women from myriad locations. Claudia Jones, in many ways, anticipated and ushered in these combinations and therefore these movements.

If what I say here serves even one whit to further dedicate growing millions of Americans to fight for peace, and to repel the fascist drive on free speech and thought in our country, I shall consider my rising to speak worthwhile indeed. (Jones, from "Speech to the Court, February, 1953.")

1,000 WOMEN VISIT UN TO URGE PEACE

Daily Worker

Vol. XXVII, No. 213   New York, Wednesday, October 25, 1950
(12 Pages) Price 5 cents

SENATE TO INVESTIGATE

TRUMAN'S UN TALK CALLS
FOR BIGGER ARMAMENTS

GOVERNMENT OFFICIALS

Korea Tells UN of Deliberate Bombing and Strafing of Civilians

Daily Worker

Vol. XXVII, No. 150   New York, Wednesday, August 9, 1950
(12 Pages) Price 5 cents

1,000 WOMEN IN CAPITAL DEMAND PEACE

NEW YORK DELEGATES to the national women's peace pilgrimage to Washington board the train at the Baltimore and Ohio station in Jersey City. The delegation was sponsored by American Women for Peace.

25–26. *Daily Worker* front page articles on women's peace protests, August and October 1950.

27. Claudia Jones with Martin Luther King on his way to Oslo. London, December 11, 1964. WIG photo.

28. Claudia Jones with Jomo Kenyatta, London. WIG photo.

29. Claudia Jones with Norman Manley, London. WIG photo.

30. Claudia Jones with Cheddi Jagan, London. WIG photo.

31. A photograph of Claudia Jones as a guest at the wedding of Fitz Gore and Patricia Reid, September 1959. WIG photo.

NOTES

Preface

1. Through Carolyn Cooper, who was then on a fellowship at the University of Birmingham, England.
2. See note 42 to the introduction for discussion of some of the processes leading up to and following the tombstone placement at the grave site in Highgate Cemetery by the London Caribbean community. The Friends of Highgate Cemetery, who provide tours through Highgate Cemetery, had no information on the person buried to the left of Marx. In fact, they asked me to send them a copy of this book (as other authors who have written on people buried in Highgate have sent theirs) so they can identify Claudia Jones appropriately, since there are numerous visitors to the Marx grave.
3. See McLendon's three-page entry, "Claudia Jones (1915–1964)," subtitled by the editor "Political Activist, Black Nationalist, Feminist, Journalist." See also Kelley's entry on Jones in *Black Women in America*.
4. Books on this subject are beginning to appear. Eric McDuffie's dissertation is based on oral histories of four left women: Queen Mother Moore, Claudia Jones, Louise Patterson, and Esther Jackson.
5. Since then published as Ransby, *Ella Baker and the Black Freedom Movement*. I have also learned that Sharon Harley is working on a history of radical black women, as is Mary Helen Washington, of the University of Maryland.
6. A photographic exhibition in London (February 2005) by Buzz Johnson, which I was not able to visit, reveals that Buzz's project may be reinvigorated now.
7. Between 1995 and 1997, I conducted interviews and conversations with Ranjana Ash, Donald Hinds, Beryl Gilroy, Billy Strachan, Pansy Jeffries, Jessica and Eric Huntley, Ricky Cambridge, and John La Rose.
8. Based on interview with Pansy Jeffries at her flat in Tollington Way, London,

April 4, 1997. Mrs. Jeffries bemoaned the fact that a lot of their papers, particularly those of her husband Lionel, were lost following his passing when she returned to Guyana and Barbados during her grieving period. She called me back several times to invite me to various functions such as lunch at the Pepper Pot in Ladbroke Grove, one of the black community organizations for Caribbean seniors that she had founded. Each interviewee recommended others. She recommended Billy Strachan, Corrine Skinner, Trevor Carter, and the Huntleys.

9. May, "Nuances of Un-American Literature(s)." The dissertation is part historical exploration and part imaginative and concentrates on the years 1940–1955.

10. Yumeris Morel, a former student of mine, has written an M.A. thesis at SUNY-Binghamton under the direction of Tiffany Patterson, titled "Claudia Jones: Race, Class and Feminist Consciousness." One other student, at University of Michigan, Ann Arbor, worked on Claudia Jones for her dissertation during the early 1990s, but subsequently changed focus.

11. Alexis (Misani) De Veaux speaks in this way about her work on Audre Lorde, now published as *Warrior Poet*. Personal conversation, Buffalo, New York, April 2001.

12. Present were Jan Shinebourne, Meredith Gadsby, and Conrad James. We had just left the classroom of Joan Anim-Addo at Goldsmith's College.

13. A London-based black radical journal, *The Black Liberator* was subtitled *Theoretical and Discussion Journal for Black Liberation* and published throughout the 1970s; it was on the order of *The Black Scholar* (United States) but explicitly Marxist-Leninist in orientation, providing space for the discussion of culture, labor, education, and popular issues in Europe and the Caribbean and the larger black world.

14. Harry Goulbourne (in his *Caribbean Transnational Experience*, 81, 86–87) describes well the contributions of Alrick (Ricky) Xavier Cambridge to black organizing in London, via the Black Unity and Freedom Party and the subsequent development, contribution, and ideological orientation of *The Black Liberator*.

15. This manuscript is in progress and will be the next component of my work on Claudia Jones.

16. Published subsequently with the title "Beyond Unicentricity."

17. Jan Shinebourne, author of *The Last English Plantation* and *Timepiece*, which won the 1987 Guyana Prize for a first novel (Leeds: Peepal Tree Press, 1986).

18. The material itself had had many journeys. It had just come back from a stay in Maryland with Merle Collins and was being held for Marika Sherwood, who was researching her book project. The BBC had borrowed it for a special they did on Claudia Jones at one point. Diane Langford reported that Sherwood had left with it on the back of her bicycle, and that Donald Hinds had another portion of material, which he had not returned to her. Interviews with Hinds indicated that he had a great deal of material, related largely to journalism and the newspaper,

and that he was himself planning a book. He also told me that Buzz Johnson's collection, which was the first major assemblage done, is perhaps the best available and that he had given Buzz a substantial amount of material. Despite several phone conversations throughout my London stay, I was not able to set up an appointment to meet Buzz in the same place as the collection.

19. Colin Prescod ends his introductory essay in Sherwood et al.'s book on Jones in a very unfortunate way: ("Claudia was magnificent—and a woman alone" (175); it minimizes a series of friendships and relationships that Jones developed in London, as my interviews with people like Ranjana Ash and Ricky Cambridge reveal. Many people in London were in awe of Claudia Jones and loved and respected her deeply. She did socialize and make time for friends, but she was also always a busy, dignified, and active woman, one who spent a great deal of time writing and/or reading. It is said that when she was found after her passing, she was in the reading posture and alone in her apartment. But she had been scheduled to go to dinner with friends on Christmas Day, and it was her not showing up there that alerted them to the fact that something was wrong. Additionally, people who work internationally and diasporically operate with friendships that transcend local geographies.

Introduction: Recovering the Radical Black Female Subject

1. Her comments at the trial (excerpted in the epigraph to this chapter) were reprinted as "Limits of Tyranny Are the Measure of Our Resistance," *West Indian Gazette and Afro-Asian-Caribbean News*, February 1965, 6–7.

2. This title came to me during a symposium sponsored by the Coloniality Working Group in Binghamton University. A student asked if it was true that Claudia Jones was buried next to Karl Marx. I responded that she was actually buried "left of Karl Marx." The instant response from the audience and the recognition from Sylvia Wynter (who was in attendance) that this captured Claudia's position, clarified that this was indeed the title of what would become a book project.

Marx's analyses of the movement of history and the creation of economic classes for the expropriation of labor are still important and incisive; they are best represented by Marx's theory of surplus value as the fundamental feature of capitalist exploitation; see Marx, *Capital*.

3. See Zetkin, *Lenin on the Woman Question*.

4. It is important to note that Davis would consistently address issues of transnational capitalism. See, for example, her address marking the twenty-fifth anniversary of the University of California, Los Angeles, Center for African American Studies, quoted in my introduction to *Decolonizing the Academy*, "Decolonizing the Academy: Advancing the Process."

5. See, for example, my *Black Women, Writing and Identity*, "Hearing Black Wom-

en's Voices: Transgressing Imposed Boundaries," and "Black Women Writing Worlds."

6. See Johnson, "*I Think of My Mother*," 35–53.

7. Interviews and conversations with Alrick Cambridge, 1997–2000.

8. She acquired the name Jones as an adult, in New York. The name change may have been a means to hide her identity. It was certainly effective in deflecting the investigations of the FBI, who did not discover her birth name and place of birth for many years after their investigation began.

9. These descriptors have also been applied to Angela Davis and Assata Shakur. See their autobiographies, *Angela Davis* and *Assata*. James's *Shadowboxing*, 78–83, offers useful discussion of some of these distinctions.

10. In Sherwood et al., *Claudia Jones*, 114.

11. Du Bois, *The Souls of Black Folk* (Chicago: A. C. McClurg and Co., 1903); Carla Kaplan, ed., *Zora Neale Hurston: A Life in Letters* (New York: Doubleday, 2002). Hortense Spillers has a helpful overview of the debates in her "The Crisis of the Negro Intellectual."

12. See Gramsci, "The Intellectuals"; and Mugo, "The Role of African Intellectuals."

13. Angela Davis and her consistent intellectual-activist work, for example, on the prison industrial complex, may be cited here as the transformative intellectual.

14. In the contemporary, post-September 11 United States, a variety of intellectuals have come under attack from both their institutions and the state. Ward Churchill, ordered fired by the University of Colorado is one example, as is Amiri Baraka, who was threatened with removal as the poet laureate of New Jersey because of a poem he wrote, titled "Who Blew Up America?" David Horowitz's *The Professors: The 101 Most Dangerous Academics in America* (2006) — published by Regnery, a right wing publishing house in Washington, D.C. — presents a list of intellectuals who can be targeted for academic work defined as critical of U.S. policies. This kind of listing is dangerous, particularly since some on the list have been already targeted for reprisals.

15. See as well her more recent *Dark Designs and Visual Culture*.

16. First published in *Z Magazine* and later reprinted in *Yearning: Race, Gender, and Cultural Politics*.

17. Greg Thomas in "The Geo-Cultural Economy of Race?" critiques this tendency in U.S. scholarship on race. See also his more recent work, *The Sexual Demon of Colonial Power*.

18. See Nnaemka's *Sisterhood, Feminisms and Power* and Oyewumi's *African Women and Feminism*.

19. See, for example, the *Sunday Trinidad Express*, Woman Magazine, July 4, 2004, which has a beautiful cover photo and the story "Baroness Valerie Amos Leading the Way," which details the moves that led to Valerie Amos's being named bar-

oness. "Amos was created a Labour peer in the House of Lords — acquiring the title Baroness — when the party came to power in 1997" (4). Originally from Guyana, she was the first black woman to hold a British Cabinet post and the first black person to be appointed leader of the House of Lords and lord president of the Privy Council, the monarch's advisory body. Amos is described as having "test[ed] her mettle in women's and racial equality causes" after undertaking sociology studies and postgraduate cultural studies. Clearly accomplished, Valerie Amos, after a series of positions, was from 1998 to 2001 the spokesperson on social security, international development, and women's issues in the House of Lords. Tony Blair also appointed her his special envoy to Africa (5).

20. See Ronke Oyewumi's *The Invention of Women: Making an African Sense of Western Gender Discourses*. See also my response, "A View from the Palace: Oyewumi's *The Invention of Women*" (paper presented at the annual meeting of the African Studies Association, Washington, D.C., December 5–8, 2002).

21. Much of this erasure is clearly the result of the U.S. government intention that her name not be mentioned in the United States again, but it also has to do with her deportation to England despite her long residence in the United States, and her being in London for the last ten years of her life.

22. The erasure of Claudia Jones from U.S. black intellectual-activist rolls is linked to the McCarthyite project of deportation and harassment that was meted out to her even though she had lived in the United States for over thirty years and it was her primary home. In England, where she ended her years, she is now a respected figure in the development of the Black British community. Much less is known about her in the United States, but this is beginning to change. Indeed, it is my project that Jones be restored into the discussion of U.S. black intellectuals.

23. See James, *Resisting State Violence, Shadowboxing, States of Confinement, The Angela Y. Davis Reader*, and *Transcending the Talented Tenth*.

24. An example of those black women radicals was Grace Campbell (of Caribbean origin), who appears repeatedly in all of the lists of organizers in Harlem in the 1930s and is identified at one time as leading the African Blood Brotherhood. She is clearly someone deserving of separate study.

25. The work of Amadiume (*Male Daughters, Female Husbands*), Butler (*Gender Trouble*), and others challenge, revise and expand on Scott (1986). Oyeronke Oyewumi's recent work has been the subject of much debate and critique from scholars of Yoruba culture, including women who have done significant work on Yoruba women's culture, e.g., the African Studies Association panel on Oyewumi's book, Washington, D.C., 2002.

26. See my *Black Women, Writing and Identity*.

27. See also Mohanty and Alexander, *Feminist Geneaologies, Colonial Legacies, Democratic Futures*.

28. See Sherwood et al., *Claudia Jones*, 110. She is also identified as representing Trinidad and Tobago in two other socialist conferences, in Tokyo and Japan.

29. Hall, "The Local and the Global: Globalization and Ethnicity."

30. In *Scattered Hegemonies*, 137–152.

31. See again Alexander and Mohanty, *Feminist Geneaologies*.

32. Examples include Shell, a transnational corporation whose responsibility for the pollution of a Nigerian community (and the resultant execution of Ken Saro Wiwa) cannot be minimized. Another example is the practical effect of U.S. plant closings, the relationship of those closings to *maquiladoras* in the third world, and the parallel relationships and emigration of displaced workers worldwide.

33. See discussions on internationalizing woman's human rights in Wing, *Global Critical Race Feminism*.

34. See *New York Times*, April 24, 1996, and May 5, 1996.

35. Dirie's personal narrative of gendered nomadism and migrancy, in my view, rewrites the theoretical definition of the nomadic subject advanced by Rosi Braidotti in *Nomadic Subjects*. Living a nomadic life did not, for example, spare her from female genital mutilation: "You can't escape it. They catch you, tie you down and then do it. It's done for men" (65). She says that it was only by becoming an emigrant, coming to London as a maid to a relative, and—when she and her relatives were due to return home—burying her passport in the garden (so that she had no documents to travel and thus had to be left behind) that she was able to access an identity that she could shape.

36. Dirie (with Miller), *Desert Flower*.

37. See Lorde, *Sister Outsider*.

38. Winston James's early classic, *Holding Aloft the Banner of Ethiopia*, for example, does not present in any depth the women who appear in his book. See also Moten's study of the black radical tradition (focusing mainly on music), *In the Break*. Tony Bogues's recent *Black Heretics, Black Prophets* is an exception in that it includes a good account of Ida Wells-Barnett.

39. See Sherwood et al., *Claudia Jones*, based on a symposium on Jones, held at the Institute of Commonwealth Studies, London; the conference also included a contribution by Gertrude Elias, "Claudia Jones (Trinidad 1915–London, 1964)." See also Johnson, *"I Think of My Mother,"* and Tyson and the Camden Black Sisters, *Claudia Jones, 1915–1964*.

40. See Boyce Davies, "A Guide to Claudia Jones Papers."

41. It is important that the name registered was Claude Vera. The more feminized version, Claudia, was no doubt acquired in childhood.

42. Jones's final resting place and the placing of a headstone on it was not without controversy. Several letters were exchanged between Abhimanyu Manchanda (nicknamed "Manu"), who identified himself as the secretary of the Claudia Jones

Memorial Committee, her friend, colleague, and coworker, the "person closest to her, her confidant and sole repository of her worldly assets and behests" (letter, September 8, 1983), and a variety of people who wanted to take in their own hands the right to recognize Claudia as community property (see, for example, a letter dated September 24, 1982, from Geo. J. Dowse and Co., solicitors to the secretary, Afro-Caribbean Organisation, 355 Gray's Inn Road, London). Manchanda, who had been out of the country when Claudia died, was shocked to learn that Mikki Doyle of the Communist Party had arranged for her to be buried, without any say from her family and close friends. An injunction was filed by a cousin in London, a Mr. Cumberbatch, to halt the planned burial. Manchanda then arranged for her cremation at the Golders Green Crematorium on January 9, 1965; purchased the burial plot of land next to the grave of Karl Marx at Highgate Cemetery, as was her wish; and arranged for the interment of her ashes on February 27, 1965. (Correspondence dated July 9, 1982, between J. H. Kenyon, funeral directors, 26 Connaught Street, London, and Mr. A. Manchanda). The story continues though with Bill Fairman, who tended to the Karl Marx tomb and noted that the burial plot next to it was covered with weeds. From there began a process to have a proper headstone erected on the site, a plan that was finally carried out by the Afro-Caribbean Organisation, which had launched a fund to erect a headstone after learning that there was nothing marking the place where Jones's ashes had been interred. Manchanda withheld permission until the end of 1983. A letter dated January 4, 1983, from the Afro-Caribbean Organisation, signed by W. S. Pinder, the general secretary, and copied to Trevor Carter and Mr. Hickey, indicates that the organization was ready to erect a headstone to honor Claudia: "We see the memory of our dear Sister Claudia belonging to all conscious black people. We believe that Claudia['s] contributions to our struggle and the struggles of all oppressed people, as one of the most outstanding contributions of a black Communist. . . .We look forward to meeting members of your committee by mid January to assist in the planning for what we hope will be a memorable occasion. We at [the] Afro-Caribbean Organisation look forward to your Committee['s] cooperation and the end of these solicitors' letters, so we can behave as two progressive groups of people should do."

In the end, it seems, Manchanda, who was in ill health at the time, wanted no more than to honor Claudia with a substantial monument in a proper way. He was unable to do so and therefore relented. The final piece of correspondence in the file comes from Bill Fairman, who, in a letter to Manu's solicitors dated August 14, 1983, indicated that preparations for the unveiling of the headstone go forward. A letter dated January 10, 1984, came from Manchanda, by then very ill and unable to pursue all the relevant documents and legal turns, but still questioning the right of the organization to erect a headstone.

1. Recent theses and dissertations include May, "Nuances of Un-American Literature(s)," and Morel, "Claudia Jones: Race, Class and Feminist Consciousness." Morel finds Weigand's Ph.D. dissertation ("Vanguards of Women's Liberation") too dismissive of the importance of Jones's contributions to feminist ideology in the United States. Weigand's position clearly changed over time, as her chapter on Jones ("Claudia Jones and the Synthesis of Gender, Race, and Class," 97–113) in her 2001 book *Red Feminism: American Communism and the Making of Women's Liberation* demonstrates. The work of an emerging new group of historians on the left has been formidable in pursuing the archival work in this regard, e.g., Solomon's *The Cry Was Unity*; McDuffie's two-volume dissertation, "Long Journeys"; and Shapiro's dissertation, "Red Feminism." Other theses and dissertations are listed by McDuffie. Along with the ongoing work of historians such as Gerald Horne and Robin Kelley on the black Left and Rosalyn Baxandall on communist women, they clarify many of these positions.

2. The *Worker* was a weekend newspaper published by CPUSA between 1958 and 1968. It succeeded a daily paper, the *Daily Worker*, founded in 1924. Although the *Daily Worker* is sometimes referred to as the *Worker* (particularly when discussing the Sunday edition), all references here will use the full name of the paper to avoid confusion with the later publication.

3. Weigand, "Vanguards of Women's Liberation." See also Hill's "Fosterites and Feminists." Both works document the resistance of white women in the Communist Party to Claudia Jones's positions on the importance of advancing black women in the party.

4. Personal communications, 2000 and 2001. See McClendon's essay "From Cultural Nationalism to Cultural Criticism" and his *CLR James Notes on Dialectics* for some of his ideas on related subjects. McClendon makes it clear that the subtitle to his "Claudia Jones (1915–1964)" ("Political Activist, Black Nationalist, Feminist, Journalist") was provided by the editor and was not his, particularly the identifications "Black Nationalist" and "Feminist."

5. Claudia Jones identifies "Women in the Struggle for Peace and Security" as the "overt act" accompanying her indictment. The published essay with that title is a republished version of "International Women's Day and the Struggle for Peace," which appeared in *Political Affairs* in March 1950. (Thanks are due to Lydia Lyndsey for her help in ascertaining this.) There is considerable overlap between various versions of these essays. For example, "Women Crusade for Peace," (March 1950) is a shortened version of this essay, and "For the Unity of Women in the Cause of Peace" (February 1951) is a subsequent essay published with similar themes and elements in its title. The FBI files (volume 2) indicate twenty-nine

essays (many of them published in the *Daily Worker*) as making the case for the charge of teaching and advocating the violent overthrow of the U.S. government.

6. Angela Davis's *Blues Legacies and Black Feminism*, as we have already shown, is one of these. Guy-Sheftall's work on black feminism and black women's studies also pursues this reasoning. See her introduction to *Words of Fire* for discussion.

7. Interview with George Bowrin, quoted in Johnson, *"I Think of My Mother,"* 129–132.

8. Weigand, *Red Feminism*, 109. Weigand sees in this the influence of historian Herbert Aptheker, e.g., his "The Negro Woman."

9. McDuffie's dissertation is based on oral histories and interviews with former American Communist Party activists, including the New York University's Tamiment Library collection of oral histories on radical women.

10. Black, communist, and a labor organizer, White articulated the special needs of black working-class women and their superexploitation in party journals as early 1932. Starting in 1930, White was an organizer for the party's Needle Trades Workers Industrial Union, which organized garment workers. She published two important articles on special needs and discrimination: "Special Negro Demands," *Labor Unity* 7.5 (May 1932), and "Fighting Discrimination," *Labor Unity* 7.11 (November 1932). Jones was not only a fellow black communist woman but, since her mother was a garment worker who died as a result of superexploitation, it is quite possible that Jones had read White's articles. See Solomon, "Rediscovering a Lost Legacy."

11. According to Rebecca Hill, "the last major theoretical work on the woman question" was a pamphlet entitled *Questions and Answers on the Woman Question* (1953) by Doxie Wilkerson and Irene Epatein that "indicated a high degree of influence from Claudia Jones's work [as] the pamphlet also dealt with the 'triple oppression' of Negro women" ("Fosterites and Feminists," 85).

12. An account of Claudia Jones's direct impact on a succeeding generation is expressed in the words of Pat Ellis, a young black woman who became a communist and describes this influence. Ellis describes a mass rally in Buffalo circa 1943–44 at which they were addressed by Jones and the ways this provided example for her subsequent activism. See Wheeler, "Black Women Workers." Weigand and Hill report that some white women in the Communist Party saw Jones as too critical of them (see Hill, "Fosterites and Feminists," 86; Weigand, *Red Feminism*, 107). There are also accounts where she seemed to come across to other black women as having too much of a communist position. McDuffie reports of an altercation between Claudia and Beulah Richardson, the leader of the Sojourners for Truth, which reveals the kind of negotiations that Claudia was engaged in, both inside and outside of the Communist Party (see McDuffie, "Long Journeys," 459).

13. Combahee River Collective, "A Black Feminist Statement," 16. See also Guy-Sheftall's definition, that while "black feminism is not a monolithic, static ideology, and there is considerable diversity among African American feminists, certain premises are constant." She identifies five premises, the first of which is that "Black women experience a special kind of oppression and suffering in this country which is racist, sexist, classist because of their dual racial and gender identity and their limited access to economic resources" (*Words of Fire*, 2).

14. Some accounts say that her mother died of emphysema (i.e., not as dramatic as collapsing on her machine at work). Jones nevertheless attributed her death to "speed-up" factory practices, which claimed the lives of many working-class women. See Johnson, "*I Think of My Mother*," 6.

15. See the film *Beah: A Black Woman Speaks* (2003), where Beah Richards describes the genesis of the Sojourners. McDuffie notes that their formal call to rally black women opens defiantly, and quotes: "The time has come for us Negro women of these United States to personally address this government for absolute, immediate and unconditional redress and grievances" ("A Call to Negro Women" issued by the Initiating Committee of the Sojourners for Truth and Justice in September 1951 for the Inaugural Convention in Washington, D.C.; a copy of the document can be found in the Louise Thompson Patterson Papers at Emory University). The "Call" condemns Jim Crow, police brutality, lynching, the death penalty, sexual violence against African American women, and the impoverishment of black Americans, making reference to a notorious case of the time, that of Mrs. Rosa Lee Ingram, who was on trial for defending herself against a racist and sexist attack. It calls on the federal government to enforce the Thirteenth, Fourteenth, and Fifteenth Amendments and to protect civil liberties. The document then steps directly into cold war politics: it charges that racism is the United States' Achilles heel and weakens the country on the global stage, and it demands an end to the Korean War. The final section of the statement calls on African American women: "Dry your tears, and in the spirit of Harriet Tubman and Sojourner Truth, ARISE and attend the group's opening meeting in Washington." Paraphrase and final quotation from the "Call" from McDuffie's "Sojourners for Truth and Justice" entry in *Encyclopedia of the African Diaspora* (ABC-CLIO, forthcoming). In the film *Beah*, Richardson indicates that her poem was chosen as best representative of the theme of peace for a Chicago Peace Conference in 1951. With the help of Patterson, she moves to New York and enters a left activist community meeting that Robeson and others admired from afar.

16. Thanks to John McClendon for help in fleshing out a dialectical materialist reading of Jones's "neglect thesis." For McClendon it "follows in a materialist way the principle that K. Marx's evokes about how White workers cannot be free as long as Black workers remain as slaves" (personal communication, January 2005). That

this position is resisted by white women is testified to by both Hill and Weigand and in fact is the basis for the charge by white women that Jones was guilty of "reverse chauvinism." See Hill, "Fosterites and Feminists," 68–70, for a discussion of this charge.

17. Kelley, in the chapter " 'The Negro Question': Red Dreams of Black Liberation," in *Freedom Dreams*, 25.

18. A line of reasoning within feminist theory on the role and construction of motherhood would develop throughout the eighties. Some of this work is included in Brenda O. Daly and Maureen T. Reddy, eds., *Narrating Mothers: Theorizing Maternal Subjectivities* (Knoxville: University of Tennessee Press, 1991).

19. See *The World's Women*, published biannually by the United Nations, for relevant statistics.

20. Amadiume's *Reinventing Africa* advances from some of Cheikh Anta Diop's work in this area. See also her earlier *Male Daughters, Female Husbands*. Moynihan clearly had not read Claudia Jones's essay.

21. Jones's FBI file quotes the text of this essay. It also discusses in detail her political organizing of various chapters across the United States, including her work as secretary of the Communist Party's National Women's Commission. "An End to the Neglect of the Problems of Negro Women" is perhaps the most available of Jones's articles (reprinted in Guy-Sheftall's *Words of Fire*) and can be read as a follow-up and detailed working-out of ideas introduced in her earlier "We Seek Full Equality for Women."

22. Jones, "Foster's Political and Theoretical Guidance to Our Work among Women," 77.

23. 1998 National Occupational Employment and Wage Estimates from Occupational Employment Statistics, U.S. Bureau of Labor Statistics. According to these statistics, in 1998, white women earned 72 cents for every dollar earned by white men, while black women earned 65 cents. This is a 10-cent increase from 1982, when black women are listed as earning 56 cents for every dollar made by white men. Among the ten lowest-paying jobs in the United States in 1998 are waiters and waitresses, fast-food cooks, food and fiber-crop farm workers, food preparation, and service workers — that is, the jobs that most black women workers are employed in.

24. I quote and paraphrase from the discussion of surplus value in Bottomore et al., *A Dictionary of Marxist Thought*, 472–475. The editors draw on a variety of sources, ranging from Marx's *Capital*, chap. 10, to the work of several Marxist scholars who have elaborated on this point. For the purposes of accuracy I have selected this standard definition. I also quote herein its entirety some comments by John McClendon, which I consider a well-reasoned fleshing out of this issue (e-mail to author, January 2005): "Marx does not hold to the notion that unequal exchange is

the source of surplus value. This is because the concept of labor power ([LP] one's capacity to labor) is distinct from labor. First, labor is the source of value. Wages fluctuate (around socially necessary) labor (which is a medium) and hence wages are subject to the law of value. Value is embodied in commodities and under capitalism labor power becomes a commodity thus it too embodies value. Thus selling one's labor power amounts to selling a commodity. What LP sells for (its value) is less than the value of what labor produces in capitalist production and thus you have surplus value according to Marx. [The selling of commodities is another issue about realization of surplus value and is not necessary to the explanation of surplus value.] Rather than unequal exchange what you have are two different operative categories, labor and labor power. Labor (socially necessary labor) is the source of value and labor power is a commodity. The value of labor power is the amount of labor needed to produce it. (What it takes for a worker to survive based on certain level of social development. Wages tend to be lower in the third world than in developed capitalist countries.) So it is the difference between labor and labor power which is the source for surplus value. Both are subject to the same law of value therefore you have *equal exchange* not unequal exchange. However, they are different categories with different functions and this is how Marx discovered the secret of surplus value. See Marx, *Wages, Price and Profit*—especially chap. 6, "Value and Labor," and chap. 7, "Laboring Power," and also see F. Engels, *On Marx's* Capital."

25. Bottomore et al., *A Dictionary of Marxist Thought*, 157.

26. Cox, also a Trinidadian, is now identified as one of the best political sociologists of his time. His books are being reprinted and awards given in his name. He is recognized as providing excellent analyses of class and race, though gender was not considered a category by him at the time.

27. Hill recaptures this point well in her article "Fosterites and Feminists." In her account, "An End to the Neglect" was written by Jones in part as a reponse to Betty Millard's "Women against Myth" (86).

28. I develop some of these arguments in Boyce Davies, "Caribbean Women, Domestic Labor and the Politics of Transnational Migration."

29. For an overview, see also Deborah Gray White, *Too Heavy a Load*.

30. Letter from J. M. Wade, vice president of the Domestic Workers of America, 2015 Ridge Avenue, Philadelphia, Pa., to Sadie T. M. Alexander, no date (Alexander Family Papers, University of Pennsylvania, STMA, box 2, ff. 16). Also, "Dr. Sadie Alexander in Domestic Bill Fight," *Afro-American* (Baltimore), February 23, 1935 (clipping in STMA, box 2, ff. 16). Sadie T. M. Alexander was author of "Negro Women in Our Economic Life," and also wrote on the international as it relates to the domestic in a piece titled "Sugar without Security," an unpublished paper available in the STMA collection and cited by Wilson in "Becoming 'Woman of the Year.'"

31. Solomon, "Rediscovering a Lost Legacy," 8.

32. See also Silvera, *Silenced*; Brand, *No Burden to Carry*; and Boyce Davies, "Caribbean Women, Domestic Labor and Transnational Migration."

33. In *Red Feminism*, Weigand reports that the party position, which came out under Foster's name, was written by the Subcommittee on Theoretical Aspects of Work among Women (86–87). Publishing it under the national party chairman's name gave the position the legitimacy and attention that was wanted.

34. This article argued for "the decisive role American women can play in the political life of the nation" ("For New Approaches to Our Work among Women," 738) and was written in preparation for the CPUSA's annual convention. In it, concepts like "equal pay for equal work" and "protective legislation for women" are offered as major issues with which to reach the woman wage earner; they are central to the position that Claudia Jones would take in party debates about gender. Her conclusions seem commonplace now: for example, calls for babysitter funds and services, which Jones had championed, were common in the 1980s and 1990s.

35. See, for example, Martin, *Race First*.

36. Lynn, "Women and the Black Radical Tradition."

37. Payne, "Ella Baker and Models of Social Change." See also Ransby, *Ella Baker and the Black Freedom Movement*; Taylor, *Black Religious Intellectuals*, chap. 8.

38. "For the Unity of Women in the Cause of Peace!" 166; Jones would make similar assertions in "Foster's Political and Theoretical Guidance to Our Work among Women."

39. Diane Langford, concerned with her daughter, about the maligning of Manchanda's name, indicates (in conversation and in a letter to Morika Sherwood dated July 10, 2000) that Manchanda kept Claudia's clothes for a long time and during the course of their marriage would affectionately, almost ritually, bring out items and memorabilia from their relationship.

40. This work identified by different titles was originally published as "International Women's Day and the Struggle for Peace" and republished by the National Women's Commission as a pamphlet. See chapter 1, note 5.

41. Kelley, in "But a Local Phase of a World Problem," notes that an internationalist vision has been present consistently throughout African American history.

42. See, for example, Mohanty, "Under Western Eyes"; Carby, "White Woman Listen!"; Hull, Scott, and Smith, *All the Women Are White*; Amos and Parmar, "Challenging Imperial Feminism"; and Spivak, *In Other Worlds*.

43. See Wynter, "Beyond Miranda's Meanings."

44. An initiative based at the University of Arizona launched an ongoing series of projects to internationalize women's studies, drawing participants from the southwest United States. A number of essays from their various meetings appear in *Women's Studies International Forum* 14.4 (1991) under the rubric "Reaching

for Global Feminism: Approaches to Curriculum Change in the Southwestern United States." There is also the New Jersey Project, headed by Paula Rothenberg, which published the journal *Transformations*. See also Rothenberg, *Race, Class, and Gender in the United States*.

45. Hennessey prefers the term "materialist feminism": "In the late 1970's materialist feminism emerged from feminist critiques of Marxism" (xi).

46. Haywood was citing Jones's article published in *Political Affairs*, August 1945, 717–720.

47. Buxenbaum, "Marxism and the Woman Question Today," 7. See also *The Woman Question: Selections from the Writings of Karl Marx, Frederick Engels, V. I. Lenin and Joseph Stalin*, which singles out this issue for full analysis and application.

48. Hill, "Fosterites and Feminists," 69.

49. In the "Communist Women" chapter of her *Women, Race and Class*, Davis gives a brief overview of the participation of women in the Communist Party, which she follows with biographical sketches of five communist women, including Claudia Jones.

50. This argument is developed fully in Boyce Davies and Jardine, "Imperial Penetrations and Caribbean Nationalism."

51. Conversation with John La Rose, New Beacon Books, London, February 1997.

52. The quotation is from "Remembering Claudia Jones," unpublished manuscript prepared for the Institute of Commonwealth Studies symposium, given to this author during interview. Ms. Ash was very supportive of some study of Claudia Jones, spoke with fondness about her, and expressed regret at her passing. Many of my interviewees indicated that they never knew that she was as ill as she was, for she never talked about her condition or let her illness keep her back from her many activities.

53. The essay was written in response to an article by Earl Browder (secretary general of CPUSA until 1945), "On the Negroes and the Right of Self-Determination," which argued that integration into the American system meant that black nationalism was technically not an important consideration. Claudia Jones, from all accounts, maintained a consistent challenge to Communist Party recalcitrance on issues of race (black empowerment) and gender, arguing that both were fundamental to their political agenda. Many identify Browder's article as pivotal in shaping CPUSA policy on race. Heywood, *Black Bolshevik*, 551, is the best source on this point, indicating further that it is Claudia Jones's 1945 "Pre-Convention Discussion Article" that fundamentally brought the issue of race squarely back on the Communist Party agenda.

54. Much of the identification of Caribbean feminism has come from Caribbean woman scholars at home and abroad. Symposia and conferences organized by the University of the West Indies Centres for Gender and Development (in St. Augustine, Trinidad and Tobago; Mona, Jamaica; and Bridgetown, Barbados) and

grassroots organizations in the various Caribbean islands, and in particular the Caribbean Association for Feminist Research and Action and its journal, have contributed significantly to the development of Caribbean feminism. For examples, see the special issue "Rethinking Caribbean Difference"; Mohammed, *Gendered Realities*; and the earlier work of Una Marson, Sylvia Wynter, Jacqui Alexander, Audre Lorde, Merle Hodge, Boyce Davies, Elaine Savory Fido, Rhoda Reddock, Andaiye, Olive Senior, Erna Brodber, Christine Barrow, and others.

55. A letter in Jones's FBI file, dated January 4, 1950, sent to the director of the FBI from "SAC, San Juan, the 10th Naval District Intelligence Officer," with the subject "Claudia Jones, Langston Hughes et al., Internal Security — C," notes the formation of a new communist group in Trinidad, and warns of a possible "liaison between Communists in the British West Indies and Communists in the United States, particularly in New York."

56. Guy-Sheftall, "The Evolution of Feminist Consciousness among African American Women," 11. Tony Martin's *Amy Ashwood Garvey* provides details of Garvey's 1953 tour through the Caribbean and her friendship with Claudia Jones (243–255; 271–273).

57. From "I Was Deported Because I Fought the Colour Bar," interview quoted in Johnson, *"I Think of My Mother,"* 131–132.

58. Personal communication and conversation with Reddock during her semester as Claudia Jones Visiting Professor at Florida International University, spring 2000.

59. One possible link was James Headley, a seaman, who had lived for a time in the United States, been a colleague of George Padmore there, and been active in the Young Communist League at the same time as Jones; he subsequently became one of the founders of the National Unemployed Movement and was active in the Negro Welfare Cultural and Social Association upon his return to Trinidad, where he also advocated the formation of trade unions. Headley is identified as responsible for introducing Francois to socialist philosophy. See Reddock, *Women, Labour and Politics in Trinidad and Tobago*, 135. Jim Barrette is identified as a partner of Elma Francois, but beyond that the organization advocated that men and women be liberated partners inside and outside the home, for the advancement of their movement. See also Reddock, *Elma Francois*, 18.

60. Caribbean scholars are beginning to define some of the terms of Caribbean feminism, and although it seems much after the fact, it is still a necessary step. Conferences on this subject have been held in Barbados. The work of the Caribbean Association for Feminist Research and Activism continues across the language groups and geographies of the Caribbean and extends diasporically.

Chapter 2: From "Half the World" to the Whole World

1. Aptheker, "A Fabulous Black Woman." Several other black women would do the same before and after Claudia Jones. Maude White is perhaps the closest example

to Jones, becoming managing editor of the black Communist newspaper, the *Harlem Liberator* in 1933. In that same period, Benjamin Davis came to New York as editor of the *Harlem Liberator*, having served successfully as the lawyer for Angelo Herndon. See Solomon, "Rediscovering a Lost Legacy." Charlotta Bass also ran her own newspaper, the *California Eagle*. See Bass, *Forty Years*. According to the website, http://www.socallib.org/bass: "Charlotta Bass, publisher, managing editor, and reporter of the *California Eagle* from 1912 to 1951, used the newspaper as a powerful tool in her pioneering fight for social justice and equality in Los Angeles and the nation . . . Like most black newspapers of that period, the *California Eagle* served as a source of both information and inspiration for the black community, which was largely ignored or negatively portrayed by the white press. With national and international coverage, the *California Eagle* brought black Angelenos in touch with struggles for civil rights taking place in other parts of the country and across the globe. The paper also helped to bring Los Angeles–based civil rights struggles to the national stage."

2. Tony Martin suggests that this could perhaps be the *West Indian American*, since she had identified that her father had also written for the paper. Conversation with Martin, Miami, Florida, August 2003.

3. The FBI file for Claudia Jones (NY 100–18676) lists a range of early articles, many of which I have identified and which are available in a collection I am preparing, provisionally titled "Beyond Containment: The Collected Essays of Claudia Jones." Several of these articles are in issues of the *Daily Worker* from 1946 and after.

4. See also the "Autobiographical History" that Jones directed to "Comrade Foster" (William Zane Foster, head of the Communist Party USA), June 1954, describing her professional trajectory as a journalist. Marika Sherwood identifies Jones as writing for a Harlem journal (the name of which is not known), for which she contributed a weekly column, "Claudia's Comments"; Sherwood also mentions that Jones's father lost his job as "the editor of a West Indian newspaper" during the Depression.

5. As editor of *Spotlight*, she wrote to Rev. Adam Clayton Powell, March 8, 1944, inviting an article from him. The letter is included in her FBI file, largely in order to ascertain her signature.

6. I have selected only the lines related to her journalism from one of the few autobiographical fragments available in her papers in the Claudia Jones Memorial Collection (Schomburg Center for Research in Black Culture, New York), this one written to "Comrade [William Z.] Foster" and dated December 6, 1955.

7. Von Eschen also identifies "the collapse of a transnational black press" (*Race against Empire*, 118–121). There are several Web listings of library collections that include chronologies of black newspapers.

8. Reddock, *Elma Francois*, 13.

9. McDuffie found no evidence of her father's work as editor in the copies of *West Indian-American* newspapers in the Schomburg Library, though he quotes Irma Watkins-Owens, *Blood Relations: Caribbean Immigrants and the Harlem Community, 1900–1930* (Bloomington: Indiana University Press, 1996), 158–159, on the development of "Charles Cumberbatch's *West Indian-American* [which] assisted in the creation of new, Caribbean, Pan-African group identities" (57).

10. Jones's FBI file identifies her association with two other newspapers in this period, the *Harlem Bulletin* and the *Amsterdam News*.

11. McDuffie, "Long Journeys," 345.

12. I plan to reprint the two cited essays in a volume provisionally titled "Beyond Containment: The Collected Essays of Claudia Jones."

13. Chaneta Holden was abducted as a newborn by a deranged woman who had lost twins in miscarriage and who cared for her in an improvised incubator. Jones criticized the press for giving no attention to the "millions of tiny Negro infants who die at birth because of primitive conditions in the richest city in the world."

14. *Daily Worker*, February 10, 1952.

15. *Daily Worker*, September 20, 1951.

16. See my chapter in *Migrations of the Subject* on black British women writers writing the anti-imperialist critique. In hindsight, the anti-imperialist critique that has since been written at the site of empire, and collaborations between black women of Asian descent, Caribbean women, and African women, have a pre-text in Claudia Jones's activism and the model of her work. In fact, many black women's organizations, such as the Camden Black Sisters, identify her as their founding mother. The Camden Black Sisters produced an early text on Claudia Jones with limited circulation, but see themselves importantly as maintaining the meaning and presence of Claudia Jones before the interest of, say, Marika Sherwood in London.

17. Interview with Billy Strachan (a London communist from the Caribbean, now deceased) at his home where he showed me copies of the *Caribbean News*. For his comments on the production of the paper ("he [Strachan's comrade] printed it for free because of my relationship with him," 201) and on the falling out between him and George Bowrin, which led to the ending of the *Caribbean News* and the birth of the *Gazette*, see his contribution to the symposium on Claudia Jones held at the Institute of Commonwealth Studies, London, and documented in Sherwood et al., *Claudia Jones* (200–201). (Bowrin was a Trinidadian labor activist affiliated with the Oilfield Workers Trade Union, who was studying in London and became a close associate of Claudia Jones.) Strachan notes that Claudia edited the last issue of the *Caribbean News* before its demise. Clearly, because the *Caribbean News* (an organ of the Caribbean Labor Congress) was printed only as a personal favor to Strachan

and was not self-supportive, it was not sustainable and therefore could not be the basis of an independent paper. Managing the *Gazette* as a community-supported paper was not without its own financial difficulties, but this is only because support for black newspapers at that time (the 1950s) was not strong. Subsequent papers have had a comparatively easier time and now have a steady and larger readership and income from advertising. According to Donald Hinds, at the same Institute of Commonwealth Studies symposium, "Whenever I read some of the black papers now I am seized with envy and jealousy at the amount of money they seem to have. We were so short on cash!" (*Claudia Jones: A Life in Exile*, 198).

18. See Sherwood et al., *Claudia Jones*, 130, for the text of the letter.

19. Quoted in Hinds, "The *West Indian Gazette*," 143.

20. Hinds, *Journey to an Illusion*, 150.

21. Hinds, "The *West Indian Gazette*." A variety of documents and letters in the Claudia Jones Memorial Collection, Schomburg Library, New York, testify to the financial difficulties the paper endured.

22. Claudia Jones Memorial Collection, Schomburg Library, New York.

23. Billy Strachan was among those who confirmed this point (interview, March 1997).

24. I am grateful to novelist George Lamming for bringing Schwarz's essay to my attention and for sending me an offprint. Much of this chapter was written before I saw the essay, which covers similar ground to my research but uses different issues of the *Gazette* to make its points.

25. Jones, "A People's Art Is the Genesis of Their Freedom."

26. C. L. R. James is widely known for his pan-Africanism, leftist activism, and cricket journalism. The nature of the interaction between him and Claudia Jones in London continues to excite interest. This is an example. In interviews, Alrick Cambridge, Donald Hinds, and George Lamming report that the divergent political positions of James and Jones (Trotskyist vs. Communist Party faithful) kept them on separate tracks, though James indicated support for Claudia Jones when she was in difficulty, as when she was incarcerated on Ellis Island. Much is left to be discovered on this subject. For example, they shared a mutual friendship with Amy Ashwood Garvey.

27. There is clearly a missing gendered subject in Gilroy's *The Black Atlantic*, as I have previously noted (in "Absent Black Women in Gilroy's Black Atlantic," a paper presented at the Black Women in the Academy Conference held at MIT in 1994 and "The Missing African and Caribbean Texts in Current Black Atlantic Formulations," presented at the Harvard/Sorbonne Conference in Honor of Michel and Geneviève Fabre, December 15–18, 2004). Claudia Jones should figure in the account, since connections across the Atlantic were a major part of her central project. I argue in this book that Claudia Jones is the missing figure in several

analyses, not just Gilroy's. See also my essay "Against Race or the Politics of Self–Ethnography" on Gilroy's *Against Race*, which critiques Gilroy's attempt to delineate "black fascism" without really discussing that fascism, which Jones's writings so aptly decry.

28. Schwarz, "Claudia Jones and the *West Indian Gazette*."

Chapter 3: Prison Blues

1. The Last Poets — popular performance poets of the 1960s and 1970s whose words accompanied the then burgeoning Black Power movement — were the featured performers at a concert sponsored by Florida International University's African–New World Studies Program, April 6, 2002, and were led in by a range of spoken-word artists. The Florida concert is just one example of widespread and frequent spoken-word activity — in cafés, contests, and concerts — which allows a variety of voices to be heard. This pattern repeats itself across the United States and re-affirms one's faith in the poetry of resistance. Events like the def poetry jam sessions, poetry slam festivals, and the Calabash Festival in Jamaica are other examples. The Nuyorican Café in New York has maintained spoken-word performances from the 1970s to the present.

2. Greg Thomas has produced a range of papers, lectures, and a very controversial course on Lil' Kim at Syracuse University. Some of these discussions are available on his e-journal *www.proudflesh.com*. See Cooper's recent book *Sound Clash*.

3. In *Sister Outsider*, 36–39.

4. See Wiwa, *A Month and a Day* and *Before I Am Hanged*.

5. See also Harlow's *Barred*.

6. See also Harlow, *Resistance Literature*, 138–140.

7. Kenyatta, *Facing Mount Kenya*; Shakur, *Assata*; Nelson Mandela, *Long Walk to Freedom*; Winnie Mandela, *Part of My Soul Went with Him*; Jackson, *Blood in My Eye* and *Soledad Brother*; Davis, *If They Come in the Morning* and *Angela Davis: An Autobiography*; Nkrumah, *Ghana*; Barios de Chungara, *Let Me Speak!*

8. See Shakur's book *The Rose That Grew from Concrete*. See also Dyson, *Holler If You Hear Me*.

9. Martha Stewart was sentenced to five months in Alderson for lying to government investigators about a stocks trade deal. As we will see, however, Alderson has also been the prison of choice for a variety of women political prisoners.

10. See also James, *States of Confinement*.

11. See Gramsci, *Selections from the Prison Notebooks*.

12. James identifies what she calls "a schism in alignment with 'foreign' political prisoners housed in the United States and awaiting deportation to hostile nations and U.S. citizens who are political prisoners in other countries" (*Imprisoned Intellectuals*, 13).

13. The letter was published as "Claudia Jones Writes from Ellis Island," in the *Daily Worker*.

14. Letter to Comrade [William Z.] Foster, December 6, 1955, in Claudia Jones Memorial Collection, Schomburg Research Center, New York.

15. Baxandall, *Words on Fire*.

16. Flynn, *Alderson Story*, 117; Buzz Johnson, *"I Think of My Mother,"* 45, reports this event similarly.

17. Unpublished poem among Claudia Jones Papers, Claudia Jones Memorial Collection, Schomburg Research Center, New York. About fifteen poems are in the Claudia Jones Papers. Two ("To Elizabeth Gurley Flynn" and "Morning Mists") have been published in the Association of Caribbean Women Writers and Scholars journal *Macomère*.

18. Jones wrote a note to the "Consuela" poem: "Dedicated to Blanca Consuela Torresola, now serving 4 years in the Federal Reformatory for Women in Alderson, W. Va., U.S.A. and who, upon completion of this sentence faces a 140 year jail term in her native Puerto Rico for her heroic participation in the struggle for Puerto Rican independence." (See Mini Seijo Bruno, *La Insurrección Nacionalista en Puerto Rico — 1950*, section entitled "The Participants." This information was provided by my colleagues and friends from Binghamton University, Kelvin Santiago-Valles and Miriam Jimenez-Munoz.) Jones also saw her situation, with less than two years total in prison, as minor compared to Torresola's. The references to fascism are clear, especially in the evocation of "Guernica's songs" — Guernica was the Basque town in northern Spain that was destroyed by German bombs in 1937, during the Spanish Civil War. Jarama, also mentioned in the poem, was the site of the first aggressive act of World War II, also in 1937. According to my daughter, Dalia Davies, Jones may also be invoking here Picasso's famous painting *Guernica*.

19. Flynn reports that there were three other Puerto Rican nationalist women in Alderson. Carmen Torresola, a young woman, was the widow of Guisello Torresola, a relative of Blanca who was killed in 1950 by a guard at a nationalist demonstration in Washington, D.C. Another was a tall, stately woman, Rosa Collazo, wife of Oscar Collazo, who was serving a life sentence in Leavenworth prison, charged with shooting a guard in Washington, D.C., in one of their demonstrations. Neither of these women had been in Washington, nor had they participated in either demonstration, but they were still charged with conspiracy under the "Acts of Violence" section of the Smith Act. Writes Flynn, "We had become acquainted with Carmen and Rosa in the New York House of Detention. There was a third Puerto Rican nationalist there but on another floor, so we did not see her. Shortly after I came to the weave shop in Alderson she was assigned there. Lolita Lebrun was a tiny little woman, sentenced to from eight to fifty years, virtually for life" (*Alderson Story*, 142–143).

20. The poem is titled "A Friend (To Claudia, June, 1956)" and also appears in Buzz Johnson's *"I Think of My Mother,"* 64; *The Alderson Story,* 212.

21. In a letter to Abhimanyu Manchanda ("Manu"), written from Russia, Jones expressed sadness about Flynn's passing.

22. Quoted in Buzz Johnson, *"I Think of My Mother,"* 46.

23. In Claudia Jones Papers, Claudia Jones Memorial Collection, Schomburg Research Center, New York.

24. Carole Boyce Davies, "Interview with Billy Strachan," London, March 1997. Strachan was one of the members of the London Communist Party who had been assigned to meet and welcome Jones and assist in the settling and organizing of her first months in London.

25. Echeruo, "The African Diaspora: The Ontological Project," in Okpewho, Boyce Davies, and Mazrui, *The African Diaspora.*

26. From conversations about Claudia Jones, Miami, Florida, 1998–2000. Cambridge was the first Claudia Jones Visiting Professor in the African–New World Studies Program at Florida International University.

27. In chap. 9, "Caribbeans and an Atlantic Fate" of his *Caribbean Transnational Experience,* 211.

28. See Sherwood et al., *Claudia Jones.*

29. See Barksdale and Kinnamon, *Black Writers of America.*

30. See the American Experience film for PBS, *The Murder of Emmett Till,* 2003. See also the book *Mississippi Trial* by Crowe.

31. See Barksdale and Kinnamon, *Black Writers of America,* which anthologizes this poem.

32. Flynn, *Alderson Story;* also quoted in Johnson, *"I Think of My Mother,"* 39.

33. From Jones, "First Lady of the World." See also Claudin, "The Chinese Revolution."

34. In the Claudia Jones Memorial Collection, Schomburg Research Center, New York.

35. Lorde, "For Assata — New Brunswick Prison, 1977."

36. The author is identified as Label Nibur, writing in the *Daily Worker.*

Chapter 4: Deportation

1. U.S. Immigration and Naturalization Service, 1997. *Statistical Yearbook of the Immigration and Naturalization Service,* http://www.ins.uscis.gov (accessed September 29, 2001).

2. Some material for this chapter appeared previously in my article "Deportable Subjects." However, I have substantially revised and expanded the argument to target the issue of Claudia Jones's deportation and the variety of contexts for, and responses to, the state's actions.

3. People classified as "enemy combatants" following the war on Afghanistan have

also been unjustly and inhumanely treated by the United States government. The legality of holding prisoners on the off-shore U.S. Naval Base in Guantanamo Bay, Cuba, without charging them or providing access to lawyers or other humanitarian services according to the Geneva Conventions, has been challenged in the media and in international law by many countries on behalf of their citizens, ending in the release of some prisoners who were found not guilty of any crimes.

4. Conversation with official of Trinidad and Tobago High Commission, Washington, D.C., who gave information freely but preferred, for obvious reasons, not be cited by name. See also Taylor and Aleinkoff, "Deportation of Criminal Aliens."

5. In the end, the court decided in both cases that the "Attorney General could not indefinitely detain lawfully admitted, but subsequently ordered removed, aliens during the post-removal period, i.e. the time after a 90-day statutory removal period, while they awaited deportation. Instead, the Court limited detention to no more than a presumptive 'reasonable time' of six months, unless the government can establish that there is a 'significant likelihood of removal in the reasonable foreseeable future' " (533 U.S. at 701).

6. The American Civil Liberties Union (ACLU) has been actively monitoring a range of deportations before and after September 11, 2001. See their website for details of cases, http://www.aclu.org.

The United States Immigration and Naturalization Service (INS) was terminated in 2003, and its responsibilities were transferred to the U.S. Citizenship and Immigration Services, which as a part of the Department of Homeland Security has combined authority over investigations, deportation and intelligence. A number of deportation cases continue to make their way through the various court systems, some reaching the U.S. Supreme Court. (One useful site for information on these cases is http://www.visalaw.com.) "Outline of Issues from Important Recent Federal Court Immigration Cases," a list of important recent federal court immigration cases (including deportation cases) compiled by Nadine K. Wettstein of the American Immigration Law Foundation, Washington, D.C., is available at http://www.vkblaw.com/news/fourhundredsixtyseven.htm (accessed March 1, 2007). One interesting case is that of Sami Al-Arian, a Palestinian professor and activist from the University of South Florida who was arrested as a terrorist supporter, imprisoned, tried and eventually sentenced to 18 months in addition to the time he had already served. The length of his sentence was based on a deal with federal prosecutors; Al-Arian pleaded guilty to a lesser charge after agreeing to deportation. See http://jurist.law.pitt.edu for details. Statistics on deportation are available from the U.S. government archives at www.dhs.gov in detailed tables that indicate the administrative reasons for removal and categories of deportations. The list indicates a rise in deportations during times of intense activism, such as the period between 1931 and 1960 during the HUAC period; and again from 1971 to 1980, which would correspond to the Black Power period; and then again from 2001 to the present, following the terrorist attacks on the United States and the subsequent "War on Terrorism."

7. For a study of this situation, see Henderson et al., *Law Enforcement and Arab American Community Relations after September 11, 2001: Engagement in a Time of Uncertainty*. New York: Vera Institute of Justice, June 2006 (available at http://www.vera.org/policerelations, accessed March 1,2007). This report offers a detailed examination of what were termed "voluntary interviews" in which federal, state, and local law enforcement were involved in gathering information from Arab Americans in the U.S. on student, business, and tourist visas.

8. Letter from David Rowe to Carole Boyce Davies, dated August 26, 2003, p. 2.

9. *Daily Worker*, October 24, 1950.

10. "80 Notables Protest Widening Attacks on Gov't on Foreign Born," *Daily Worker*, October 30, 1952.

11. *Daily Worker*, October 30, 1952.

12. Quoted in Johnson, "*I Think of My Mother*," 28–29.

13. Letter from Rowe to Boyce Davies, August 26, 2003. Correspondence with David Rowe was instrumental in forming the argumentative framework for this discussion.

14. The Immigration and Naturalization Act of 1952 (McCarran-Walter Act), the Illegal Immigration Reform and Immigrant Responsibility Act of 1996, and the Patriot Act of 2001 have provided the legal bases for deportation and incarceration.

15. See, for example, Harris, *Global Dimensions of the African Diaspora*; Lemelle and Kelley, *Imagining Home*; and Okpewho, Boyce Davies and Mazrui, *The African Diaspora*.

16. Gerald Horne's *Black Liberation/Red Scare* details how Ben Davis was criminalized for black activism. Additionally his *Communist Front?* identifies how black organizations were targeted as communist for black community organizing. See also Carmichael (with Thelwell), *Ready for Revolution*, in which Thelwell notes, "According to some written sources I've seen, the Tennessee legislature then passed a resolution calling for Carmichael's DEPORTATION. Since he was a United States citizen, the legislative intent must have been a revival of the medieval practice of BANISHMENT" (556).

17. "Letter to John Gates," *Daily Worker*, November 8, 1950.

18. *Daily Worker*, Monday February 25, 1952.

19. *Daily Worker*, March 7, 1955.

20. *Daily Worker*, Friday December 2, 1955.

21. *Daily Worker*, November 21, 1955. See also *Daily Worker*, November 13, 18, and 27, 1955. Clippings available in Claudia Jones Memorial Collection, Schomburg Research Center, New York.

22. "CP Hits Deportation of Claudia Jones," *Daily Worker*, December 1, 1955. Lydia Lindsey identifies that Du Bois sent a public statement to the United States Judiciary Subcommittee on Immigration and Naturalization and the Senate Subcommittee on Constitutional Rights (November 28, 1955) concerning the deportation of Jones. National Committee to Defend Negro Leadership, December 3, 1955, 3, DHC.

23. Stretch Johnson's remarks at Claudia Jones symposium, Schomburg Library, New York, December 2, 1998, indicate that through Claudia he met everybody from Queen Mother Moore to Lorraine Hansberry, as well as African leaders. Johnson was a former romantic interest of Claudia Jones and is named in Jones's "Ship's Log: Paean to the Atlantic" as one of the well wishers who came to the ship to see her off.

24. See *Daily Worker*, September 1, 1953. Another plea had come from the Jamaican Federation of Trade Unions, signed by Ferdinand Smith; it asked for the immediate parole of Claudia Jones; *Daily Worker*, July 6, 1955.

25. Sherwood et al., *Claudia Jones*, documents much of this activity.

26. Many of the original copies of the *West Indian Gazette and Afro-Asian-Caribbean News* that I surveyed are available at the Institute of Race Relations, London, which publishes the journal *Race and Class*. The institute was an excellent source for studying the content of these newspapers. Some copies of the newspaper are on microfilm at the Brixton Library, but they are not good copies and/or the machines to view them were not very efficient when I visited this library in 1997.

27. Elias, "Claudia Jones," identifies the ways that Africa Unity House became the venue of many important events which Claudia had arranged (Africa Unity House was founded by Kwame Nkrumah in London in 1963 and served as a forum for the third world). One of the most notable guests was Dr. Martin Luther King, who came to address a meeting when he passed through London on his journey from Stockholm to receive the Peace Nobel Prize in 1964 (Elias, "Claudia Jones," 73).

28. Ranjana Sidhanta Ash ("Remembering Claudia," and interview by Boyce Davies at the University Women's Club, Audley Square, London, May 12, 1997) identifies numerous ways that Claudia bridged the gap between Afro-Caribbean and Asian communities.

29. Quoted in Strong, "Hundreds Say Last Goodbye."

30. Interview with George Bowrin in *Caribbean News*, June 1956, quoted in Johnson, "*I Think of My Mother*," 132.

31. This point has been made by Crenshaw and Davis. See Crenshaw, *Critical Race Theory*; Davis, *Are Prisons Obsolete?*; Davis, foreword to Wing, *Global Critical Race Feminism*; Davis essay, "Race and Criminalization," in Lubiano, *The House That Race Built*; Davis, "Slavery and the Prison Industrial Complex." See also Ogletree, *All Deliberate Speed*.

32. Jones had applied for United States citizenship many years before, but since she had joined the Communist Party and been active at such a young age, her application was held up and she was never granted citizenship.

33. In the Claudia Jones Memorial Collection, Schomburg Research Center. A copy of this letter is also in this author's files. Her last passport (also in the Schomburg) is dated 1962.

34. *Daily Worker*, Thursday December 7, 1950; and December 28, 1950.

35. *Daily Worker*, December 4, 1950.

36. Campi, "The McCarran-Walter Act," 2.

37. See "Statement on Un-American Activities Committee," news release, Council on African Affairs, New York City, July 20, 1949, in *Paul Robeson Speaks*, ed. Philip S. Foner (New York: Citadel Press, 1978), 218.

38. Jones, "Speech to the Court, February, 1953."

39. Identified as defendants in the trial and subsequent appeals (argued through 1954 and 1955) are: Elizabeth Gurley Flynn, Pettis Perry, Claudia Jones, Alexander Bittelman, Alexander Trachtenberg, Victor Jeremy Jerome, Albert Francis Lannon, Louis Weinstock, Arnold Samuel Johnson, Betty Gannett, Jacob Mindel, William Wolf Weinstone, and George Blake Carney (216 F.2d 354, *389, p. 33).

40. See Boyce Davies and M'bow, "Towards African Diaspora Citizenship."

41. A great deal of organizing around the fate of political prisoners such as Mumia Abu Jamal and others make similar arguments in the contemporary period.

42. "Hundreds Say Last Goodbye to Claudia Jones Who Sails Today." *Daily Worker*, December 9, 1955.

43. Unpublished autobiographical notes, December 6, 1955. Claudia Jones Memorial Collection, Schomburg Research Center, New York Public Library.

44. William L. Patterson, "Remarks on the Eve of the Deportation of Claudia Jones," December 8, 1955. Copy available in Claudia Jones Memorial Collection, Schomburg Library, New York.

45. Letter at the Claudia Jones Memorial Collection, Schomburg Center, New York.

46. Clipping in Claudia Jones Papers. Claudia Jones Memorial Collection, Schomburg Research Center, New York Public Library.

47. Claudia Jones is the founder of the Caribbean Carnival, which became the Notting Hill Carnival. See also "Claudia Jones in Britain — Symposium on Claudia Jones," Session 4: Carnival. Audiotapes archived at ICS; and Colin Prescod's chapter "Carnival" in Marika Sherwood, Donald Hinds and Colin Prescod, *Claudia Jones: A Life in Exile*.

Chapter 5: Carnival and Diaspora

1. Since the early work of Errol Hill and J. D. Elder, a number of scholars in the Caribbean have defined an entire field of carnival study within the larger context

of black popular culture studies. Conferences on the subject engage areas such as performativity in the African diaspora, globalization and carnival, and the various aesthetic principles and politics of carnival.

2. The essay was republished in the *Black Liberator: A Theoretical and Discussion Journal for Black Liberation* (London), which served as an important site for discussions about issues pertaining to the black community in London and internationally throughout the 1970s.

3. I detail the range of these publications through the mid-1990s in "From 'Postcoloniality' to Uprising Textualities: Black Women Writing the Critique of Empire," chap. 4 of *Migrations of the Subject*. See also Carby, *Cultures in Babylon*, which includes her early piece "Schooling in Babylon" (189–218), which had previously been included in *The Empire Strikes Back*, a pivotal work produced by the Centre for Contemporary Cultural Studies under the leadership of Stuart Hall.

4. These include Cambridge and Feuchtwang, *Where You Belong*. See Cambridge's introduction and his "The Beauty of Valuing Black Culture." Another collection, also edited by Cambridge and Feuchtwang, is *Anti-racist Strategies*.

5. Hinds, "The *West Indian Gazette*," 148.

6. Goulbourne details some of this history in chap. 4, "Africa and the Caribbean," in *Caribbean Transnational Experience*, 79–111.

7. In Sherwood et al., *Claudia Jones*, 62–88. Sherwood's introductory historical essay, along with other chapters in *Claudia Jones*, provides the documentary evidence for understanding this split with the Communist Party Great Britain when she arrives there.

8. Jones's later affiliation with A. Manchanda allowed her to operate in a different field — more linked to decolonization struggles across the third world.

9. John Cowley, author of *Carnival, Canboulay and Calypso*, in a personal communication, Paris, December 2004.

10. Byam, "Carnival: New York's Caribbean Connection," 2.

11. Thanks are due to Winston James for reminding me of this important point (e-mail, September 1, 2004).

12. Hinds, "The *West Indian Gazette*" provides a detailed history of the founding and development of the *Gazette* from the early *Caribbean News*. In my interview with Billy Strachan, who showed me copies of the *Caribbean News*, I detected some bitterness for the way the *Gazette* supplanted the *Caribbean News*, largely due to the energy of Jones and her "let's get on with it" style of operation, which rubbed some people the wrong way.

13. Interviews with Donald Hinds, Alrick Cambridge, Billy Strachan, and Pansy Jeffries in London, January to June 1997.

14. See also James, "Migration, Racism and Identity Formation," for a discussion of the range of issues that have confronted the Caribbean community in London historically.

15. Lindsey, "Claudia Jones," 19.

16. A play was developed and staged in London based on this struggle between Jones and the more hard-line members of the communist network in London.

17. A play by Winsome Pinnock, *Rock in the Water*, staged at the Royal Court Theatre in London, January 1989, used this controversy as the central dramatic conflict. The play was reviewed in the *Guardian*, the *Sunday Times*, and the *Times Educational Supplement*, but they varied in their assessments. Sherwood reports some of this in *Claudia Jones*, 172–174. A film, *Claudia Jones: A Woman of Our Times*, aired in London.

18. Jones, "A People's Art Is the Genesis of Their Freedom."

19. See Cambridge, "The Beauty of Valuing Black Culture."

20. The London activists I interviewed in 1990 and 1995 all reported that they had supported the West Indian Federation unquestioningly and felt betrayed by the national and island leaders, whom many of them had helped get into power. See, in particular, interview with Billy Strachan, London, May 1998 (audiotape available).

21. Boyce Davies, "Carnivalised Caribbean Female Bodies," 333.

22. The second antiblack race riots in the city of Nottingham happened simultaneously with those in Notting Hill and led many to define them in relation to each other.

23. Gutzmore presented a paper titled "Yu can ben wire?," on this subject at the conference *Carnival and the Caribbean Diaspora*, Florida International University, 1999, in which he identifies some of the internal contradictions of the carnival.

24. See my "Carnivalised Caribbean Female Bodies."

25. Sparrow was invited in 1960 and subsequently went on tour in England. He told me in an interview in Brooklyn in June 2006 that this was the occasion on which he prevailed on Kitchener, who was living in London at the time, to return home to Trinidad. He was less familiar with or interested in the Jones narrative than he was in Kitchener's calypso history when we spoke. He remembered Jones, but only marginally. What he remembered was meeting Kitchener.

26. In Sherwood et al., *Claudia Jones*, See also Carter, *Shattering Illusions*, an insightful work from a communist activist working inside and outside the party. Carter dedicated his book to his parents and to Jones.

27. Connor cites as sources of information on this topic D. Howe and M. Phillips, "So, Whose Carnival Is It Anyway?" *London Evening Standard*, Notting Hill Carnival Supplement, 1994; J. La Rose, *Kaiso, Calypso Music*; M. La Rose, *Newsletter of the Association for a People's Carnival* (London: New Beacon Books, March 1995); and Oliver, *Young Gifted and Black*.

28. *Masquerade Politics* (1993). Cohen is a British anthropologist who obviously had done limited research on the subject and who since then has been refuted by almost all London activists and scholars of black culture and history in England.

29. "Notting Hill Carnival Committee Draft Constitution" and "Notting Hill Carnival Development Committee," documents given to the author by Pansy Jeffries in London, May 1995; interviews conducted with Mrs. Jeffries, who made the distinction between the efforts of the Notting Hill Carnival Committee and the initial work of Jones and the Caribbean Carnival Committee, each fulfilling different functions even though the intent was similar.

30. Symposium contributions, documented in Sherwood et al., *Claudia Jones*, 178–248.

31. The newsletter was issued from 76 Stroud Green Road, London, a committee functioning out of the New Beacon collective.

32. Some accounts give the starting date as 1964.

33. Accounts of Jones's death and the responses to it are testimony to a community outpouring of tremendous proportions, national and international. Jones was embraced by the Caribbean community for her leadership roles and consciousness-raising activism.

34. Quoted in Connor, "Culture, Identity and the Music of Notting Hill Carnival," 12.

35. Carmen England, friend and community organizer with Jones, now lies directly across from the Marx bust and the Jones grave site in Highgate Cemetery, London. This entire corner of Highgate is the location in death of a number of London activists.

36. One can of course make the same assertion of the movement from the *West Indian Gazette and Afro-Asian-Caribbean News*, which continued with some issues after the death of Jones, and the subsequent founding of more developed journals like the *Black Liberator* throughout the 1970s, as political legacies of Jones — particularly since the founder and editor of the *Black Liberator*, Alrick Cambridge, had been Claudia Jones's last assistant at the *West Indian Gazette* and in other forms of political organizing of the London Caribbean community.

37. In "An End to the Neglect of the Problems of Negro Women."

38. See Boyce Davies, "Feminism and Anti-Imperialism: The Black Feminist Politics of Claudia Jones," paper presented at Spelman College, June 1998, and at the Walter Rodney Conference, Binghamton University, September 1998.

39. Since carnival is not the intellectual property of any one individual but community property, it has to be asserted that similar narratives no doubt exist in various locations where carnival has followed the Caribbean diaspora, as Dale Byam reveals happened in New York.

40. In her contribution to the Institute of Commonwealth Studies symposium on Jones, as documented in Sherwood et al., *Claudia Jones*, 211. Connor, an ethnomusicologist, is the author of the *Carnival Messiah*, which ran to great acclaim in London's West End. She is the daughter of Edric Connor, musician and member of the Carnival Organising Committee put together by the *West Indian Gazette*.

41. See, for example, James and Harris, *Inside Babylon*, which is dedicated to Jones and Kelso Cochrane. See, in particular, Gutzmore, "Carnival the State and the Black Masses in the United Kingdom." Gutzmore has since presented a paper, "Yu can ben wire?," at the *Carnival and the Caribbean Diaspora* symposium at Florida International University.

42. Boyce Davies, "Taking Space."

Chapter 6: Piece Work/Peace Work

1. Poulantzas, *Political Power and Social Classes*. Thanks to Monica Jardine for this helpful reference and discussion.

2. In the title of this chapter I am deliberately using "peace work" to rewrite as well the notion of "piece work," which is fundamental to Fordist factory practices, as in the sweat shops of New York of Claudia's time, and which devoured her mother and from which she escaped.

3. This letter is dated July 2, 2002.

4. One obtains the FBI file of an individual by writing to the FBI with a formal request under the Freedom of Information and Privacy Act, which allows material previously classified to be released to the public for research purposes. The actual providing of this massive assemblage of documents, articles, testimonies, reports, letters, once these conditions are satisfied, takes close to eight weeks.

5. Horne's *Black Liberation/Red Scare* provides some of that detail throughout the 1940s and 1950s.

6. See, for example, Churchill and Vander Wall, *Agents of Repression*; Carmichael with Thelwell, *Ready for the Revolution*.

7. Quoted in Fletcher, Jones, and Lotringer, *Still Black, Still Strong*, 79. The role of the FBI in the demise of the Black Panther Party has been documented by a series of researchers (a number of Ph.D. dissertations were written on this subject in the 1990s).

8. Schrecker, *The Age of McCarthyism*, is a very helpful accounting of these activities.

9. See O'Reilly, *Hoover and the Un-Americans*.

10. "The Assault on the Communist Party," *The Age of McCarthyism: A Brief History with Documents* (Boston: Palgrave Macmillan, 2002), 48.

11. When Jones was arrested for the second time on June 29, 1951 (her earlier arrest came in 1948 under the McCarran Act), the grounds for this action was laid by a Supreme Court decision that upheld the Smith Act. The decision on Eugene Dennis v. the United States, 341 U.S. 494 (1951) was handed down in June 1951, and only a few days thereafter Jones was incarcerated. Of particular note is the fact that one of the lawyers for the defendants in the *Dennis* case was the African American George W. Crockett. Crockett also served time in prison (in 1950) on contempt of court charges in connection with the *Dennis* case. Crockett was later elected a judge on the Recorder's Court in Detroit from 1966 to 1978 and later

served in the U.S. Congress. In 1969, during his tenure as a judge in Detroit, Crockett ordered the release of members of the Republic of New Africa group after they were jailed following a police attack on the group. The attack occurred when the group (which included men, women and children) was holding a meeting in a local church. The Republic of New Africa was one of the groups on the Cointelpro hit list.

12. Interviews with Alrick Cambridge, Ranjana Ash, and Gertrude Elias (March to June 1997) and George Lamming (June 2002) testify to this.

13. Another possibility is that U.S. government forces, in conjunction with their British counterparts, could have taken some of her papers and the manuscript under question. The government seizure of a black communist woman's papers has a precedent in the instance of Lucy Parsons. When Parsons died in 1942, at the age of eighty-nine, the government immediately ransacked her home and confiscated her papers and books. See Ashbaugh, *Lucy Parsons, American Revolutionary*.

14. George Bowrin seemed to have served an important role in connecting Claudia Jones to Caribbean organizations. His presence in London at the same time, as a student, reveals him as one of the important members of her London supportive team. Bowrin himself had prior to his arrival in London and subsequently been an active official of the radical Oilfield Workers Trade Union and edited its newsletter as well.

15. Jones's FBI file indicates that the speaker was James Ashford; it quotes a biographical sketch from *New Masses* (May 16, 1939, 11) as follows: "a Negro YCL leader to whom belongs most of the credit for the strong organization in Harlem. Claudia joined the YCL after hearing Jimmie Ashford's arguments. Now she does a good deal of work with members of the Harlem Branch. Jimmie worked himself to death a couple of years ago." Maude White and other women were in the Communist Party at the same time, all doing influential work in Harlem.

16. The impact of Jones's leadership particularly as a journalist, on other women activists started as early as her membership in the Young Communist League (YCL). While a member of the YCL, Jones functioned as editor of its paper. One woman in particular that Jones influenced was Pat Ellis. Ellis was an African American migrant worker from Florida. After arriving in New York, Ellis joined the YCL and served as the press director of its paper, under Jones's editorship. Ellis rose to become the organizational secretary of the Communist Party in Harlem but had to go underground during the McCarthy era. See Tim Wheeler, "Black Women Workers."

17. Scholnick is identified in the FBI file as a Jew, the information coming from FBI interviews with the building superintendent; the couple was described as "quiet tenants with no children" and as having moved subsequently to Gavine Farms, Chelsea-on-Hudson, New York.

18. The government's ability to detain suspects without any hearing or evidence has been challenged in court, on behalf of prisoners in Guantanamo and in the case of Jose Padilla; Padilla, an American, was arrested as an "enemy combatant" and held incommunicado, without legal counsel and without charges being formally brought against him.

19. Most work on autobiography makes this point. See my "Collaboration and the Ordering Imperative in Life Story Production" and "Private Selves and Public Spaces."

20. From "Private Lives and Public Spaces," 207.

21. *Towards a Poetics of Women's Autobiography*, 44.

22. Ruth Prager's interviews with black communist women are a significant effort to bring their stories to light. They were conducted in conjunction with the Radical Oral History Project of the Tamiment Library in New York City. Both Maude White and Louise Thompson Patterson were interviewed under this project. See Solomon, "Rediscovering a Lost Legacy," 13. McDuffie also reports, "There are many primary sources on Louise Thompson Patterson. Her rich personal papers, including several transcribed interviews and her unfinished memoir, are available at the Special Collections Department, Robert W. Woodruff Library, Emory University, Atlanta, Ga. Information can also be found about her in the Matt N. and Evelyn Graves Crawford Papers, Special Collections, Emory University; Langston Hughes Papers, Beinecke Rare Book and Manuscript Library, Yale University, New Haven, Conn.; and in the Communist Party, USA Files, Library of Congress, Washington, D.C." See McDuffie, "Thompson Patterson, Louise."

23. A version of this speech, narrated by Ruby Dee, is listed in the program of Claudia's funeral.

24. Originally published in *Caribbean News*, June 1956. Quoted in Johnson, *"I Think of My Mother,"* 129–132.

25. See also Horne *Black Liberation/Red Scare* and Davis's autobiography, *Communist Councilman from Harlem*.

26. Letter dated August 16, 1959, Claudia Jones Memorial Collection, Schomburg Library, New York.

27. The FBI Files indicate that the officers spent a substantial amount of time on the Lawrenceville, Virginia end but were unable to find any information.

28. The FBI had to devote substantial time and research activity to determine her name, as an entry dated March 17, 1943, indicates. Another entry dated May 19, 1943, indicates (erroneously) that she was — according to one source of information — born in New York City, the daughter of Charles Jones and the former Sybil Lewis; no verification of this statement was found in the records.

29. Perhaps the most exciting connection for the FBI was this putting together of the names Claudia Vera Cumberbatch and Claudia Jones, which they had not been

able to from 1942 to 1947. Once they did this, on April 28, 1947, they began aggressively to document her various CPUSA positions and then to decide that "she is one of the most prominent of the younger leading Negro communists. . . . In view of the foregoing important positions held by Claudia Jones, the New York Office considers her to be a top functionary in the Communist Party, therefore, necessitating that continuous active investigative attention be given this case."

30. Her divorce papers are in the Claudia Jones Papers, Claudia Jones Memorial Collection, Schomburg Library and Research Center, New York.

31. One of the important revelations in the examination of the FBI file is that Claudia Jones remained under FBI surveillance until her death: a final entry documenting her death closes out the case. The various visits by Paul Robeson, also under surveillance, would have been similarly observed.

32. "Women in the Struggle for Peace and Security." See chapter 1, notes 5 and 40.

33. Elias, reporting on a conversation with Jones soon after Jones's arrival in the United Kingdom, in "Claudia Jones (Trinidad 1915–London, 1964)." Elias, who was eighty when I met her, was a friend and comrade of Jones. I spoke with her in December 1997 in her flat in Hampstead, about three or four streets from where Claudia Jones spent her last years. I visited Jones's last home on Meadow Street and took a photograph of it. Elias, I would learn later, died in 1999. The meeting with Elias was facilitated by the presence of Alrick Cambridge, whom she referred to as comrade throughout the evening, as she and a visiting cousin made us tea in a flat that smelled of onions. Elias was evidently excited that Cambridge had come to see her and that there was renewed interest in Claudia. She chatted about her first meetings with Jones and their fast friendship from that time. She was more pleased to see Cambridge again than she was to see me, and they shared many memories. She lived then in what to me seemed a damp apartment, recounting stories of growing up in Eastern Europe with a cousin, of similar age who was visiting her. A cartoonist by profession, she also showed me some of her early cartoons, which she claimed was the early idea for Orwell's *Animal Farm*, with the pigs as characters, which she had shared with Orwell prior to his writing his classic *Animal Farm*.

34. Charlotta Bass stressed world peace and the banning of the bomb during her unsuccessful run for Congress for the state of California on the Independent Progressive party ticket in 1950 (Chase, "Bass, Charlotta Spears"). Charlotta Bass, who was not a communist, was so branded by the government. And as with Jones, she was also subject to government harassment during the McCarthy period. Of note, Bass openly supported the fight against Jones's deportation. See Bass, *Forty Years*. Bass continued her fight for peace during her vice presidential campaign on the Progressive Party ticket in 1952 (Gill, " 'Win or Lose — We Win.' ")

35. Interview with George Lamming, Atlantis Hotel, Batsheba, Barbados, June 18, 2002. Lamming spoke at length of the importance of "peace work" to Claudia and

to the authorities. Both Lamming and Jan Carew would make this point in different ways at the Schomburg Symposium, "The Life and Times of Claudia Jones," December 2, 1998.

36. Harold Cruse writes, "From 1932 onward, of course, the Communists had their biggest propaganda windfall in the infamous Scottsboro Case," *The Crisis of the Negro Intellectual*, 148.

37. See, for example, Hampsch, *The Theory of Communism*; Narkiewicz, *Marxism and the Reality of Power*; Deakin, Shukman, and Willetts, *A History of World Communism*; and Kilroy-Silk, *Socialism since Marx*. Marx's *The Communist Manifesto* and other writings are widely available in collections such as *The Portable Karl Marx*. Another useful source is Bottomore et al., *A Dictionary of Marxist Thought*.

38. "On the Right to Self-Determination for the Negro People in the Black Belt" is one of the essays in which she makes some explicit and direct claims for communism.

39. Bottomore et al., p. 279.

40. She cites Lenin's "Miscellany" on p. 71 of her essay.

41. Earl R. Browder was general secratary of the CPUSA from 1932 to 1945; he was expelled from the party in 1946. See his 1944 article "On the Negroes and the Right of Self-Determination."

42. According to John McClendon, the debates at that time in the Communist Party were not around Stalin the person but more about policies, especially since the CPUSA was coming under heavy attack from the state. At that time, as well, the Soviet Union would have been the most supportive it ever was of struggles against imperialism. Jones was consistently focused on anti-imperialism. McClendon sees Claudia Jones as the most astute communist of the period. (Telephone conversation, September 13, 2004.)

43. Cruse, "Jews and Negroes in the Communist Party," in *The Crisis of the Negro Intellectual*, 147–170.

44. Thanks to Monica Jardine for conversation and clarification on this issue; telephone conversation, August 21, 2004.

45. Indirect sources are Naison, *Communists and Harlem During the Depression* (Naison's interpretation is different from Cruse's, but he does not mention Jones); Kelley, *Hammer and Hoe*; Solomon, *The Cry Was Unity*; Maxwell, *Old Negro, New Left*; Mullen, *Popular Fronts*; and Smethurst, *The New Red Negro*. Some direct sources are in Watts, *The Crisis of the Negro Intellectual Reconsidered*; see especially the essays by Alan Wald (chap. 7), Penny Von Eschen (chap. 9), Kevin Gaines (chap. 10), and Guy-Sheftall (chap. 12).

46. May, "Nuances of Un-American Literature(s) In Search of Claudia Jones," 2.

47. See, for example, Claudin, *The Communist Movement*.

48. Gertrude Elias, *Suspect Generation*, 1994. See also her comment in Sherwood et al., 191–92.

49. Quoted in Sherwood et al., *Claudia Jones*, 201. See also Sherwood's discussion under "Activities Abroad" (108–114).

50. See, for example, Cambridge, "C.L.R. James, Socialist Future and Human Happiness." There is a very nice letter from John Henrik Clarke to Claudia Jones on the *Freedomways* issue dated May 11, 1964, ending: "Both Esther and Louise send regards and would appreciate learning from you" (Claudia Jones Memorial Collection, Schomburg Library.

51. See McClendon, *C. L. R. James's Notes on Dialectics*.

52. Jones wrote about the experience in a letter to Manchanda dated September 7, 1964. A photograph of Jones meeting Madame Soon Ching Ling appears in the *West Indian Gazette*, October 1964, 5. See also Johnson, "Claudia Jones: Freedom Fighter," 10.

53. In Claudia Jones Memorial Collection, Schomburg Library.

54. Hinds, "People of all Races Pay Homage to Claudia Jones."

55. Marika Sherwood makes this point in her *Kwame Nkrumah*. Nkrumah knew Jones well. There is a letter from him to Claudia, dated October 27, 1942, in which he thanks Claudia for courage and insprration and aid during his time in the United States. Nkrumah Collection, Ghana National Archives. Thanks to Michael Hanchard for sharing this reference with me.

56. Besides his obvious importance as a role model, and thus "teacher," W. E. B. Du Bois also offered courses for progressive New Yorkers in the 1940s and 1950s; the *Daily Worker* reports at least two such courses.

57. See, for example, Kelley, *Freedom Dreams*; and Haywood, *Black Bolshevik*. See also Richards, *Maida Springer*, for a discussion of a similar combination.

58. Hayes's work on the formation of a black international that was pan-Africanist and leftist in orientation examines collaborations across languages, in particular French and English, in the emergence of a black radicalism. See also Michelle Stephens, *Black Empire: The Masculine Global Imaginary of Caribbean Intellectuals in the United States, 1914–1962*.

59. For example, in 1946 W. E. B. Du Bois appeared before the U.N. Commission on Human Rights on behalf of the Negro National Congress; NAACP published "An Appeal to the World: A Statement on the Denial of Human Rights to Minorities in the Case of Citizens of Negro Descent in the United States of America and an Appeal to the United States for Redress," a 155-page document endorsed by black organizations, cited in Kelley, *Freedom Dreams*, 58–59. See also Foner, *American Socialism and Black Americans*, 218–219 and 306–311.

60. See Sherwood et al., *Claudia Jones*.

61. The logic of internal colonialism of course does not begin here. One could go to David Walker's *Appeal* for an early assertion of this position of black people as a colonized nation, and linked to other black subjects around the world.

62. Letter from Benjamin Davis, September 2, 1957, p. 2. In the Claudia Memorial Collection, Schomburg Library. See Boyce Davies, "A Guide to the Claudia Jones Collection." Davis talks in other ways about the difficult task ahead of rebuilding the party after the U.S. government's onslaught. About twelve letters from Benjamin Davis are in the Claudia Jones collection.

63. See Alrick Cambridge's summary of Marx's fundamental teachings, the first being that socialism is vastly superior to capitalism as a form of organization of modern society: *Decolonizing the Academy*, 65–66.

64. Sylvia Wynter, interview with Greg Thomas, *Proud Flesh* on-line journal: www .proudfleshjournal.com/issue4/wynter.html.

BIBLIOGRAPHY

Works by Claudia Jones

"American Imperialism and the British West Indies." *Political Affairs* 37 (April 1958): 9–18.

"Autobiographical History." Unpublished manuscript, December 6, 1955. Claudia Jones Memorial Collection, Schomburg Center for Research in Black Culture, New York Public Library.

Ben Davis—Fighter for Freedom. Introduction by Eslanda Goode Robeson. New York: National Committee to Defend Negro Leadership, November 1954.

"Call Negro Women to Sojourn for Justice." *Daily Worker*, September 20, 1951.

"The Caribbean Community in Britain." *Freedomways* (Summer 1964): 340–357.

"Claudia Jones Writes from Ellis Island." *Daily Worker*, November 8, 1950.

"Discussion Article." *Political Affairs* 25 (August 1943): 67–77.

"An End to the Neglect of the Problems of Negro Women." June 1949. *Political Affairs* 53 (March 1974): 28–42.

"First Lady of the World: I Talk with Mme Sun Yat–Sen." *West Indian Gazette and Afro-Asian Caribbean News*, November 1964.

"For New Approaches to Our Work among Women." *Political Affairs* 27 (August 1948): 738–743.

"For the Unity of Women in the Cause of Peace!" *Political Affairs* 30 (February 1951): 151–168.

"Foster's Political and Theoretical Guidance to Our Work among Women." *Political Affairs* 30 (March 1951): 68–78.

"Half the World" (weekly column). *Daily Worker*, 1948–55.

"Her Words Rang Out beyond the Walls of the Courthouse." *Daily Worker*, November 21, 1952.

"International Women's Day and the Struggle for Peace." *Political Affairs* 29 (March 1950): 32–45.

"I Was Deported Because I Fought the Colour Bar." Interview with George Bowrin. *Caribbean News* (June 1956). Quoted in Buzz Johnson, *"I Think of My Mother"*: *Notes on the Life and Times of Claudia Jones* (London: Karia Press, 1985).

Jim-Crow in Uniform. New York: New Age Publishers, 1940.

"Letter to John Gates." *Daily Worker*, November 8, 1950.

Lift Every Voice — For Victory! Pamphlet. New York: New Age Publishers, 1942.

"The Meaning of Dr. Du Bois's Life." *West Indian Gazette and Afro-Asian Caribbean News* (September 1963): 4.

"New Problems of the Negro Youth Movement." *Clarity* 1.2 (Summer 1940): 54–64.

"On the Right to Self-Determination for the Negro People in the Black Belt." *Political Affairs* (January 1946): 67–77.

"A People's Art Is the Genesis of Their Freedom." *Caribbean Carnival 1959.* Souvenir program.

"Pre-Convention Discussion Article." *Political Affairs* 25 (August 1945): 67–77.

"Ship's Log: Paean to the Atlantic." Unpublished manuscript. December 10, 1955.

"Sojourners for Truth and Justice." *Daily Worker*, February 10, 1952.

"Speech to the Court, February, 1953." In *13 Communists Speak* (New York: New Century Publishers, 1955); reprinted in Buzz Johnson, *"I Think of My Mother"*: *Notes on the Life and Times of Claudia Jones* (London: Karia Press, 1985): 121–126.

"The Story of Bigger Thomas." *Weekly Review*, April 11, 1940: 6.

"The Struggle for Peace in the United States." *Political Affairs* 31 (February 1952): 1–20.

"To Elizabeth Gurley Flynn" and "Morning Mists." *Macomère* 1.1 (1998): 35–37.

"Visit to the USSR." *West Indian Gazette and Afro-Asian Caribbean News* (December 1962): 5–9.

"We Seek Full Equality for Women." *Daily Worker*, September 4, 1949.

"West Indies Federation." *West Indian Gazette* (March 1958): 2.

"Why a Paper for West Indians?" *West Indian Gazette* (March 1958): 1.

"Women Crusade for Peace." In "Woman Today," International Women's Day issue of *Daily Worker*, March 12, 1950.

"Women in the Struggle for Peace and Security"; reprinted from *Political Affairs* (March 1950). New York: National Women's Commission of the Communist Party, 1950.

"Women's Organizations in the Struggle for Peace." *Daily Worker*, February 13, 1951.

Secondary Sources

Alexander, Jacqui, and Chandra Talpade Mohanty, eds. *Feminist Geneaologies, Colonial Legacies, Democratic Futures.* London: Routledge, 1996.

Alexander, Sadie T. M. "Negro Women in Our Economic Life." *Opportunity* (July 1930): 201–203.

Amadiume, Ifi. *Male Daughters, Female Husbands: Gender and Sex in an African Society.* London: Zed Books, 1987.

———. *Reinventing Africa: Matriarchy, Religion and Culture.* London: Zed Books, 1997.

Amos, Valerie, and Pratibha Parmar. "Challenging Imperial Feminism." *Feminist Review* 17 (July 1984): 3–19.

Anzaldua, Gloria. *Borderlands La Frontera: The New Mestiza.* 1990; San Francisco, Calif.: Aunt Lute Books, 1999.

Aptheker, Herbert. "A Fabulous Black Woman," *Political Affairs* 50.3 (March 1971): 54–57.

———. "The Negro Woman." *Masses and Mainstream* 2 (January 1949): 10–17.

Ash, Ranjana Sidhanta. "Remembering Claudia." Unpublished manuscript, ca. 1996. Copy in possession of Boyce Davies.

Ashbaugh, Carolyn. *Lucy Parsons, American Revolutionary.* Chicago: Charles Kerr Publishing, 1976.

Baker, Ella, and Marvell Cooke. "The Bronx Slave Market." *The Crisis* 42 (November 1935): 330–331, 340. Republished in *Afro-American History: Primary Sources*, edited by Thomas R. Frazier, 265–271 (Chicago: Dorsey Press, 1988).

Baldwin, Kate A. *Beyond the Color Line and the Iron Curtain: Reading Encounters between Black and Red, 1922–1963.* Durham: Duke University Press, 2002.

Barios de Chungara, Domitila. *Let Me Speak! Testimony of Domitila, a Woman of the Bolivian Mines.* New York: Monthly Review Press, 1979.

Barksdale, Richard, and Kenneth Kinnamon, eds. *Black Writers of America.* Upper Saddle River, N.J.: Pearson Education P.O.D., 1997.

Barriteau, [Violet] Eudine, ed. *Confronting Power, Theorizing Gender: Interdisciplinary Perspectives in the Caribbean.* Kingston, Jamaica: University of the West Indies Press, 2003.

———. "Issues and Challenges of Caribbean Feminisms." Keynote address at "Caribbean Feminisms Workshop: Recentring Caribbean Feminism," University of the West Indies, Cave Hill, Barbados, June 17, 2002.

Bass, Charlotta. *Forty Years: Memoirs from the Pages of a Newspaper.* Los Angeles: privately printed, 1960.

Basu, Amrita. *The Challenge of Local Feminisms: Women's Liberation in Global Perspective.* Boulder, Colo.: Westview Press, 1995.

Baxandall, Rosalynn Fraad. *Words on Fire: The Life and Writing of Elizabeth Gurley Flynn.* New Brunswick, N.J.: Rutgers University Press, 1987.

Beah: A Black Woman Speaks. Written and directed by LisaGay Hamilton. Clinica Estetico, Ltd. and LisaGay, Inc. for HBO/Cinamax, 2003.

Beale, Francis. "Double Jeopardy to Be Black and Female." In *The Black Woman*, edited by Toni Cade, 94–95. New York: New American Library, 1970.

Bogues, Tony. *Black Heretics, Black Prophets: Radical Political Intellectuals.* London: Routledge, 2003.

Bottomore, Thomas, Laurence Harris, V. G. Kiernan, and Ralph Miliband, eds. *A Dictionary of Marxist Thought.* Cambridge, Mass.: Harvard University Press, 1983.

Boyce Davies, Carole. "Absent Black Women in Gilroy's Black Atlantic." Paper presented at the Black Women in the Academy: Defending our Name 1894–1994 Conference, MIT, January 13–15, 1994. Published as "Politicizing a Pre-existing Global Geography," in *Black Geographies and the Politics of Place*, edited by Katherine McKittrick and Clyde Woods, 14–15. Toronto: Between the Lines Press/Boston: South End Press, 2007.

———. "African Diaspora Citizenship: A Policy Oriented Approach to Its Problems and Possibilities." Paper submitted to African Union deliberations in Maputo, July 2003, through Western Hemisphere African Diaspora Network.

———. "Against Race or the Politics of Self–Ethnography" and "Remembering Beryl Gilroy." *jendajournal* 2.1 (2002). http://www.jendajournal.com.

———. "Beyond Unicentricity: Trans-Cultural Black Intellectual Presences." *Research in African Literatures* 30.2 (Summer 1998): 96–109.

———. *Black Women, Writing and Identity: Migrations of the Subject.* London: Routledge, 1994.

———. "Black Women Writing Worlds: Textual Production, Dominance and the Critical Voice." In *Moving beyond Boundaries*, vol. 2, *Black Women's Diasporas*, 1–15. New York: New York University Press; London: Pluto Press, 1995.

———. "Caribbean Women, Domestic Labor and the Politics of Transnational Migration." In *Women's Labor in the Global Economy*, edited by Sharon Harley, 116–133. New Brunswick, N.J.: Rutgers University Press, 2007.

———. "Carnivalised Caribbean Female Bodies: Taking Space/Making Space," *Thamyris* 5.2 (Autumn 1998): 333–346.

———. "Collaboration and the Ordering Imperative in Life Story Production." In *De/Colonizing the Subject: The Politics of Gender in Women's Autobiography*, edited by Sidonie Smith and Julia Watson, 3–19. Minneapolis: University of Minnesota Press, 1992.

———. "Decolonizing the Academy: Advancing the Process." Introduction to *Decolonizing the Academy: African Diaspora Studies*, edited by Carole Boyce Davies, et al., x–xi. Trenton, N.J.: Africa World Press, 2003.

———. "Deportable Subjects: U.S. Immigration Laws and the Criminalizing of Communism." *South Atlantic Quarterly* 100.2 (Fall 2002): 950–966.

———. "A Guide to the Claudia Jones Papers Deposited at the Schomburg Center and Research Library, Harlem, New York." Centre for Gender and Development, University of the West Indies, St. Augustine, Trinidad, April 2002.

———. "Hearing Black Women's Voices: Transgressing Imposed Boundaries." In *Moving beyond Boundaries*, vol. 1, *International Dimensions of Black Women's Writing*, 3–14. London and New York: New York University Press / Pluto Press, 1995.

———. "Private Selves and Public Spaces: Autobiography and the African Woman Writer." *Neohelicon* 17.2 (1990): 183–213.

———. "Taking Space: Carnival, Freedom and Self-Articulation." In "Miami Carnival 1999," supplement to *Caribbean Today* (April 1999): 13.

———. "A View from the Palace: Oyewumi's *The Invention of Women*." Paper presented at the annual meeting of the African Studies Association, Washington, D.C., December 5–8, 2002.

Boyce Davies, Carole, and Elaine Savory Fido, eds. *Out of the Kumbla: Caribbean Women and Literature*. Trenton, N.J.: Africa World Press, 1990.

Boyce Davies, Carole, and Monica Jardine. "Imperial Penetrations and Caribbean Nationalism: Between 'A Dying Colonialism' and Rising American Hegemony." *New Centennial Review* 3.3 (Fall 2003): 131–149.

Boyce Davies, Carole, and Babacar M'bou. "Towards African Diaspora Citizenship: Politicizing a Pre-existing Global Geography." In *Black Geographies and the Politics of Place*, edited by Katherine McKittrick and Clyde Woods, 14–15. Toronto: Between the Lines Press/Boston: South End Press, 2007.

Boyer, Richard. "Why 6 Negro Leaders Defend Claudia Jones." *Daily Worker*, February 25, 1952.

Braidotti, Rosi. *Nomadic Subjects*. New York: Columbia University Press, 1994.

Brand, Dionne. *No Burden to Carry: Narrratives of Black Working Women in Ontario 1920's to 1950's*. Toronto: Women's Press, 1991.

Browder, Earl. "On the Negroes and the Right of Self-Determination." *Communist* (January 1944): 83–85.

Bruno, Mini Seijo. *La Insurrección Nacionalista en Puerto Rico — 1950*. [The Revolution of 1950.] Rio-Pedras, P.R.: Editorial Edil, 1989.

Bryan, Beverley, Stella Dadzie, and Suzanne Scafe. *The Heart of the Race: Black Women's Lives in Britain*. London: Virago, 1985.

Butler, Judith. *Gender Trouble: Feminism and the Subversion of Identity*. New York: Routledge, 1990.

Buxenbaum, Alva. "Marxism and the Woman Question Today." *Political Affairs* 50 (March 1971): 6–14.

Byam, Dale. "Carnival: New York's Caribbean Connection." Paper presented at the World Conference on Carnival: Showcasing the Caribbean, Trinity College, Hartford, Connecticut, September 9–12, 1998.

Cade, Toni, ed. *The Black Woman*. New York: New American Library, 1970.

Cambridge, Alrick X. "The Beauty of Valuing Black Cultures." In *Re-Situating Identities: The Politics of Race, Ethnicity and Culture*, edited by Vered Amit-Talai and Caroline Knowles, 161–183. Peterborough, Ontario: Broadview Press, 1996.

———. "Choosing Our Family Forms in Order to Survive." London: Sabbokai Gallery (Brixton), 1996.

———. "C.L.R. James' Socialist Future and Human Happiness." In *Decolonizing the Academy: African Diaspora Studies*, edited by Carole Boyce Davies, 61–91. Trenton, N.J.: Africa World Press, 2003.

Cambridge, Alrick X., and Stephan Feuchtwang, eds. *Antiracist Strategies*. Research in Ethnic Relations Series. Aldershot, England: Avebury Press, 1990.

——, eds. *Where You Belong: Government and Black Culture*. Aldershot, England: Avebury Press, 1992.

Campi, Alicia. "The McCarran-Walter Act: A Contradictory Legacy on Race, Quotas, and Ideology." Immigration policy brief. Washington D.C.: Immigration Policy Center, American Immigration Law Foundation, June 2004. http://www.ailf.org/ipc/policy_reports_2004_mccarranwalter.asp (accessed September 5, 2006).

Carby, Hazel. *Reconstructing Womanhood: The Emergence of the Afro-American Woman Novelist*. Oxford: Oxford University Press, 1995.

——. "Schooling in Babylon." In *Cultures in Babylon. Black Britain and African America*, 189–218. London, Verso, 1999.

——. "White Woman Listen! Black Feminism and the Boundaries of Sisterhood." In *The Empire Strikes Back: Race and Racism in Seventies Britain*, 212–235. London: Hutchinson, 1982.

Carew, Jan. "British West Indian Poets and their Culture" *Phylon* 14:1 (1953): 71–73.

Carmichael, Stokely, with Ekwueme Michael Thelwell. *Ready for Revolution: The Life and Struggles of Stokely Carmichael [Kwame Ture]*. New York: Scribner, 2003.

Carter, Trevor. *Shattering Illusions: West Indians in British Politics*. London: Lawrence and Wishart, 1986.

Carty, Linda. "Not a Nanny": A Gendered, Transnational Analysis of Caribbean Domestic Workers in New York City." In *Decolonizing the Academy: African Diaspora Studies*, edited by Carole Boyce Davies, 269–282. Trenton, N.J.: Africa World Press, 2003.

Centre for Contemporary Cultural Studies. *The Empire Strikes Back: Race and Racism in Seventies Britain*. London: Hutchinson, 1982.

Cesaire, Aime. *Discourse on Colonialism*. 1955; New York: Monthly Review Press, 1972.

Chang, Grace. *Disposable Domestics: Immigrant Women Workers in the Global Economy*. Cambridge, Mass.: South End Press, 2000.

Chase, Norah C. "Bass, Charlotta Spears." In *American National Biography Online*. Oxford: Oxford University Press, February 2000. http://www.anb.org/articles/15/15-00043.html (accessed January 7, 2005).

Childress, Alice. *Like One of the Family: Conversations from a Domestic's Life*. Boston: Beacon Press, 1986.

Chrisman, Robert. Foreword to *Voices of a Black Nation: Political Journalism in the Harlem Renaissance*, edited by Theodore G. Vincent. Trenton, N.J.: Africa World Press, 1991.

Churchill, Ward, and James Vander Wall. *Agents of Repression: The FBI's Secret Wars against the Black Panther Party and the American Indian Movement*. Cambridge, Mass.: South End Press, 1988.

Claudia Jones: A Woman of Our Times. Directed by Ingrid Lewis for BBC Television. Broadcast on *Eye to Eye*, BBC London, September 18, 1989. (Includes footage of interview with Claudia Jones on the Commonwealth Immigration Act from *To-night* show, BBC 1963.)

"Claudia Jones Denied Diet Prescribed for Heart Illness." *Daily Worker*, March 7, 1955.

"Claudia Jones in Britain—Symposium on Claudia Jones," Institute of Commonwealth Studies, University of London, September 28, 1996. Audiotapes archived at ICS.

"Claudia Jones Will Go to London: Too Ill to Fight Deportation Order." *Daily Worker*, November 21, 1955.

"Claudia Jones, February 21, 1915–December 25, 1964." *Political Affairs* 44 (February 1965): 63–64.

Claudin, Fernando. "The Chinese Revolution." In *The Communist Movement*, 271–294. New York: Monthly Review Press, 1975.

———. *The Communist Movement: From Cominterm to Cominform*. New York: Monthly Review Press, 1975.

Cohen, Abner. *Masquerade Politics: Explorations in the Structure of Urban Cultural Movements*. Los Angeles: University of California Press, 1993.

Collins, Patricia Hill. *Black Feminist Thought*. London: Routledge, 1991.

———. *Fighting Words: Black Women and the Search for Justice*. Contradictions of Modernity 7. Minneapolis: University of Minnesota Press, 1998.

———. "Learning from the Outsider Within: The Social Significance of Black Feminist Thought." *Social Problems* 33.6 (December 1986): 514–532.

Connor, Geraldine. "Culture, Identity and the Music of Notting Hill Carnival." Master's thesis. School of Oriental and African Studies, University of London, 1995.

Cock, Jacqueline. *Maids and Madams: Domestic Workers under Apartheid*. London: Women's Press, 1990.

Cooper, Carolyn. *Sound Clash: Jamaican Dancehall Culture at Large*. New York: Palgrave Macmillan, 2004.

Cowley, John. *Carnival, Canboulay and Calypso: Traditions in the Making*. Cambridge: Cambridge University Press, 1996.

Cox, Oliver Cromwell. *Caste, Class and Race: A Study in Social Dynamics*. Garden City, N.Y.: Doubleday, 1948.

———. *Race: A Study in Social Dynamics*. Fiftieth anniversary edition of *Caste, Class and Race*. New York: Monthly Review Press, 2000.

"CP Hits Deportation of Claudia Jones." *Daily Worker*, December 1, 1955.

Crenshaw, Kimberle, ed. *Critical Race Theory: The Key Writings That Formed the Movement*. New York: New Press, 1996.

Crowe, Chris. *Getting Away with Murder: The True Story of the Emmett Till Case*. New York: Dial, 2003.

Crowe, Chris. *Mississippi Trial*. New York: Puffin Books, 2003.

Cruse, Harold. *The Crisis of the Negro Intellectual: A Historical Analysis of the Failure of Black Leadership*. 1967; New York: Quill, 1984.

Davis, Angela Y. *Angela Davis: An Autobiography*, New York: International Publishers, 1989.

——. *Are Prisons Obsolete?* New York: Seven Stories Press, 2003.

——. *Blues Legacies and Black Feminism: Gertrude "Ma" Rainey, Bessie Smith, and Billie Holiday*. New York: Random House / Vintage, 1998.

——. *If They Come in the Morning*. New York: New American Library, 1971.

——. "Race and Criminalization: Black Americans and the Punishment Industry." In *The House that Race Built*, edited by Wahneema Lubiano, 264–279. New York: Pantheon, 1997.

——. "Slavery and the Prison Industrial Complex." Fifth annual Eric E. Williams Lecture, African New World Studies, Florida International University, Miami, September 19, 2003. Available as videocassette.

——. "Women and Capitalism: Dialectics of Oppression and Liberation." In *The Angela Y. Davis Reader*, edited by Joy James, 161–192 (Malden, Mass.: Blackwell, 1998).

——. *Women, Race and Class*. New York: Random House, 1981; London: Women's Press, 1982.

Davis, Benjamin. *Autobiographical Notes Written in a Federal Penitentiary*. New York: International Publishers, 1969.

De Veaux, Alexis. *Warrior Poet: A Biography of Audre Lorde*. New York: W. W. Norton, 2004.

Deakin, F. W., H. Shukman, and H. T. Willetts. *A History of World Communism*. London: Harper and Row, 1975.

Dirie, Waris, with Cathleen Miller. *Desert Flower: The Extraordinary Journey of a Desert Nomad*. New York: Perennial, 1999.

Douglass, Frederick. *Narrative of the Life of Frederick Douglass, an American Slave, Written by Himself*. Boston: Bedford, St. Martin's, 1993.

Dunayevskaya, Raya. *Women's Liberation and the Dialectics of Revolution: Reaching for the Future*. Atlantic Highlands, N.J.: Humanities Press International, 1985.

Dyson, Michael Eric. *Holler If You Hear Me: Searching for Tupac Shakur*. New York: Basic Civitas Books, 2001.

Edwards, Brent Hayes. *The Practice of Diaspora: Literature, Translation, and the Rise of Black Internationalism*. Cambridge, Mass.: Harvard University Press, 2003.

el Saadawi, Nawal. *Memoirs from the Women's Prison*. Translated by Marilyn Booth. London: Women's Press, 1986.

——. *Woman at Point Zero*. London: Zed Books, 1983.

Elias, Gertrude. "Claudia Jones (Trinidad 1915–London, 1964)." In *The "Suspect Generation."* London: privately printed, 1994.

Engels, Friedrich. *On Marx's "Capital."* Moscow: Progress Publishers, 1965.

Fletcher, Jim, Tanaquil Jones, and Sylvere Lotringer. *Still Black, Still Strong: Survivors of the U.S. War against Black Revolutionaries. Dhoruba Bin Wahad, Mumia Abu-Jamal, Assata Shakur.* Cambridge, Mass.: Semiotexte, 1993.

Flynn, Elizabeth Gurley. *The Alderson Story: My Life as a Political Prisoner.* New York: International Publishers, 1972.

———. "Miss Liberty's Torch Grows Dim." *Daily Worker*, November 9, 1950.

———. *The McCarran Act: Fact and Fancy.* Pamphlet. New York: Gus Hall–Benjamin J. Davis Defense Committee, ca. 1950.

Foner, Philip S. *American Socialism and Black Americans: From the Age of Jackson to World War II.* Westport, Conn.: Greenwood Press, 1977.

Foner, Philip S., and James S. Allen, eds. *American Communism and Black Americans: A Documentary History, 1919–1929.* Philadelphia, Pa.: Temple University Press, 1987.

Foner, Philip S., and Herbert Shapiro, eds. *American Communism and Black Americans: A Documentary History, 1930–1934.* Philadelphia, Pa.: Temple University Press, 1991.

Foster, William Z. "On Improving the Party's Work among Women (A Report to the Party Commission on Theoretical Aspects of Work among Women, August 9, 1948)." *Political Affairs* 27 (November 1948): 987–990.

Gill, Gerald. " 'Win or Lose — We Win': The 1952 Vice Presidential Campaign of Charlotta Bass." In *The Afro-American Women: Struggles and Images*, edited by Sharon Harley and Rosalyn Terborg-Penn, 109–118. Port Washington, N.Y.: National University Publications, 1978.

Gilroy, Paul. *The Black Atlantic: Modernity and Double Consciousness.* Cambridge, Mass: Harvard University Press; London: Verso, 1993.

———. *There Is No Black in the Union Jack.* London: Hutchinson, 1987.

Gordon, Eugene, and Cyril Briggs. *The Position of Negro Women.* Pamphlet. New York: Workers Library Publishers, 1935.

Goulbourne, Harry. *Caribbean Transnational Experience.* London: Pluto Press; Kingston, Jamaica: Arawak Publications, 2002.

———. *Ethnicity and Nationalism in Post-Imperial Britain.* London: Cambridge University Press, 1991.

Gramsci, Antonio. "The Intellectuals." In *Selections from the Prison Notebooks of Antonio Gramsci.* Edited and translated by Quintin Hoare and Geoffrey Nowell Smith, 2–23. New York: International Publishers, 1971.

Grant, Joanne. *Ella Baker: Freedom Bound.* New York: John Wiley and Sons, 1998.

Grewal, Inderpal, and Caren Kaplan. *Scattered Hegemonies: Postmodernity and Transnational Feminist Practices.* Minneapolis: University of Minnesota Press, 1994.

Gutzmore, Cecil. "Carnival, the State and the Black Masses in the United Kingdom."

In *Inside Babylon: The Caribbean Diaspora in Britain*, edited by Winston James and Clive Harris, 207–230. London: Verso, 1993.

———. "Yu can ben wire? The Politics of Organizing in Notting Hill (London) Carnival." Paper presented at the "Carnival and the Caribbean Diaspora" symposium at Florida International University, Miami, October 8, 1999.

Guy-Sheftall, Beverly. "The Evolution of Feminist Consciousness among African American Women." Introduction to *Words of Fire: An Anthology of African-American Feminist Thought*, 1–22. New York: New Press, 1995.

———. "Speaking for Ourselves: Feminisms in the African Diaspora." In *Decolonizing the Academy: African Diaspora Studies*, edited by Carole Boyce Davies, 27–43. Trenton, N.J.: Africa World Press, 2003.

———, ed. *Words of Fire: An Anthology of African-American Feminist Thought*. New York: New Press, 1995.

Hall, Stuart. "The Local and the Global: Globalization and Ethnicity" and "Old and New Identities, Old and New Ethnicities." In *Culture, Globalization and the World System: Contemporary Conditions for the Representaion of Identity*, edited by Anthony King, 19–39, 41–68. London: Macmillan, 1991.

Hampsch, George H. *The Theory of Communism*. New York: Citadel Press, 1965.

Hanchard, Michael. "The Color of Subversion: Racial Politics and Immigration Policy in the United States." Paper prepared for the International Center for Migration, Ethnicity and Citizenship's project, "Negotiating Difference," New School University, 1999.

———. "Identity, Meaning and the African-American." *Social Text* (1990): 31–42.

Harlow, Barbara. *Barred: Women, Writing and Political Detention*. Middletown, Conn.: Wesleyan University Press, 1993.

———. *Resistance Literature*. New York: Methuen, 1987.

Harris, Joseph, ed. *Global Dimensions of the African Diaspora*. Washington, D.C.: Howard University Press, 1993.

Haywood, Harry. *Black Bolshevik: Autobiography of an Afro-American Communist*. Chicago: Liberator Press, 1978.

Hennessy, Rosemary. *Materialist Feminism and the Politics of Discourse*. London: Routledge, 1992.

Hill, Errol. *The Trinidad Carnival: Mandate for a National Theatre*. 1972; London: New Beacon Books, 1997.

Hill, Rebecca. "Fosterites and Feminists, or 1950s Ultra-Leftists and the Invention of AmeriKKKa." *New Left Review*, no. 228 (March–April 1998): 67–90.

Hinds, Donald. *Journey to an Illusion: The West Indian in Britain*. London: Bogle L'Ouverture Press, 2001.

———. "People of All Races Pay Homage to Claudia Jones." In *"I Think of My Mother": Notes on the Life and Times of Claudia Jones*, by Buzz Johnson, 161–162. London: Karia Press, 1985.

———. "The *West Indian Gazette*." In *Claudia Jones: A Life in Exile*, by Marika Sherwood, with Colin Prescod, Donald Hinds, and the 1966 Claudia Jones Symposium, 125–149. London: Lawrence and Wishart, 2002.

Hine, Darlene Clark, Elsa Barkley Brown, and Rosalyn Terborg-Penn, eds. *Black Women in America: An Historical Encyclopedia*. New York: Carlson Publishing, 1993.

hooks, bell. "Third World Diva Girls: Politics of Feminist Solidarity." In *Yearning: Race Gender and Cultural Politics*, 89–102. Boston, Mass.: South End Press, 1990.

Horne, Gerald. *Black Liberation/Red Scare: Ben Davis and the Communist Party*. Newark, N.J.: University of Delaware Press, 1994.

———. *Communist Front? The Civil Rights Congress, 1946–1956*. Madison, N.J.: Fairleigh Dickinson University Press, 1988.

———. *Race Woman: The Lives of Shirley Graham Du Bois*. New York: New York University Press, 2000.

Hull, Gloria T., Patricia Bell Scott, and Barbara Smith, eds. *All the Women Are White, All the Blacks Are Men, But Some of Us Are Brave: Black Women's Studies*. New York: Feminist Press, 1982.

"International Women's Day." Editorial. *Political Affairs* 50.3 (March 1971): 1.

Jackson, George. *Blood in My Eye*. New York: Random House, 1972.

———. *Soledad Brother: The Prison Letters of George Jackson*. New York: Bantam Books, 1970.

James, Joy, ed. *The Angela Y. Davis Reader*. London: Blackwell, 1998.

———, ed. *Imprisoned Intellectuals: America's Political Prisoners Write on Life, Liberation and Rebellion*. Lanham, Md.: Rowman and Littlefield, 2003.

———. *Resisting State Violence: Radicalism, Gender, and Race in U.S. Culture*. Minneapolis: University of Minnesota Press, 1996.

———. *Shadowboxing: Representations of Black Feminist Politics*. New York: Palgrave Macmillan, 2002.

———, ed. *States of Confinement: Policing, Detention and Prisons*. New York: Palgrave Macmillan, 2000.

———. *Transcending the Talented Tenth: Black Leaders and American Intellectuals*. London: Routledge, 1997.

James, Joy, and T. Denean Sharpley-Whiting, eds. *The Black Feminist Reader*. London, Blackwell, 2000.

James, Winston. "Being Red and Black in Jim Crow America: Notes on the Ideology and Travails of Afro-America's Socialist Pioneers." *Souls* 1.4 (Fall 1999): 45–63.

———. *Holding Aloft the Banner of Ethiopia: Caribbean Radicalism in Early Twentieth-Century America*. London: Verso, 1999.

———. "Migration, Racism and Identity Formation: The Caribbean Experience in Britain." In *Inside Babylon: The Caribbean Diaspora in Britain*, edited by Winston James and Clive Harris, 231–287. London: Verso, 1993.

James, Winston, and Clive Harris, eds. *Inside Babylon: The Caribbean Diaspora in Britain*. London: Verso, 1993.

Johnson, Buzz. "Claudia Jones: Freedom Fighter." *Dragon's Teeth* 16 (Winter 1983): 8–10.

———. *"I Think of My Mother": Notes on the Life and Times of Claudia Jones*. London: Karia Press, 1985.

Kaplan, Judy, and Linn Shapiro, eds. *Red Diapers: Growing up in the Communist Left*. Urbana-Champaign: University of Illinois Press, 1998.

Kelley, Robin D. G. " 'But a Local Phase of a World Problem': Black History's Global Vision, 1883–1950." *Journal of American History* 86.3 (December 1999): 1045–1077.

———. "Claudia Jones." In *Black Women in America: An Historical Encyclopedia*, edited by Darlene Clark Hine, Elsa Barkley Brown, and Rosalyn Terborg-Penn, 1:647–648. New York: Carlson Publishing, 1993.

———. *Freedom Dreams: The Black Radical Imagination*. Boston: Beacon Press, 2002.

———. *Hammer and Hoe: Alabama Communists During the Great Depression*. Chapel Hill: University of North Carolina Press, 1990.

Kenyatta, Jomo. *Facing Mount Kenya*. New York: Vintage Books, 1962.

Kilroy-Silk, Robert. *Socialism since Marx*. New York: Taplinger Publishing, 1972.

Kornweibel, Theodore, Jr. *Seeing Red: Federal Campaigns against Black Militancy, 1919–1925*. Bloomington: Indiana University Press, 1998.

Langford, Diane, and Claudia Manchanda. Letter to Marika Sherwood. July 10, 2000.

Langston, Donna. "The Legacy of Claudia Jones." *Nature, Society and Thought* 2.1 (1989): 76–96.

La Rose, J. *Kaiso, Calypso Music: David Rudder in Conversation with John La Rose*. London: New Beacon Books, 1990.

Lemelle, Sidney, and Robin D. G. Kelley. *Imagining Home: Class, Culture and Nationalism in the African Diaspora*. London: Verso, 1994.

"The Life and Times of Claudia Jones," symposium at the Schomburg Center for Research in Black Culture, New York Public Library, New York, December 2, 1998. Videotapes archived at the Schomburg Center.

Lindsey, Lydia. "Claudia Jones: A Black Political Theoretician and Social Activist in the United States and England, 1915–1964." Unpublished manuscript, ca. 1999.

Lorde, Audre. *The Black Unicorn*. New York: W. W. Norton, 1978.

———. "For Assata — New Brunswick Prison, 1977." In *The Black Unicorn*, 28. New York: W. W. Norton, 1978.

———. *Sister Outsider*. Freedom, Calif.: Crossing Press, 1984.

Lubiano, Wahneema, ed. *The House That Race Built*. New York: Pantheon, 1997.

Lynn, Denise. "Women and the Black Radical Tradition: Claudia Jones and Ella Baker." *Binghamton Journal of History* (Fall 2002). http://history.binghamton.edu/resources/bjoh/WomnBlkTrad.htm.

Mandela, Nelson. *Long Walk to Freedom: The Autobiography of Nelson Mandela*. Boston: Back Bay Books, 1995.

Mandela, Winnie. *Part of My Soul Went with Him*. New York: W. W. Norton, 1985.

Marshall, Paule. *Brown Girl: Brownstones*. 1959; New York: Feminist Press, 1996.

Martin, Tony. *Amy Ashwood Garvey. Pan-Africanist, Feminist, and Mrs. Marcus Garvey No. 1, or, A Tale of Two Armies*. Dover, Mass.: The Majority Press, 2007.

——. *Race First: The Ideological and Organizational Struggles of Marcus Garvey and the Universal Negro Improvement Association*. Wellesley, Mass.: Majority Press, 1986.

Marx, Karl. *Capital: A Critique of Political Economy*. Vol. 1. New York: International Publishers, 1957.

——. *The Communist Manifesto*. In *The Portable Karl Marx*, by Karl Marx and Eugene Kamenka. New York: London, Penguin Books, 1983.

——. *Wage-Labour and Capital and Value, Price and Profit*. New York: International Publishers, 1933.

Marx, Karl, et al. *Woman Question: Selections from the Writings of Karl Marx, Frederick Engels, V. I. Lenin and Joseph Stalin*. New York: International Publishers, 1951.

Maxwell, William J. *New Negro, Old Left: African-American Writing and Communism between the Wars*. New York: Columbia University Press, 1999.

May, Claudia. "Nuances of Un-American Literature(s): In Search of Claudia Jones. A Literary Retrospective of the Life, Times and Works of an Activist Writer." Ph.D. dissertation, University of California, Berkeley, 1996.

McClendon, John. "Claudia Jones (1915–1964): Political Activist, Black Nationalist, Feminist, Journalist." In *Notable Black American Women*, edited by Jessie Carney Smith, 2:343–346. Detroit: Gale Research, 1996.

——. *CLR James's Notes on Dialectics: Left Hegelianism or Marxism-Leninism?* Lanham, Md.: Lexington Books, Rowman and Littlefield, 2005.

——. "From Cultural Nationalism to Cultural Criticism: Philosophical Idealism, Paradigmatic Illusions and the Politics of Identity." In *Decolonizing the Academy: African Diaspora Studies*, edited by Carole Boyce Davies, 4–25. Trenton, N.J.: Africa World Press, 2003.

McDuffie, Erik S. "Long Journeys: Four Black Women and the Communist Party, USA, 1930–1956." 2 vols. Ph.D. dissertation, New York University, 2003.

——. "Sojourners for Truth and Justice." In *Encyclopedia of the African Diaspora*, edited by Carole Boyce Davies. Oxford: ABC-Clio, forthcoming.

——. "Thompson Patterson, Louise." *American National Biography Online*. Oxford: Oxford University Press, 2003. http://www.anb.org/articles/15/15-01299.html (accessed January 7, 2005).

Mies, Maria, Veronika Bennholdt-Thomsen, and Claudia von Werlhof. *Women: The Last Colony*. London: Zed Books, 1988.

Milner, David Roussel. "False History of Notting Hill Carnival: A Review of Abner

Cohen's *Masquerade Politics.*" *Association for a People's Carnival Newsletter*, no. 7 (August 1996): 8–10.

Mohammed, Patricia, ed. *Gendered Realities: Essays in Caribbean Feminist Thought.* Kingston, Jamaica: University of the West Indies Press, 2002.

Mohammed, Patricia, and Catherine Shepherd, eds. *Gender in Caribbean Development.* Papers presented at the inaugural seminar of the University of the West Indies Women and Development Studies Project. Mona, Jamaica: The University of the West Indies, 1988. Reprinted with new foreword by Elsa Leo-Rhynie. Kingston, Jamaica: Canoe Press, 1999.

Mohanty, Chandra Talpade. *Feminism without Borders: Decolonizing Theory, Practicing Solidarity.* Durham: Duke University Press, 2003.

———. "Under Western Eyes: Feminist Scholarship and Colonial Discourses." In *Third World Women and the Politics of Feminism,* edited by Chandra Talpade Mohanty, Anna Russo, and Lourdes Torres, 51–80. Bloomington: Indiana University Press, 1991.

Mohanty, Chandra Talpade, and Jacqui Alexander, eds. *Feminist Geneaologies, Colonial Legacies, Democratic Futures.* London: Routledge, 1996.

Mohanty, Chandra Talpade, Anna Russo, and Lourdes Torres, eds. *Third World Women and the Politics of Feminism.* Bloomington: Indiana University Press, 1991.

Momsen, Janet Henshall, ed. *Women and Change in the Caribbean: A Pan Caribbean Perspective.* Kingston, Jamaica: Ian Randle, 1993.

Morel, Yumeris. "Claudia Jones: Race, Class and Feminist Consciousness." M.A. thesis, Binghamton University, 2000.

Moten, Fred. *In the Break: The Aesthetics of the Black Radical Tradition.* Minneapolis: University of Minnesota Press, 2003.

Mugo, Micere. "The Role of African Intellectuals: Reflections of a Female Scholar, University of Nairobi, 1973–82." In *The Role of African Intellectuals,* edited by Ibbo Mandaza. Harare: SAPES, forthcoming.

Mullen, Bill V. *Popular Fronts: Chicago and African-American Cultural Politics, 1935–46.* Urbana: University of Illinois Press, 1999.

Naison, Mark. *Communists in Harlem During the Depression.* Champaign-Urbana: University of Illinois Press, 1983.

Narkiewicz, Olga A. *Marxism and the Reality of Power, 1919–1980.* London: Croom-Helm, 1981.

Nibur, Label. "A Ballad to Claudia Jones." *Daily Worker,* February 25, 1952.

Nkrumah, Kwame. *Ghana: The Autobiography of Kwame Nkrumah.* New York: International Publishers, 1970.

Nnaemka, Obioma. *Sisterhood, Feminisms and Power: From Africa to the Diaspora.* Africa World Press, 2000.

Noguera, Pedro. "Exploring the Undesirable: An Analysis of the Factors Influencing the Deportation of Immigrants from the United States and an Examination of their Impact on Caribbean and Central American Societies." *Wadabagei: A Journal of the Caribbean and Its Diaspora* 2.1 (Winter–Spring 1999): 1–28.

Noh, Eliza. "Problematics of Transnational Feminism and Asian American Women." *New Centennial Review* 3.3 (Fall 2003): 131–149.

Ogletree, Charles J., Jr. *All Deliberate Speed: Reflections on the First Half of Brown v. Board of Education*. New York: W. W. Norton, 2004.

Okome, Onookome, ed. *Before I Am Hanged: Ken Saro-Wiwa, Literature, Politics and Dissent*. Trenton, N.J.: Africa World Press, 1999.

Okpewho, Isidore, Carole Boyce Davies, and Ali Mazrui, eds. *The African Diaspora: African Origins and New World Identities*. Bloomington: Indiana University Press, 1999.

Oliver, Paul. *Young, Gifted and Black: Black Music in Britain*. London: Open University Press, 1990.

O'Reilly, Kenneth. *Hoover and the Un-Americans: The FBI, HUAC, and the Red Menace*. Philadelphia, Pa.: Temple University Press, 1983.

O'Reilly, Kenneth, and David Gallen. *Black Americans: The FBI Files*. New York: Carroll and Graf, 1994.

Oyewumi, Ronke. *The Invention of Women: Making an African Sense of Western Gender Discourses*. Minneapolis: University of Minnesota Press, 1997.

Padmore, George. *Pan-Africanism or Communism?: The Coming Struggle for Africa*. London: D. Dobson, 1961.

Patterson, William L. "Remarks on the Eve of the Deportation of Claudia Jones." Unpublished manuscript, December 8, 1955. Claudia Jones Memorial Collection, Schomburg Center for Research in Black Culture, New York Public Library.

Payne, Charles. "Ella Baker and Models of Social Change." *Signs* 14.1 (Spring 1989): 877–899.

Perry, Pettis. "The New 'Alien and Sedition' Law." *Catholic Worker*, November 15, 17, 19, 1952.

Pery, Imani. *Prophets of the Hood: Politics and Poetics in Hip Hop*. Durham: Duke University Press, 2004.

Philip, Marlene Nourbese. "Negro in America: Evaluating the *New Yorker*'s 'Black in America' Issue." Special issue of *Border/Lines* 41 (July 1996).

Pilkington, Edward. *Beyond the Mother Country: West Indians and the Notting Hill White Riots*. London: I. B. Tauris, 1988.

Pinnock, Winsome. *Rock in the Water*. Play. Staged at Royal Court Theatre, London, January 1989.

Poulantzas, Nicos. *State, Power, Socialism*. Introduction by Stuart Hall. London: Verso, 2000.

Ransby, Barbara. *Ella Baker and the Black Freedom Movement: A Radical Democratic Vision*. Chapel Hill: University of North Carolina Press, 2003.

Raymond, Harry. "Illegal Gestapo Buildup by the FBI against the Foreign-Born." *Daily Worker*, December 7 and December 28, 1950.

Reddock, Rhoda. *Elma Francois: The NWCSA and the Workers Struggle for Change in the Caribbean*. London: New Beacon Books, 1988.

———. *Women, Labour and Politics in Trinidad and Tobago: A History*. Kingston, Jamaica: Ian Randle, 1994.

"Rethinking Caribbean Difference." Special issue of *Feminist Review* 39.59 (Summer 1998).

Richards, Yvette. *Maida Springer: Pan Africanist and International Labor Leader*. Pittsburgh: University of Pittsburgh Press, 2001.

Riley, Joan, *The Unbelonging*. London: Women's Press, 1985.

Robeson, Paul. "Statement on Un-American Activities Committee." News release, Council on African Affairs, New York City, July 20, 1949. In *Paul Robeson Speaks*, edited by Philip S. Foner. New York: Citadel Press, 1978.

Robinson, Cedric J. *Black Marxism: The Making of a Black Radical Tradition*. London: Zed Books, 1983.

Rothenberg, Paula S., *Race, Class, and Gender in the United States: An Integrated Study*. New York: St. Martins Press, 1992.

Roussel-Milner, David. "False History of Notting Hill Carnival: A Review of Professor Abner Cohen's *Masquerade Politics.*" *Newsletter, Association for a People's Carnival*, no. 7: 8–10. London: New Beacon Books, 1996.

Said, Edward. "The Limits of the Artistic Imagination and the Secular Intellectual." In "Literature, the Creative Imagination and Globalization," special issue of *Macalester International* 3 (Spring 1996): 3–34.

Sandoval, Chela. "U.S. Third World Feminism: The Theory and Method of Oppositional Consciousness in the Postmodern World." *Genders* 10 (Spring 1991): 1–24.

Sargent, Lydia, ed. *Women and Revolution: A Discussion of the Unhappy Marriage of Marxism and Feminism*. Cambridge, Mass.: South End Press, 1981.

Saro Wiwa, Ken. *A Month and a Day: A Detention Diary*. New York: Penguin, 1995.

Schrecker, Ellen. *The Age of McCarthyism: A Brief History with Documents*, 2nd ed. Boston: Bedford–St. Martin's, 2002.

———. *No Ivory Tower: McCarthyism and the Universities*. New York: Oxford University Press, 1986.

Schwarz, Bill. "Claudia Jones and the *West Indian Gazette*: Reflections on the Emergence of Post-colonial Britain." *Twentieth Century British History* 14.3 (2003): 264–285.

Scott, Joan. "Gender: A Useful Category of Historical Analysis." *American Historical Review* 91.5 (1996): 1053–75.

"17 Foreign-Born Jailed under McCarran Act: 107 File Suit to Void McCarran Act." *Daily Worker*, October 24, 1950.

Shakur, Assata. *Assata: An Autobiography*. Chicago: Lawrence Hill, 1988.

Shakur, Tupac. *The Rose That Grew from Concrete*. New York: MTV, 1999.

Shapiro, Linn. "Red Feminism: American Communism and the Women's Rights Tradition, 1919–1956." Ph.D. dissertation, American University, 1997.

Shepherd, Claire. "Who Controls the Future of the Notting Hill Carnival?" Unpublished manscript, London, 1999. Copy in Boyce Davies's possession.

Sherwood, Marika. *Kwame Nkrumah: The Years Abroad*. Legon: Freedom Publications, 1996.

Sherwood, Marika, with Donald Hinds, Colin Prescod, and the 1966 Claudia Jones Symposium. *Claudia Jones: A Life in Exile*. Report of the Institute for Contemporary Arts Claudia Jones Symposium, London, 1996. London: Lawrence and Wishart, 1999.

Shinebourne, Jan. *The Last English Plantation*. Leeds, England: Peepal Tree Press, 1988.

Silvera, Makeda. *Silenced: Life Stories of Domestic Workers in Canada*. Toronto: Sister Vision Press, 1989.

Smethurst, James Edward. *The New Red Negro: The Literary Left and African American Poetry, 1930–1946*. New York: Oxford University Press, 1999.

Smith, Sidonie. *Towards a Poetics of Women's Autobiography*. Bloomington: Indiana University Press, 1980.

Solomon, Mark. *The Cry Was Unity: Communism and African Americans, 1919–1936*. Jackson: University Press of Mississippi, 1998.

———. "Rediscovering a Lost Legacy: Black Women Radicals Maude White and Louise Thompson Patterson." *Abafazi* (Fall–Winter 1995): 6–13.

Spillers, Hortense. "The Crisis of the Negro Intellectual: A Post-date." *boundary 2: An International Journal of Literature and Culture* 21.3 (Fall 1994): 65–116.

Spivak, Gayatri. *In Other Worlds: Essays in Cultural Politics*. New York: Methuen, 1987; New York: Routledge, 1988.

Stephens, Michelle Ann. *Black Empire: The Masculine Global Imaginary of Caribbean Intellectuals in the United States, 1914–1962*. Durham, N.C.: Duke University Press, 2005.

Strong, Augusta. "Hundreds Say Last Goodbye to Claudia Jones Who Sails Today." *Daily Worker*, December 9, 1955.

Taylor, Clarence. *Black Religious Intellectuals*. London: Routledge, 2002.

Taylor, Margaret H., and T. Alexander Aleinkoff. "Deportation of Criminal Aliens: A Geopolitical Perspective." *Inter-American Dialogue*. Working paper. June 1998. http://www.thedialogue.org/publications/program _ reports/taylor _ criminal .htm (accessed march 3, 2007).

Taylor, Ula Yvette. *The Veiled Garvey: The Life and Times of Amy Jacques Garvey*. Chapel Hill: University of North Carolina Press, 2002.

Thomas, Elean. "Remembering Claudia Jones." *World Marxist Review* 30 (March 1987): 67–69.

Thomas, Greg. "The Geo-Cultural Economy of Race? Omi and Winant 'Nation State' Americanism and the Global Turn." Unpublished manuscript, 1994. Copy in Boyce Davies's possession.

———. *The Sexual Demon of Colonial Power: Pan-African Embodiment and the Erotic Schemes of Empire.* Bloomington: Indiana University Press, 2007.

Turner, W. Burghardt, and Joyce Moore Turner. *Richard B. Moore: Caribbean Militant in Harlem. Collected Writings, 1920–1972.* Bloomington: Indiana University Press, 1988.

Tyson, Jennifer, and the Camden Black Sisters. *Claudia Jones, 1915–1964: A Woman of Our Times.* London: Camden Black Sisters Publications, 1988.

Vincent, Theodore G., ed. *Voices of a Black Nation: Political Journalism in the Harlem Renaissance.* Trenton, N.J.: Africa World Press, 1991.

Von Eschen, Peggy M. *Race against Empire: Black Americans and Anticolonialism, 1937–1957.* Ithaca: Cornell University Press, 1997.

Wallace, Michelle. *Black Macho and the Myth of the Superwoman.* London: Verso, 1999.

———. *Dark Designs and Visual Culture.* Durham: Duke University Press, 2004.

Washington, Mary Helen. "Alice Childress, Lorraine Hansberry, and Claudia Jones: Black Women Write the Popular Front." In *Left of the Color Line: Race, Radicalism, and Twentieth-Century Literature of the United States,* edited by Bill V. Mullen and James Smethurst, 183–204. Chapel Hill: University of North Carolina Press, 2003.

Watkins-Owen, Irma. *Blood Relations: Caribbean Immigrants and the Harlem Community.* Bloomington: Indiana University Press, 1996.

Watt, George. "Negro Slave Market." *Review* 6.3 (February 3, 1941): 1, 12.

Watts, Jerry, ed. *The Crisis of the Negro Intellectual Reconsidered.* New York: Routledge, 2004.

Weigand, Kate. *Red Feminism: American Communism and the Making of Women's Liberation.* Baltimore: Johns Hopkins University Press, 2001.

———. "Vanguards of Women's Liberation: The Old Left and the Continuity of the Women's Movement in the United States, 1945–1970's." Ph.D. dissertation, Ohio State University, 1995.

Wheeler, Tim. "Black Women Workers." *People's Weekly World* (February 11, 1995): 1–4.

White, Deborah Gray. *Too Heavy a Load: Black Women in Defense of Themselves, 1894–1994.* New York: W. W. Norton, 2000.

White, Maude. "Special Negro Demands." *Labor Unity* 7.5 (May 1932).

———. "Fighting Discrimination." *Labor Unity* 7.11 (November 1932).

Williams, Eric. *The Negro in the Caribbean.* Washington, D.C.: Associates in Negro Folk Education, 1942.

Wilson, Francille Rusan. "Becoming 'Woman of the Year': Sadie T. M. Alexander and the Construction of a Public Persona as a Professional and a Race Woman." Paper presented at the "Work in the Lives of Women of Color" Bellagio Seminar, August 2004.

Wing, Adrienne Katherine, ed. *Global Critical Race Feminism*. New York: New York University Press, 2000.

Wynter, Sylvia. "Beyond Miranda's Meanings: Un/silencing the Demonic Ground of Caliban's Woman." Afterword to *Out of the Kumbla*, edited by Carole Boyce Davies and Elaine Savory Fido, 355–366. Trenton, N.J.: Africa World Press, 1990. Reprinted in *The Black Feminist Reader*, edited by Joy James and T. Denean Sharpley-Whiting, 109–130. Oxford: Blackwell, 2000.

———. "On How We Mistook the Map for the Territory, and Re-Imprisoned Ourselves in Our Unbearable Wrongness of Being, of Désêtre: Black Studies Toward the Human Project." In *Not Only the Master's Tools: African-American Studies in Theory and Practice*, edited by Lewis R. Gordon and Jane Anna Gordon, 107–169. Boulder, Colo.: Paradigm Publishers, 2006.

Zetkin, Clara. *Lenin on the Woman Question*. New York: International Publishers, 1934.

INDEX

Abu Jamal, Mumia, 262 n.41
Acheson, Dean, 82
African Americans: African diaspora and,
12–16; black feminism and, 36–40;
Caribbean diaspora and, 162, 165–
66; citizenship rights denied to, 144–
47; civil rights violations against,
147–59; Jones's involvement with, 8–
10; transnational black feminism and,
21–25
African Blood Brotherhood, 18, 50, 73,
243 n.24
African Democratic Rally, Women's
Committee of, 81
African diaspora: African American intellectuals and, 12–16; Caribbean diaspora and, 159, 162, 165–66;
deportation politics and, 137–47; international identity in, 137–38;
Jones's legacy in, xiii–xv, xix–xx, 5, 7;
pan-Africanism and, 229–32; performativity in, 263 n.1; transnational
black feminism and, 22; in United
Kingdom, 85–97, 142–47, 254 n.16
African National Congress, 231
Africa Unity House, 143, 261 n.27

Afro-Asian Caribbean News. See West In-
dian Gazette and Afro-Asian Caribbean
News
Afro-Asian Conference, 174
Afro-Caribbean Organisation, 162, 245
n.2
Age of McCarthyism, The, 196
Al-Arian, Sami, 259 n.6
Alderson Federal Prison: Jones's incar-
ceration in, 107–17, 140; women im-
prisoned in, 103–4, 257 n.10
Alderson Story, The, 103–4, 107–9, 112, 156
Alexander, Jacqui, 22
Alexander, Sadie T. M., 45
Alien Registration Act of 1940, 25, 34,
72, 138, 147–50, 194–98, 206. See
also McCarran-Walter International
Security Act
All the Women Are White, All the Blacks
Are Men, But Some of Us Are Brave, 11
Amadiume, Ifi, 39
American Civil Liberties Union, 259 n.6
"American Imperialism and the British
West Indies," 60–65
American left, black communists and,
17–20

American Women for Peace, 81

Amos, Valerie, 14, 242 n.19

Amsterdam News, 254 n.10

Anglo-American Commission, 61

Animal Farm, 269 n.33

Anti-imperialism: black feminism and, 14–16, 38, 54–55, 254 n.16; Caribbean feminism and, 65–68; feminist solidarity against, 110–17; in Jones's poetry, 110–17; Jones's writings on, 60–65, 86–87, 222, 270 n.42; transnational feminism and, 21–25

Aptheker, Herbert, 69–70

Aptheker's Documentary History of the Negro People in the U.S., 80

Arab Americans, deportation proceedings against, 133, 148, 260 n.7

Ash, Ranjana, 63–64, 241 n.19, 252 n.52

Ashford, James, 267 n.15

Asian diaspora, in United Kingdom, 143, 261 n.28

Association for a People's Carnival, 182

Association for the Study of African American Life and History Conference, xvii

Atlantic. *See* "Ship's Log: Paean to the Atlantic"

"Autobiographical History" (Jones), 197–208, 212

Autobiography/autobiographical writings, 202–3, 212–13, 268 n.22

Baker, Ella, xv, 6, 15, 46, 50, 124

Baldwin, James, 91, 95

"Ballad to Claudia, A," 128–29

Baraka, Amiri, 242 n.14

Barios de Chungara, Domitila, 103

Barrette, Jim, 253 n.59

Bass, Charlotta, 19, 35, 82, 213, 269 n.34

Basu, Amrita, 21–22

Baxandall, Rosalyn Fraad, 113–14, 117

Beah: A Black Woman Speaks, 37, 248 n.13

Beale, Francis, 4

Bennett, Louise, 167

Bethune, Mary McCleod, 33

"Better World, A," 78

"Beyond Miranda's Meanings: Unsilencing the Demonic Ground of Caliban's Woman," 16

Beyond the Mother Country: West Indians and the Notting Hill White Riots, 85, 93, 173

Bibb, Henry, 73

Bittelman, Alexander, 148

Black and Red, 214

Black Bolshevik, 56

"Black British" discourse, Jones's contributions to, 168–69

Black British feminism, 65–68, 85–97, 168–69

Black communist women, 17–20, 47–55, 74

Black feminism: anti-imperialist critique of, 14–16, 38, 54–55, 254 n.16; autobiographical writings of, 202–3, 268 n.22; blues legacy and, 101–2; critique of Western feminist scholarship by, 55; current research on, 10; definitions of, 34–35, 247 n.13; Jones's influence on, 10–20; pacificist movement and, 217–33; "second wave" of, 37–40; superexploitation of black women and, 2–4; theoretics of, 32–40; transnational black feminism, 20–25; U.S.-centeredness of, xv, 4, 16, 20

Black Feminist Reader, The, 16

Black Feminist Thought, 13

"Black Feminist Thought: Dancing at the Borders," xv

Black international movement, 229–30

Black Liberation/Red Scare, 137, 260 n.16

Black Liberator: A Theoretical and Discussion Journal for Black Liberation, xviii, 85, 169, 240 n.13, 263 n.2, 265 n.36

Black Macho and the Myth of the Superwoman, 12

Black Marxism, 223

Black Panther Party, 124, 193, 266 n.7

Black Power movement, 256 n.1, 259 n.6

Black Scholar, The, 240 nn.13–14

"Black Woman Speaks of White Womanhood, of White Supremacy, of Peace, A," 37

Black Women in America, 16

Black Women, Writing and Identity, 54

Blues Legacies and Black Feminism, 101–2

Blues music and lyrics, poetics and aesthetic of, 101–4

Bogle L'Ouverture Publications, 85, 169

Boscoe Holder, 93, 180

Bowrin, George, 29, 198, 205, 255 n.17, 267 n.14

Boyer, Richard, 139

Briggs, Cyril, 18, 45, 229

"Bronx Slave Market, The," 14, 46

Browder, Earl, 221, 252 n.53, 270 n.41

Brown, Elsa Barkley, 16

Brown Girl, Brownstones, 14, 46

Brown v. Board of Education, 145

Bryan, Beverly, xiv

Burroughs, Williana, 50

Byam, Dale, 170–71

California Eagle, The, 19, 35

"Call Negro Women to 'Sojourn for Justice,'" 37, 82, 248 n.15

Cambridge, Ricky (Alrick), xviii–xix, 85, 120, 169, 240 n.14, 241 n.19, 265 n.36, 269 n.33

Camden Black Sisters, xvii, 254 n.16

Campbell, Grace, 18, 50, 229, 243 n.24

Campi, Alicia J., 134

Capitalism: international, and black women domestic workers, 44–49; socialist feminism's view of, 57–60; super-exploitation of working-class black women and, 41–44; transnational feminism and, 23–25, 244 n.32

Carew, Jan, xvii, 93, 173, 213–14, 270 n.35

Caribbean Artists Movement, 230–31

Caribbean Association for Feminist Research and Activism, 253 n.60

Caribbean Carnival Committee, 176, 179–80, 183

Caribbean Commission, 61

"Caribbean Community in Britain, The," 88, 167–69, 263 n.2

Caribbean diaspora: Communist Party and, 18; cultural identity of, 167–89; demographic statistics on, 167–68; deportation of "returnees" and, 132; as domestic laborers in New York City, 15; feminist history and, 25, 65–68, 244 n.38; international identity in, 138; in Jones's poetry, 111–17; Jones's work with, xix–xx, 1–2, 7–10, 25–27, 60–65, 162, 165–66, 167–89; newspapers of, 199–200; in New York City, 170–74; political activism of, 168–74; in United Kingdom, xx–xxi, 65–68, 85–97, 143–47, 169–74, 224–33

Caribbean feminism, Jones's involvement in, 65–68, 252 n.54, 253 n.60

Caribbean Labor Congress, 224–25, 255 n.17

Caribbean News, 86, 94, 255 n.17

Caribbean Transnational Experience, 85, 168–69

Carmichael, Stokely (Kwame Ture), 27, 124, 137, 146–147, 260 n.16

Carnival Development Committee, 179

Carnival Messiah, 266 n.40

Carnivals, Caribbean diaspora and role of, 167–89, 170–84, 263 n.1

"Carnival, the State and Black Masses in the United Kingdom," 179

Carter, Trevor, 180, 224, 245 n.2, 264 n.26

Carty, Linday, 46

Caste, Class and Race, 42

Castle, Barbara, xvi

Catholic Worker, 147

Center for Research on Women, 41

Césaire, Aime, 60, 62

Challenge of Local Feminism, The, 21–22

"Challenging Imperialist Feminism," 14

Chang, Grace, 46

Chase, Norma, 213

Children, Jones's columns on behalf of, 81–82

Childress, Alice, 45, 82

China, Jones's visit to, 126–27, 221–22, 225–28

Chrisman, Robert, 73, 89

Churchill, Ward, 242 n.14

Citizenship rights: denial of, to African Americans, 144–45; deportation policies and, 135–47, 157, 159

Civil rights violations: under Smith and McCarran Acts, 147–59; United States deportation policies and, 132–34, 259 nn.3, 5, 6, 260 n.7

Class struggle: black feminism and role of, 4, 11–16, 38; superexploitation theoretics and, 42–44, 250 n.26; transnational black feminism and, 20–25

Claudia Jones: A Life in Exile, xvi

"Claudia Jones and the *West Indian Ga-*

zette: Reflections on the Emergence of Post-colonial Britain," 91–92

Claudia Jones beyond Containment, xviii

Claudia Jones Memorial Committee, 245 n.2

Claudia Jones Organisation, xvii

"Claudia's Comments," 75–77, 200

Claudin, Fernando, 214

"Clay Sculpture," 124–25

Cochrane, Kelso, 172, 176, 178, 182–83

Cock, Jacquelyn, 46

Cohen, Abner, 181, 265 n.28

Collazo, Oscar, 257 n.19

Collazo, Rosa, 257 n.19

Collins, Merle, 240 n.18

Collins, Patricia Hill, 13–14

"Colonization in reverse," Caribbean diaspora culture as, 167–68

Combahee River Collective, 11, 34–36, 59–60

Committee of Afro-Asian and Caribbean Organisations, 64, 174, 177

Commoditized intellectual, emergence of, 8–10

"Common Differences: Third World Women and Feminist Perspectives," 58

Commonwealth Immigration Act, 88

Communist International, 74

Communist Movement, The, 214

Communist Party Great Britain (CPGB): Jones's work with, 170, 230–32, 263 n.7; racial and cultural barriers in, 174–84, 223–33, 264 n.16

Communist Party of USA (CPUSA): black feminism and, 30–40, 246 n.3; black women's leadership in, 49–55; black working women and, 46–49; criminalization of, 135–47, 151–59, 193–97; Du Bois's membership in, 17; FBI persecution and investigation of, 193–197, 210–212; government persecution of, 115–17, 149–50; Jones's role in, xix, 30–32, 56–60, 74–75, 200–201, 210–12, 219–33; male supremacy in, 50–55; pacifist activities of, 214–33; protests against Jones's deportation by, 140–41; racial tensions in, 38–40, 174–75, 262 n.53; Women's Commission of, 34–36, 51, 54, 72, 77, 79, 212; women's rights issues and, 29–30

Communists in Harlem During the Depression, 74

Community, black women's role in, 37–38

Congressional Record, 152

Connor, Cedric, 181, 185

Connor, Eric, 180

Connor, Geraldine, 181, 184, 266 n.40

Constantine, Learie, 91

Cooke, Marvel, xv, 15, 46

Cooper, Anna Julia, 22, 37

Cooper, Carolyn, 100

Cotton, Eugenie, 81

Council of African Affairs, 229

Counter Intelligence Program (COIN-TELPRO), 137

Court, Jones' testimony before, 1, 6, 203–4

Cox, Oliver Cromwell, 42–43, 250 n.26

Crockett, George W., 267 n.11

Crusader, 73

Cry Was Unity: Communists and African Americans, 1917–1936, The, 18

Cuban Revolution: Caribbean diaspora and, 63; Jones's support of, 223

Culture: of Caribbean diaspora, 167–68, 174–84, 263 n.1; Jones on importance of, xviii, 167, 175–84

"Culture, Identity and the Music of Notting Hill Carnival," 181

Dadzie, Stella, xiv

Daily Express, 61

Daily News, 81

Daily Worker, The: "Ballad to Claudia" in, 128–29; deportation articles in, 134–35, 138–42, 147–48, 161; "Half the World" column in, 77–84, 96, 215; Jones's imprisonment and, 99; Jones's writing for, xvii, 6–7, 30, 34, 37, 41, 70–72, 87, 95–97, 107, 254 n.3; "Letter to John Gates" in, 105–7, 121, 153–54, 198, 201–2; peace activism articles in, 214–34; as research source, xv, 246 n.2; Till case coverage in, 156–57

Damon, Anna, 50

Dark Designs and Visual Culture, 12

Davis, Angela, xiv, 242 n.9; black communism and, 17, 19, 247 n.6; on the blues, 101–2; intellectual-activist work, 8–10, 242 n.13; on Jones, 30, 38; Marxist-feminist politics of, 59, 144, 252 n.49; prison literature of, 103; "talented tenth" formation critiqued by, 15; on transnational capital, 241 n.4; on "triple jeopardy" theory of black women's exploitation, 4; on white women progressives, 48–49

Davis, Benjamin, 19, 77, 140, 198, 205–7, 231–32, 260 n.16, 272 n.61

Decolonization, 22, 167–68

Deportation: African-American targets of, 152–53, 262 n.39; African diaspora and, 137–47; gendered aspects of, 159, 162, 165; protests against, 147–58; U.S. policies concerning, 131–37, 259 nn.3, 6

Dill, Bonnie Thornton, 41
Dimock, Edward J., 1, 6, 116–17, 203–4
Dirie, Waris, 24, 244 n.36
Discourse on Colonialism, 60, 62
Disposable Domestics: Immigrant Women Workers in the Global Economy, 46
Dixielanders, 180
Dixieland Steelband, 93
Domestic service: black working-class women's relegation to, 41–44; Caribbean emigration as source for, 61–65; international capitalist economy and, 44–49
Domingo, W. A., 76
Dominican Republic, "returnees" deported back to, 132
"Double Jeopardy: To Be Black and Female," 4
Douglass, Frederick, 73, 107
Doyle, Mikki, 245 n.2
Dred Scott decision, 144
Du Bois, W. E. B., 1, 95; Communist Party USA and, 17; Jones influenced by, 271 nn.56, 59; pan-Africanism and, 229–30; persecution of, 137, 140, 148, 206, 214; "talented tenth" formation of, 8, 15
Dunayevskaya, Raya, 58–59

Earnings data for working-class black women, 41, 249 n.23
Echeruo, Michael, 119
Economic conditions for black women: Jones's discussion of, 37–38, 80; super-exploitation theory and, 41–44
Elder, J. D., 263 n.1
Elias, Gertrude, 213–19, 223–24, 269 n.33
Ellis, Pat, 247 n.12, 267 n.16

Ellis Island, 105–7, 120–22, 154–55, 200, 202
Elma Francois, the NWCSA and the Workers Struggle for Change in the Caribbean in the 1930s, 66–67
"Elms at Morn, The," 99, 120–22
Employment, black women's struggle for, 49
"End to the Neglect of the Problems of Black Women, An," 16, 33, 37–40, 47–49, 251 n.34
"Enemy combatants," inhumane treatment of, 259 n.3
England, Carmen, xx–xxi, 183, 265 n.35
Equal Rights Amendment, Jones's discussion of, 68
Ethiopia, Mussolini's invasion of, 66
Eugene Dennis v. the United States, 193, 267 n.11
Exile: gendered aspects of, 24; Jones's discussion of, 157–58

Fairman, Bill, 245 n.2
"False History of Notting Hill Carnival," 183
Families: black woman's role in, 37–39; super-exploitation of women and, 41–44
Federal Bureau of Investigation (FBI): Black Panther party surveillance by, 193, 266 n.7; criminalization of communism by, 193–97; deportation case against Jones, 150–59; file on Jones, xvii, 59, 141, 201, 207–12, 242 n.8, 252 n.55, 253 n.3, 254 n.5, 266 n.4, 269 nn.28, 29; Jones's imprisonment and, 191–97
Feminism without Borders, 22
Feminist movement: Jones's legacy in,

xix–xx; Marxism and, 31–32, 246 n.4; nonhierarchical feminism in, 55; pacificist activities of, 214–33; "prison blues" literature and, 102–4; racial tensions in, 4, 41–44, 48, 248 n.16. *See also* Black British feminism; Black feminism; Caribbean feminism; Imperialist feminism; Materialist feminism; Socialist feminism; Third world feminism

Fighting Words, 14

Firdaus, or Woman at Point Zero, 102–3

Fire Next Time, The, 91, 95

"First Lady of the World: I Talk with Mme Sun Yat-sen," 226

Flynn, Elizabeth Gurley, 34, 257 n.19; on economic conditions for black women, 80; imprisonment of, 103–4, 107–10; in Jones's poetry, 112–17; on McCarran Act, 134–36, 156; Women's Commission of the CPUSA and, 77–78

"For Assata," 128

"For Consuela-Anti-Fascista," 62, 110–17, 257 n.18

"For the Unity of Women in the Cause of Peace," 29, 31, 50–52, 215, 246 n.5

Forty Years, 19

Foster, William Zane, 47, 51, 109, 140–41, 197–99, 209, 221, 250 n.33, 253 n.4

"Foster's Political and Theoretical Guidance to our Work among Women," 51–52, 221–22

Francois, Elma, 66–67, 253 n.59

Franklin, John Hope, xvii

Freedman's Journal, 73

Freedom Dreams, 214

Freedomways, 17, 88, 167, 225

"Friend, A," 114–17

Fugitive Slave Act, 144

Fundi, xv

Garment workers, Communist organization of, 35, 248 n.14

Garvey, Amy Ashwood, 2, 22, 66, 231

Garvey, Marcus, 73, 95, 104, 145, 229–30

Gates, John, 105–7, 121, 153–54, 198, 201–2

Gender: British Communist Party's sexism and, 170–74; Communisty Party conflicts concerning, 51–55; political exile and, 24; racial emancipation and issues of, 46–49; transnational black feminism and, 20–25, 243 n.25

Geopolitics, black feminism and, 11–16

Gilroy, Paul, 95, 120, 168–69, 256 n.27

Globalization, transnational feminism and, 22–25

Golders Green Crematorium, 245 n.2

Goldman, Emma, 104

Gordon, Eugene, 45

Goulbourne, Harry, 85, 120, 168–69

Graham Du Bois, Shirley, 17, 82, 226

Grayson, Josephine, 82

Grewal, Inderpal, 25

Grimke, Angelina, 123

Guantanamo detainees, 259 n.3, 268 n.18

"Guerilla intellectual," 8–10

Guernica, images in Jones's poetry of, 112, 257 n.18

Gutzmore, Cecil, 179, 264 n.23

Guy-Sheftall, Beverly, 16, 22, 37, 247 nn.6, 13

"Half the World" column, 77–84, 96, 215

Hall, Stuart, 8, 22–25, 169

Hanchard, Michael, 14, 147–48

Hansberry, Lorraine, 1, 261 n.23

Harlem Bulletin, 254 n.10

Harlem Riot of 1935, 17

Harlow, Barbara, 99–100, 102

Harris, Clive, 168

Harris, Joseph, 137

Harrison, Hubert, 229

Hayes Edwards, Brent, 229, 271 n.58

Haywood, Harry, 56

Headley, James, 253 n.59

Heart of the Race: Black Women's Lives in Britain, The, xiv

Hennessey, Rosmary, 32, 58

Herndon, Angelo, 19, 66

"Her Words Rang Out beyond the Walls of the Courthouse," 116–17

Highgate Cemetery, Marx's and Jones's graves in, xiv, 239 n.2, 245 n.2

Hill, Errol, 180–81, 263 n.1

Hinds, Donald, xvi, 84–89, 94, 169, 172, 240 n.18, 254 n.17, 263 n.12

Hine, Darlene Clark, 16

Hip-hop movement poetics, 100–101

Holden, Chaneta, 82, 254 n.13

Holder, Claire, 183

Holiday, Billie, 101, 103–4

Hooks, bell, 13

Hoover, J. Edgar, 194

Horne, Gerald, xvii, 17, 137, 214, 226, 260 n.16

Horne, Lena, 80

Horowitz, David, 242 n.14

House Un-American Activities Committee (HUAC): civil rights violations of, 134, 149–50, 194; Jones's trial and, 34

Howe, Darcus, 181

Hughes, Langston, 37

Huiswood, Otto, 18

Hull, Gloria T., 11

Huntley, Jessica and Eric, 85, 169

Hunton, Dorothy, 82

Hurston, Zora Neale, 8

Ibarruri, Dolores, 112

"Identity, Meaning and the African-American," 14

"If We Must Die," 124, 213

Illegal Immigration Reform and Immigrant Responsibility Act of 1997, 131, 136–37, 260 n.14

Immigration and Nationality Act of 1952. *See* McCarran-Walter International Security Act

Immigration and Naturalisation Acts (U.K.), 120

imperialist feminism: black feminism and, 14–16, 54–55; transnational black feminism and, 21–25

Imprisoned Intellectuals, 104

Imprisonment: black feminism and, 21–25; politics of, 148–50; prison blues and, 101–4; spoken-word poetics in, 99–100

Ingram, Rosie Lee, 47–48, 57, 248 n.15

Inside Babylon: The Caribbean Diaspora in Britain, 168

"Insider within" scholarship, black feminism and, 15–16

Institute of Commonwealth Studies (ICS), xvi

Institute of Race Relations, 261 n.26

Intellectual property issues, in London Carnival, 184–89, 266 n.39

Intellectuals: imprisonment of, 104–29; post–September 11 targeting of, 9, 242 n.14

"Internal colonialism," Jones's discussion of, 64–65, 231–33

Internal Security Act of 1950 (McKarran

Act), 134–36, 138, 141, 147–57, 159, 164, 194–97. *See also* McCarran-Walter International Security Act

International capitalism, domestic service and, 44–49

International law: transnational feminism and, 24–25; U.S. deportation policies and, 133, 259 n.5

International Negro Workers Review, 74

"International Women's Day and the Struggle for Peace," 50, 57, 59–60, 67–68, 151, 214–17. *See also* "Women in the Struggle for Peace and Security"

Intersectionality, black feminism and, 10–16

"I Think of My Mother": Notes on the Life and Times of Claudia Jones, xiv, 205–6

Jackson, Esther Cooper, 17, 19
Jackson, George, 103
Jackson, James, 17
Jagan, Cheddi, 236
"Jail House Blues," 101
Jamaica, "returnees" deported back to, 132
Jamaican dub poetry, 100
Jamaican Federation of Trade Unions, 261 n.24
James, C. L. R., 2, 25, 27, 94, 104, 185, 255 n.26; Jones's relationship with, 225–26; pan-Africanism and, 230; persecution of, 145–48
James, Joy, xv, 2, 15, 17, 32, 104, 257 n.12
James, Winston, 168, 244 n.38
Jefferson School of Social Science, 210
Jeffries, Lionel, 240 n.8
Jeffries, Pansy, xvi, 240 n.8
Jewish People's Fraternal Order, 147–48

Jim Crow in Uniform, 76, 213
Jobs, black women's struggle for, 49
Johnson, Buzz, xiv–xvi, 5, 169, 205, 239 n.6, 240 n.18
Johnson, Howard "Stretch," xvii, 53, 261 n.23
Johnson, Linton Kwesi, 169
Joint Congressional Committee on the Economic Report, 80
Jones, Claudia: activist-intellectual work of, 8–10; autobiographical writings of, 198–208; birth certificate of, 6, 145–47; black feminism and, 10–16, 32–40; Bowrin interview of, 29; Caribbean diaspora and, 1–2, 7–10, 25–27, 65–68, 167–74; chronology of life of, xxiii–xxvii; citizenship application of, 144–47, 201, 262 n.32; court testimony of, 1, 6, 203–4; cultural work of, xviii, 167–89; current scholarship on, xvi–xvii; death of, 182–84, 265 n.33; deportation of, 2, 4–5, 7, 25–26, 117–20, 135–47, 150–57, 159, 164–66, 243 n.21; erasure and silencing of, 5–7, 15–16, 243 nn.21, 22; grave of, xiv, xx–xxi, 2, 27, 239 n.2, 241 n.2, 244 n.42; health of, 112–17, 140–42, 171–72, 199–201, 228; imprisonment of, 99–129, 138, 140, 191–97, 200, 267 n.11; journalism career of, xvii, 6–7, 30, 34, 37, 41, 70–97, 143–44, 172–74, 185–89, 200, 254 nn.4, 6; legacy of, xiii–xv; literary output of, 6–7, 104, 109–29; London Carnival and, xvi, 2, 25–26, 91–92, 165–66, 172–84, 262 n.64; passport of, 160–61; peace activism of, 191–233; personal papers of, xix–xx, 240 n.18; personal relationships of, 52–53; poetry of, 101, 104, 109–29;

Jones, Claudia (*continued*)
  research sources on, xv–xvi; transnational feminism and, 20–25; trial and
  incarceration of, 1–2, 5; Trinidad
  roots of, 26–27; "Unity of Women"
  speech by, 29
Jones, Clinton, 91
Jordan, June, 100
Journal of Women's Liberation Front, 165

Kaplan, Caren, 25
Karia Press, 169
Karnak House, 169
Kasinga, Fauziya, 24
Kelley, Robin, xv, 38, 56, 214
Kenyatta, Jomo, 18, 103, 235
Khelifa, H. E. L., 231
Khruschev, Nikita, 221–22
King, Martin Luther, Jr., 95, 137, 234,
  261 n.27
Ku Klux Klan, London branch of, 87
Kunene, Raymond, 231
Kuti, Ransome, 22

Labor issues: sexual divisions in, 41–44,
  58–60; transnational feminism and,
  23–25, 244 n.32; U.S. imperialism in
  the Caribbean region and, 61–65;
  women's rights and, 29–68
"Lament for Emmet Till," 123–24, 127
Lamming, George, xvii, 213–14, 255
  n.24, 270 n.34
Langford, Diane, xix, 240 n.18, 251 n.39
La Rose, John, 63, 85, 143, 169, 181
Last Poets movement, 100, 256 n.1
Lawal, Amina, 24
Lawson, Sonora B., 82
Lazlett, Rhaume, 181, 183
Leadership roles for black women,
  Jones's advocacy for, 49–55

"Learning from the Outsider Within:
  The Social Significance of Black
  Feminist Thought," 13
Lebrun, Lolita, 112
Legal structures, superexploitation
  of working black women fostered
  by, 46–49
Lenin, Vladimir Ilyich, 3, 57, 220–
  22
Lenin on the Woman Question, 57
Lewis, Christina, 66
Library of Congress, files on Jones at,
  192–93
Lift Every Voice-For Victory, 76
Lightcap, Rose Nelson, 147–48
Like One of the Family, 45
"Limits of the Artistic Imagination and
  the Secular Intellectual," 9
Lindsey, Lydia, xvii, 175
Lil' Kim, 100, 257 n.2
London Carnival: intellectual property
  issues with, 184–89; Jones's founding
  of, xvi, 2, 25–26, 91–92, 160, 172–84,
  188–89, 262 n.64
"Long Journeys," 17
Loomis, Everett, 75
"Loom of Language and in the Family
  Man," 233
Lorde, Audre, 7, 16, 25, 55, 127–28
Lord Kitchener, 93, 180, 264 n.25
Lowenfels, Walter, 79
Lumumba, Patrice, 89–90

Maathai, Wangari, 24
*Maids and Madams: Domestic Workers
  Under Apartheid*, 46
*Making Ends Meet on Less than $2,000 a
  Year*, 80–81
Malcolm X, 231
Mallard, Amy, 82

Manchanda, Abhimanyu, xix, 53–54, 89, 227, 245 n.2, 251 n.39, 263 n.9

Manchanda, Claudia, xix

Manley, Norman, 173, 236

Mao Tse-tung, 226

Maquiladoras, labor displacement and, 244 n.32

Marshall, Paule, 15, 46

Marx, Karl: grave of, xiv, xx, 239 n.2, 245 n.2; theories of, 2, 241 n.2

Marxist-Leninist theory: anti-imperialism and, 65; black feminism and, 31–32, 40, 52, 246 n.4; Caribbean feminism and, 67–68; Jones's cultural aesthetics and, 175–84; Jones's ideology and, 2–3, 5–7, 30–32, 34–40, 219–33; Jones's self-identity and, 203–6; socialist feminism and, 57–60

Masquerade Politics, 181, 265 n.28

Materialist feminism, 38, 58, 251 n.45. *See also* Socialist feminism, in Jones's "Half the World " columns, 78–84

Materialist Feminism and the Politics of Discourse, 32, 58

Matriarchal tradition, Jones's discussion of, 39

Maxwell, William, 75

May, Claudia, xvii, 222–23

McCarran, Pat, 134

McCarran Act. *See* Internal Security Act of 1950

"McCarran-Walter Act: A Contradictory Legacy ond Race, Quotas, and Ideology," 134

McCarran-Walter International Security Act: criminalization of communism in, 134–47; deportation provisions in, 131, 136–37, 147–50, 260 n.14; Jones's deportation under, 25, 34, 72, 106–7, 138–47, 194–97, 200–201

McCarthy period, Jones's activism during, 6–7, 194, 196–97, 243 n.22

McClendon, John, xv, 31, 33, 230, 248 n.16, 249 n.24, 270 n.42

McDuffie, Erik, xvii, 17, 33, 36, 76

McGee, Rosalie, 82

McKay, Claude, 124, 229

Mandela, Nelson, 103

Mandela, Winnie, 103

Miami Carnival, 176

Mies, Maria, 58

Mighty Sparrow, The, 93, 180, 264 n.25

Migration, of African and Caribbean diaspora, 162, 165–66

Migratory subjectivity: black feminist history and, 20–25; Jones's deportation as example of, 142–47

Militancy of black women, Jones's "neglect thesis" concerning, 38

Mindel, Jacob, 138

"Miss Liberty's Torch Grows Dim," 134–35

Mitchell, Bessie, 83

Mohanty, Chandra Talpade, 22–23

Moore, Audley ("Queen Mother"), 17, 261 n.23

Moore, Richard, 18

Morel, Yumeris, xvii, 77

"Morning Mists," 121–22

Motherhood, Jones's discussion of, 38–39, 249 n.18

Naison, Mark, 74

Narrative of the Life of Frederick Douglass, 107

National Association for the Advancement of Colored People (NAACP), 76

National Black Feminist Organization, 11, 36, 58–59
National Council of Negro Women, 35
National Defense Committee for Claudia Jones, 140
National Security Entry-Exit Registration System, 133
National Unemployed Movement, 253 n.59
Native Son, 75
"Native Sons Strive for Freedom," 75
Needle Trades Workers Industrial Union, 45, 247 n.1
"Neglect thesis" in black feminism, 38–40, 248 n.16
Negro Welfare Cultural and Social Association (NWCSA), 66–67, 253 n.59
Negro Worker, 74
Negro World, The, 95
Negro World Unity Congress, 229
"New 'Alien and Sedition' Law, The," 147
New Beacon Books, 85, 169
New Jersey Project, 251 n.44
New Masses, 267 n.15
New Negro, Old Left, 75
New Novels about the Negro, 209–10
"New Problems of the Negro Youth Movement," 76
Newspapers: Jones's criticisms of mainstream press, 82; radical black intellectuals' use of, 73–75, 85–97, 254 n.7
New Yorker magazine, 14
New York Public Library, files on Jones at, 192–93
New York Times, 81
Nigeria: adultery laws in, 24; oil degradation in, 102, 244 n.32
Nkrumah, Kwame, 103, 229, 261 n.27, 271 n.55

Noguera, Pedro, 132
Noh, Eliza, 23
Nomadism, gender and, 24, 244 n.35
"Notes on Dialects," 225
Notting Hill Carnival, 25–26, 178–84, 264 n.22
Notting Hill Carnival Committee, 181–82
Notting Hill riots, 87, 172–74, 178–79, 264 n.22
"Nuances of Un-American Literature(s)," 240 n.9

Ogletree, Charles J., 145
Oilfield Workers Trade Union, 255 n.17, 267 n.14
Oliver, Paul, 181
"On Improving the Party's Work Among Women," 51
"On the Cult of Personality," 222
"On the Right of Self Determination for the Negro People in the Black Belt," 64, 212, 220–21, 252 n.53
Oyewumi, Oyeronke, 243 n.25

Pacifism, Jones's involvement in, 191–233
Padilla, Jose, 268 n.18
Padmore, George, 27, 229–30, 253 n.59
"Paean to Crimea," 125, 228
Pan-Africanism: African diaspora focus on, 137; Jones's legacy and, 228–32; in United Kingdom, 142–43, 170, 225, 263 n.8
Parmar, Partibha, 14
Parsons, Lucy, 267 n.13
Patterson, Louise. *See* Thompson Patterson, Louise
Patterson, William, 157
Payne, Charles, 50

Peace activism, Jones's involvement in, 49, 191–233

Peking Meeting Tribute, 165

"People's Art Is the Genesis of Their Freedom, A," 176, 264 n.22

People's National Movement, 146

Perry, Imani, 100

Philip, Marlene Nourbese, 14

Pilkington, Edward, 85, 93, 172–73, 178–79

Pinder, W. S., 245 n.2

Pinnock, Winsome, 264 n.17

Plessey v. Ferguson, 144

"Poetry for the people" movement, 100

Poetry of resistance: evolution of, 99–129, 256 n.1; Jones's contributions to, 101–29

Political Affairs, 6–7, 57; Jones's articles in, 30, 210

"Political Score, The" (column), 77

Politics of location: Jones's poetry and, 123–29; transnational feminism and, 23–25

Position of Negro Women, 45

Postcolonial theory, African American intellectuals and, 13–16

Practice of Diaspora, The, 229

Prager, Ruth, 268 n.22

Prescod, Colin, xvi, 180, 241 n.19

Presence Africaine, xviii

Primus, Pearl, 135

"Prison blues" literature, 102–4

"Problematics of Transnational Feminism and Asian American Women," 23

Professors: The 101 Most Dangerous Academics in America, The, 242 n.14

Prophets of the Hood, 100

Protofeminist theory, black feminism and, 32

Provincial Freeman, 73

Puerto Rican nationalism: Jones's discussion of, 62; in Jones's poetry, 111–17, 257 n.18

Race against Empire, 73

Race and Class, xv, 261 n.26

"Race first" theoretics, black feminism and, 48

Race Policy Unit, 169

Race Woman: The Lives of Shirley Graham Du Bois, 17, 226

Racism: capitalism's nurturing of, 42–44; Caribbean diaspora in United Kingdom and experiences of, 170–74; Communism and, 223–33; in feminist movement, 4, 41–44, 48, 248 n.16; Jones's discussion of, 7, 215–33; in Jones's poetry, 124–29

"Radiant Season," 122–23

"Radical black female subject," Jones characterized as, 5–7

Rainey, Ma, 101

Randolph, A. Philip, 76

Ransby, Barbara, xv

Raymond, Henry, 148

Reddock, Rhoda, 66–67, 74

Red Feminism: American Communism and the Making of Women's Liberation, 18, 30

"Rediscovering a Lost Legacy: Black Women Radicals Maude White and Louise Thompson," 18

"Remarks on the Eve of the Deportation of Claudia Jones," 157

"Report to the Party Commission on Theoretical Aspects of Work among Women, August 1948," 47, 250 n.33

Republic of New Africa, 267 n.11

Resistance literature, evolution of, 99–101

Resistance Literature, 99–100, 102

"Reverse chauvinism," Jones charged with, 48–49, 248 n.16

Revolution, in Jones's poetry, 123–29

Rich, Adrienne, 23

Richards, Beah, 19, 37

Richardson, Beulah, 82, 247 n.12

Robeson, Eslanda Goode, 1, 22, 83, 95, 150

Robeson, Paul, 1, 95, 149–51, 177, 186, 209, 269 n.31

Robinson, Cedric, 223

Rock in the Water, 264 n.17

Rodney, Walter, 8–10, 86

"Role of African Intellectuals, The," 8–10

Rossia Sanitorium, Jones's stay at, 125

Roussel-Milner, David, 183

Rowe, David P., 133, 136

Russo, Anna, 23

Saadawi, Nawal el, 102

Saakana, Amon Saba, 169

Said, Edward, 9

Saro-Wiwa, Ken, 102, 244 n.32

Scafe, Suzanne, xiv

Scattered Hegemonies: Postmodernity and Transnational Feminist Practices, 23

Scholnick, Abraham, 52–53, 201, 209, 268 n.17, 269 n.30

Schomburg Library, Claudia Jones Memorial Collection in, xix–xx

Schrecker, Ellen, 195–96

Schwarz, Bill, 91–92, 173–74

Scott, Patricia Bell, 11

Scottsboro Boys case, 19, 66, 197, 200, 219–20

Seamen and Waterfront Workers' Trade Union, 74

Secular intellectual, emergence of, 9

Sellins, Fanny, 50

September 11, 2001 attacks: civil rights abuses following, 193; deportation legislation following, 133

Seretse-Khama, 133, 259 n.5

Shadd, Mary Ann, 73

Shakur, Assata, 48, 103, 242 n.9

Shakur, Tupac, 103

Shattering Illusions, 224

Shell Oil, environmental damage in Nigeria by, 244 n.32

Shepherd, Claire, 177–78, 183

Sherwood, Marika, xvi, 7, 170, 240 n.18, 241 n.19, 254 n.4, 263 n.7, 270 n.55

"Ship's Log: Paean to the Atlantic," 117–20, 157, 159, 261 n.23

Siskind, George, 148

Sister Outsider, 55

Slam, 100

Slavery: African diaspora focus on, 137; domestic service as form of, 46; Jones's discussion of, 39

Smith, Barbara, 11

Smith, Bessie, 101

Smith, Elsie, 50

Smith, Ferdinand, 136, 261 n.24

Smith, Moranda, 33

Smith, Sidonie, 203

Smith Act. *See* Alien Registration Act of 1940

Socialism: black activists and, 229–32; black women's leadership issues in, 49–55; liberation of black working women through, 46, 250 n.33

Socialist feminism, Jones's legacy in, 56–60

Socialist Party of America, 229

Socialist Party of Jamaica, 91

Sojourners for Truth and Justice, 18–19, 35–37, 47–49, 82–84, 214, 247 n.12

"Sojourners for Truth and Justice" (Jones), 83–84

Solomon, Mark, 17–18, 44
Soong Ching Ling, 226–27
Southern Christian Leadership Conference, 50
Southern Negro Youth Conference, 19
Soviet Union: Jones's view of, 125–26, 221–22, 225–27, 270 n.42; women's status in, 52
Spotlight, 76, 254 n.5
Stalin, Joseph, 221–22, 270 n.42
Standpoint epistemology, black feminism and, 13–14
Stewart, Maria, 13
Stewart, Martha, 257 n.9
Still Black, Still Strong, 137
Stokes, Rose Pastor, 50
"Storm at Sea," 120, 122
Strachan, Billy, xvi, 225, 255 n.17, 258 n.24, 263 n.12
Student Nonviolent Coordinating Committee, 124
Super-exploitation of working black women: black feminism and, 2–4; in domestic service, 46–49; Jones's personal experiences with, 53–54; Jones's theoretics concerning, 37–44, 184; Thompson-Patterson's work on, 33, 247 n.10
Surplus value: Marxist theory of, 2–3, 241 n.2; super-exploitation theoretics and, 42–44, 249 n.24

Taylor, Pauline, 83
Terborg-Penn, Rosalyn, 16
Terrell, Mary Church, 33
"There Are Some Things I Always Remember," 123
There Is No Black in the Union Jack, 168
Third World and Radical Book Fair, 85

"Third World Diva Girls: Politics of Feminist Solidarity," 13
Third world feminism, black intellectuals and, 13–16
Third World Women and the Politics of Feminism, 23
Thomas, Greg, 100, 256 n.2
Thompson Patterson, Louise, 17–19, 33, 37, 44, 52, 83, 248 n.135
Till, Emmet, 123–24, 156–57
"To a Dear Friend on Her Birthday," 117
Torres, Lourdes, 23
Torresola, Blanca Canales, 110–17, 257 n.18
Torresola, Carmen, 257 n.19
Torresola, Guisello, 257 n.19
Trade unions: in Caribbean region, 62–65; domestic workers excluded from, 44–49
"Trans-cultural Black Intellectual Presences," xviii–xix
Transformative intellectuals, Jones's involvement with, 8–10
Transnational black activism: deportation politics and, 162, 165–66; Jones's legacy in, 20–25, 57–60, 72–73
Transnational capitalism, Davis's work on, 241 n.4
Trinidad: Jones's involvement with activists in, xix–xx, 170–74; Jones's status as national from, 145–47; "returnees" deported back to, 132; U.S. corporate imperialism and, 60–65
Trinidad All Stars, 180
Trinidad Carnival, 180–81
Trinidad Carnival (London), 177–78
Trinidad Independence Party, 143
"Triple oppression" logic: in Jones' theoretics, 30, 39–40; in socialist feminism, 56–60

Troupe, 180

Truth, Sojourner, 12, 32–33, 36 80

Tshombe, Moise, 89–90

Tubman, Harriet, 13, 19, 33, 80

Ture, Kwame (Stokely Carmichael), 27,
124, 137, 146–147, 260 n.16

Ulasi, Adora Lily, 19

United Front (Harlem), 17

United Kingdom: Caribbean diaspora in,
xviii, 25–27, 66–68, 85–97, 143–47,
167–89, 240 n.14; corporate imperialism in, 60–65; Jones's activism in, 142–
47, 223–33; Jones's deportation to, 7,
25–27, 141–47, 243 nn.21–22; Jones's
journalism career in, 84–97

United Nations: CPUSA petitions to, 136;
women's delegation to, 81

United States: corporatist domination of
Caribbean by, 60–65; deportation
statistics and policies, 131–32; dominance in feminism of, 20; Jones's deportation from, 2, 4–5, 7, 25–26, 243
n.21; Jones's legacy in, xix–xx

United States Citizenship and Immigration Services, 259 n.6

United States Department of Homeland
Security, 259 n.6

U. S. Department of Labor Handbook of
Facts on Women, 80

United States Immigration and Naturalization Service, 131, 259 n.6

United States of America v. Elizabeth
Gurley Flynn, et al., 136

Universal Negro Improvement Association, 73

University of Arizona, feminist initiative
at, 251 n.44

USA Patriot Act, 133–37, 155–56, 260
n.14

Vera, Claude, 26, 244 n.41

Vincent, Theodore, 73, 89

"Visit to the U.S.S.R.," 125

Voice of the Fugitive, 73

Voices of a Black Nation, 73, 88

Von Eschen, Penny, 73

Voting Rights Act, 148

Wahad, Dhoruba bin, 137

Walker, David, 272 n.61

Wallace, Michelle, 12

Walter, Francis, 134

Weekly Review, 71–72, 75–77, 87

Weigand, Kate, 18, 30, 56, 246 n.3

Wells-Barnett, Ida B., 13, 15, 33, 69–70,
244 n.38

"We Seek Full Equality for Women,"
39–40, 249 n.21

West Indian American, 73, 92, 253 n.2;
Jones's father's work with, 75, 92, 254
n.9

West Indian Federation, 60, 62–63, 69,
87, 90–91, 174, 176–77, 264 n.20

West Indian Gazette and Afro-Asian Caribbean News, xv; Caribbean issues in,
63–64; carnivals sponsored by, 172–
74, 176–84; as community force, 168,
183–89, 265 n.36; founding of, 25–
27, 172, 263 n.12; Jones's work with,
2, 6, 66, 69–70, 72, 84–97, 125, 143,
185–89, 226, 261 n.26; pan-
Africanism discussed in, 230–31

White, Maude, 17–18, 33, 44–45, 247
n.10; in Soviet Union, 52, 65

White, Walter, 76

White women progressives, racial tensions with black feminists, 4, 41–44,
48, 55, 248 n.16

"Who Controls the Notting Hill Carnival?" 177–78, 183

"Why Six Negro Leaders Defend
Claudia Jones," 139
Wilkins, Roy, 76
Williams, Eric, 27, 61, 145–46
Williams, Frances, 83
Williams, Saul, 100
Williams, Sylvester, 27
Wilson, Francille Rusan, 45
Winston, Harry, 75, 125
Woman Question, The, 80
Women: Jones on super-exploitation of
black working, 2–4; Jones's activism
on behalf of, 51–55; Jones's "Half the
World" columns on rights of, 79–84;
Lenin on exploitation of, 3, 57;
workers' rights for, 29–68
"Women and Capitalism: Dialectics of
Oppression and Liberation," 38
Women in the Last Colony, 58
"Women in the Struggle for Peace and
Security," 54–55, 57, 59–60, 151–52,
251 n.40. *See also* "International
Women's Day and the Struggle for
Peace"
*Women, Labour and Politics in Trinidad
and Tobago*, 66
Women, Race and Class, xiv, 30, 48–49,
59
Women's International Democratic
Federation, 49, 81

*Women's Liberation and the Dielectics of
Revolution*, 58
*Words of Fire: An Anthology of African-
American Feminist Thought*, 16, 37,
113–14
Working-class black women: census data
on earnings of, 41, 249 n.23; interna-
tional capitalist economy and, 44–49;
Jones's activism concerning, 204–5;
super-exploitation thesis concerning,
40–44
Working-class intellectuals, 9–10
World Congress of Intellectuals for
Peace, 214
World Peace Appeal, 81–82
Wright, Richard, 75
Wynter, Sylvia, 16, 241 n.2

Yates v. United States, 208
"Yenan — Cradle of the Revolution,"
126–27, 226
Yoruba culture, black feminist history
and, 243 n.25
"You Can't Have Guns and Butter Too," 80
Young Communist League, 70–72, 75–
76, 96, 204–5, 209–12, 253 n.59, 267
n.16
Young Communist Review, xxi

Zetkin, Clara, 57, 216–17

Carole Boyce Davies is a professor of African-New World studies and professor of English, Florida International University. She is the author of *Black Women, Writing, and Identity: Migrations of the Subject* (1994) and has coedited *Decolonizing the Academy: African Diaspora Studies* (2003), *The African Diaspora: African Origins and New World Identities* (1999), *Moving beyond Boundaries* (1995), *Out of the Kumbla: Caribbean Women and Literature* (1990), and *Ngambika: Studies of Women in African Literature* (1986).

Library of Congress Cataloging-in-Publication Data
Boyce Davies, Carole.
Left of Karl Marx : the political life of black communist Claudia Jones /
Carole Boyce Davies.
p. cm.
Includes bibliographical references and index.
ISBN 978-0-8223-4096-6 (cloth : alk. paper)
ISBN 978-0-8223-4116-1 (pbk. : alk. paper)
1. Jones, Claudia, 1915–1964. 2. Women communists — United States — Biography.
3. Women communists — Great Britain — Biography. 4. West Indians — United States —
Biography. 5. West Indians — Great Britain — Biography. 6. Women journalists — United
States — Biography. 7. Women journalists — Great Britain — Biography. 8. Feminists —
United States — Biography. 9. Feminists — Great Britain — Biography. 10. Women and
communism — United States — History — 20th century. 11. Women and communism —
Great Britain — History — 20th century. 12. Women's rights — United States — History —
20th century. 13. Women's rights — Great Britain — History — 20th century. I. Title.
HX84.J66B69 2007
941.085'092 — dc22
[B] 2007029291